CW00553189

Anonymous

Civil Procedure Reports

Vol. III

Anonymous

Civil Procedure Reports

Vol. III

Reprint of the original, first published in 1883.

1st Edition 2023 | ISBN: 978-3-36863-531-2

Verlag (Publisher): Outlook Verlag GmbH, Zeilweg 44, 60439 Frankfurt, Deutschland
Vertretungsberechtigt (Authorized to represent): E. Roepke, Zeilweg 44, 60439 Frankfurt, Deutschland
Druck (Print): Books on Demand GmbH, In de Tarpen 42, 22848 Norderstedt, Deutschland

CIVIL PROCEDURE REPORTS.

CONTAINING CASES UNDER THE

CODE OF CIVIL PROCEDURE

AND

THE GENERAL CIVIL PRACTICE

OF THE

STATE OF NEW YORK.

REPORTED WITH NOTES

BY

HENRY H. BROWNE

OF THE NEW YORK BAR.

WITH A REFERENCE TO THE SECTIONS OF THE CODE CONSTRUED OR CITED IN THE REPORTS ISSUED BETWEEN JANUARY 1, 1883, AND JULY 31, 1883.

VOLUME III.

NEW YORK:

S. S. PELOUBET & CO.,

LAW PUBLISHERS AND BOOKSELLERS,

80 NASSAU STREET.

1883.

CONTENTS.

CONTENTS.

TABLE OF CASES REPORTED.

TABLE OF CASES CITED

IN THE OPINIONS.

A.

B.

CASES.	WHERE REPORTED.	PAGE CITED.
Dickens *v.* N. Y. Cent. & Hudson R. R. R. Co.	13 How. Pr. 228	204
Dickson, Estate of	11 Phil. 86	55
Doe *v.* Stickland	8 C. B. 724	67
Don *v.* Lippman	5 Clark & Fin. 1	115
Donnell *v.* Williams	21 Hun, 216	346
Dubois *v.* Marshall	3 Dana, 336	408
Duckworth *v.* Roach	18 N. Y. 46	135
Duncan *v.* Katen	6 Hun, 1; affd. 64 N. Y. 625	692
Dyster *v.* Battye	3 Barn. & Ald. 438	425

E.

CASES.	WHERE REPORTED.	PAGE CITED.
East River Bank *v.* Rogers	7 Bosw. 493	265
Edwards *v.* Bishop	4 N. Y. 61	406
Elme *v.* Da Costa	1 Phil. 173	127
Ely *v.* Cook	28 N. Y. 372	120
Es *v.* Curry	22 Hun, 584	255

F.

CASES.	WHERE REPORTED.	PAGE CITED.
Farmers' Loan & Trust Co. *v.* Henning, receiver, &c.	17 Am. Law Reg. N. S. 266	24
First Nat'l. Bank, Meadville *v.* Fourth Nat'l. Bank, N. Y.	84 N. Y. 469	88
Fisher *v.* Bassett	9 Leigh (Va.) 133	107
Fisher *v.* Hunter	15 How. Pr. 156	170
Fisher *v.* Mayor	67 N. Y. 86	97
Fisher *v.* Pond	1 Hill, 672; S. C., 2 Id. 338	425
Fitzgerald *v.* Quann	1 N. Y. Civ. Pro. 273	394
Flynn *v.* Equitable Life Ins. Co.	18 Hun, 212	411
Forman's will, Matter of,	54 Barb. 274	67
Fosdick *v.* Delafield	2 Redf. 404	127
Fox *v.* Fox	5 Hun, 53	161
French Mfg. Co., *Ex parte*	12 Hun, 488	134

G.

CASES.	WHERE REPORTED.	PAGE CITED.
Gardner *v.* Locke	2 N. Y. Civ. Pro 252	8, 204
Gibbons *v.* Berhard	3 Bosw. 635	63
Giles, Estate of	11 Abb. N. C. 57	55
Gillett *v.* Stanley	1 Hill, 121	406

H.

I.

J.

R.

T.

U.

V.

W.

STATUTES, ETC., CITED.

SECTIONS OF THE CODE OF CIVIL PROCEDURE CITED.

SECTION	PAGE	SECTION	PAGE
66	146, 255	723	380, 382
263	37	731	154
266	37	732	153
382	95	733	154, 155
383	95, 96	755	58, 447
410	96, 97, 98	756	58, 447
413	190, 424, 427	768	387
414	181	769	136
438	71	779	359
439	70, 72	803, *et seq.*	336
450	394	829	35, 330
469, subd. 3	187	868	374
500	228	869	374
501	211	870	362
531	413, 414	871	362
549, subd. 4	113	872	103
550, subd. 2	111	885	451
553	392, 395	893	362
587	366, 367	911	259
595	366	992	178, 179
600	366	993	179
635	108	994	179
644	186	995	179
647	186	996	179
650	356	1180	178
651	356	1207	5
655	356	1266	196
677	356	1335	61
682	293, 419	1351	306
683	108, 293	1352	61
687	293	1366	193
688	293	1421	167

SECTIONS OF THE CODE OF PROCEDURE CITED.

SESSION LAWS CITED.

NEW YORK REVISED STATUTES CITED.

FIRST EDITION.

SIXTH EDITION.

SEVENTH EDITION.

ACTS RELATING TO CIVIL PRACTICE CONTAINED IN THE SESSION LAWS OF 1883.

SECTIONS OF THE CODE OF CIVIL PROCEDURE AMENDED BY SESSION LAWS OF 1883.

CONSTITUTION OF THE STATE OF NEW YORK CITED.

GENERAL RULES OF PRACTICE CITED.

UNITED STATES STATUTES CITED.

SECTIONS OF CODE OF CIVIL PROCEDURE.

Construed or Cited, in the opinions contained in the following Reports, issued during the Period Covered by this Volume: N. Y. Reports, Vols. 89, 90; Hun's Reports, Vols. 28, 29; Abbott's New Cases, Vol. 11; Howard's Pr. Vol. 64; and N. Y. Civil Procedure Reports, Vol. 3.

190, subd. 2. McHenry *v.* Jewett............ 90 N. Y. 58.
239 Matter of Wadley.................... 29 Hun, 12.
243 Woodruff *v.* I. F. Ins. Co. .... 90 N. Y. 521.
266 Brooks *v.* Mexican Nat. Const. Co...... 3 N. Y. Civ. Pro. 36.
340 Coe *v.* Raymond..................... 89 N. Y. 612.
383 Dickenson *v.* Mayor of N. Y.......... 3 N. Y. Civ. Pro. 93.
383 People *ex rel.* Byrne *v.* French......... 3 N. Y. Civ. Pro. 180.
395 Anderson *v.* Sibley.................. 28 Hun, 16.
410 Dickenson *v.* Mayor of N. Y.......... 3 N. Y. Civ. Pro. 93.
413 Plimpton *v.* Bigelow... .... 3 N. Y. Civ Pro. 182.
413 Budd *v* Walker..................... 3 N. Y. Civ. Pro. 422.
414 People *ex rel.* Byrne *v.* French...... . 3 N. Y. Civ. Pro. 180.
438, 439 Williamson *v.* Williamson.......... 3 N. Y. Civ. Pro. 69.
440, 441 M. N. Bank *v.* P. N. Bank.... .... 89 N. Y. 397.
450 Muser *v.* Miller...................... 3 N. Y. Civ. Pro. 388.
454 Quinn *v.* Bowe........................ 11 Abb. N. C. 115.
481 Dorr *v.* Mills..................... ... 3 N. Y. Civ. Pro. 7.
481 Velie *v.* Newark City Ins. Co......... 3 N. Y. Civ. Pro. 202.
499 Farwell *v.* I. & T. Nat. Bank......... 90 N. Y. 483.
500 Leary *v.* Boggs...................... 3 N. Y. Civ. Pro. 227.
507 Boreel *v.* Lawton .. .. 90 N. Y. 293.
501 Denny *v.* Horton....... .... 3 N. Y. Civ. Pro. 255.
501 Heidelback *v.* Kilpatrick... .... 3 N. Y. Civ. Pro. 209.
521 Edwards *v.* Woodruff.. .... 90 N. Y. 396.
522 Fleischman *v.* Stern.................. 90 N. Y. 110.
531 Shaffer *v.* Holm...................... 3 N. Y. Civ. Pro. 81.
531 Schulhoff *v.* Co-operative Dress Ass..... 3 N. Y. Civ. Pro. 412.
532 Albert Palmer Co. *v.* Shaw. . ... 64 How. Pr. 80.
545 Nehresheimer *v.* Bowe.. .... 3 N. Y. Civ. Pro. 368.
546 Velie *v.* Newark City Ins. Co.......... 3 N. Y. Civ. Pro. 202
549, 550 Ætna Ins. Co. *v.* Schuler.......... 28 Hun, 338.
550, subd. 2 Arnold *v.* Shapir... .... 29 Hun, 478.
550, subd. 2 Claflin *v.* Frenkel... .... 3 N. Y. Civ. Pro. 109.
553 Muser *v.* Miller......................... 3 N. Y. Civ. Pro. 388.
587 Nehresheimer *v.* Bowe .... 3 N. Y. Civ. Pro. 368.
600 Nehresheimer *v.* Bowe................. 3 N. Y. Civ. Pro. 363.
603 McHenry *v.* Jewett..................... 90 N. Y. 58.
635 Hamilton *v.* Penney...... .... 29 Hun, 265.
635, 636 Weiller *v.* Schreiber............... 11 Abb. N. C. 175.
635, 636 Alford *v.* Cobb.................. 28 Hun, 22.
635, 636 Hirsch *v.* Hutchison............... 3 N. Y. Civ. Pro. 106.
636 Murray *v.* Hankin... ... . 3 N. Y. Civ. Pro. 343.
636 Smith *v.* Davis....... .... 3 N. Y. Civ. Pro. 75.
636 Doltz *v.* Atlantic &c., Trans. Co........ 3 N. Y. Civ. Pro. 162.
644 Plympton *v.* Bigelow.... .... 11 Abb. N. C. 180.

827 Matter of Booth........ 11 Abb. N. C. 145.
829 Sprague v. Swift........ 3 N. Y. Civ. Pro. 34.
829 Bristol v. Sears........ 3 N. Y. Civ. Pro. 329.
829 MacDonald v. Woodbury........ 3 N. Y. Civ. Pro. 337.
829 Pope v. Allen........ 90 N. Y. 298.
829 Smith v. Cross........ 90 N. Y. 549.
829 Maverick v. Marvel........ 90 N. Y. 656.
829 Lathrop v. Hopkins........ 29 Hun, 608.
829 Brown v. Brown........ 29 Hun, 498.
829 Cannon v. North West. M. Ins. Co........ 29 Hun, 470.
829 Sweet v. Low........ 28 Hun, 432.
829 Smith v. Meagher........ 28 Hun, 423.
829 Corning v. Walker........ 28 Hun, 435.
832 People v. McGloin........ 28 Hun, 150.
837 Canada S. S. Co. v. Sinclair........ 3 N. Y. Civ. Pro. 284
853 Carrington v. Hutson........ 28 Hun, 371.
870 *et seq.* Hutchinson v. Lawrence........ 3 N. Y. Civ. Pro. 99.
870 *et seq.* Canada S. S. Co. v. Sinclair........ 3 N. Y. Civ. Pro. 284.
870 *et seq.* Cooke v. Lalance Grosjean Mfg. Co........ 3 N. Y. Co. Pro. 333.
872 Knowlton v. Bannigan........ 11 Abb. N. C. 419.
872 subd. 4 Fourth Nat'l. Bank v. Boynton. 29 Hun, 441.
873 Kirkland v. Moss........ 11 Abb N. C. 421.
880 Canada S. S. Co. v. Sinclair........ 3 N. Y. Civ. Pro. 284.
881 MacDonald v. Woodbury........ 3 N. Y. Civ. Pro. 337.
885 Williams v. West. U. Tel. Co........ 3 N. Y. Civ. Pro. 448
887–913 Champlin v. Stodard........ 64 How. Pr. 378.
887, 888, 889 Clark v. Candee........ 29 Hun, 139.
910 Denny v. Horton........ 3 N. Y. Civ. Pro. 255.
911 Denny v. Horton........ 3 N. Y. Civ. Pro. 255.
970 Lorillard v. Clyde........ 3 N. Y. Civ. Pro. 307.
983 Ackerman v. Delude........ 29 Hun, 137.
984 Smith v. Danzig........ 3 N. Y. Civ. Pro. 127.
992, 993 Mead v. Smith........ 3 N. Y. Civ. Pro. 171.
1015 Jones v. Easton........ 11 Abb. N. C. 114.
1041 People v. Petrea........ 64 How. Pr. 139.
1207 Murtha v. Curley........ 3 N. Y. Civ. Pro. 1.
1216, 1217 Plympton v. Bigelow........ 11 Abb. N. C. 180.
1241 Noland v. Noland........ 29 Hun, 630.
1266 Adams v. Bowe........ 3 N. Y. Civ. Pro. 191.
1268 Arnold v. Oliver........ 64 How. Pr. 452.
1269 Blumenthal v. Anderson........ 28 Hun, 93.
1303 Lavalle v. Skelly........ 90 N. Y. 546.
1323 Kidd v. Curry........ 29 Hun, 215.
1327 Grow v. Garlock........ 29 Hun, 598.

1331 Grow *v.* Garlock .... 29 Hun, 598.
1335 Manning *v.* Gould .... 3 N. Y. Civ. Pro. 58.
1342 Matteson *v.* Hall .... 64 How. Pr. 515.
1351 Baker *v.* Hatfield .... 3 N. Y. Civ. Pro. 303.
1353 Matter of Swezey .... 64 How. Pr. 331.
1356 Matter of Swezey .... 64 How. Pr. 331.
1361 Matter of Swezey .... 64 How. Pr. 331.
1366 Ansonia Brass & Cop. Co. *v.* Conner.... 3 N. Y. Civ. Pro. 88.
1371 Felt *v.* Dorr .... 29 Hun, 14.
1380, 1381 Kerr *v.* Kreuder .... 28 Hun, 452.
1421 Hessberg *v.* Riley .... 3 N. Y. Civ. Pro. 165.
1422 Hessberg *v.* Riley .... 3 N. Y. Civ. Pro. 165.
1423 Hessberg *v.* Riley .... 3 N. Y. Civ. Pro. 165.
1426 Hessberg *v.* Riley .... 3 N. Y. Civ. Pro, 165.
1487 Keller *v.* Strasburger .... 90 N. Y. 399.
1487 Ætna Ins. Co. *v.* Shuler .... 28 Hun, 338.
1500 Smith *v.* Long .... 3 N. Y. Civ. Pro. 396.
1501 Smith *v.* Long .... 3 N. Y. Civ. Pro. 396.
1501 Adriance *v.* Sanders .... 11 Abb. N. C. 422.
1525, 1526 Howell *v.* Leavitt .... 90 N. Y. 238.
1776 Bengtson *v.* Thingvalla S. S. Co....... 3 N. Y. Civ. Pro. 263.
1778 Hutson *v.* Morrisania Steamboat Co.. . 64 How. Pr. 268.
1780 Merchants' Manufacturing Co. *v.* Grand Trunk R. R. Co. .... 11 Abb. N. C. 183.
1780 Ervin *v.* Oregon R. & Nav. Co. .... 28 Hun, 269.
1780 Brooks *v.* Mexican National Construction Co. .... 3 N. Y. Civ. Pro. 36.
1788 Smith *v.* Danzig .... 3 N. Y. Civ. Pro. 127.
1788 Eddy *v.* Co-operative Dress Ass'n...... 3 N. Y. Civ. Pro. 434, 442.
1789 Smith *v.* Danzig .... 3 N. Y. Civ. Pro. 127.
1793 Eddy *v.* Co-operative Dress Ass'n...... 3 N. Y. Civ. Pro. 442.
1806 Smith *v.* Danzig .... 3 N. Y. Civ. Pro. 127.
1810 Smith *v.* Danzig .... 3 N. Y. Civ. Pro. 127.
1835, 1836 Horton *v.* Brown .... 29 Hun, 684.
1835, 1836 Daggett *v.* Mead .... 11 Abb. N. C. 116.
1861 Younger *v.* Duffie .... 28 Hun, 242.
1909 Carpenter *v.* Butler .... 29 Hun, 251.
1912, 1913 Carpenter *v.* Butler .... 29 Hun, 251.
1926 Farnham *v.* Benedict .... 29 Hun, 44.
1930 Farnham *v.* Benedict .... 29 Hun, 44.
1933 Richardson *v.* Case .... 3 N. Y. Civ. Pro. 295.
1939 Richardson *v.* Case .... 3 N. Y. Civ. Pro. 295.
1948 *et seq.* Morris *v.* Whelan .... 11 Abb. N. C. 64; 64 How. Pr. 109.

3256 Douglis v. Atwell.................... 3 N. Y. Civ. Pro. 80.
3256 Sanders v. Townshend............... 11 Abb. N. C. 217.
3264 Matthews v. Matson.................. 3 N. Y. Civ. Pro. 157.
3265 Matthews v. Matson.................. 3 N. Y. Civ. Pro. 157.
3267 Robitzek v. Hect .... 3 N. Y. Civ. Pro. 156.
3268 Buckley v. Gutta Percha, &c. M'f'g. Co. 3 N. Y. Civ. Pro. 428.
3268 Boylan v. Mathews.................... 3 N. Y. Civ. Pro. 38.
3271 Sharp v. Fancher...................... 29 Hun, 193.
3272 Buckley v. Gutta Percha, &c. M'f'g. Co. 3 N. Y. Civ. Pro. 428.
3272 Robertson v. Brown.................. 29 Hun, 657.
3331 Woodruff v. I. F. Ins. Co.............. 90 N. Y. 521.
3343 Woodruff v. I. F. Ins. Co.............. 90 N. Y. 521.
3343 subd. 10 Weiller v. Schreiber .... 11 Abb. N. C. 175.
Wertheim v. Continental R. R. & Trust Co.................................. 3 N. Y. Civ. Pro. 371.

CIVIL PROCEDURE REPORTS.

MURTHA, APPELLANT, v. CURLEY, IMPLEADED, &c., RESPONDENT.

N. Y. COURT OF APPEALS; OCTOBER, 1882.

§ 1207.

Judgment.—Demand for wrong, does not prevent recovery where answer was interposed.—Action, when equitable, and in nature of creditor's bill.—Trial, findings and judgment in such actions.

Under the present system of practice a plaintiff is not to be turned out of court, when an answer has been interposed, because he has prayed for too much, or too little, or for wrong relief; but he can have any relief consistent with the case made by the complaint and embraced within the issues. [3, 4]

The complaint in an action alleged that D., a defendant, was, in April, 1872, indebted to the defendant C. in the sum of $500; to one F. in the sum of $300, and to plaintiff in the sum of $500, which were all the debts he then owed; that at that time he executed to and delivered to C. a mortgage for $3,100 on his personal property, which was worth at least $3,500; that this security, by renewals or new mortgages, was kept in force until October 10, 1878, when C. foreclosed the last mortgage, although there was then nothing due thereon, and converted the proceeds of the property to his own use; that all the mortgages were made and kept in force for the purpose of hindering, delaying and defrauding the plaintiff and other creditors of D.; that on October 10, 1878, the plaintiff recovered judgment on his claim, and thereafter an execution was issued, and returned unsatisfied, and prayed judgment against the defendants, that they and each of them be required to pay the amount of the judgment against D. *Held*, that the complaint contained all the allegations requisite for what is commonly known as a creditor's bill;[1] also *Held*, that there could be no reasonabl ojection to the judgment prayed for;[2, 3] the only relief the plaintiff needed being that C. should pay him out of the money received by him out of the debtor's property, or to the extent of the value of the property taken and converted by him. [2] A judgment in the plaintiff's favor for the precise sum of money claimed was, under all the circumstances, the proper judgment.[9] *Held*, further, that the form of the judgment does not stamp this as a legal, rather than an equitable action. [9]

Where, in such a case, there was evidence that the property couverted was, when first mortgaged—six years before—worth the sum of $3,000, but no evidence as to its value when converted, the court was justified in finding that when couverted it was worth at least the amount of plaintiff's claim, $734.18. [7]

Where an action, in the nature of a creditor's bill, was tried by a judge just as equitable actions are required to be tried,—*Held*, that it mattered not that the cause was noticed for trial at a jury term.[8]

Where an execution was returned on the day the complaint was sworn to, and the summons dated, the court is justified holding that it was returned before the commencement of the action, in the absence of proof as to when the action was commenced. [8]

(*Decided November* 21. 1882.)

Appeal from judgment of general term, reversing judgment of special term.

The facts are fully stated in the opinion.

Adolphus D. Pape, for appellant.

George H. Starr (*Starr & Hooker*, attorneys), for respondent.

Earl, J.—The complaint in this action alleges that, in and prior to April, 1872, the defendant, Doyle, was indebted to the plaintiff in the sum of $500, to the defendant Curley, in the sum of $500, and to one Fitzsimmons, in the sum of $300, and that these were all the debts that he owed; that in April, 1872, he, Doyle, owned a large amount of personal property, worth at least $3,500, and at that time gave the defendant Curley a mortgage thereon for the nominal amount of $3,100, and that that security, by renewals or new mortgages, each year executed, was kept in force until October 10, 1878, when the defendant Curley foreclosed the last mortgage, although there was nothing actually due thereon, and converted the proceeds of the property to his own use; that all the mortgages were made and kept in force for the purpose of hindering, delaying and defrauding the plaintiff and the other creditors of Doyle; that on October 10, 1878, the plaintiff recovered judgment upon his demand against Doyle for upwards of $700, and that an execution upon the judgment was issued and returned unsatisfied; and the plaintiff prayed judgment against the defendants, that they and each of them be compelled to pay him the aforesaid sum of $734.18, with interest, besides costs.

The defendant Curley, in his answer, admitted the giving of the mortgage referred to in the complaint, and the foreclosure of the last mortgage, and denied the other allegations contained in the complaint. The defendant Doyle suffered default.

The cause was noticed for trial for "a jury or trial term," as stated in the printed case, and a trial by jury having been waived, it was tried before a judge without a jury.

Upon the trial, the plaintiff gave evidence tending to prove all the allegations contained in the complaint, his only witness being Doyle, and the defendant Curley, as a witness in his own behalf, gave evidence tending to show that the mortgages were given in good faith, to secure an indebtedness actually due him.

The trial judge found all the allegations of fact contained in the complaint to be substantially true. Among his findings of fact, was one "that said chattel mortgages were made by said Doyle, and received by said Curley, with intent to hinder, delay and defraud this plaintiff and said Fitzsimmons of their lawful suits, damages, debts and demands," and he found as conclusions of law, that the mortgages were fraudulent and void as against the plaintiff, and were made with the intent to hinder, delay and defraud him, and that they did hinder, delay and defraud him in the collection of his claim, and that, by reason thereof, he suffered damages to the amount of his judgment; that the defendant Curley, was liable jointly with Doyle, for the amount of plaintiff's damages, and he directed that judgment be entered in favor of plaintiff and against the defendants, for the amount of the judgment, with interest and costs.

The defendant, Curley, filed exceptions to the findings of the judge, and his refusal to find as requested, and appealed from the judgment entered in favor of the plaintiff to the general term, and there the judgment was reversed and a new trial granted for errors of law. It appears, from the opinion pronounced at general term, that the action was there treated not as a creditor's bill, but as an action at law to recover damages for the fraud alleged, and the conclusion reached was that such an action could not be sustained, and the decision of the general term was sought by Curley's counsel to be sustained in his argument before us upon the same ground.

We are of opinion that the learned general term fell
into error. The complaint contains all the alle-
[1] gations requisite for what is commonly called a
creditor's bill, to wit, that the plaintiff was a creditor of Doyle, having a judgment and execution returned unsatisfied, that the mortgages were executed by Doyle with the intent to hinder, delay and defraud his creditors, and that Curley had converted the mortgaged property by a sale, and had taken the proceeds to his use. The facts alleged show that the mortgages were void as to the plaintiff, and the only
[2] relief the plaintiff needed was that Curley should
pay him out of the money received by him

from the debtor's property, or to the extent of the value of such property taken and converted by him. Hence there can be no reasonable objection to the judgment prayed for. Even if the prayer for judgment
[3] was defective for equitable relief, an answer having been interposed, the plaintiff could have any relief "consistent with the case made by the complaint, and embraced within the issues" (*Code*, § 1207).*

Under our present system of practice a plaintiff
[4] is not to be turned out of court when an answer has been interposed, because he has prayed for too much or too little, or for wrong relief.

It matters not that the cause was noticed for
[5] trial at a jury term. It does not appear that either party claimed that the action was a legal action, triable by a jury. It was, in fact, tried by the judge, just as equitable actions are required to be tried.

No claim was made upon the trial that this was not an equitable action. The judge found all the facts requisite to sustain a creditor's bill. It is said that there was no proof that the execution was returned before the commencement of the action. But it does not appear when the action was commenced. The summons is dated October 12, 1878, and the complaint was
[6] sworn to on the same day, and alleges that the execution had been issued and returned unsatisfied. It was proved that the execution was returned in the usual form unsatisfied on October 12, 1878, and the judge found that it was returned before the commencement of the action. There was no claim at the trial that the execution was returned after the commencement of the action, and we think the finding that it was returned before was justified. There was proof
[7] sufficient to justify a finding that the property taken by Curley was worth much more than the

* A demurrer is not an answer within the meaning of this section. Kelly v. Downing, 42 *N. Y.* 71.

plaintiff's judgment. At the time the first mortgage was given in 1872, the property mortgaged was worth upwards of $3,000. No other proof as to its value was given. There was no claim upon the trial, and no request to find that it was not worth at least the amount of plaintiff's claim, and in the absence of other proof the judge was justified in finding, as we must assume he did, that it was worth, when taken and converted by Curley, at least that sum. It cannot be alleged for legal error that the judge based his decision upon the evidence of Doyle, which was in direct conflict with that of Curley. That conflict raised a question of credibility which was to be settled by the trial judge.

There can be no valid objection to the form of the judgment ordered. Curley did not ask that any
[*] other judgment should be given to the plaintiff. He did not claim that any accounting should be ordered between him and Doyle, or as to the proceeds of the property sold by him. He gave all the
[*] proof he desired to, to defeat plaintiff's action. Under the circumstances of the case, this judgment for the recovery of the precise sum of money claimed, was the proper judgment, and the form of the judgment does not stamp this as a legal rather than an equitable action. A court of equity adapts its relief to the exigencies of the case in hand. It may restrain or compel the defendant; it may appoint a receiver or order an accounting; may compel specific performance or order the delivery to the plaintiff of specific real or personal property, or it may order a sum of money to be paid to the plaintiff, and give him a personal judgment therefor. Here no accounting was needed. Even if something was honestly due from Doyle to Curley, on account of the fraud, Curley could not retain the property, or use its proceeds against a pursuing creditor to pay his debt. The transaction between

him and Doyle was, as to the plaintiff, void, and he could take no benefit from it. The plaintiff was the vigilant debtor, and had priority over other creditors, if there were any. But there appears to have been but one other creditor of Doyle, and that one Fitzsimmons, and his claim was apparently barred by the statute of limitations. Besides, the property was sufficent to pay the plaintiff, Fitzsimmons, and Curley. Under such circumstances, all the relief that plaintiff needed was to compel Curley to pay him. There was no property to be sold. He had converted it, and had the proceeds. No receiver was needed, and there were no accounts to be taken or stated. The judgment ordered was therefore proper. The order of the general term should be reversed, and the judgment of the trial term affirmed, with costs.

All concur.

DORR v. MILLS ET AL.

CITY COURT OF BROOKLYN; SPECIAL TERM, DEC., 1882.

§§ 481, 547.

Complaint.—Setting out two causes of action on same claim should be amended.—When, should be required to be made more definite and certain.

A complaint alleged that certain services and materials sued for "were reasonably worth the sum of $1523.85, and defendants promised and agreed to pay therefor the sum of $1,523.85." *Held*, that the complaint should amend so as to state a cause of action in one form, either on *quantum meruit* or a promise to pay.

Where a complaint averred, on a day named that, "the defendants were indebted to 'one D.' in the sum of $80, which sum the defendants promised and agreed to pay," and set up the assignment of the claim to plaintiff,—*Held*, that it should be amended so as to set out the nature, character and terms of the contract, and with whom the same was made.

Gardner *v.* Locke (2 *N. Y. Civ. Pro.* 252), approved.
(*Decided December* 15, 1882.)

Motion (1) to compel plaintiff to elect upon which of two causes of action, set out in his complaint, as a first cause of action, *quantum meruit*, or special contract, he will rely; (2) to make the second cause of action more definite and certain.

The complaint set out two causes of action. The first of which was for services rendered, and materials furnished defendants by plaintiff. It stated "that said services and materials were reasonably worth the sum of $1,523.85, and defendants promised and agreed to pay therefor the sum of $1,523.85." For a second cause of action, the complaint alleged, "that on or about the 25th day of November, 1879, the defendants were indebted to Henry J. Dorr, upon a contract, in the sum of $80, which said sum the defendants promised and agreed to pay," and then set up the assignment of that claim to the plaintiff.

Alexander R. Thompson, Jr. (*Thompson Bros.*, attorneys), for motion:

Cited, in support of motion to compel plaintiff to elect, etc., Gardner *v.* Locke, 2 *N. Y. Civ. Pro. R.* 252; Churchill *v.* Churchill, 9 *How. Pr.* 552; Waler *v.* Raskan, 12 *Id.* 28. In support of motion to make second cause of action more definite and certain, Wiggin *v.* Gans, 3 *Sandf.* 646.

Mirabeau L. Towns, opposed.

NEILSON, J.—The case of Gardner *v.* Locke (2 *N. Y. Civ. Pro. R.* 252) is an authority in support of this claim, that the complaint should be amended as to the first cause of action stated. The same principle applies as to the second cause of action.

Let the complaint be amended: First, as to the first cause of action, by electing or by stating one form, that is, as to the value, or as to the promise to pay. Second, as to the other cause of action, by alleging nature, character and terms of the contract mentioned, and with whom the same was made.

Defendant's costs of motion, $10, to abide the event.

COOPER ET AL. v. JOLLY.

SUPREME COURT, FOURTH DEPARTMENT; ONEIDA COUNTY SPECIAL TERM, JANUARY, 1883.

§ 3234.

Costs.—When both parties to action entitled to.

Where in an action for the recovery of money only, the complaint set forth separately twenty-three causes of action, upon each of which an issue of fact was joined by the answer, and upon the trial evidence was given tending to establish thirteen of the alleged causes of action, and a verdict was found on two of them in favor of plaintiff, and there was no certificate that the substantial cause of action was the same in each case,—*Held*, that each party was entitled to costs against the adverse party.

(*Decided January* 3, 1883.)

Watson M. Rogers (*Lansing & Rogers*, attorneys), for the motion.

Charles W. Thompson, opposed.

MERWIN, J.—This was an action for the recovery of money only. The complaint sets forth, separately, twenty-three causes of action, upon each of which an issue of fact was joined by the answer. The action is for penalties under chapter 518 of Laws of 1864, as amended by chapter 237 of Laws of 1878. Upon the trial evidence was given tending to establish thirteen of the alleged causes of action. The verdict was "for the plaintiff for two counts at $50 each, amounting to $100."

By section 3234 of the Code of Civil Procedure, it is provided that in an action, specified in section 3228, wherein the complaint sets forth separately two or more causes of action upon which issues of fact are joined, if the plaintiff recovers upon one or more of the issues, and the defendant upon the other or others, each party is entitled to costs against the adverse party, unless it is certified that the substantial cause of action was the same upon each issue; in which case the plaintiff only is entitled to costs. There is no certificate bringing this case within the exception in the last clause, there is no question but that the action is specified in section 3228. But the point is made by the counsel for plaintiff that the failure of plaintiff to recover on all the counts, is not equivalent to a recovery by defendant, within the meaning of the section. Upon all the counts but two, the defendant was certainly successful. The verdict, however, was not in terms in his favor on those counts, but it was so in effect, and would be a bar to any further prosecution of defendant on those counts. (Guenther *v.* People, 24 *N. Y.* 100, 101.) If so, he, to all intents and purposes, recovered on the issues made as to those counts. I cannot, as it seems to me, reasonably hold any other way. The effect of such a holding may operate as a hardship in this and other similar cases. It may be that there was no occasion for such a provision, in view of the opportunity that a defendant has to protect himself by an offer of judgment. These considerations are for the legislature, not for this court.

In the case of Thayer *v.* Holland, 63 *How.* 179, cited by plaintiff's counsel, the operation of the section in question was not considered. In Hudson *v.* Guttenburg, 9 *Abb. N. C.* 415, the defendant was allowed costs, although there was no specific finding in his favor, the plaintiff having failed to recover on one count. No point is made in the present motion as to the necessity of a certificate under section 3248.

In my opinion, the situation of the defendant brings him within the provision of section 3234, and he is entitled to recover costs against the plaintiff, such costs to be taxed by the clerk, and offset against the costs or recovery of the plaintiff.

No costs on this motion.

THE PEOPLE OF THE STATE OF NEW YORK, APPELLANTS, v. THE NEW YORK CENTRAL AND HUDSON RIVER RAILROAD COMPANY, RESPONDENT.

THE SAME, APPELLANTS, v. THE NEW YORK, LAKE ERIE AND WESTERN RAILWAY COMPANY, RESPONDENT.

SUPREME COURT, FIRST DEPARTMENT, GENERAL TERM; OCTOBER, 1882.

§§ 1993, 2067, 2070.

Mandamus.—Motion to quash application for, not proper practice.—May be granted to compel railroad corporation to perform public duties.—Duties of railroads to receive, transport and deliver freight, are public.—Railroads are public highways.

Where an alternative writ of mandamus has been granted, the defendant may move to quash or set the same aside. Such a motion is in the nature of a demurrer, and should be made before the return to the writ, unless the motion to quash is based upon a defect in substance, in which case it may be taken advantage of at any time before a peremptory mandamus is awarded. Upon such a motion the moving party holds the affirmative. [1]

Where, upon the return of an order to show cause why a mandamus should not issue, the defendant's counsel objected that the moving papers failed to show any grounds for the relief prayed for, and moved "to quash and dismiss said petitions and order to show cause," and the court entertained and granted the motion,—*Held*, that no alternative writ having been granted, there was nothing to quash;[3] that the usual and proper course was to proceed to a hearing of the motion for the writ, the moving party holding the affirmative.[1]

On motions at special term it is not very material which party opens or closes, and the general term on appeal will only inquire into the correctness of the decision where the order denies or grants the motion. [4]

Railroads are, in every essential quality, public highways, created for public use, but permitted to be owned, controlled and managed by private persons. [6, 8, 9, 12] All public highways are subjects of general State jurisdiction, because their uses are the common property of the public. [10]

The State has no power to grant the right of eminent domain to any corporation or person for other than a public use. [7]

The general railroad act, which authorizes the organization of corporations for "the construction, maintaining and operating" of railroads "for public use," imposed upon them the duty "to furnish accommodations for all passengers and property, and to transport all persons and property on payment of fare or freight." [11] These duties are consigned to them as public trusts, and the acceptance of such trusts on the part of a corporation makes it an agency of the State to perform public functions which might otherwise devolved ed upon public officers. [13, 14]

While it is not the duty of the State to be or become a common carrier upon the public highways which it is its duty to make and maintain, [17] it may in some cases assume that duty, and whenever it lawfully does so, the execution of the duty may be enforced against the agents or officers upon whom the law devolves it. [18]

A railroad corporation is compellable by mandamus to exercise its duties as a common carrier of freight and passengers. [19, 20] The power so to compel it rests (1) upon the ground that that duty is a public trust, which, having been conferred by the State and accepted by the corporation, may be enforced for the public benefit; [11, 13, 14, 20] (2) upon the contract between the corporation and the State, expressed in its charter, or implied by the acceptance of the franchise; [20] and (3) upon the ground that the common right of all the people to travel and carry upon every public highway of the State, has been changed in the special instance by the legislature into a corporate franchise, to be exercised solely by a corporate body for the public benefit, to the exclusion of all other persons, whereby it has become the duty of the State to see that the franchise so put in trust be faithfully administered by its trustees. [18, 19, 20]

The fact that the State suffers no pecuniary injury by the neglect, misuse or abuse of any public function vested by it in any person, natural or artificial, for the common good, is no test of the power or duty of the State. [21] In every such case the sovereignty of the State is injured. [22] While the State may proceed, where a corporation neglects public duties, to annul it, its only adequate remedy is by mandamus to compel the performance of such duties. [23] A sound discretion is vested in its law officer to decide whether the exigency is such as to call for the use of either remedy, as it is ultimately for the court to decide whether the elected remedy should be applied. [24] The fact that injured individuals may have private remedies for the damages they have sustained by neglect of the duties, does not preclude the State from its remedy by mandamus. [25] If the people have a right to the remedy, the attorney-general is the proper officer to set it in effective operation on their behalf. [6]

Chapter 133 of the Laws of 1880, which provides that railroad corporations shall have power "to regulate the time and manner in which passengers and property shall be transported," gives them a discretion, but does not justify a general or partial suspension of the duty of receiving and transporting freight. [27]

Railroad corporations cannot refuse or neglect to perform their public duties upon a controversy with their employees over the cost or expense of doing them. [30, 31] Their duties must be discharged at whatever cost, and can not be laid down, or abandoned, or suspended without the legally expressed consent of the State. [31]

On an application of the State for a mandamus requiring a railroad company to resume its duties as a common carrier, it appeared that for about two weeks the company failed and neglected to receive from three-quarters to seven-eighths of the goods offered for transportation from and to the city of New York, and in many instances refused to receive goods offered, and turned them back and closed their gates during business hours, thus causing a stoppage of all delivery of freight, and in some instances unusual terms were sought to be imposed as a condition of receiving goods, which would increase the risks of the owner; that the refusal to receive goods did not arise from any unwillingness or inability on the part of the shipper to pay charges, but was wholly the act of the railroad company: that it was so continuous and extensive that it seriously interfered with the business operations of the citizens of New York, deteriorated the value of many commodities, and caused a diversion of trade from the city; that great losses were caused, and large quantities of perishable goods, by reason of non-delivery, were destroyed, to the value of many thousand dollars, and that a vast amount of freight was thus detained and refused carriage. *Held*, That these facts, being true and unexcused, showed a strong case for the interference of the State; [29] that the fact that certain employees of the company, who had been working at the rate of seventeen cents per hour, refused to work unless twenty cents per hour were paid, and their abandonment of the work, and the inefficiency of the unskilled men afterwards employed caused the neglect and refusal complained of, is not a sufficient excuse. [30] Also *Held*, that the writ of mandamus, in such case, should require the company to resume the duties of carriers of goods and passengers—that is, to receive, carry and deliver the same under the existing rules and regulations; that there was no necessity to specify what kinds of goods should be first received and carried, or whose goods, or to take any notice of the details of the established usages of the companies. [32] Upon the return to the writ all questions whether what had been done was a sufficient compliance with its commands may properly arise and become a subject of further consideration. [33]

Bloodgood v. Mohawk and Hudson R. R. Co. (18 *Wend.* 9); [8] Olcott v. Supervisors (16 *Wall* 678); [9] Messenger v. The Pennsylvania R. R. Co. (36 *N. J.* 107); [12] Talcott v. Township of Pine Grove (1 *Flippin U. S. Cir. Ct.* 144); [13] Railroad Commissioners v. Portland and Oxford R. R. Co. (63 *Maine*, 269); [28] approved; Ohlen v. Erie Railway Company (22 *Hun*, 533), distinguished. [36]

(*Decided January* 17, 1883.)

Appeals from orders of the special term, granting motions to quash and dismiss the petitions and orders to show cause, of the appellants, and denying the application of the appellants for peremptory writs of mandamus (Reversing 2 *N. Y. Civ. Pro. R.* 82).

The opinion states the facts.

Leslie W. Russell, attorney-general, *E. C. James*, *Simon Sterne* and *Daniel G. Thompson*, for appellants.

Roscoe Conkling and *William D. Shipman*, for respondents.

Davis, P. J.—The appellants, upon the petition of their attorney-general, and affidavits accompanying the same, obtained orders from one of the justices of this court, requiring the respondents respectively to show cause, upon service of less than eight days, at a special term sitting at chambers, why a peremptory writ of mandamus should not issue, commanding the respondents respectively to forthwith resume the discharge of their duties as common carriers, and the exercise of their franchises, by promptly receiving, transporting and delivering all such freight or other property as may be offered to or heretofore received by them for transportation at their stations, in and to the city of New York, upon the usual and reasonable terms and charges.

Upon an adjourned day for the hearing of the motion, the respondents appeared by counsel and objected that the moving papers failed to show any grounds for the relief prayed for, and moved "to quash and dismiss said petitions and orders to show cause." The court entertained this motion, and, against the objection of the appellants, awarded the right to open and close the argument on the hearing to the counsel for the respondents; and after hearing the respective counsel, the court ordered as follows: "That the said preliminary objection be and the same is hereby sustained, and that the motion to quash the said petition and order to show cause be and the same is hereby granted, and the said application of the said petitioner denied."

It is now objected that this mode of disposing of the motions was so far irregular as to render the orders erroneous.

It certainly was an unusual mode of proceeding. The motions came to the special term precisely as though upon an ordinary notice. The order of the judge simply limited the time of notice, and when the respondents appeared in answer to the notice, if they

were willing to come to a hearing upon the petition and affidavits, the usual and proper course was to proceed to a hearing of the motions upon those pa-
[1] pers, the moving party holding the affirmative, and being entitled to the right to open and close. A motion to quash a motion is a novel proceeding. Motions to quash usually apply to existing writs or process, and not to mere attempts to obtain them. The court doubtless regarded the action of the respondent's counsel as in the nature of a demurrer *ore tenus* to the petition, and affidavits on the part of the appellants.

Where an alternative writ has been granted, the
[2] defendant may move to quash or set the same aside (People *ex rel.* Knapp *v.* Judges, &c. of Westchester, 4 *Cow.* 73), and such a motion is in the nature of a demurrer (People *ex rel.* Barnet *v.* College of Physicians, &c., 7 *How. Pr.* 290) and should be made before the return to the writ, unless the motion to quash is based upon a defect in substance, in which case it may be taken advantage of at any time before a peremptory mandamus is awarded (Commercial Bank of Albany *v.* Canal Commissioners, 10 *Wend.* 25; People *ex rel.* Post *v.* Ransom, 2 *N. Y.* 490). Of course, upon such a motion the moving party holds the affirmative, but that was not this case. In this case, no alternative writ having been issued, there was nothing to quash; and the objection made was simply an assertion that
[3] the appellants were not, upon their own showing, entitled to have the motion granted; and such assertion did not change the rights of the respective parties as to the order of proceeding on the hearing. The court of appeals have held that the according of the affirmative to the wrong party on a trial before a jury is an error fatal to the judgment. But, on motions at special term, it is not very material which party opens or closes; and this court on review will only in-
[4] quire into the correctness of the decision where

the order denies or grants the motion. In this case, although the order directs that the petition and proceedings be quashed, yet the motion for the mandamus was also denied, and both the denial and the order to quash were based upon the merits of the motion. The right of appeal was not affected, and we think it is our duty to hear and dispose of the appeal upon the merits. The practice at the special term should, however, be discountenanced as a precedent.

The question presented by the motion is one of signal importance. It is whether the people of the state can invoke the power of the courts to compel the exercise by railroad corporations of the most useful public functions with which they are clothed. If the people have that right, there can be no doubt that their attorney-general is the proper officer to set it in effective [5] operation on their behalf (1 *R. S.* 179, § 1, *Code C. Pro.* § 1993; People *ex rel.* Stephens *v.* Halsey, 37 *N. Y.* 344; People *ex rel.* Case *v.* Collins, 19 *Wend.* 56).

The question involves a consideration of the nature of this class of corporations, the objects for which they are created, the powers conferred and the duties imposed upon them by the laws of their creation and of the State. As bodies corporate, their ownership may be, and usually is, altogether private, belonging wholly to the holders of their capital stock; and their management may be vested in such officers or agents as the stockholders and directors, under the provisions of law, may appoint. In this sense they are to be regarded as trading or private corporations, having in view the profit or advantage of the corporators. But these conditions are in no just sense in conflict with their obligations and duties to the public. The objects of their creation are, from their very nature, largely different from those of ordinary private and trading corporations. Railroads are, in every essential quality, public highways, created for public use, but per-

[6] mitted to be owned, controlled and managed by private persons. But for this quality, the railroads of the respondents could not lawfully exist. Their construction depended upon the exercise of the right of eminent domain, which belongs to the State in its in the corporate capacity alone, and cannot be conferred, except upon a "public use." The State has no power to grant the right of eminent domain to any
[7] corporation or person for other than a public use. Every attempt to go beyond that is void by the constitution, and although the legislature may determine what is a necessary public use, it cannot by any sort of enactment divest of that character any portion of the right of eminent domain which it may confer. This characteristic of "public use" is in no sense lost or diminished by the fact that the use of the railroad by the corporation which constructs or owns it must, from its nature, be exclusive. That incident grows out of the method of use, which does not admit of any enjoyment in common by the public. The general and popular use of a railroad as a highway is, therefore, handed over exclusively to corporate management and control, because that is for the best and manifest advantage of the public. The progress of science and skill has shown that highways may be created for public use, of such form and kind that the best and most advantageous enjoyment by the people can only be secured through the ownership, management and control of corporate bodies created for that purpose, and the people of the State are not restricted from availing themselves of the best modes for the carriage of their persons and property. There is nothing in the constitution hostile to the adoption and use by the state of any and every newly developed form or kind of travel and traffic which have a public use for their end and aim, and giving to them vital activity by the use of the power of eminent domain.

When the earliest constitution of our State was adopted, railroads were unknown. The public highways of the State were its turnpikes, ordinary roads and navigable waters. The exercise of eminent domain in respect of them was permitted by the constitution, for the same reasons that adapt it now to the greatly improved methods of travel and transportation; and in making this adaptation, there is no enlarged sense given to the language of the constitution, so long as its inherent purpose,—the creation only of public uses,—be faithfully observed.

These principles are abundantly sustained by authority. In Bloodgood *v.* Mohawk & Hudson R. R. Co. (18 *Wend.* 9), the court of last resort in this [*] State first announced them, and affixed to railroads their true character as public highways. It is there declared that the fact that railroad corporations may remunerate themselves by tolls and fares "does not destroy the public nature of a road, nor convert it from a public to a private use. . . . If it is a public franchise, and granted to the company for the purpose of providing a mode of public conveyance, the company, in accepting it, engages on its part to use it in such manner as will accomplish the object for which the legislature designed it." And in Olcott *v.* The Supervisors (16 *Wall.* 678) the su- [*] preme court of the United States adjudge "That railroads, though constructed by private corporations and owned by them, are public highways, has been the doctrine of nearly all the courts, ever since such conveniences for passage and transportation have had any existence. Very early the question was whether a State's right of eminent domain could be exercised by a private corporation created for the purpose of constructing a railroad. Clearly it could not, unless taking land for such a purpose by such an agency is taking land for public use. The right of eminent domain nowhere justifies taking property for private use. Yet it is a doctrine universally accepted that a State legislature may authorize a private corporation to take land for the construction of such a road, making compensation to the owner. What else does this doctrine mean, if not that building a railroad, though it be built by a private corporation, is an act done for a public use? And the reason why the use has always been held a public one is that such a road is a highway, whether made by the government itself, or by the agency of corporate bodies, or even by individuals when they obtain their power to construct it from legislative grant. Whether the use of a railroad is a public or a private one depends in no measure upon the question who constructed it or who owns it. It has never been considered a matter of any importance that the road was built by the agency of a private corporation. *No matter who is the agent, the function performed is that of the State. Though the ownership is private, the USE is public.* The owners may be private companies, *but they are compellable to permit the public to use their works in the manner in which such works can be used.* That all persons may not put their own cars upon the road, and use their own motor power, has no bearing upon the question whether the road is a public highway. It bears only upon the mode of use, of which the legislature is the exclusive judge."

All public highways are subjects of general State jurisdiction, because their uses are the common property of the public. This principle of the common
[10] law is, in this State, of universal application. As to the class of public highways known as railroads, the common law is fortified by the express conditions of the statutes creating or regulating or controlling them.

The General Railroad Act of this State may now be

regarded as the general charter of all such corpora-
[11] tions. It authorizes the organization of corporations
for "the constructing, maintaining and operating" of railroads "*for public use*," and it imposes upon them the duty "to furnish accommodations for all passengers and property, and to transport all persons and property on payment of fare or freight" (*Laws of* 1850, chap. 140, §§ 1, 36). These words are a brief summary in respect of the duties imposed upon such corporations by all the provisions of the act. Those duties are consigned to them as public trusts, and, as was said in Messenger *v.* Pennsylvania R. R. Co. (36 *N. J.* 407), "although in the hands of a private cor-
[12] poration, they are still sovereign franchises, and
must be used and treated as such; they must be held in trust for the public good." This relation of such a corporation to the State is forcibly expressed by EMMONS, J., in Talcott *v.* Township of Pine Grove
[13] (1 *Flippin U. S. C. C.* 144): "The road, once
constructed, is, instanter, and by mere force of the grant and law, embodied in the governmental agencies of the State and dedicated to public use. All and singular its cars, engines, rights of way and property of every description, real, personal and mixed, are but a trust fund for the political power, like the functions of a public office. The artificial personage—the corporation created by the sovereign power expressly for this sole purpose and no other—is, in the most strict, technical and unqualified sense, but its trustee. This is the primary and sole legal political motive for its creation. The incidental interest and profits of individuals are accidents, both in theory and practice."

The acceptance of such trusts on the part of a corporation, by the express and implied contracts already referred to, makes it an agency of the State to
[14] perform public functions which might otherwise
be devolved upon public officers. The maintenance

and control of most other classes of public highways are so devolved, and the performance of every official duty in respect of them may be compelled by the courts on application of the State, while private damages may also be recoverable for individual injuries. The analogy between such officials and railroad corporations, in regard to their relations to the State, is strong and clear, and, so far as affects the construction and proper and efficient maintenance of their railways, will be questioned by no one. It is equally clear, we think, in regard to their duty as carriers of persons and property. This springs sharply out of the
[15] exclusive nature of their right to do those things.

On other public highways every person may be his own carrier; or he may hire whomsoever he will to do that service. Between him and such employee a special and personal relation exists, independent of any public duty, and in which the State has no interest. In such a case, the carrier has not contracted with the State to assume the duty *as a public trust*, nor taken the right and power to do it from the State by becoming the special donee and depositary of a trust. A good reason may, therefore, be assigned why the State will not, by mandamus, enforce the performance of his contract by such a carrier. But the reason for such a rule altogether fails when the public highway is the exclu-
[16] sive property of a body corporate, which alone has power to use it, in a manner which of necessity requires that all management, control and user for the purposes of carriage must be limited to itself, and which, as a condition of the franchise that grants such absolute and exclusive power over and user of a public highway, has contracted with the State to accept the duty of carrying all persons and property within the scope of its charter, as a public trust. The relation of the State to such a body is entirely different from that which it bears to the individual users of

a common highway, as between whom and the State no relation of trust exists; and there is small reason for seeking analogies between them. It is the duty
[17] of the State to make and maintain public highways. That duty it performs by a scheme of laws, which set in operation the functions of its political divisions into counties, towns and other municipalities, and their officers. It can and does enforce those duties, whenever necessary, through its courts. It is not the duty of the State to be or become a common
[18] carrier upon its public highways; but it may, in some cases, assume that duty, and, whenever it lawfully does so, the execution of the duty may be enforced against the agents or officers upon whom the law devolves it. It may grant its power to construct a public highway to a corporation, or an individual, and, with that power, its right of eminent domain, in order to secure the public use; and may make the traffic of the highway common to all on such terms as it may impose. In such case, it is its duty to secure that common traffic, when refused, by the authority of its courts (19 *Wend.* 56;* 1 *Cow.* 23†). Or it may grant the same powers of construction and maintenance, with the exclusive enjoyment of use which the manner of use requires, and, if that excludes all common travel and transportation, it may impose on the corporation or person the duty to furnish every requisite facility for carrying passengers and freight, and to carry both in such manner and at such times as public needs may require. Why is that duty, in respect of the power to compel its performance through the courts, not in the category of all others entrusted to such a body? The writ of mandamus has been awarded to compel a company to operate its road as one continuous line (Union Pacific R. R. Co. v. Hall,

* People *ex rel.* Case v. Collins.

† People *ex rel.* McFarland v. Commissioners of Highways, &c.

91 *U. S.* 343); to compel the running of passenger trains to the terminus of the road (State *v.* N. Y., N. H. & H. R'y Co., 29 *Conn.* 538); to compel the company to make fences and cattle-guards (People *ex rel.* Garbutt *v.* Rochester & State Line R. R. Co., 14 *Hun*, 373; affirmed, 76 *N. Y.* 294); to compel it to build a bridge (70 *N. Y.* 569);* to compel it to construct its road across streams so as not to interfere with navigation (State *v.* Northern R. R. Co., 9 *Rich.* [*S. C.*] 247); to compel it to run daily trains (*Re* New Brunswick & Canada R. R., 1 *P. & B.* [*New Brunswick*] 667); to compel the delivery of grain at a particular elevator (Chicago, etc. R. R. Co. *v.* People, 56 *Ill.* 365); to compel the completion of its road (Farmers' Loan & Trust Co. *v* Henning, receiver, &c., 17 *Am. Law Reg. N. S.* 266); to compel the grading of its track so as to make crossings convenient and useful (58 *N. Y.* 152;† 12 *Hun*, 175;‡ 74 *N. Y.* 302;‡ Indianapolis R. R. Co. *v.* State, 37 *Ind.* 489; 35 *N. J. L.* 396); to compel the re-establishment of an abandoned station (State *v.* N. H. & N. R. R. 37 *Conn.* 154); to compel the replacement of a track taken up in violation of its charter (King *v.* Severn & Wye Railway Co., 2 *Barn. & Adol.* 644); to prevent the abandonment of a road once completed (Talcott *v.* Township of Pine Grove, *supra*, 1 *Flippin*, 145); and to compel a company to exercise its franchise (People *v.* Albany & Vermont R. R. Co., 24 *N. Y.* 261. These are all express or implied obligations arising from the charters of the railroad companies, but not more so than the duty to carry freight and passengers. That duty is indeed the *ultima ratio* of their existence; the great and sole public good for the attainment and accomplishment of which all the other powers and duties are given or imposed. It is strangely illogical to

* People *ex rel.* Kimbal *v.* Boston & A. R. R. Co.

† People *ex rel.* Green *v.* Dutchess & Columbia R. R. Co.

‡ People *v.* New York Central & Hudson River R. R. Co.

[19] assert that the State, through the courts, may compel the performance of every step necessary to bring a corporation into a condition of readiness to do the very thing for which it is created, but is then powerless to compel the doing of the thing itself.

We cannot bring our minds to entertain a doubt that a railroad corporation is compellable by mandamus to exercise its duties as a carrier of freight
[20] and passengers, and that the power so to compel it rests equally firmly on the ground that that duty is a public trust, which, having been conferred by the State and accepted by the corporation, may be enforced for the public benefit, and also upon the contract between the corporation and the State, expressed in its charter or implied by the acceptance of the franchise (Abbott *v.* Johnson, &c. Horse R. R. Co., 80 *N. Y.* 31), and also upon the ground that the common right of all the people to travel and carry upon every public highway of the State has been changed in the special instance by the legislature, for adequate reasons, into a corporate franchise, to be exercised solely by a corporate body, for the public benefit, to the exclusion of all other persons, whereby it has become the duty of the State to see to it that the franchise so put in trust be faithfully administered by its trustee.

But it is said that the State is not injured, and has no interest in the question whether the corporation
[21] perform the duty or not. The State may suffer no direct pecuniary injury, as it may not by the neglect of one or more of its numerous political officers, who hold, in trust for the people, the official duties reposed in their hands; but that is no test of the power or duty of the State in either case. The sovereignty of the State is injured whenever any public function vested by it in any person, natural or artificial, for
[22] the common good, is not used or is misused, or is abused; and it is not bound to inquire whether

some one or more of its citizens has not thereby received a special injury for which he may recover damages in his private suit. Such an injury wounds the sovereignty of the State and thereby, in a legal sense, injures the entire body politic. The State in such a case as this has no other adequate remedy. It may proceed, it is true, to annul the corporation, as has [23] been held in many cases where corporations had neglected public duties (People *v.* Fishkill, &c. Plank-road Co., 27 *Barb.* 452, 458; People *v.* President, &c. Hillsdale & Chatham Turnpike Co., 23 *Wend.* 254; Turnpike Co. *v.* State, 3 *Wall.* 210; People *ex rel.* Bishop *v.* Kingston & Middletown Turnpike Road Co., 23 *Wend.* 208; People *ex rel.* M'Kinch *v.* President, &c. Bristol & Rensselaerville Turnpike Road, *Id.* 222; Charles River Bridge Co. *v.* Warren Bridge Co., 7 *Pick.* 344); but that remedy is not adequate, for it only destroys functions where the public interests require their continued existence and enforcement. It has, therefore, an election which of these remedies to pursue (State *v.* H. & N. H. R. R. Co., 29 *Conn.* 538; People *v.* Albany & Vermont R. R. Co., 24 *N. Y.* 261; Talcott *v.* Township of Pine Grove, *supra*).*

Undoubtedly a sound discretion is vested in its law officer to decide whether the exigency is such [24] as to call for the use of either remedy, as it is ultimately for the court to judge whether the elected remedy should be applied. But upon the question of power and of sufficient legal injury to justify its use, where the corporation neglects or refuses to exercise its franchises or perform its duties, there seems to us no reason to doubt.

Nor do we think the fact that injured individuals may have private remedies for the damages they [25] have sustained by neglect of duties, precludes the

* 1 *Flippin* (*U. S. Cir Ct.*) 144.

State from its remedy by mandamus. Where the injury is to a single person under circumstances which do not affect the general public, the courts, in the exercise of their discretion, have properly refused this remedy on his relation. The injured party is then the suitor; he has an adequate remedy by private action for damages. That was the case of The People *ex*
[26] *rel.* Ohlen *v.* N. Y., Lake Erie & Western Ry. Co. (22 *Hun*, 533), relied upon by the court below, in which the court held that the relator's remedy was by suit for damages and not by mandamus. That case is not authority for denying the writ to the attorney-general, for a neglect or refusal by corporations to exercise their franchise, to an extent which affects a great number of citizens and continues for a considerable period of time; nor does it deny the right of the people, acting on their own behalf and in their own suit, to pursue this remedy inany case of neglect or refusal to exercise a public function which the interest of the people require should be kept in vigorous and efficient use.

The court in that case recognizes the distinction when it says: "An exception exists . . . . where a corporation suspends the exercise of its functions." The suspension of the exercise of corporate functions is the gravamen of the complaint in this case, and the case cited is no authority for denying the writ when the people come into court with their own suit, by their attorney-general, to move for a writ of mandamus on allegations of an alleged long-continued and very general suspension of a corporate duty.

It was supposed by the court below that the provisions of section 28 of the act of 1850,* as amend-
[27] ed by chapter 133 of the Laws of 1880, which provides that railroad corporations shall have power "to regulate the time and manner in which passengers

* Chap. 140.

and property shall be transported," interfere in some way with the power to grant the writ. Undoubtedly it gives the discretion which the learned judge states,* but it cannot be so construed as to justify a general or partial suspension of the duty of receiving and transporting freight. Language of that kind in a similar act was correctly construed by DICKERSON,
[28] J., in Railroad Commissioners v. Portland & Oxford R. R. Co. (63 *Maine*, 269). We adopt, but have not room to quote his language. Having determined the question of the right of the State to prosecute the writ of mandamus on the ground of refusal or neglect of a corporation to exercise its duty of carrier, it remains to be seen whether a case which would justify the granting of the writ was presented. The case stands altogether upon the facts presented by the appellants. The course taken by the respondents must be regarded as an admission of the material facts contained in the petition and affidavits.

The petition alleges that the said railroad company, since about the 16th day of June, 1882, "has substantially refused to discharge its duties as a common carrier and has, to a material degree, suspended the exercise of its franchises by refusing to take freight which has been offered at its stations in the city of New York for transportation, at the usual rates, and upon the usual terms," and that said railroad company has refused to accept and transport the greater part of the outgoing, and to deliver the incoming freight and property of the merchants doing business in the city of New York, who have relations with, and need for, the services of such railway, and has refused to them to furnish adequate transportation for the same, so that from that date the business community of the city of New York "are unable to obtain sufficient and adequate

* See opinion of HAIGHT, J., 2 *N. Y. Civ. Pro. R.* 93.

transportation for their goods on said railroad, although they have offered the same on the usual terms and rates of transportation; but said railroad has uniformly delayed, and sometimes peremptorily refused to receive, and deliver freight, and to transport the outgoing freight as aforesaid, and at certain points within the State have declined to receive incoming freight, whereby great loss and damages accrue to the people of the State of New York, for which there is no adequate remedy in damages," and that the trade and commerce of said city is greatly injured by the action of the said railroad.

These allegations are broad enough to show a quite general and largely injurious refusal and neglect to perform the duties of carrier. The affidavits go far to sustain these allegations; but it is not important to examine them minutely, because the admission of a demurrer *ore tenus*, extends to, and admits the well pleaded averments of the petition. Stated very briefly, the affidavits show that for about two weeks the respondents failed and neglected to receive from three-quarters to seven-eighths of the goods offered for transportation from the city, and large quantities seeking transportation to the city, and in many instances refused to receive goods offered, and turned them back and closed their gates during business hours, thus causing a stoppage of all delivery of freight; that in some instances unusual terms were sought to be imposed as a condition of receiving goods, which would increase the risks of the owner; that the refusal to receive goods did not arise from any unwillingness or inability on the part of the shipper to pay charges, but was wholly the act of respondents; that it was so continuous and extensive that it seriously interfered with the business operations of the citizens of New York, deteriorated the value of many commodities, and caused a diversion of trade

from the city; that great losses were caused, and especially that large quantities of perishable goods, by reason of non-delivery, were destroyed, to the value of many thousand dollars: that a vast amount of freight, equal, as estimated, to 360,000 tons, was thus detained or refused carriage; that large numbers of carmen were detained in their efforts to deliver freight, and the injury to that branch of business is estimated at not less than $50,000, while the aggregate of injuries is estimated at some millions. These are the substantial facts conceded by the respondents at the special term. Surely it cannot be doubted that
[29] these facts, being true and unexcused, showed a strong case for the interference of the State.

The only question is whether the course and conduct of the respondents was so far excused by anything appearing in the petition and affidavits that the court was justified in denying the motion for the writ on its merits, or in a wise exercise of its judicial discretion.

The excuse appears only in the statements of the reasons assigned by the respondents for their refusal to accept, transport and deliver the freight and property. In the petition it is stated in these words: "that the persons in their employ handling such freight, refuse to perform their work unless some small advance, said to be three cents per hour, is paid them by the said railroad corporation." The affidavits show, it may in short be said, that the skilled freight handlers of the respondents, who had been working at the rate of seventeen cents per hour (or $1.70 for ten hours), refused to work unless twenty cents per hour or $2 per day of ten hours, were paid; and that their abandonment of the work and the inefficiency of the unskilled men afterwards employed, caused the neglect and refusal complained of.

It is not alleged or shown that the workmen com-

mitted any unlawful act; and no violence, no riot and no unlawful interference with other employees of the respondents appear. It is urged, in effect, that the court should regard the case as one of unlawful duress caused by some breach of law sufficiently violent to prevent the reception and transportation of freight. There is nothing in the papers to justify this contention. According to the statements of the case, a body of laborers acting in concert fixed a price for their labor, and refused to work at a less price. The respondents fixed a price for the same labor, and refused to pay more. In doing this, neither did an act violative of any law, or subjecting either to any penalty. The respondents had a lawful right to take their ground in respect of the price to be paid, and adhere to it if they chose; but if the consequence of doing so were an
[30] inability to exercise their corporate franchises, to the great injury of the public, they cannot be heard to assert that such consequence must be shouldered and borne by an innocent public, who neither directly nor indirectly participated in their causes.

If it had been shown that a "strike" of their skilled laborers had been cansed or compelled by some illegal combination or organized body which held an unlawful control of their actions, and sought through them to enforce its will upon the respondents, and that the respondents in resisting such unlawful efforts had refused to obey unjust and illegal dictation, and had used all the means in their power to employ other men in sufficient numbers to do the work, and that the refusal and neglect complained of had grown out of such a state of facts, a very different case for the exercise of the discretion of the court, as well as of the attorney-general, would have been presented. Whether such a state of facts could have been shown, we cannot judicially know. The present case must stand or fall upon the papers before us; and we are not to be swerved from thus disposing of it by any suggestion of facts not in the case, which might lead, if they appeared, to some other result. The most that can be found from the petition and affidavits is that the skilled freight handlers of the respondents refuse to work without an increase of wages to the amount of three cents per hour; that the respondents refuse to pay such increase; that the laborers then abandoned the work; and that the respondents did not procure other laborers competent or sufficient in number to do the work, and so the numerous evils complained of fell upon the public, and were continuous until the people felt called upon to step in and seek to remedy them by proceedings for mandamus.

These facts reduce the question to this: can railroad corporations refuse or neglect to perform
[31] their public duties upon a controversy with their
employees, over the cost or expense of doing them? We think this question admits of but one answer. The excuse has in law no validity. The duties imposed must be discharged at whatever cost. They cannot be laid down or abandoned or suspended without the legally expressed consent of the State. The trusts are active, potential and imperative, and must be executed until lawfully surrendered; otherwise a public highway of great utility is closed or obstructed *without any process recognized by law.* This is something no public officer charged with the same trusts and duties in regard to other public highways can do without subjecting himself to mandamus or indictment.

We are not able to perceive the difficulties that embarrassed the court below as to the form of a writ of mandamus in such cases. It is true the writ must be specific as to the thing to be done; but the thing to
[32] be done in this case was to resume the duties of
carriers of the goods and property offered for transportation. That is, to receive, carry and deliver

the same under the existing rules and regulations as the business had been accustomed to be done. There was no necessity to specify what kinds of goods should be first received and carried, or whose goods; or indeed to take any notice of the details of the established usages of the companies. It was the people who were invoking the writ, on their own behalf, and not for some private suitor, or to redress individual injuries. The prayer of the petition indicated the proper form of the writ. Upon the return to the writ all questions
[33] whether what has been done is a sufficient compliance with its command, may properly arise and become a subject of further consideration (People *ex rel.* Green *v.* D. & C. R. R. Co., 58 *N. Y.* 152, 160, 161). They need not have been anticipated. It is suggested that the time has now past when such a writ can be of any valuable effect. That is probably so; but we are governed by the record in disposing of the appeal, and not by subsequently occurring events.

The appellants labor now under a judgment alleged to be injurious to the rights they possessed when it was pronounced, and harmful to them as a precedent. If erroneous, they are entitled to have that judgment reversed, and to be indemnified in the discretion of the court for the costs incurred on the appeal made necessary by the error.

We think the court below had power to award the writ, and that, upon the case presented, it was error to refuse it.

The order should be reversed with the usual costs, and an order entered, if deemed advisable, from any existing circumstances, by the attorney-general, awarding the writ.

BRADY and DANIELS, JJ., concurred.

SPRAGUE, RESPONDENT, v. SWIFT, APPELLANT.

SUPREME COURT, FOURTH DEPARTMENT; GENERAL TERM, JUNE, 1882.

§ 829.

Witness.—When party not incompetent.

Where, in an action against one of the makers of a joint and several promissory note, the court overruled the defendant's objection, and allowed the plaintiff to testify to conversations between himself and the other maker of the note, who was then deceased,—*Held*, that the objection was properly overruled; that the note being several as well as joint, the defendant was liable to a separate action as well before as after the death of the other maker, and the defendant was not a survivor within the meaning of section 829 of the Code. (*Decided October*, 1882.)

Appeal from a judgment entered on a verdict rendered at the Erie circuit, and from an order denying a motion for a new trial on a case.

The facts are stated in the opinion.

Osgoodby, Titus & Moot, for appellant.

Lewis & Rice, for respondent.

SMITH, P. J.—The action is upon a joint and several promissory note alleged to have been made by one Stillwell and the defendant. The defense was a denial of the execution of the note by defendant, and payment by Stillwell, for whose accommodation the note was made. Stillwell died before the action was commenced.

We are satisfied, upon reading the entire case, that the position of the defendant's counsel, that the verdict is against the weight of evidence, cannot be sustained.

We have examined the numerous exceptions taken to rulings of the court upon the rejection or admission of testimony. None of them, in our opinion, point to any error, except in some instances where immaterial testimony, objected to as such, was received by the court; but in every such instance, the testimony received manifestly did no harm. One exception only, need be more particularly commented on.

The plaintiff, to establish the issues on his part, was permitted as a witness in his own behalf, to testify to transactions and conversations between himself and Stillwell. The defendant objected at the trial, and he now contends, that the plaintiff was incompetent to testify to those matters, under section 829 of the Code, on the ground that the defendant is sought to be charged in the action, as the "survivor" of Stillwell. The objection was properly overruled. The defendant is not a "survivor" within the meaning of the section. As the note sued on was several as well as joint, he was liable to a separate action, as well before, as after, the death of Stillwell.

The judgment and order should be affirmed.

HARDIN, J., concurred.

BROOKS ET AL. v. THE MEXICAN NATIONAL CONSTRUCTION CO.

NEW YORK SUPERIOR COURT, SPECIAL TERM, JANUARY, 1883.

§§ 266, 1780.

Foreign corporations.—When superior city court no jurisdiction of action against.—Objection to jurisdiction may be taken at any time.

The superior court of the city of New York has no jurisdiction over a foreign corporation in an action brought against it by a non-resi dent, and the objection to its jurisdiction may be taken at any time, and although it has not been taken in the answer. [2]

Section 266 of the Code does not provide that the jurisdiction of a superior city court must be presumed, and that a want of jurisdiction by reason of any of the jurisdictional facts specified in section 263 of the Code is a matter of defense and is waived by the appearance of the defendant, but it means that the plaintiff need not set forth these facts, but that in a case in which the supreme court has jurisdiction, if the non-existence of these facts is not set up in the answer, the court will presume that they do exist. [1]

(*Decided January* 8, 1883.)

Motion to vacate attachment, on the ground that the court has not jurisdiction of the action.

Theodore F. H. Meyer, for motion.

Henry D. Hotchkiss, opposed.

TRUAX, J.—If the plaintiff's view of the meaning of sections 266 and 1780 of the Code of Civil Procedure is the right one, this court would have jurisdiction of an action brought by a non-resident, against a foreign corporation, where the supreme court has not jurisdiction. I do not think, that such was the intention

of the legislature. Section 1780 provides, that in certain cases only, shall any of the courts of this State have jurisdiction over a foreign corporation, in actions brought by a non-resident plaintiff, and there mentions the cases. This is not one of the cases mentioned in that section. But, the plaintiffs contend, section 266 provides that the jurisdiction of a superior city court must be presumed, and that a want of jurisdiction by reason of the non-existence of any of the jurisdictional facts specified in section 263 is a matter of defense, and is waived by the appearance of the defendant, unless it is pleaded in defense, and that the defendant, not having pleaded that the plaintiffs are non-residents, he cannot raise the question of jurisdiction, on a motion to vacate an attachment. Such, however, is not the meaning of those sections. They mean, that the plaintiff need not set forth in his complaint, that
[*] the contract sued on was made, executed, or delivered within the State, or that the cause of action arose within the State, or that a warrant of attachment, has been actually served within this city, but that, in a case in which the supreme court has jurisdiction, if the non-existence of these facts is not set up in the answer, the court will presume that they do exist.

I am therefore of the opinion, that this court has
[*] no jurisdiction over a foreign corporation, in an action brought by a non-resident, against such corporation, and that the objection to the jurisdiction of the court may be taken at any time, although it has not been taken in the answer. The motion to vacate the attachment is granted, with ten dollars costs.

BOYLAN, AN INFANT, BY BOYLAN, HIS GUARDIAN AD LITEM, v. MATHEWS.

NEW YORK SUPERIOR COURT; SPECIAL TERM, FEBRUARY, 1883.

§ 3268

Security for costs.—When court may deny application for.

Where, in an action by an infant, the defendant delays applying for the security for costs, to which the Code entitles him, until after the plaintiff has been examined before trial, and the case has been called on the calendar of the court and marked ready for trial, and is about to be tried,—*Held*, that the court has the power to and should deny a motion for such security.*

(*Decided February* 2 *and* 5, 1883.)

Motion by defendant that plaintiff be required to give security for costs.

The plaintiff, an infant, by his guardian *ad litem*, brought this action to recover damages for a personal injury. Issue was joined, and the case thereafter noticed for trial. The plaintiff had been examined before trial, at the instance of the defendant, and the case had been upon the day calendar of the court, and marked ready for trial.

Hart & Price, for motion.

C. D. Rust, opposed.

INGRAHAM, J.—I think, under the circumstances in this case, the motion should be denied.

* As to the loss of the right to security for costs by laches, see Healy v. Twenty-third Street Railway Co. (1 *N. Y. Civ. Pro.* 15), and case cited in note thereto.

On a reargument of the same motion, the following decision, was rendered.

INGRAHAM, J.—I think the court has the power to deny a motion for security, where defendant has waited until after he has examined the plaintiff before trial, and the case has been called on the calendar, is ready for trial, and about to be tried. Under these circumstances, I think the former decision was right, and the motion should be denied.

IN RE FINAL ACCOUNTING OF THE EXECUTORS, &c., OF ADOLPH BROWN, DECEASED. (CASE NO. 1.)

IN RE FINAL ACCOUNTING OF THE ADMINISTRATRIX, &c., OF ELIZABETH BAUER, DECEASED. (CASE NO. 2.)

SURROGATE'S COURT, NEW YORK COUNTY, JANUARY, 1883.

§§ 2514, 2743.

Surrogate.—Authority of, to adjudicate upon the validity, etc., of claims against an estate or to a share therein on the final accounting of an executor or administrator.

Under the Revised Statutes of this State the surrogate had authority to decree, upon the final accounting of an executor or administrator, a distribution to claimants according to their respective rights, and to ascertain and determine the nature and extent of these rights only in cases where they were conceded to exist, [1] and the imposition upon the surrogate of the duty "to settle and determine all questions concerning any debt, claim, legacy, bequest or distributive share," empowered him to settle and determine such questions only as were not matters of dispute between the parties. [2]

Prior to the Code of Civil Procedure a surrogate had no power to inquire into the validity of a release of an interest in or claim against an estate. [3]

By the limited grant of authority to surrogates to determine, upon the final accounting of an executor or administrator, all questions concerning "debts, claims and distributive shares," where their validity is not disputed or has been established, conferred by section 2743 of the Code, it is intended that, whenever the executor or administrator shall dispute the validity of a debt, claim or right to a distributive share, the jurisdiction of the surrogate to adjudicate upon it is straightway suspended until such debt, claim or right shall have been established by the judgment of some competent tribunal, and of some tribunal, of course, other than the surrogate's court itself. [4]

The term "debt, claim or distributive share," as used in section 2743 of the Code, is designed to comprehend every species of claim or demand against a decedent's estate which may be or can be preferred by any creditor, or legatee, or next of kin, or husband or wife of decedent, or by the assignee of any one of such persons, [5] and a dispute about the validity of any such debt, claim or distributive share, whose payment is sought to be obtained or secured at a final accounting, is a dispute about whether the right to such debt, claim or distributive share at the time exists. [6]

Whenever anyone, as next of kin or legatee, claims, upon a final accounting of an executor or administrator, a share in the decedent's estate, and the accounting party disputes his claim and interposes against it a lease or assignment, which is assailed by its maker as invalid and ineffectual by reason of fraud, the surrogate should hold in abeyance his decree of distribution, so far, at least, as concerns that interest in the estate to which the assignment or release relates, until the rights of the parties can be determined in another forum. [7]

Where, on the final settlement of the accounts of an executor or administrator, a claim to a share in the estate is interposed, which is contested by the accounting party on the ground that it has been released or assigned, the proceedings should not be conducted to a decree as if such claim had not been filed, [8] but the inquiry into the correctness of the accounts should be postponed until an adjudication is had in the matters as to which the surrogate's court lacks jurisdiction, or, if the inquiry is suffered to proceed, every person who claims a share or an interest in the estate should be allowed to take part therein, despite the fact that he is alleged to have assigned or released such share or interest, provided that he interposes allegations of facts disputing the validity of such assignment or release, and that, but for such assignment or release, he would be entitled to such share or interest. [9]

(*Decided January* 10, 1883.)

Motion to dismiss objections to the account of executors (in one case), and to that of an administratrix (in the other case).

The opinion states the facts.

Sigismund Kaufman, for executors, *in re* Brown.

Coleridge A. Hart, opposed.

Randolph Guggenheimer, for administratrix, *in re* Bauer.

Henry Metzinger, opposed.

ROLLINS, S.—The above entitled cases have been coupled, and will be considered together, though they neither concern the same parties nor relate to the same estate.

Indeed, the two proceedings somewhat differ from each other in respect to the nature of the issue submitted for the determination of the court. Each involves, however, an important question as to the jurisdiction of the surrogate and as to the construction of a provision of the Code from which that jurisdiction, if it exists at all, is solely derivable.

Brief statements of the facts of these cases will disclose the nature of the controversies.

CASE NO. 1.

Brown's executors filed their accounts in October, 1880, and commenced proceedings before my predecessor for their judicial settlement.

Two daughters of the testator, who were legatees under his will, interposed objections. This the executors insisted they had no right to do, because of the execution of certain releases whereby their respective interests in the estate are claimed to have been absolutely extinguished.

The legatees denied the validity of these releases on the ground of alleged fraud in their procurement, and the surrogate (after overruling the objection that he had no jurisdiction to inquire into and determine the matter), decided, upon the facts as then presented, that the releases should be upheld, and that their effect was to deprive the objectors of any right to contest the accuracy of the accounts filed by the executor.

The objectors subsequently applied to the present surrogate for a reargument, and such reargument was permitted for reasons stated in an opinion on file.

The inquiry is now presented anew, whether these contestants can avail themselves of their objections, and, so far at least as relates to one of them, whether the surrogate should inquire into and determine the validity of the release with which she is confronted.

Case No. 2.

Catherine Kostner has filed her account as administratrix of the estate of Elizabeth Bauer.

John Bauer, the husband of decedent, whose right to be a party to this proceeding is attacked for reasons which are foreign to the present inquiry, and which will be elsewhere considered, has heretofore assigned to the administratrix whatever interest he may have had in his wife's estate. He claims, however, that this assignment was procured by fraud, that the circumstances under which it was executed should be investigated by the surrogate, and that, as a result of such investigation, it should be pronounced invalid.

The administratrix insists that the issue thus presented is not triable in this court; that the contestants' objections should be ignored, and that the estate should be distributed as if they had never been interposed.

Two questions are thus presented for my determination—

1st. Has the surrogate jurisdiction to inquire into and pass upon the validity of the release and of the assignment in the above entitled proceeding?

2d. If he is without jurisdiction, should the objections on file be entertained, or should they be disregarded?

I. The Authority of the Surrogate under the Provisions of the Revised Statutes.

Prior to the adoption of the present Code of Procedure, the surrogate derived from section 71, title 3, chap. 6, part 2 of the Revised Statutes* (3 Banks' 6th ed. 104), whatever authority he possessed in reference to the determination of—

(*a*) The validity and effect of releases and assignments by persons interested in estates; and,

(*b*) The validity of disputed claims of creditors.

The provisions of section 71 were as follows:

"Whenever an account shall be rendered and finally settled, ... if it shall appear to the surrogate that any part of the estate remains to be paid or distributed, he shall make a decree for the payment and distribution of what shall so remain, to and among the creditors, legatees, widow and next of kin of the deceased, *according to their respective rights;* and in such decree *shall settle and determine all questions* concerning any debt, claim, legacy, bequest or distributive share; to whom the same shall be payable, and the sum to be paid to each person."

This language was very comprehensive, and was doubtless supposed to be plain and unequivocal when it was adopted into the statutes.

Its meaning, however, at once became the subject of

* 2 *R. S.* 93.

spirited contention in the various courts of this State, and forms the topic of a multitude of reported decisions (Estate of Martine, 11 *Abb. N. C.* 50).

The court of appeals finally determined, in the case of Tucker *v.* Tucker (4 *Keyes*, 136), that, so far at least as concerned the matter of disputed claims of creditors, the surrogate's court had no jurisdiction to adjudicate upon them.

This doctrine has since been frequently re-asserted, and is maintained in the very recent case of Glacius *v.* Fogel (88 *N. Y.* 434).

It is a doctrine which, as I have elsewhere stated, seems to me to demand such an interpretation of section 71 as is fairly summed up in these two propositions:

1st. The delegation to surrogates of authority to decree, upon the final accounting of an executor or
[1] administrator, a distribution to claimants *according to their respective rights*, gave power to ascertain and determine the nature and extent of those rights, *only in cases where they were conceded to exist*, and

2nd. The imposition upon the surrogate of the duty "to settle and determine *all questions* concerning
[2] any debt, claim, legacy, bequest or distributive share," empowered him to settle and determine such questions, and such only, as were not a matter of dispute, between the parties, or, in simpler phrase, *such questions as there was no question about* (Estate of Martine, *supra*).

Nearly all the decisions which I have condensed into the two propositions just stated, relate to matters involving the demands of persons claiming to be creditors of a decedent's estate, but not conceded to be such by the executor or administrator.

Though not authoritative upon the precise questions here at issue, I am nevertheless at loss how to put any interpretation upon section 71 which would at once consist with those decisions, and sustain the right of this court to exercise such authority as is invoked in the present proceedings; and I should probably hold, without further inquiry, that I had no jurisdiction to pass upon the release and assignment which are respectively interposed in the cases at bar, but for certain recent decisions to which I feel bound to refer.

II. Judicial Decisions in Respect to Releases.

In Strong *v.* Strong (3 *Redf.* 480) it was decided, that prior to the adoption of the Code, the surrogate's court possessed the power to inquire into the validity of releases.

But, the argument by which that conclusion is supported is substantially the same as that which was persistently but vainly urged in Tucker *v.* Tucker and in a score of supreme court decisions relating to disputed claims.

It has been urged, that the intimation of the court of appeals in Harris *v.* Ely (25 *N. Y.* 142) should be regarded as authoritative in this matter.

The question there at issue was, whether an executor was properly required to account at the instance of a legatee.

This legatee, the widow of decedent, had twelve years previous given the executor a receipt in full of all demands *up to that date*, and had also executed a deed conveying to him, as trustee for herself, all her personal estate.

The court held that the receipt was no bar to the accounting, as it did not profess to be an admission that the executor had fully administered the estate, and that the deed, which was in the nature of an antenuptial settlement, was not intended in any respect to discharge the executor, and did not in fact discharge him from the liability of filing an account.

In pronouncing the opinion of the court, Judge

DENIO cited the case of Kenny *v.* Jackson (1 *Hagg. Eccl.* 105), wherein it was held, that though a residuary legatee had executed a release, whose validity was disputed and could not be determined in the prerogative court, the executor should, nevertheless, at his instance, be required to account. Judge DENIO made a passing comment, to the effect that the jurisdiction of our surrogate's courts so exceeded that of the English ecclesiastical tribunals as to permit an adjudication upon the validity of releases interposed in bar of an accounting.

So far as I have discovered, from the time when the decision in Harris *v.* Ely was rendered (1862) it was never, for the succeeding sixteen years, referred to in any cases included in the Reports of this State.

In 1878 the court of appeals passed upon the appeal of Bevan *v.* Cooper (72 *N. Y.* 317).

At the trial below, the then surrogate of this county had adjudicated upon the question whether under a will certain legacies were, or were not a charge, upon a testator's real estate. In this the court of appeals, held that he had exceeded his authority. In discussing the general subject of the nature and extent of the surrogate's jurisdiction, the court said:

"There is an intimation in Harris *v.* Ely, that a surrogate on an accounting may try the validity of a release, but the remark was *obiter*." So far as this allusion has any significance, it must be deemed, when read in the light of its context, as a disapproval of the *dictum* in Harris *v.* Ely. But it will be observed that the more recent intimation is itself *obiter*, and should not, therefore, be regarded as a final determination of the question.

By its decision in People *ex rel.* Wright *v.* Coffin (7 *Hun*, 60) the supreme court, general term, of the second department, seems to maintain the right of a Surrogate before the repeal of section 71 of the Revised

Statutes (*supra*) to exercise such authority as is here invoked by the contestants. An offshoot of the same litigation is the case of Wright *v.* Fleming (12 *Hun*, 469), wherein it is claimed that the general term of the supreme court, in the first department, took the same view of the surrogate's jurisdiction. It does not seem to me, however, that the question here under consideration was intended to be passed upon in that case. From the recital of facts which accompanies the opinion of the presiding justice, his statement that under the circumstances there disclosed "the surrogate committed a palpable error by his decision to *disregard* the releases" which were the subject of that contention, by no means involves the notion that it was within the scope of the surrogate's authority to receive and weigh the evidence for and against those releases and then to decide upon their validity.

The allegations of the complaint were opposed only by a demurrer, and, for aught that appeared by the pleadings, the defendants had executed releases against which there was no opposing evidence, but which, nevertheless, the surrogate utterly disregarded.

To say that this disposition of the matter was error, was to say somthing which is not decisive of the present contention. Nor, on the other hand, does the language of the court of appeals in its review of this decision, seem to me to mean what is claimed by the opposing counsel (See Wright *v.* Fleming, 76 *N. Y.* 517).

It seems, that after the surrogate had announced his purpose of "disregarding" the releases, (though without an adjudication that they were invalid), he directed a distribution of the estate, as if they had never existed. Thereupon the accounting administrator commenced an action in the supreme court, whereby he sought to enjoin the entry of any decree which should require him to pay, to the parties who had given the releases, large sums of money to which, but for such releases, they would admittedly have been entitled from the funds of the estate. The defendants in that action demurred. At special term, the demurrer was overruled, and judgment was rendered for the plaintiff.

The general term reversed this judgment on the merits, holding that an appeal was the proper remedy for the error into which, in its judgment, the surrogate had fallen, and that the circumstance did not call for the intervention of a court of equity.

The court of appeals, in a *per Curiam* opinion, sustained the judgment of the general term, but intimated that the injunction ought to have been granted if the complaint had not been deficient in some of its allegations.

The court said: "The facts alleged to sustain the prayer of the complaint for an injunction are not sufficient. It alleges the giving of releases and assignments, and that the surrogate disregarded them when presented to him in the proceedings in his court. It is not alleged that he had, or had not, the power to consider and pass upon them. . . . . It is plain that there can be no final and complete settlement of the plaintiff's accounts. . . . . until it is determined by an authentic adjudication whether the releases and assignments are valid, and what is the force and effect of them. It is therefore well that, if the plaintiff is so advised, he should amend his complaint, and make averments which will render an issue upon the validity of the releases, and the effect of them, to relieve him from liability to the makers of them, and to vest in him their interest in the estate of said intestate, so that there may be such an adjudication. . . . . The proceedings before the surrogate should not go forward, so far as that the releases, if upheld, will be of no avail to him. . . . . The accounting may be had so far forth as that the balances for or against him may be ascertained, and all things be in readiness for the entry of a final decree. Hence he ought to have an injunction upon his complaint, if he shall amend it as above indicated, restraining the proceedings in the surrogate's court beyond the point mentioned above."

This is the full opinion of the court of appeals, so far as relates to the subject of the present inquiry. It seems to me that there is room for great divergence of opinion as to the application of this decision to the facts of such a case as the present. It is certainly not squarely determined that under the Revised Statutes the surrogate's court *had* jurisdiction or *had not* jurisdiction to inquire into the force and effect of releases whose validity had been assailed by the parties executing them.

It was urged by the appellants in that action that the remedy by injunction should be accorded because of the alleged misconduct and irregularity of the trial court in "disregarding" the releases there in question after having admitted them in evidence.

A simple question of law, they said, would have been raised if the surrogate had refused, for lack of jurisdiction, to permit the introduction of those instruments; and, on the other hand, if, after they had been admitted, evidence had been offered tending in any wise to impair their validity and effect, a question of fact would have arisen. In either contingency, as they argued, error could have been effectually corrected by resort to the ordinary remedy of appeal. But they claimed that—

1st. The "disregard" of an instrument which had been admitted in evidence, whose validity, force and effect had not been attacked by evidence in opposition, and which purported to be a "full, absolute and final release" of the defendant's claims; and,

2d. The avowal of a purpose on the part of defendants to enter a decree in harmony with this "disregarding" were circumstances which afforded sufficient grounds for the interference of a court of equity.

How far the court of appeals acted upon this view is not apparent from the language of its decision.

It is fairly open to dispute, whether its determination that the plaintiff would be entitled to an injunction upon making the suggested amendments in his complaint, was based on the theory that the surrogate had absolutely no jurisdiction in the premises, or merely upon the theory that his decision was erroneous, and that any decree by which it should be made effective would inflict upon the plaintiff an injury against which he should be permitted to interpose the shield of an injunction.

So, too, when the court says that the proceedings before the surrogate ought to stop short of the entry of a final decree, it is by no means clear whether these remarks were intended to be limited to a class of cases wherein, as in the one then under review, the surrogate had indicated his purpose of ignoring the effect of releases without adjudging them to be invalid, or whether, on the other hand, that language was designed to have a wider reach, and to declare that until a controversy over the validity and effect of a release should be determined by another tribunal, the surrogate ought under no circumstances to enter a decree of distribution as to any portion of the estate to which such release appertained.

This case is certainly not decisive of the present contention, and if the Code of Procedure had made no substantial change in the statutes, I should feel
[*] bound to adhere, until otherwise advised by an appellate tribunal, to the position which seems to have the sanction of the supreme court in the second department, and which, in this very proceeding (Estate of Adolph Brown), was maintained by my predecessor.

This I should do with the greater confidence in view of the recent decision of the recent decision of the court of appeals in Riggs *v.* Cragg (*Daily Register*, October 21, 1882), a decision which certainly gives a more liberal interpretation to section 71 than it has hitherto received, and settles in the affirmative the much mooted question whether, upon a final accounting, to which all persons interested were made parties, the surrogate had power under that section to construe a will.

III. As to Assignments.

Before examining the meaning of the Code provisions which have supplanted that section, it is proper to consider briefly the question, What authority is conferred upon the surrogate to pass upon the validity of assignments made by persons interested in an estate? In Bonfanti *v.* Deguerre (3 *Bradf.* 429), the plaintiff, legatee sought to procure from the defendant, executor, an accounting. The executor set up in answer that the plaintiff had executed to one W. assignments of his entire interest in the decedent's estate.

The applicant alleged in opposition that the assignment was procured by misrepresentations for which the executor was himself responsible. Surrogate Bradford refused to inquire into the validity of the assignment, but as the only reason which he gave for his action was his lack of jurisdiction, because of the fact that the assignee was not a party to the proceedings, the case is of little utility.

Hitchcock *v.* Marshall (2 *Redf.* 174) is, however, directly in point. Surrogate Coffin there held that even where no question arose as to the validity of an assignment executed by a person entitled to a distributive share, he did not feel authorized, under the law as it stood prior to the enactment of the Code, to recognize such an assignment, and to direct distribution accordingly. This view he reasserted in Haskin *v.* Feller (3 *Redf.* 321), and in Strong *v.* Strong (*Id.* 481), and in Leviness *v.* Cassebeer (*Id.* 491).

I am informed that in New York county it has been for years the practice of this court to recognize and give effect to assignments when they have not been attacked, but that, whenever their validity has been the subject of controversy, the court has refused to exercise any jurisdiction concerning them.

IV. The Surrogate's Authority under the Code Provisions.

We are now brought to the consideration of the question to what extent, if at all, the authority of the surrogate has been affected by the substitution of the existing law in place of the repealed provisions of the Revised Statutes.

It has been necessary to examine those repealed provisions and the decisions to which they have given rise, because the section of the Code which will presently be quoted, and which is now the sole source of the surrogate's authority in these matters, was designed to bring the very letter of the new law into exact conformity with the interpretation which the courts had put upon the language of the old, and thus to prevent in the future all doubts and disputation as to its meaning. Such is declared by Mr. Commissioner Throop (see note to section 2743 of his edition of the Code) to have been the aim of the commissioners in changing the phraseology of the statute. The new provision is as follows:

"Where an account is judicially settled, ... and any part of the estate remains, and is ready to be distributed to the creditor, legatees, next of kin, husband or wife of the decedent, or their assigns, the decree must direct the payment and distribution thereof to the persons so entitled, according to their respective rights." * * * * * *

"Where the validity of a debt, claim or distributive share is not disputed or has been established, the decree must determine to whom it is payable, the sum to be paid by reason thereof, and all other questions concerning the same (*Code*, § 2743).

I do not share the confidence of the commissioners that these provisions have been so skillfully worded as to leave no room for future contention. But my own interpretation of them and of their application to the cases now before the court is as follows:

First. By this limited grant of authority to determine all questions concerning "debts, claims and distributive shares," when their validity "*is not disputed* or has been established," it is intended that when-
[4] ever the executor or administrator *shall dispute* the validity of a debt, claim or right to a distributive share, the jurisdiction of the surrogate to adjudicate upon it is straightway suspended until such debt, claim or right shall have been established by the judgment of some competent tribunal, and of some tribunal, of course, other than the surrogate's court itself.

Second. The term "claim, debt or distributive share," as used in section 2743, is designed to comprehend every species of claim or demand against a
[5] decedent's estate, which may be or can be preferred by any individual belonging to any of the classes of persons previously enumerated in that section, *i. e.*, by any creditor, or legatee, or next of kin, or husband or wife of decedent, or by the assignee of any one of such persons. Indeed, the word "debt" of itself must be deemed to have a significance almost as broad as this, if we are to heed its definition in section 2514. "The word debts," says that section, "includes every claim and demand upon which a judgment for a sum of money, or directing the payment of money, could be recovered in an action."

Third. That a dispute about the *validity* of any such debt, claim or distributive share, whose pay-
[6] ment is sought to be obtained or secured at a final accounting, is a dispute about whether the right to such debt, claim or distributive share at the time exists.

Fourth. That accordingly, whenever one, as next of kin or legatee, claims upon a final accounting a share in the decedent's estate, and the accounting party [*] disputes his claim and interposes against it a release or an assignment, which is assailed by its maker as invalid and ineffectual by reason of fraud, a contingency has arisen which requires the surrogate, in obedience to section 2743, to hold in abeyance his decree of distribution, so far, at least, as concerns that interest in the estate to which such assignment or release relates, until the rights of the parties can be determined in another forum.

If the provisions of the Revised Statutes were still in force, it might be claimed, with some show of reason, that the surrogate's right to determine a controversy between an accounting executor or administrator and a person claiming as legatee or next of kin, touching the validity and effect of a release or assignment *to the accounting party himself*, might be defended as within the spirit, if not the letter, of recent decisions of the court of appeals. See, for example, the cases of Kyle *v.* Kyle, 67 *N. Y.* 400; Shakespeare *v.* Markham, 72 *N. Y.* 400; Boughton *v.* Flint, 74 *N. Y.* 476, which lend some support to the notion that whatever claims of interest in an estate its executor or administrator sets up may be passed upon by the surrogate.

But section 2739 of the Code seems to have established certain restrictions in this regard which are too plain to be overlooked. It provides that a contest between the accounting party and any other party in interest may be determined by the surrogate when it relates to a debt alleged to be due by such accounting party to the decedent, or by the decedent to the accounting party, or when it relates to property of the estate to which the latter lays claim. The provision is manifestly too narrow to include such cases as the present.

V. SHALL THE CONTESTANTS' OBJECTIONS BE CONSIDERED.

Having no power to pass upon the validity of either the release in the Brown estate or of the assignment in the estate of Bauer, what disposal ought I to make of the objections which have in each case been interposed? It is insisted by the accounting parties that the claims of the objectors to appear as such should be denied, and that the proceedings should be conducted to a final decree as if their objections had not been filed.

[*] But would not such a course imply an assumption that the instruments whose validity is attacked are in fact valid?

In other words, would it not practically involve just such a determination of their validity as the court has no right to make?

It seems to me that one or the other of two courses should be taken for protecting the rights of all parties in such controversies as these.

Either the inquiry into the correctness of the accounts should be postponed until an adjudication is had in the matters as to which the court lacks jurisdiction, or if the inquiry is suffered to proceed, every person who claims a share or an interest in the estate should be allowed to take part therein, despite the fact that he is alleged to have assigned or released such share or interest, provided that he interposes allegations of fact disputing the validity of such assignment or release, and that but for such assignment or release, he would be entitled to such interest or share (Thomson *v.* Thomson, 1 *Bradf.* 24; Burwell *v.* Shaw, 2 *Bradf.* 322; Dickson's Estate, 11 *Phil.* 86; Wister's Estate, 12 *Phil.* 48; Kenny *v.* Jackson, 1 *Hagg. Eccl.* 105; Estate of Martine, 11 *Abb. N. C.* 50; Estate of Giles, 11 *Abb. N. C.* 57; Buchan *v.* Rintoul, 70 *N. Y.* 1).

Which of these two courses should be pursued in any

given case must depend upon a variety of circumstances that need not be here considered or enumerated.

In both of the present proceedings I have decided to permit the contestants to go on at once. Orders may therefore be presented for submission to a reference of the accounts and of the objections thereto.

CONCORD GRANITE COMPANY v. FRENCH, IMPLEADED, &c.

NEW YORK MARINE COURT; TRIAL TERM, NOVEMBER, 1882.

§§ 755, 756.

Effect of payment of note by indorser upon action brought against maker prior thereto.

Where the indorser of a promissory note paid it after an action there on had been commenced against the maker,—*Held*, that plaintiff, being the holder of the note at the time he commenced the action, was then the real party in interest; [1] that the subsequent payment of the note by the indorser relieved him only from liability to the plaintiff, and did not in any way impair the legal remedy against the maker or furnish him with any defense to the action; [2, 3] that it entitled the indorser to be subrogated to any right the plaintiff had acquired, including the right to prosecute the action, [2] but to nothing more, and the pendency of the action would have furnished the maker with a good plea in bar of an independent action by such indorser, his proper remedy being either to continue the action or direct its discontinuance. [5] The indorser not applying for leave to continue the action in his own name, it is properly continued in the name of the original plaintiff, who becomes the trustee of the indorser as regards the moneys sued for, when recovered. [4]

(*Decided December* 1, 1882.)

Action against the maker of a promissory note.

The opinion states the facts.

Cephas Brainerd, for plaintiff.

Lyman B. Bunnell, for defendant.

McAdam, J.—This action is against the defendant as the maker of a promissory note. After suit brought, but before the time to answer therein had expired, the payee and first indorser of the note paid the amount thereof to the plaintiff, whereupon the maker (the defendant) interposed, as a defense to the action so commenced, the plea of payment by the payee, claiming that, in consequence, the latter had become the owner of the note and the real party in interest. The plea is substantially true as matter of fact, and the point is whether it presents a legal defense.

My conclusions are: 1st. That the plaintiff, being the owner of the note at the time the action was commenced, was the real party in interest within the
[1] meaning of the term as used in the Code, and that the action was properly brought in its name. 2d.
[2] That the subsequent payment of the note by the payee and indorser operated to discharge the latter only from further liability to the plaintiff, and entitled the payee who made the payment to be subrogated to any right which the plaintiff had in the meantime acquired against the maker of the note, including the right to prosecute the present action. But that
[3] such payment in no way impaired the legal remedy which had been invoked against the defendant as the principal debtor, and that no benefit inured to the latter from the circumstance of such payment, and that it furnishes him with no defense hereto. 3d. That the payee and indorser who paid the note not having applied for leave to continue the action in his name, it was properly continued in the name of

[*] the original plaintiff (*Code*, §§ 755, 756), the money sued for, when recovered, being held for the benefit of the payee and indorser, to whom, in consequence of such payment, they rightfully belong, the plaintiff in this regard becoming the trustee of the assignee of the cause of action (*Wait's Actions and Defenses*, 360). 4th. The present action having been commenced against the maker of the note, prior to the payment there-
[*] of by the payee and indorser, such payment subrogated the latter to the then existing rights of the plaintiff, but to nothing more (*Baylies on Sureties*, 362), and the pendency of this action would furnish the maker with a good plea in bar to an independent action by such payee and indorser for the same cause, the proper remedy of the latter being to continue this action, if he desired to enforce a legal remedy against the maker (*Code*, § 756) or to direct its discontinuance, if he did not desire the proceedings then pending to proceed further. From these conclusions I must direct a judgment in favor of the plaintiff for $517.49, the amount claimed, and interest. The defendant may have thirty days to make a case, with a like stay of execution.

MANNING, RESPONDENT, *v.* GOULD & ANO., APPELLANTS.

COURT OF APPEALS; OCTOBER, 1882.

§ 1335.

Undertaking on appeal.—Failure of sureties to, to justify when excepted to, relieves them from liability thereon.

Failure of the sureties to an undertaking upon an appeal, to justify, when excepted to, defeats entirely the object and purpose of the undertaking. [1, 2] Where security is required to perfect the appeal, the appeal is not perfected, and the party having the judgment may proceed thereon as if no appeal had been taken. Where it required to stay execution of the judgment, the judgment may be enforced pending the appeal as if no undertaking to stay the execution thereof had been given. [1]

Where sureties to an undertaking given on appeal, either to perfect the appeal or to stay the execution of the judgment, are excepted to and fail to justify, and the respondent does not waive their justification, the sureties are not bound by the undertaking executed by them. [3, 10]

Decker v. Anderson (39 *Barb.* 346) ; [4] Ballard v. Ballard (18 *N. Y.* 491) ; [5] Gibbons v. Berhard (3 *Bosw.* 635) ; [6] Hill v. Burke (62 *N. Y.* 111); [7] Knapp v. Anderson (71 *N. Y.* 466; affirming 7 *Hun,* 295); [8] McSpedon v. Bouton (5 *Daly,* 30), [9] distinguished.

(*Decided December* 12, 1882.)

Appeal from judgment of general term of N. Y. superior court affirming judgment, etc., of the trial term of said court. (Reported below, 47 *N. Y. Super. Ct.* 387.)

A judgment was recovered, January 11, 1880, in the superior court of the city of New York in favor of the plaintiff and against one S. Starr Rowland for $555.49. Said Rowland appealed, February 9, 1880, to the general term of said court, and an undertaking was made and executed by the defendants in this action conditioned "that the appellant would pay all costs or damages which may be awarded against the appellant on said appeal, not exceeding $500, and, also, that if the judgment so appealed from or any part thereof is affirmed or the appeal is dismissed, the appellant will pay the sum directed to be paid by the judgment, or that part thereof as to which the judgment shall be affirmed." The sufficiency of the sureties was duly excepted to by plaintiff and a notice of their justification duly served.

Upon the day set for their justification, the sureties

were duly sworn, and the examination of one of them, the defendant Gould, was taken; but before it was signed by him news came of the death of Rowland, and he refused to sign his examination, and the other surety, the defendant King, whose examination had been adjourned, failed and refused to appear on the adjourned day and submit to an examination.

Thereafter, the action was revived and continued against Domitila D. Rowland as administratrix, etc., of S. Starr Rowland, and on the 6th day of November, 1880, the said judgment was in all respects affirmed.

This action was thereafter brought on the undertaking. Upon the trial, at the close of plaintiff's case, each defendant moved for a nonsuit. Their motions were denied, and they excepted. A verdict in favor of plaintiff for $692.75 was found by direction of the court, and judgment thereupon entered for $833.74, from which an appeal was taken to the general term, which affirmed the judgment.

This appeal was taken from that judgment of affirmance.

N. C. Moak (*James R. Carmichal & N. W. Newhall*, attorneys), for appellants.

Fred. M. Littlefield, for respondent.

Sureties upon an undertaking are not released from liability by their failure to justify, if excepted to . . . McSpedon v. Bouton, 5 *Daly*, 30; Hill v. Burke, 62 *N. Y.* 111; Gibbons v. Berhard, 3 *Bosw.* 635; Knapp v. Anderson, 7 *Hun*, 295; Ballard v. Ballard, 18 *N. Y.* 491; Decker v. Anderson, 39 *Barb.* 346; Gusthal v. Reinhardt, 1 *Law Bul.* 37; Van Duyne v. Coope, 1 *Hill*, 557.

TRACY, J.—The question to be determined in this case is whether the sureties to an undertaking given on appeal to the general term of the supreme court or of a superior city court, when excepted to, and they fail or refuse to justify, and justification is not waived by the respondent, are nevertheless bound by the conditions of their undertaking. This depends upon the construction to be placed upon sections 1352 and 1335 of the Code. Security is not required to perfect an appeal to the general term from a final judgment rendered in the same court, but such appeal does not stay proceedings upon the judgment, and the party having the judgment may proceed to enforce it as if no appeal had been taken. If the appellant desires to stay the execution of the judgment pending the appeal, section 1352 of the Code requires that he must give the security required to perfect an appeal to the court of appeals. Upon giving such security, the execution of the judgment appealed from is stayed, as upon an appeal to the court of appeals, and subject to the same conditions. Section 1335 of the Code provides that it is not necessary that an undertaking upon an appeal to the court of appeals should be approved, but the attorney for the respondent may, within ten days after service of a copy of the undertaking, except to the sufficiency of the sureties. Within ten days thereafter, the sureties, or other sureties in a new undertaking to the same effect must justify before a judge of the court below or a county judge. If the judge, after examination of the sureties, finds them sufficient, he must indorse his allowance of them upon the undertaking or a copy thereof. The section then declares: "The effect of a failure so to justify and to procure an allowance is the same as if the undertaking had not been given."

[1] The meaning of this language is too obvious to admit of doubt. Failure of the sureties to an undertaking upon an appeal, to justify when expected to, defeats entirely the object and purpose of the undertaking. Where security is required in order to perfect the appeal, the appeal from the judgment is not per-

fected, and the party having the judgment may proceed thereon as if no appeal had been taken. Where security is not required to perfect the appeal, but is required to stay the execution of the judgment, the judgment may be enforced pending the appeal as if no undertaking to stay the execution thereof had been given.

So much is clear. The remaining question to be considered is, whether the respondent may insist upon his right to disregard the appeal or the stay of proceedings, as the case may be, because of the failure of the sureties to justify, and at the same time hold the sureties upon their undertaking.

We think not. Upon the service of a notice of appeal with an undertaking, the respondent may accept the undertaking, and thereupon it becomes effectual and the sureties will be bound. But he may say, "I will not accept the sureties tendered by the undertaking, except upon condition that they appear before a judge, are examined as to their responsibility and the judge approves them after such examination." Thereupon the appellant may undertake to meet this condition and give notice of justification of the sureties, or he may tender other sureties in a new undertaking to the same effect, who must justify before a judge of
[2] the court below or a county judge. If he does neither then the case stands at if no attempt to give an undertaking had been made. No reason can be suggested why the respondent should be permitted to disregard the undertaking and proceed upon the judgment as if none had been given, and yet have all the advantages
[3] that the undertaking was intended to secure. The only object and purpose of the undertaking was to stay the execution of the judgment until the appeal had been heard and determined. The respondent cannot have the dual right to enforce the judgment pending the appeal as if no undertaking had been given, and at the same time treat it as valid security for the

payment of the judgment. The undertaking was tendered by the appellant and rejected by the respondent, and never perfected by the appellant. It is unnecessary to determine whether or not the exceptant might have waived her exception at any time before the refusal of the surety to justify. No waiver in this case was made or attempted. We have carefully examined the numerous authorities cited by the respondent, and none of them are in conflict with the conclusion in this case.

The case of Decker v. Anderson (39 *Barb.* 346) arose [4] on an undertaking given upon the bringing of an action to recover possession of personal property under the Code. The cases are not analogous. In an undertaking given in an action of replevin, the sureties being approved by the sheriff, he is required to take the property of the defendant, and becomes liable to the defendant therefor in case the sureties fail to justify, if excepted to.

In such a case it would be unreasonable to hold that, after the defendant's property has been taken upon the faith of the undertaking, the sureties could relieve themselves from liability by refusing to justify when excepted to. Besides, the Code does not declare that the effect of a failure to justify is the same as if no undertaking had been given. On the contrary, the effect of a failure to justify is to subject the sheriff to liability to the defendant for the property taken. Ballard v. Ballard (18 *N. Y.* 491), simply decides that an [5] exception duly taken to sureties on appeal is waived by the failure of the respondent to attend the officer before whom the notice of justification is given, although the sureties also fail to attend. It holds that the party excepting is the actor in the proceeding, and no step is necessary to be taken except upon his requisition.

The question involved in the case of Gibbons v. Ber-

[6] hard (3 *Bosw.* 635) was one of pleading. It was there held that a complaint upon an undertaking, executed upon an appeal to the court of appeals, sufficient in other respects, is not demurrable as not stating facts sufficient to constitute a cause of action, merely because it omits to aver that the undertaking was accompanied by the affidavits of the sureties that they were worth double the sum specified therein. Such affidavit was intended for the protection of the respondent, and it was competent for him to waive it. In
[7] Hill *v.* Burke (62 *N. Y.* 111) the respondent accepted the undertaking, and never excepted to the sureties. The only defect the sureties claimed was that they did not originally justify in a sufficiently large
[8] amount. Knapp *v.* Anderson (7 *Hun,* 295; 71 *N. Y.* 466) decides nothing except that the discharge of the judgment debtor in bankruptcy did not discharge his sureties.

The case of McSpedon *v* Bouton (5 *Daly,* 30) was an action brought upon an undertaking given upon
[9] an appeal to the court of appeals. Although no such defense was set up in the answer, proof was given upon the trial that the respondent excepted to the sureties, and that after repeated attendance by the respondents on notice for their justification and their failure to attend and justify, the proceedings for justification were abandoned without formal order, and the appeal proceeded, and was regularly heard and disposed of in the court of appeals. Judge Robinson held that the failure of the sureties to justify, constituted no defense, and cited Decker *v.* Anderson (39 *Barb.* 346). But that case, as we have already seen, did not arise upon an undertaking given upon an appeal, and cannot be considered an authority upon the question now before the court. We think the court was misled by the supposed analogy of this case.

Furthermore, the language of the Code under which

the undertaking was given in that case, is not the same as the present Code. The intent of the legislature to make the effect of a failure to justify and to procure an allowance, the same as if an undertaking had not been given, is more strongly expressed in the present code, than it was in section 334 of the old Code.

The sureties were not bound; and the judgment of the general and special terms must be reversed,
[10] and a new trial granted: costs to abide the event.

All concurred.

In re HENRY CROSSMAN, Deceased.

Surrogate's Court, Kings County; November, 1882.

§ 2647.

Will executed in duplicate.—While two testamentary instruments, executed by same testator at same time, are to be considered as one will, when a will is executed in duplicate, each is a complete will.—Either duplicate may be admitted to probate.—When petition for probate in such case irregular.

It is the general rule that two or more testamentary instruments, executed at the same time, by the same testator, are to be construed together, and viewed as one will and must be admitted to probate as such. [1]

Where a will is executed in duplicate, each is a complete will, [2] and it would be unnecessary to admit to probate and record both duplicates. [3]

Where the petition for the probate of a will does not properly describe it as having been executed in duplicate, and one of the duplicates is thereupon admitted to probate, the probate is irregular, but will not be revoked for that reason, as the irregularity does not affect the validity of the will, or the competency of the proof thereof. [4]

(*Decided November* 16, 1882.)

Petition to revoke the probate of a will.

Sufficient facts are stated in the opinion.

Henry L. Clinton and *Nathaniel H. Clement*, for petitioner.

Henry W. Bookstaver, and *James R. Steers, Jr.*, opposed.

LIVINGSTON, Surrogate.—This is an application under sections 2647 and 2653 of the Code, to revoke the probate of the will of Henry Crossman, deceased.

The will was executed in duplicate, but only one of the duplicate parts was produced and proved on the probate, and no mention was then made of the other part, nor did it then appear that the will had been executed in duplicate.

That fact was first made apparent, on this proceeding, by the testimony of Mr. Zener, one of the subscribing witnesses, and the duplicate part of the will not produced on the probate was admitted in evidence in this proceeding, for the purpose of showing that it was in every respect an exact duplicate of the will admitted to probate, and had not been in any way altered since its execution.

The proponents having rested their case, a motion is now made for a decree revoking the probate of said will, on the ground that only part of it was admitted to probate.

No question arises as to the destruction, alteration or revocation of the duplicate part not produced on the original probate; it is not pretended that it is not now in the same condition in every respect, as the other part which was produced on that occasion; the contention is, that a will executed in duplicate consists of both duplicate parts; that neither constitutes the whole will and that consequently such a will, has not been admitted to probate if only one of its duplicate

parts has been proved. This would no doubt be so, if the several instruments, instead of being duplicates, contained different provisions. It is undoubtedly the
general rule that two or more testamentary instru-
[1] ments executed at the same time, by the same
testator, are to be construed together, and viewed as one will, and must be admitted to probate as such. (In the matter of Forman's will, 54 *Barb.* 274, 284, 285) But where a will is executed in duplicate, although
each duplicate may be said to be part of the will
[2] in the sense that it is not a separate will, yet from
the very nature of duplicates, each is the complete will in itself, since each part is a duplicate *original*. (*The Touchstone*, 1 Am. ed. p. 53, note 1; (2 *Phillips on Ev.* 544). As was said by Judge MAULE, in Doe *v.* Strickland (8 *C. B.* 724): "Each part, fully and entirely expresses the will and intention of the testator." And it is upon this theory, that the revocation or intentional and final alteration of one of the parts by the testator, is held to be a revocation or alteration of the whole will.

So considered, it would be unnecessary to admit to
probate, and record both duplicates. And this
[3] view is sustained by the practice followed in the
surrogate's court of New York, on the probate of the will of Ann Seaman, and in this court in the case of the will of Austin D. Moore. Both of those wills were executed in duplicate, but only one part was admitted to probate and recorded. So in Doe *v.* Strickland (*supra*), only the altered duplicate part found in the possession of the testator was proved and admitted to probate, and yet, if the theory of counsel for the petitioners is correct, there is the same necessity for admitting to probate and recording both duplicates where one of them has been altered, as where no alteration has been made in either, since the change in the one does not destroy or annul the other, but only

effects the same alteration in both. Still, on the probate of a will executed in duplicate, the petition should describe the will as having been so executed, so as to inform the parties in interest of that fact, which it is very material for them to know; and the part kept by the testator must be produced or accounted for, as in case it cannot be found, the presumption is that he has destroyed it with the intention of revoking his will (*Wms. on Executors*, 158). But as said before, no such question arises in this case, as it appears that both duplicate parts were in the possession of the testator, and that neither was destroyed or altered by him.

The petition for probate of the will probably was irregular in not properly describing the will as having been executed in duplicate; but the probate is not
[*] to be revoked, in this proceeding, for that reason. The irregularity does not affect the validity of the will, or the competency of the proof thereof. (*Code*, § 2647).

The motion to revoke the probate, must be denied on the evidence as it now stands, and this proceeding may be entered on the day calendar for contested matters for further hearing, on the application of either side, on eight days' notice to the other.

Let an order be entered accordingly.

WILLIAMSON v. WILLIAMSON.

SUPREME COURT, FIRST DEPARTMENT; SPECIAL TERM, FEBRUARY, 1883.

§ 439.

Complaint verified before a commissioner for New York in another State must have certificate of secretary of state.—Order for service of summons by publication granted on complaint so verified, but not having such certificate, is void.

Where an order for the service of the summons in an action by publication was founded upon a complaint purporting to have been verified before a commissioner for this State resident in Philadelphia, Pa., to which there was not attached any certificate of the secretary of state certifying that the commissioner was duly authorized to administer such oath or affirmation, etc.,—*Held*, that the objection that no verified complaint was presented to the justice who granted the order was well taken; [1] that there was no evidence before said justice that there was a verified complaint showing a sufficient or any cause of action, as required by section 439 of the Code; and hence he never acquired any jurisdiction to make the order. [2]

(*Decided February* 12, 1883.)

Motion to vacate and set aside an order for the service of the summons in an action by publication, and to set aside the service made thereunder.

The facts are stated in the opinion.

Charles H. Smith, for motion.

Arthur Furber, opposed.

LAWRENCE, J.—This is an action to obtain a judgment for an absolute divorce, on the ground of the adultery of the defendant. The plaintiff resides in the city of New York, and alleges in his affidavit that the defendant "is at present living with her infant child in the said city of Baltimore, and State of Maryland; that for the reason that defendant has not been within the State of New York for a period long prior to the commencement of this action, deponent has been unable to cause personal service of the summons herein to be made on defendant," etc.

Upon the complaint and affidavit of the plaintiff an order was made, September 5, 1882, for the service of the summons, upon the defendant by publication, and the defendant having made default, the cause was referred to a referee, who reported in favor of the plaintiff, but said report has not been confirmed.

The defendant now moves to vacate and set aside the service of the summons and order for publication, for the reason that the complaint presented to the justice granting the order of publication was not a verified complaint, no certificate of the secretary of the state of New York, certifying to the genuineness and official signature of the commissioner of the state of New York, residing in Philadelphia, where the complaint purports to have been verified, being attached to the alleged verification of the complaint. Also, on the ground that the affidavit and order for publication failed to specify defendant's precise address in Baltimore, to which the summons should have been mailed. There is also in the notice of motion a general prayer, that in case the application be denied on the above grounds, the default of the defendant be opened and that she be allowed to come in and defend the action.

In this case the order for the publication of the summons was founded upon a complaint purporting to have been verified before Lewin W. Barringer, a commissioner for the State of New York, resident in Philadelphia, Pa. By section 439 of the Code of Civil Procedure, the order for the publication of the summons must be founded upon a verified complaint, showing sufficient cause of action against the defendant, to be served, and proof by affidavit of the additional facts required by section 438.

It is claimed that in this case no verified complaint was presented to the learned justice who granted the granted the order of publication, for the reason that there was no certificate of the secretary of state certifying that such commissioner was duly authorized to administer such oath or affirmation, &c. I am inclined
[1] to the opinion that this objection is well taken, for the reason that the statutes provide that when any oath or affirmation shall be taken before any commissioner appointed in another State for this State, before the same shall be entitled to be used or read in evidence there shall be subjoined or affixed to the certificate signed and sealed by such commissioner a certificate under the hand and official seal of the secretary of state of this State, certifying that such commissioner was duly authorized to administer such oath or affirmation at the time his certificate bears date, and that the secretary is acquainted with the handwriting of such commissioner, or has compared the signature to such certificate with signature of such commissioner deposited in his office, and that he believes the signature and the impression of the seal of said certificate to be genuine (See 3 *R. S.* 7 ed. p. 2231, § 2;* *Ibid.* 2226, § 4).† Inasmuch as the statute requires that before any deed or other instrument, oath or affidavit, patent or record, shall be read in evidence the certificate of the secretary of state required by the statute shall be attached to the certificate of the commissioner residing in the sister state, it seems to me conclusively to follow that there was no evidence before the learned justice who
[2] granted the order for publication in this case, that

* Laws of 1875, chap. 136, § 2.

† Laws of 1850, chap. 270, § 4.

there was a verified complaint showing a sufficient or any cause of action against the defendant. And yet, as we have already seen, section 439 of the Code requires that the order must be founded upon a verified complaint showing such sufficient cause of action.

If the view which I take is correct, the learned justice who made the order for the publication of the summons never acquired any jurisdiction to make the order, the essential prerequisite to such jurisdiction, to wit, a verified complaint, being wanting in the case presented to him.

SMITH, Assignee, etc., Respondent, v. BOWERS, et al., Apellants.

N. Y. Court of Common Pleas; General Term, November, 1882.

§ 738.

Offer of judgment.—Must be for specified sum.—When judgment not more favorable than offer.

The offer of judgment authorized by the Code must be for a specified sum. Where an offer of judgment was for $56, "with interest," —*Held*, that the only sum specified was $56, and no significance could be given to the words, "with interest," from the impossibility of fixing any date for computation. [1]

To determine whether the judgment recovered in an action was for more or less than an offer of judgment made therein, the recovery, for the purposes of comparison, must be reduced by a part of the sum allowed as interest on the principal sum recovered, [2] so that the interest shall be computed only to the date of the offer. [3]

(*Decided December* 4, 1882.)

Appeal from order denying defendant's motion to compel the clerk to retax costs.

This action was brought to recover the sum of

$196.48, a balance due for iron sold and delivered, with interest thereon from the 1st day of April, 1881.

On July 19, 1881, the defendants offered to allow judgment for $56 with interest and costs. The time from which interest was to run, was not specified.

A trial was had November 21, 1881; the jury rendered a verdict for plaintiff and against defendants for $58.75.

Conlan & McCrea, for appellants.

Chauncey S. Truax, for respondents.

BEACH, J.—This is an appeal from an order of the special term denying the defendant's motion for a readjustment of costs. It was claimed the sum recovered was less than an unaccepted offer of judgment. The Code of Civil Procedure authorizes a written offer [1] for a *sum specified*. The offer served by the defendants was for $56, with interest. The only sum specified is the $56. No significance can be given to the words, "with interest," from the impossibility of fixing any date for computation.

While the defendants offer must be held at $56; [2] the plaintiff's recovery, for purposes of comparison, must be reduced by a part of the sum allowed as interest. His claim, in the view adopted by the jury, was thus stated by the learned judge in his charge on the trial: "If you find as claimed by the defendants . . . . . ., then the plaintiff would be entitled to a verdict at your hands for $58.70; $3.50 of which, as I make it, being for interest from April 1, 1881, to the time of the trial."

The jury found for the plaintiff $58.70. In Pike *v.* Johnson (47 *N. Y.* 1) the court says: "We hold that the defendant was entitled to recover costs." We hold that in such a case, interest added by a jury or by the court to the damages found, cannot be estimated in determining whether a judgment is more or less favorable to the appellant than the offer of the respondent."

The offer of judgment is dated July 19, 1881. The plaintiff's complaint demanded interest from April [*] 1, 1881. Interest on the principal sum of the recovery from April 1, 1881, to the date of the offer, should be computed, that is, for three months and nineteen days, being $1.01. This, added to the $55.17, aggregates $56.18; the offer having been for $56.

The propriety of the method is shown by this test. Suppose, instead of an offer, the defendants on July 19 1881, had made legal tender of $56, and being refused, had paid the money into court. To settle the adequacy of the tender, interest on plaintiff's claim would have to be reckoned to its date. This must be the course under the offer of judgment (Budd v. Jackson, 26 *How. Pr.* 398). The offer seems to fall short of the principal sum found by the jury for plaintiff with interest to its date, and therefore was less favorable than his recovery.

The order must be affirmed, with costs and disbursements.

VAN BRUNT, J., concurred.

SMITH & ANO., RESPONDENTS, v. DAVIS. CHRISTIAN, APPELLANT.

SUPREME COURT, FIRST DEPARTMENT; GENERAL TERM, JANUARY, 1883.

§ 636.

Attachment.—When person acquiring interest in attached property may move to vacate.—Affidavit on which attachment granted must show cause of action.

A person who acquires an interest in attached property subsequent to the levying of the attachment has the right, under the provisions of the Code, to make and maintain a motion to set aside the attachment where the affidavits upon which it was granted are not sufficient to warrant the issuing of an attachment. [1]

Where the affidavit upon which a warrant of attachment was granted, stated, that the "defendant is indebted to the . . . plaintiffs in the sum of $11,398.65, over and above any counter-claims or offsets, and that the grounds for plaintiffs' claim are as follows, to wit: For goods, wares and merchandise sold and delivered to the amount of said sum of $11,398.65, the whole amount whereof is now due and owing,"—*Held*, that it wholly failed to comply with the provisions of the Code requiring a cause of actions to be shown by affidavit to authorize the granting of an attachment, [2] and the attachment should be vacated. [5] The assertion of the indebtedness itself was a mere conclusion, which the facts afterwards related in no manner tended to sustain. [2]

To entitle a plaintiff to attach the defendant's property before his right to do so has been established by evidence, reasonable and satisfactory proof is required. A plain case must be made out, and where it is not, it necessarily follows that the attachment must be set aside. [4] Reed v. French (23 *N. Y.* 294), distinguished. [3]

(*Decided February* 2, 1883.)

Appeal by one Edward D. Christian from order of New York county special term denying motion to vacate attachment.

On September 15, 1882, a warrant of attachment was granted which was issued to the sheriff of the city and county of New York, who under said warrant levied and attached certain property belonging to the defendant, then in possession of H. K. & F. B. Thurber & Co. Thereafter, on September 19, 1882, the defendant executed and delivered an assignment of the property so attached to Edward D. Christian, the appellant, in trust for certain of his creditors. To cure possible imperfections in this deed, the defendant, on October 3, 1882, executed and delivered to said Christian a second deed of assignment of said property in trust for his creditors. Both assignments were recorded in the offices of the clerk and register of the city and county of New York, October 4, 1882.

On October 23, 1882, said Christian, upon an affidavit setting forth the deeds of assignment to him and claiming to have become thereby the owner of the property attached, moved to vacate said warrant of attachment upon the ground, among others, that the affidavit upon which the warrant was granted did not disclose a cause of action against the defendant.

The motion was heard November 1, 1882, and denied; and said Christian thereupon appeal from the order entered thereon.

Further facts are stated in the opinion.

William L. Royall, for appellant.

There is no averment in the affidavit that the goods were sold and delivered *to the defendant*. . . . If English cases are to count as authorities this objection to the affidavit is fatal. See Perks *v.* Severn, 7 *East*, 194; Bell *v.* Thrupp, 2 *Barn. & Ald.* 596; Fenton *v.* Ellis, 6 *Taunt.* 192; Loiscador *v.* Moryoseph, 1 *Bingh.* 357; Hopkins *v.* Vaughan, 12 *East*, 398; Visger *v.* Delyal, 2 *Barn. & Ald.* 571; Cullman *v.* Leeson, 2 *C. & M.* 406; Kelly *v.* Curzon, 4 *A. & E.* 622; Balby *v.* Batley, 6 *Taunt.* 25.

The affidavit does not state that the goods were sold and delivered to the defendant *by the plaintiff*. This is just as fatal. . . . Carthrow *v.* Haggar, 8 *East*, 106; Taylor *v.* Forbes, 11 *East*, 315. The fact that the affidavit states that the defendant is indebted to the plaintiff does not help matters; that is only a statement of the plaintiff's *opinion* that the defendant owes him. Skiff *v.* Stewart, 39 *How.* 388; Balbi *v.* Batley, 6 *Taunt.* 25; Edwards *v.* Dick, 6 *Barn & Ald.* 495.

Edwin More (*More, Aplington & More*, attorneys, for respondent.

DANIELS, J.—The applicant in whose behalf the motion to set aside the atttachment was made was

shown to have acquired an interest in the property attached, after the levying of the attachment. That entitled him to move to set it aside because of the insufficiency of the affidavit on which it had been issued
[1] (Steuben Co. Bank *v.* Alberger, 75 *N. Y.* 179; 78 *Id.*
252). When that case was last before the court of appeals it was definitely decided that such a party had the right, under the provisions of the Code, to make and maintain a motion of this nature, if in fact the affidavit was not sufficient to justify the issuing of the attachment. And that was claimed to have been the effect of the affidavit upon which the attachment in the action had been issued. The affidavit was exceedingly brief, and, after being entitled in the action, was in the following words and figures:

"City and County of New York, ss.:

"Robert T. Smith, being duly sworn, doth depose and say that he is one of the plaintiffs composing the firm of Smith & Wicks; that the above named defendant is indebted to the above named plaintiff in the sum of eleven thousand three hundred and ninety-eight and 65-100 dollars, over and above any counter-claims or offsets, and that the grounds for plaintiffs' claim are as follows, to wit: For goods, wares and merchandise sold and delivered, to the amount of said sum of $11,398.65, the whole amount whereof is now due and owing. And this deponent further says that the defendant is not a resident this State, but resides and is at Richmond, in the State of Virginia.

ROBERT T. SMITH.

"Sworn to before me, this 15th
day of September, 1882.
"ALEX. WILEY,
Notary Public, N. Y. Co."

By this affidavit no demand in favor of the plaintiffs against the defendant was established. But whatever might have existed was stated to be an indebtedness "to the above named plaintiff," who was the person alone who made the affidavit, and this indebtedness was stated to have been created for goods, &c., sold and delivered to the amount of $11,398.65, the whole of which was then due and owing. These statements, besides being insufficient to establish a cause of action in favor of the plaintiffs, were likewise insufficient to present a cause of action in favor of the one of them who made the affidavit. For it was not stated that either the plaintiffs or he himself had sold and delivered the goods, or that such sale had been made to the defendant in the action. All the facts mentioned may very well be true, and still the defendant not be liable either to the plaintiffs, or to the plaintiff making the affidavit, to the amount of a single dollar.

To authorize an attachment, the provisions of the Code require a cause of action to be shown by the affidavit, and that which was made in this case wholly [*] failed to comply with that requirement. The assertion of the indebtedness itself was a mere conclusion which the facts afterwards related in no manner tended to sustain. For nothing was inserted in the affidavit from which it could be inferred that it was intended to be stated that the goods had been sold to or even on the credit or liability of the defendant in any form. An indictment upon this affidavit, accusing the person making it of falsely swearing that the goods had been sold to or on the credit of the defendant, could not for a moment be sustained; for no such averment, by the most liberal implication, can be constructively derived from it.

The case in this respect is no more favorable to the plaintiff than that of Pomeroy *v.* Moss,* recently decided upon the effect of a similar affidavit by the

* Pomeroy *v.* Moss was digested in 15 *Weekly Dig.* 25.

general term of this department. No authority has been found under which a seizure of the defendant's property by means of an attachment can be sustained on this affidavit. It has been urged that Read *v.*
[3] French (28 *N. Y.* 294) sanctioned a practice as loose and indefinite as that which resulted in this affidavit. But that was a case arising under the provisions of the Code prescribing the statement required to be made to support the confession of a judgment, and where the defendant himself practically consented that his property might be affected and incumbered by means of the statement which he made.

The nature of the provisions made upon this subject do not require that degree of care and strictness which has been found necessary to be observed to protect the owners of property from its unauthorized and unwarranted seizure. To entitle a party to make such a
[4] seizure before his right to appropriate the defendant's property has been established by evidence, reasonable and satisfactory proof is required. A plain case must be made out; and where it is not, it necessarily follows that the attachment must be set aside. This rule imposes no hardship upon the applicant for an attachment, for he is allowed to make out his case by his own unsupported oath, and where the facts are such as will warrant him in making the statements required for this purpose, he should be obliged carefully and intelligently to embody them in the affidavit.

[5] The order should be reversed, and an order entered vacating the attachment, with the usual costs and disbursements.

DOUGLISS ET AL. v. ATWELL ET AL.

N. Y. SUPERIOR COURT; SPECIAL TERM, OCTOBER, 1882.

§ 3256.

Disbursements.—When expense of lithographing summons and complaint and for telegrams may be included in bill of costs.

Where on the adjustment of costs in an action for partition, certain items of disbursement for telegrams and lithographic copies of the summons and complaint were objected to, and there was an affidavit showing a reasonable necessity for incurring such expenses, and no affidavit to the contrary was presented,—*Held*, that the items objected to must be allowed.

(*Decided October* 31, 1882.)

Motion for a new taxation of costs.

Action for a partition or sale of certain real property. The plaintiff's attorneys presented their bill of costs to the clerk for adjustment, after notice to the defendants' attorneys. The attorneys for certain of the defendants appeared and objected to certain items of disbursements set forth therein, to wit: an item of $2.30 expended for telegrams; another of $33.84, expense of lithographing summons and complaint; and one of $4.65 disbursed for lithographing supplemental summons and complaint. The clerk struck out the items objected to, and the matter was thereupon submitted to the court. There was an affidavit showing the necessity for the disbursements.

A. H. Stoiber (*Van Schaick, Gillender & Stoiber*, attorneys), for motion.

R. B. Gwillim, opposed.

FREEDMAN, J.—In view of the character of the

action and the procedings therein, and there being a special affidavit showing a reasonable necessity for incurring the expenses for telegrams, and lithographic copies, while no affidavit to the contrary was presented, the items of $2.30, $38.84, and $4.65 must be allowed.

SHAFFER, Respondent, v. HOLM, Appellant.

Supreme Court, First Department; General Term, October, 1882.

§ 531.

Bill of Particulars.—Properly ordered in action for criminal conversation.—When right to, not lost by laches.

Where, in an action for damages for the seduction of plaintiff's wife by defendant, the complaint, verified May 23, 1881, set up that the acts complained of took place "on or about the 10th of December, 1878, and in the fall of 1879, and in every month in the year 1880, and at divers other times since the 10th of December, 1878," but did not state where,—*Held*, that a bill of particulars of the particular times and places at which plaintiff expects or intends to prove that such acts took place, should be granted.

Where, in an action for criminal conversation, the complaint was sworn to May 2, 1881, and the defendant demanded a bill of particulars on June 18, but did not move to compel the plaintiff to serve it until May 20, 1882,—*Held*, that the defendant was diligent in making the demand, and that the question of laches cannot be successfully urged against him. It was the duty of the plaintiff to have complied with that demand, and not to have driven the defendant to compulsory measures.

(*Decided, November* 24, 1882.)

Appeal from order of New York county special term, denying motion that plaintiff furnish a bill of particulars.

The opinion states the facts.

Isaac N. Mills, for appellant.

Jacob Fromme, for respondent.

The appellate court will not reverse the order in a case where the court denies a motion for a bill of particulars in an action such as this, unless it appears beyond a peradventure that the court abused its discretion. Weller *v.* Weller, 4 *Hun*, 195; Wehle *v.* Broadway Savings Bank, 8 *J. & S.* 161.

BRADY, J.—This is an action for criminal conversation. The complaint sets forth, on information and belief, that on or about the 10th of December, 1878, and in the fall of 1879, and in every month in the year 1880, and up to and including the 18th of May, 1881, and at divers other times since the 10th of December, 1878, the defendant debauched and carnally knew Catharine, the wife of the plaintiff. The complaint was sworn to the 23rd of May, 1881, and the summons bears the same date. On June 18, the defendant's attorney demanded a verified statement, in writing, of the particular times and places at which the plaintiff expected or intended to prove that any of the acts of adultery or criminal intercourse took place between the defendant and the wife of the plaintiff, and that service thereof be made at his office in Mount Vernon, Westchester county, New York. The demand was addressed to the plaintiff's attorney.

Nothing further seems to have been done on the subject to which the demand related, until May 26, 1882, when a motion was inaugurated to procure the bill of particulars demanded, and which was founded in part upon an affidavit of the defendant in which he stated, that he had no knowledge whatever of the times and places at which the plaintiff expected or intended to prove upon the trial that he had committed adultery with the plaintiff's wife, and without some knowledge upon this point, he did not, and could not know what witnesses he should subpœna to prove his whereabouts and conduct at such times; and that without such knowledge, he would be forced to enter upon the trial of the action without the benefit of the testimony of important and material witnesses, and that he could not safely proceed to trial, without a verified statement in writing from the plaintiff, of the times and places at which the plaintiff expected or intended to prove the acts of criminal intercourse, alleged to have taken place between himself and the plaintiff's wife, as he was advised by counsel and verily believed.

Upon this application the plaintiff's affidavit appears to have been read, in which he stated, that he knew nothing of his own knowledge of the matters contained in the complaint, which were set out therein, with the exception of those matters which were not set out on information and belief; and he stated further, that he was advised by his counsel and verily believed, that it would not be safe for him to give the verified statement demanded, until the defendant was examined as an adverse party before the trial. The result of this application was an order denying it, but no opinion was expressed by the learned justice in disposing of the motion.

The respondent insists that the defendant was guilty of laches in allowing a year to elapse, and when the action was about to be reached on the day calendar, before he made the application; and further, that the wrongful acts charged, were particularly within the knowledge of the defendant, who knows the places at which he and the wife of the plaintiff were, at the various times charged in the complaint. But neither of these were sufficient to require the special term to deny the motion. In the case of Tilton *v.* Beecher, 56 *N. Y.* 176, which was an action of a similar character to the one in hand, it was decided that a bill of particulars in an action for criminal conversation might be exacted, and the direction to furnish it was a proper exercise of judicial power.

In Jones *v.* Platt, 60 *How. Pr.* 278, which was an action for slander, the complaint alleged that on certain days, the defendant in the town of Western and elsewhere, and at divers and various other times and places, uttered slanderous words. The defendant, after issue was joined, applied for a bill of particulars specifying the times and places where. The motion was granted.

In Stiebling *v.* Lockhaus, 21 *Hun*, 457, which was also an action for slander, the importance of apprising the defendant with great particularity of the matters for which he was to be put on trial was recognized.

In the case of Winchell *v.* Martin, 14 *N. Y. Weekly Dig.* 468, which was also an action for criminal conversation, the complaint alleged that in the month of August, 1869, and at divers other times previous thereto, and during such marriage whilst the plaintiff and his wife were living together as man and wife, the defendant wrongfully and carnally knew the wife. It appeared that in January, 1870, although the issue was joined in September, 1869, the plaintiff noticed the cause for trial, and sometime afterwards application was made for a bill of particulars, which was denied by the learned justice at special term, on the ground of the defendant's laches in making it.

An appeal was taken to the general term of this department, and the order was reversed. The court in its opinion said, "We are unable to discover any good and satisfactory reason for refusing a bill of particulars in this case, because of delay on the defendant's part; such delay having in no way embarrassed the plaintiff, as we can see, and he can as readily comply with the demand now, as at any time since the action was commenced." And upon the merits the court said, "The defendant made a fair case for the allowance of the order, and while the determination of these applications rests somewhat in the discretion of the court, yet it is almost a matter of course to grant the demand in actions of this nature, where the complaint omits to allege time and place with particularity, as it failed to do in this instance." And the court further said, "The propriety and justice of requiring the plaintiff to supply the information sought by the defendant's motion, was stated and fully commented upon in Wood v. Wood, 2 *Paige*, 108; Tilton v. Beecher, 59 *N. Y.* 176; Stiebling v. Lockhaus, 21 *Hun*, 457."

In this case it will have appeared that the charge made against the defendant in the complaint, is without reference to place. The criminal conversation is alleged to have taken place at certain dates and between certain dates, but the place of its occurrence is not named, neither town, city nor county, and this would seem to be a strong reason why the particulars asked for should be given. It does not appear that the plaintiff is unable to give them. On the contrary, it is quite clear, that he has the ability to give the required information, because in his affidavit in answer to the application for a direction to furnish the bill, he said that he was advised by his counsel and verily believed, that it would be unsafe for him to give the verified statement, as already suggested. The case of Winchell v. Martin, *supra*, is conclusive of the right of the defendant in this case to have the particulars sought, inasmuch as it bears upon the question of laches, as well as the merits of the application made herein.

If it were necessary to sustain the power and propriety of ordering a bill of particulars in this case, the other decisions might be cited; but the adjudications mentioned are quite sufficient, and it is unnecessary to pursue the subject further.

In conclusion however, it is proper to say on the

question of laches, that although no proceeding to compel the delivery of the bill of particulars was commenced until May, 1882, yet the demand for one was made soon after the action was commenced, as already suggested, viz.: upon the 18th of June, 1881, and with which the plaintiff never complied. It must be said that the defendant was diligent in making the demand, and the question of laches cannot now be successfully urged against him. It was the duty of the plaintiff to have complied with that demand, and not to have driven the defendant to compulsory measures.

For these reasons the order appealed from should be reversed, the motion granted, and the plaintiff directed to furnish a bill of particulars of the times and places where the criminal conversation took place, within twenty days after service of a copy of the order to be entered herein; $10 costs and disbursements of this appeal allowed to the appellant.

Davis, P. J., and Daniels, J., concurred.

MURTHA, Respondent, *v.* CURLEY, Appellant.

New York Superior Court; General Term, January, 1883.

§ 3238.

Costs.—Awarded to abide event upon granting new trial on appeal.

The costs to be awarded upon the granting of a new trial are in the discretion of the general term, and may be awarded to either party, either absolutely or to abide the event.

Where the general term awarded the costs of the appeal to the defendant, and the court of appeals reversed the judgment of the general

term, "with costs,"—*Held*, that the words "with costs," in the order of the court of appeals, mean the costs in that court, and that the plaintiff could not have the costs of the appeal to the general term.

Appeal from an order made at special term directing the clerk to tax certain costs.

The plaintiff obtained, on the trial of the action, a judgment against the defendants for a certain sum of money. From this judgment the defendant Curley appealed to the general term of this court, which reversed the judgment of the court below, with costs of appeal to the appellant to abide the event of a new trial.

The plaintiff appealed to the court of appeals. The order of the general term of this court was reversed by the court of appeals and the judgment of the trial term was affirmed with costs to the plaintiff. (See *ante*, p. 1.)

The plaintiff then presented his bill of costs for taxation to the clerk, who refused to tax the costs of the general term in favor of plaintiff. The plaintiff then moved at special term for a retaxation of said costs, and the special term made an order directing the clerk to allow to the plaintiff the costs of the general term.

Starr & Hooker, for appellant.

Adolphus D. Pape and *H. S. Bennett*, for respondent.

TRUAX, J.—The order of the general term limited the recovery of the costs of the general term to the defendant Curley, who was the successful party on the appeal to the general term, only in the event that he should finally succeed in the action. The general term had the power to reverse the judgment with costs to abide the event, in which event the party finally succeeding in the action would have been entitled to tax the costs of an appeal or trial at which he had been beaten (84 *N. Y.* 469).*

The costs to be awarded upon the granting of a new trial are in the discretion of the general term, and may be awarded to either party absolutely or to abide the event (*Code Civ. Pro.* § 3238).

In this case the general term saw fit to award the costs of the appeal to the defendant Curley. It did not award them to the plaintiff. The plaintiff could not have them in any event, because he did not maintain the judgment in his favor (Howell *v.* Van Siclen, 8 *Hun*, 525). It is true that the court of appeals reversed the judgment of the general term "with costs," but the words "with costs" in the order of the court of appeals mean the costs in that court (68 *N. Y.* 628).†

The order of the special term should be reversed, with $10 costs of the appeal, and disbursements, and the taxation of the clerk should be affirmed.

O'GORMAN, J., concurred.

ANSONIA BRASS AND COPPER CO., RESPONDENT, *v.* CONNER, ET AL., AS EXECUTORS, &c., APPELLANTS.

N. Y. COURT OF COMMON PLEAS; GENERAL TERM, NOVEMBER, 1882.

§ 1366.

Execution.—Sheriff's time to return, extended by stay of proceedings

The sixty days allowed the sheriff, by law, to return an execution against the property, is for his benefit, to prevent an action or com-

---

* First National Bank, Meadville *v.* Fourth National Bank, N. Y.

† Sisters of Charity *v.* Kelly.

pulsory proceeding against him before he has had a reasonable time to execute the process ; [1] this time cannot be abridged by any order of any court,[2] but may be extended by operation of law.[3] The sheriff himself may shorten the time, by returning the execution before the expiration of the sixty days, but there is no authority for holding that the sheriff's time to collect the amount of the execution can be shortened, without his consent. [4]

Where the proceedings of a sheriff, to whom an execution against the property had been issued, were actually stayed by order of the court, he is entitled to an allowance for the time he is so stayed,[1] and this, although the stay was for a short period only, and there remained, after it was vacated, a reasonable time to levy, collect and make return of the execution.[5]

An order of the United States District Court, made in bankruptcy proceedings, pending in it, "enjoining and restraining the sheriff" from all further proceedings until the further order of the court stays a sale under execution by a sheriff, and he is bound to obey the order, under penalty.[6]

(*Decided January* 12, 1883.)

Appeal by defendants from order of general term of marine court, affirming judgment of the trial term of said court in favor of plaintiff.

This action was commenced January 27, 1876, to recover damages against defendant's testator, W. C. Conner, as sheriff of the city and county of New York, for failure to return an execution against Charles G. Wilson, upon a judgment recovered by plaintiff against him, which execution was issued to the sheriff November 22, 1875. The cause was tried by a judge without a jury, who found as matter of fact and law at the request of the defendant: "That on the 27th day of November, 1875, and five days after the issuing of the execution mentioned in the plaintiff's complaint, and after defendant's testator had levied upon property belonging to the defendant named in said execution, an order was duly made and issued out of the United States district court for the southern district of New York in bankruptcy, which order was duly served upon defendant's testator, and enjoined and restrained him from all and every proceeding under said execution until the further order of the court. That said order remained and was in full force and effect until the 14th day of December, 1875, when said order was vacated as to the defendant's testator, William C. Conner, then sheriff of the city and county of New York." The judge found, as matter of law, "That the said order of the United States court did not operate to extend the time within which said sheriff was required to return said execution." To this conclusion of law defendants excepted.

The sheriff collected $480.81 on the judgment, $387.15 of which he paid plaintiff. The court therefore found in favor of plaintiff for the balance, less the sheriff's legal fees, and judgment was thereupon entered against him for $80.79, and costs. This judgment was affirmed by the general term of the New York marine court, from whose judgment of affirmance the defendants took this appeal.

The action was commenced sixty-six days after the execution was issued, and the defendants claim that the time the sheriff was stayed should be excluded in computing the time that he had the execution in his hands.

Vanderpoel, Green & Cuming, for appellants.

M. P. Stafford, for respondent.

It is an imperative requirement of law that the execution should be returned within sixty days after its receipt by the sheriff. . . . . Wilson v. Wright, 9 *How. Pr.* 459. At the expiration of sixty days the execution was *functus officio*, invalid for any further proceedings, and the sheriff had no power under it thereafter. *Herman on Executions*, 106; Vail v. Lewis, 4 *Johns.* 450; Van Rensselaer v. Kidd, 6 *N. Y.* 333; Kingston Bank v. Eltinge, 40 *N. Y.* 395; Sherman v. Boyce, 15 *Johns.* 442. The order of the United States court was an absolute nullity. . . . *U. S. Rev. Stat.* § 720; Tenth Nat. Bank *v.* Sanger, 42 *How. Pr.* 179; Clark *v.* Binninger, 3 *N. B. R.* 518; *In re* Campbell, 1 *N. B R.* 174; . . . *In re* Dudley, 1 *Penn. L. J.* 302. A sheriff is bound to know whether an order served upon him is valid or void, and if he acts under a void order he acts at his peril. Ansonia Brass and Copper Co. *v.* Babbitt, 74 *N. Y.* 395. The order, if not void, did not extend the statutory time for returning the execution. Glover *v.* Whittenhall, 6 *Hill*, 600; Lowber *v.* Mayor, &c., 5 *Abb. Pr.* 268.

J. F. DALY, J.—The sheriff is entitled to an [1] allowance for the time he is actually stayed by order of the court. The Code in force when this action was brought provided that "the execution shall be returnable within sixty days after its receipt by the officer."* The sixty days thus allowed by law to the sheriff is for his benefit, to prevent an action or compulsory proceeding against him before he has had a reasonable time to execute the process (Renaud *v.* O'Brien, 35 *N. Y.* 99). This time, allowed by statute to the officer cannot of course be abridged by any [2] order of any court; yet we should hold that it might be, if we agreed with plaintiff's contention that the time during which a sheriff was under stay should be disregarded in computing the period between his receipt of the execution and the bringing of the action for failure to make a return. His time may be [3] extended by operation of law (Wehle *v.* Conner, 69 *N. Y.* 546–550) and by order staying proceedings (Paige *v.* Willet, 38 *N. Y.* 35; People *v.* Comley, 3 *Abb.* 217); and the sheriff himself may shorten the time by returning the process before the expiration

* Section 290 of the Code of Procedure, for which section 1366 of the Code of Civil Procedure is a substitute.

[4] of sixty days (Renaud *v.* O'Brien, *supra*); but there is no authority for holding the sheriff's time in which he may collect the amount of the execution, can be shortened without his consent.

It is not sufficient to say that the stay in this case was for a short period only, and there remained,
[5] after it was vacated, a reasonble time to levy, collect and make return of the execution before the sixty days from the issuing were up. What is a reasonable time is not left to the circumstances of the case or the judgment of courts and juries: the statute has fixed it at sixty days, in order to avoid all dispute or question, and the sheriff is entitled to every day of it.

The respondent's points claim that the order of the United States district court did not stay the sheriff. The finding of the justice is supported by the plaintiff's own admission in the case, that the order was made "enjoining and restraining the sheriff" from all further proceedings until the further order of the court; that said order remained and was of full force and effect until the 14th day of December, 1875, when the said order was vacated," &c. The admission can not now be gainsayed. The United States district court had power by statute (*U. S. Revised Statutes*, § 5024) to enjoin all persons from making any disposition
[6] of the debtor's property. This included a sale by a sheriff, and he was bound to obey the order under penalty until it was vacated, which of course it might be upon motion.

The judgment must be reversed and a new trial granted, with costs to abide event.

VAN BRUNT and VAN HOESEN, JJ., concurred.

DICKENSON, RESPONDENT, v. THE MAYOR, &c., OF NEW YORK, APPELLANTS.

SUPREME COURT, FIRST DEPARTMENT; GENERAL TERM, OCTOBER, 1882.

§§ 383, 410.

Limitation to action.—When action for personal injury must be begun within three years after cause of action accrued.—When time limited for commencement of action against the city of New York begins to run.

Where municipal authorities suffered snow and ice to accumulate on a cross-walk, in such a rough and uneven manner as to render it unsafe and dangerous to foot passengers,—*Held*, in an action against the city for damages for personal injuries received by reason thereof, that the negligence of defendant is the gist of the action, and must be affirmatively established; [1] that the negligence was wrongful only in the sense that all neglect of duty is wrongful,[2] and the action is therefore one to recover "damages for a personal injury resulting from negligence," within the meaning of section 383 of the Code,[3] and must be commenced within three years after the cause of action accrued.[4]

The time limited for the commencement of an action against the city of New York, begins to run from the time the right to make a demand upon the comptroller, pursuant to section 105 of chapter 335 of the Laws of 1873, is completed, [5, 6] and not from the expiration of thirty days after such demand.[6]

(*Decided November* 24, 1882.)

Appeal from judgment in favor of plaintiff entered on demurrer to one of the answers of the defendants.

The facts are stated in the opinion.

D. J. Dean, (*William C. Whitney*, corporation counsel), for appellant.

C. A. H. Bartlett, for respondent.

Davis, P. J.—The complaint in this case, among other things alleges that the Eighth avenue in the city of New York is a public thoroughfare, and that it was and is the duty of the defendants to keep and maintain the streets and avenues of said city, including the said Eighth avenue, in good order and repair, and not to suffer ice or snow to be or remain in such rough and uneven condition on the cross-walks thereof as to be unsafe and dangerous to foot passengers. That the defendants improperly, carelessly, negligently and unlawfully suffered ice or snow to be and remain upon the crosswalk on the east side of Eighth avenue, at the intersection of Eighteenth street, in the city of New York, in such a rough and uneven condition that a person could not walk over it without danger of falling down; and that by reason thereof the plaintiff, on or about the 10th day of January, 1877, while lawfully passing over and upon said cross-walk, and without any fault on her part, was suddenly precipitated, cast and thrown upon the ground, thereby fracturing her left thigh or hip.

It then alleges the damages suffered by her, for which she claims to recover $15,000, and that on the 28th day of April, 1881, the plaintiff presented the claim on which this action is brought in writing to the comptroller of the City of New York, and demanded payment thereof, but that he has neglected for thirty days after such presentation to pay the same.

To this alleged cause of action the defendants for their fourth answer allege that more than three years have elapsed since the cause of action set forth in the complaint accrued, and that the right of the plaintiff to make the demand necessary to entitle her to maintain an action therefor was complete more than three years before the commencement of this suit.

To this answer the plaintiff demurred.

Two questions are presented by this demurrer: first,

whether the cause of action set up in the complaint is subject to the provisions of section 382 of the Code of Civil Procedure or to those of 383. Section 382 provides, among other things, that "an action to recover damages for an injury to property or for personal injury" must be commenced within six years after the cause of action has accrued, except in a case where a different period is expressly prescribed in chapter 4 of the Code. Section 383 provides that an action to recover damages for a personal injury resulting from negligence" must be commenced within three years after the cause of action accrued.

The action set out in the complaint is undoubtedly one for personal injury, and the question to be determined is whether such injury is alleged by the complaint to have resulted from the negligence of the defendant, or from some wrongful act of the defendant independent of the question of negligence. A clear distinction between these causes of action is established by the authorities (Irvine v. Wood, 51 *N. Y.* 228; Muller v. McKesson, 73 *Id.* 204; Clifford v. Dam, 81 *Id.* 56; Sexton v. Zett, 44 *Id.* 431; Creed v. Hartman, 29 *Id.* 597; Congreve v. Smith, 18 *Id.* 82.)

In all of these cases, the cause of action arose from some wrongful act of the defendant, which resulted in an injury to the plaintiff, independently of any question of negligence on the part of the defendant. They establish that it is not necessary, where a person wrongfully places an obstruction upon a public highway by which another is injured, to prove that the wrongful act was negligently done. It is enough that it was done without lawful authority, or is wrongful in itself, and has produced the injury complained of. But a quite different rule prevails where the injury arises from an omission to perform a lawful act or duty, or from the negligent manner in which such an act or duty is performed. In that case the negligence of

[1] the defendant is the gist of the action and must be affirmatively established, and the contributory negligence of the plaintiff constitutes a defense. The cause alleged in the complaint falls within this latter rule, because the city, in constructing and maintaining the crosswalk on which the plaintiff was injured, performed merely a lawful act and duty.

It is not alleged that the city authorities placed the ice or snow upon the crosswalk by means of which the plaintiff was injured. On the contrary the snow or ice was deposited or formed upon the crosswalk by causes beyond the control of the defendant, and the allegations of the complaint only tend to show that the defendant neglected to perform, in due season and in proper manner, a duty, by removing the ice and snow from the walk.

The negligence was wrongful, but only in the sense that all neglect of duty is wrongful; and if any
[2] injury was caused by such neglect of duty it was the result of negligence and not of a wrongful act within the meaning of the law as established by the authorities above cited.

[3] Hence, there seems to be no doubt that the action set out in the complaint in this case was to one to recover "damages for a personal injury resulting from negligence."

It is subject therefore to the provisions of section 383 of the Code and the action must be commenced
[4] within three years after the cause of action has accrued. The second question is as to the effect of section 105 of chap. 335, of the laws of 1873,* in connection with section 410 of the Code of Civil Procedure. It is conceded that the provision of the charter above referred to, is still in force. That provision enacts that

* Re-enacted in the New York City Consolidation act of 1882. (*Laws of* 1882, chap. 410, § 1104.)

"no action shall be maintained against the mayor, aldermen and commonalty of the city of New York, unless the claim on which the action is brought has been presented to the comptroller, and he has neglected for thirty days after such presentment to pay the same."

The claim in this case is alleged to have been presented to the comptroller on the 28th of April, 1881, and it is alleged that the comptroller neglected to pay the same for thirty days before the action was commenced. It has been held in various cases that where the action is brought under this provision of the charter, the statute of limitations does not begin to run until the thirty days, after such presentment, have expired. (Fisher v. Mayor, 67 *N. Y.* 86; Taylor v. Mayor, 67 *N. Y.* 87; Van Wart v. Mayor, 52 *How. Pr.* 78).

The fact, therefore that the demand was not presented until 1881, would be a complete answer to the alleged defense, were it not for the provisions of section 410 of the Code of Civil Procedure, which enacts that where a right exists, but a demand is necessary to entitle the person to maintain an action, the time within which the action must be commenced must be computed from the time when the right to make the demand is complete. We think this provision is [*] applicable to the case at bar. If it were not so, there would be no limitation in cases against the city, except at the option of the plaintiff, who could delay making his demand for an indefinite period of time, and so keep his cause of action alive until the death of witnesses or any other change of circumstances rendered a defense difficult or impossible. There are special reasons why demands of this character against the city should be required to be presented promptly and without unreasonable delay, because the city necessarily acts through official agents and servants, who are frequently changed.

We have no doubt that by section 410 the legislature intended to provide for such cases, and to prevent advantage from being taken of public authorities by
[*] long delays in making demands, which might otherwise ensue. The demand in this case, therefore, ought to have been made and the action brought within three years, in ordered to maintain the action. The answer set up a good defence, and the demurrer should have been overruled. The judgment must be reversed, and judgment ordered on the demurrer with leave to amend upon the usual terms.

DANIELS and BRADY, JJ., concurred.

HUTCHINSON, RESPONDENT, v. LAWRENCE, PRESIDENT OF THE NEW YORK STOCK EXCHANGE, APPELLANT.

SUPREME COURT, FIRST DEPARMENT; GENERAL TERM, MARCH, 1883.

§ 870, *et seq.*

Examination of party before trial.—When should be ordered to enable plaintiff to frame complaint.—Not refused because liable to abuse.—Judge before whom it is taken should limit.

Where, in an action against the president of the New York Stock Exchange, an unincorporated association, to have the expulsion of the plaintiff from membership therein declared illegal and void, and restrain it from depriving him of his seat therein, or from the other rights and privileges appertaining to membership in the exchange, an order for the examination of the defendant before trial to enable plaintiff to frame his complaint, was granted, upon affidavits showing that charges had been made against the plaintiff which he had personally appeared to answer; that plaintiff had not been able to ascertain what afterwards transpired which produced his dismissal, but that, as to the fact that other proceedings were had, he had received credible information, and formed a belief; but this information was not so definite as to enable him to set forth in his complaint a history or averment of what had really taken place; that he believed that evidence had been taken in his absence, upon which a vote had been taken, but as to what the evidence was, or the number of votes given for his removal, he had no information. *Held*, that the plaintiff has a right to call upon the defendant to supply this essential information,[1] and the order for his examination before trial was, under the circumstances, a proper one.[2, 3]

The possibility that, upon the examination of a defendant before trial, to enable plaintiff to frame his complaint, an effort will be made to extend it beyond what may appear to be necessary to obtain a knowledge of the facts required to be known to present the plaintiff's case, will not justify a denial of the remedy.[3] The officer before whom the examination will be taken is vested with abundant authority to properly limit it.[3] No direction on that subject can be required on appeal from an order granting such examination.[4] (*Decided March* 9, 1883.)

Appeal from order of special term denying motion to vacate order for examination of defendant before trial to enable plaintiff to frame his complaint.

This is an action, commenced July 14, 1882, under section 1919 of the Code, against the defendant as president of the New York Stock Exchange, an unincorporated association, to obtain judgment of the court that the expulsion of the plaintiff from membership in the said Exchange is illegal and void, and to restrain it from enforcing the same or from depriving the plaintiff of his seat, which is said to have been worth not less than $30,000, and from interfering with his right to transact business in the Exchange.

An order for the examination of the defendant before trial to enable the plaintiff to frame his complaint was granted December 2, 1882, upon the summons and an affidavit of the plaintiff. From this affidavit it appears that the proceeding, which resulted in the plaintiff's expulsion from the Stock Exchange were taken under a provision of its constitution that the governing committee of the Exchange, by a vote of two-thirds of its members present may expel any member of the Exchange upon conviction of obvious fraud. The plaintiff avers in his affidavit that he was served with a notice, accompanied by certain charges stated in the notice to have been preferred against him by the governing committee; that he appeared in answer to the notice at the time designated, and put in his answer to the charges, denying all the accusations therein contained and claiming an opportunity to disprove the same, whereupon he was dismissed from the presence of the committee, who, on the following day, passed the resolution of expulsion without further communication with the plaintiff or any opportunity for him to establish his defense; that this is all the knowledge the plaintiff has in respect to the proceedings, but that he has heard and believes, that after he was dismissed from the committee, and before the resolution of expulsion, witnesses were examined and statements made, without notice to him or an opportunity to refute and answer them, and that he has no knowledge as to what was so communicated. That he has heard and believes that various motions were made and various votes taken during his absence, but he is ignorant of the nature and effect thereof and how the votes were cast on the same. That the defendant, Lawrence, was present during the whole trial, and that all these matters are peculiarly within his knowledge, and that plaintiff has not sufficient knowledge or information in respect to any of these matters, except as to his own appearance and answer and statement before the committee. That he is advised by counsel and believes that to frame his complaint it is necessary and material to take the deposition of the defendant upon the occurrences of the trial and as to the records of the committee and upon the matters above set forth. That he is informed and believes that a majority of the committee voted to sustain some of the charges and not to sustain others, and that it is material and necessary to frame his complaint, that he should ascertain by the examination of defendant, which of the charges were sustained and which were not sustained. That, as he is informed and believes, some of the governing committee, who voted in favor of the resolution of expulsion, accepted the charges as proof of the accusations. That some of the members of the committee, before the trial, in his absence and without notice to him, had prejudged the case, and upon the final vote decided the case without reference to the testimony taken before them. That, as he is informed and believes, after the governing committee had, in his absence and without notice to him, received the evidence of hostile witnesses, a motion was made by one of the committee to recall plaintiff and give him an opportunity to answer the same, but that the motion was overruled. That plaintiff is advised that he has a good cause of action for damages against the members of the committee who voted to expel him. That the deposition and testimony of the defendant are material and necessary for the prosecution of the action and to enable plaintiff to frame his complaint. That he does not know the names of certain necessary parties defendant, and that the deposition of defendant is necessary and material to enable him to ascertain these names. That his counsel advise him he has a good cause of action against the Exchange and the persons aforesaid, and that the testimony of defendant is necessary and material, and that the application is made in good faith.

On December 20, 1882, an order to show cause was obtained why the order of December 2 should not be vacated for the insufficiency of the affidavit.

This order was obtained upon the affidavit of defendant, setting out that the Exchange is an unincorporated association of over one thousand members, governed by a constitution and by laws, signed by the members, and that plaintiff had been an active member for several years. That the whole government of the Exchange is vested in a governing committee, of which defendant was president at the times mentioned in plaintiff's affidavit. That by the constitution if any member is guilty of obvious fraud, of which the committee is the judge, he shall, on conviction by a vote of two-thirds of the members present, be declared expelled and his membership shall escheat to the Exchange. That the committee has power to try all offenses against the laws of the Exchange and all charges against members, and their decision is final. That by the constitution any member who applies for a legal instrument restraining any officer or committee of the Exchange from performance of his acts and duties, thereby ceases to be a member of the association. That plaintiff, prior to May 17, 1882, demanded an investigation of current rumors of dishonest practices, as a member of the Exchange; that a committee was appointed by the governing committee, before whom plaintiff appeared, by whom an investigation was had; that the substance of the matters so investigated was reduced to charges, being those mentioned by plaintiff in his affidavit. That plaintiff appeared in response to the notice of the governing committee, made answers and explanations, and the committee deliberated and voted thereon. That the Exchange is an association for dealing in stocks, and the members dealing in their own name represent largely persons who are not members. It is considered the duty of members to give evidence before the governing committee bearing upon charges against members, and it is the understanding that such testimony is privileged and confidential. That defendant has no personal knowledge of the transactions alleged in plaintiff's affidavit except as presiding officer of the committee, and he claims that he is not bound to disclose any of the acts of the committee after plaintiff made his answers and explanations in answer to the charges.

This motion was heard at special term and denied, and from the order thereupon entered the defendant took this appeal.

Stephen P. Nash, *James C. Carter* and *Julien T. Davies* (*Davies, Work, McNamee & Hilton*, attorneys), for appellant.

Cited, in support of contention that the order for defendant's examination should be vacated: Greer *v.* Allen, 15 *Hun*, 435; Chapin *v.* Thompson, 16 *Hun*, 56; Winston *v.* English, 44 *How. Pr.* 390; Levy *v.* Loeb, 5 *Abb. N. C.* 157 (aff'd, 75 *N. Y.* 609); Corbett *v.* De Comeau, 5 *Abb. N. C.* 169; Beach *v.* The Mayor, 14 *Hun*, 79; Williams *v.* Telegraph Co., 40 *Super. Ct.* 580.

Joseph H. Choate and *Robert Sewell* (*Evarts, Southmayd & Choate*, attorneys), for respondent.

Cited: Heishon *v.* Knickerbocker Life Insurance Co., 77 *N. Y.* 278; Glenny *v.* Stedwell, 64 *N. Y.* 120.

DANIELS, J.—The examination provided for by the order was to afford the plaintiff an opportunity to discover facts claimed by him to be necessary to enable him to frame his complaint in the action; and that such an examination may be had under section 872 of the Code of Civil Procedure, is, in effect, settled by the case of Glenny *v.* Stedwell (64 *N. Y.* 120). That case was decided under similar provisions contained in the Code of Procedure. So far as this right was involved, those provisions have not been materially changed by the enactments in the present Code. The provisions certainly are as broad now as they were when that case was determined by the court, and it must be regarded as settling the right of the plaintiff to such an examination, where its necessity shall be reasonably evidenced by the affidavit made to obtain the order.

It appears by the affidavit made use of in this instance, that the plaintiff had been expelled from the Stock Exchange as a member of that body. His seat is averred to have been of the value of $30,000, and the proceedings resulting in his expulsion are alleged to have been unlawful, and for that reason inoperative. Precisely what those proceedings were, he states himself unable to set forth. The charges made against him were served upon him, and he personally appeared to answer them. But what afterwards transpired which produced his dismissal, he has not been able to ascertain. It is true that as to the fact that other proceedings were had, he has received credible information and formed a belief, but this information was not so definite as to enable him to set forth in his complaint a history or averment of what really had taken place. Evidence is believed to have been received in his absence and a vote to have been taken upon it; but what that evidence was or the number of votes given for his removal do not appear to have been embodied in the information received by him, and for that reason he is not able to show by his complaint, without further information upon this subject, what was done or precisely in what the illegality of his removal may be alleged to consist, and it is practically to remove this inability to state his case, as he considers it important for him to do in his complaint, that the order for the examination of the defendant has been obtained. He was apparently a party to the proceedings and is able to furnish the information required to make reasonably definite [1] allegations upon these subjects. And under the doctrine of the case to which reference has been made, and these provisions of the Code, he has the right to call upon the defendant to supply this essential in-

formation. Without it he would practically be groping in the dark, and might discover when the case came to be tried that very material variations would be found between his allegations and the proofs which would then be developed. To avoid this possibility and to prevent himself from being surprised at the trial, the precaution of taking the defendant's examination has been adopted, and no good reason is disclosed for dispensing with such an examination. The certainty in the allegations which would be required to be made for the purpose of sustaining the action, if that can be done at all, can under the circumstances be attained in no
[*] other manner. And as the law has provided the plaintiff with this mode of ascertaining the facts, the defendant should submit to the examination already ordered.

It may be that effort will be made to extend it beyond what may appear to be necessary to obtain a knowledge of the facts required to be known to
[*] present the plaintiff's case. But that possibility will not justify a denial of the remedy. The officer before whom the examination will take place is vested with abundant authority to properly limit it and prevent in that manner the authority of the law from being made the subject of abuse. If the defendant should be interrogated concerning matters not strictly relevant to what the complaint may be expected or ought to contain in such an action, ample power exists to prevent such interrogatories from being answered. In important respects the plaintiff is manifestly dependent upon the disclosures of the defendant for the information required to frame a proper complaint. And to that extent he has the right to obtain them under the authority of such an order. Beyond that he has no right to go, and the justice before whom the examination will be had, will surely restrict the proceeding within such limits. No direction upon that sub-

ject can be required in the present disposition of the case.

The order, under the circumstances, was a proper one and it should be affrmed, with the usual costs and disbursements.

DAVIS, P. J., concurred.

HIRSCH v. HUTCHISON, IMPLEADED WITH ROANY.

N. Y. MARINE COURT; SPECIAL TERM, JANUARY, 1883.

§§ 635, 636, 683.

Attachment.—Granted in action against firm where one partner has fraudulently transferred his interest therein to another.—Action for goods sold and delivered, is for breach of contract within the meaning of section 635 of the Code.—Using new papers on motion to vacate attachment.

Where partners were jointly and individually insolvent, and one of them made a fraudulent transfer of his interest in the firm to his copartner,—*Held*, that such transfer justified the issuing of an attachment, in an action against the firm for goods sold and delivered to it. [1]

An action to recover a balance due for goods sold and delivered, is an action to recover damages for a breach of contract, within the meaning of section 635 of the Code. [2]

Section 683 of the Code of Civil Procedure is merely declaratory of the existing rule of practice, in regard to the use of new papers on motion to vacate attachment, and where defendant moves on the attachment, and the papers on which it was granted, to vacate it, an additional affidavit, offered by the plaintiff on the argument, will not be considered. [3]

Ives v. Holden, (14 *Hun*, 402), construed.

(*Decided January*, 1883.)

Motion to vacate an attachment, made by defendant upon the attachment and the papers on which it was granted.

The opinion states the facts.

Henry Arden, for motion.

Frankenheim & Rosenblatt, opposed.

McADAM, J.—The plaintiff's affidavit, after stating the amount of his demand over and above all counterclaims, proves that the defendants, who were partners, on the 25th day of September, 1882, were both jointly and individually insolvent, and that, being so insolvent and indebted to the plaintiff and others, on joint demands, the defendant Roany made a fraudulent transfer of his interest in the firm to his copartner and co-defendant, Hutchison. The defendant Hutchison moves on the original papers to vacate the attachment, and thereby admits for the purposes of this motion that the charges made are true. The sole question, therefore is whether the sale conceded to be fraudulent justifies the attachment.

[1] On first impression it would seem that a transfer from the one joint debtor to the other could not prejudice the plaintiff in collecting his debt; but this impression is removed by considering the legal effect of such a transfer, which makes the one partner the sole owner of the firm's property, and gives his individual creditors a preference over the joint creditors of the firm in the marshalling of the assets. (*Story Eq. Jur.* §§ 646–675; 2 *Spence Eq. Jur.* 213; and see 4 *Barb.* 571;* 41 *Id.* 307;† 52 *N. Y.* 146.‡)

The defendant also claims that, as the action is

* Burtus v. Tisdall. † Ransom v. Van Deventer.
‡ Menagh v. Whitwell.

[2] brought to recover a balance due "for goods sold and delivered," it is not such an action as is contemplated by section 635 of the Code, which permits an attachment "where the action is to recover a sum of money only, as damages for . . . breach of contract."

But this position is untenable. The action is for goods sold and delivered. It is founded on contract. The agreed price or the reasonable value being the measure of damages, and the breach consists in the defendants' failure to perform their part of it, to wit, by paying the price or value. The words employed in the present Code are even more comprehensive than those employed by section 227 of the old Code. When the codifiers superseded this section (227) by the new section (635) they did not intend to limit or restrict, but rather to enlarge, the right of attachment, so as to have it comprehend not only attachments in actions "arising on contract for the recovery of money only," but every action "for the recovery of damages for the breach of [any] contract." This is the more reasonable construction of the legislative intent.

The additional affidavit offered by the plain-
[3] tiff on the argument has not been considered, because I regard section 683 of the Code of Civil Procedure as merely declaratory of the (then) existing rule of practice in regard to new papers, as reaffirmed by the court of appeals in Yates *v.* North (44 *N. Y.* 271), and hold that the case of Ives *v.* Holden (14 *Hun*, 402) must be limited in its application to the practice as declared in Yates *v.* North (*supra*).

Motion to vacate attachment denied, with $10 **costs, and with leave to renew on affidavits.**

CLAFLIN et al. v. FRENKEL, Impleaded, &c.

SUPREME COURT, FIRST DEPARTMENT; GENERAL TERM, JANUARY, 1883.

§ 550, subd. 2.

Order of arrest.—May be granted where defendant has disposed of his property in another State, with intent to defraud his creditors—One who receives the benefit of an order by complying with a condition, cannot appeal from that part of the order imposing the condition.

Where an order of arrest was vacated, on condition that defendant stipulate not to sue, and the defendant so stipulated and was discharged from arrest, he cannot subsequently appeal from that portion of the order imposing the condition. [1]

Where goods were sold and delivered in this State to parties who did business in the State of Alabama, and they subsequently disposed of their property in that State with intent to defraud their creditors, —*Held*, that an order for the arrest of the defendants was properly granted in an action in this State, for the value of the goods so sold and delivered. [2, 3, 5]

Blason v. Bruno (33 *Barb.* 520), distinguished; [3] Brown v. Ashbrough (40 *How Pr.* 226), approved. [4]

(*Decided February* 2, 1883).

Appeal by plaintiff from an order vacating an order of arrest; and by defendant from that part of the order requiring him to stipulate not to sue.

Action for goods sold and delivered by plaintiffs to defendants in the State of New York. An order of arrest was issued in the action, on the ground, that the defendants who were copartners had disposed of their property with the intent to defraud their creditors. The affidavits upon which the order was granted allege that the defendants are non-residents of the State, doing business at Mobile, Alabama, and that the fraudulent disposition of their property was made at that place.

The defendant moved to vacate the order of arrest, which was granted on his stipulating not to sue. The appeals above described were thereupon taken.

Melville H. Regensburger, for the plaintiffs.

Rudolph Sampter, for defendant.

Our statutes giving a remedy extrinsic of the cause of action, to arrest a defendant upon the ground of a fraudulent disposition of property, contemplate that such disposition shall be of property within the limits of the state. Blason *v.* Bruno, 33 *Barb.* 520 ; Brown *v.* Ashbrough, 40 *How. Pr.* 226; Johnson *v.* Whitman, 10 *Abb. Pr. N. S.* 113; City Bank *v.* Lumley, 28 *How. Pr.* 401 ; Moller *v.* Aznar, 11 *Abb. Pr. N. S.* 233.

DANIELS, J.—The defendants appeal from that portion of the order which required Frenkel who was under arrest, to stipulate not to bring an action for damages because of his arrest as a defendant, after his discharge. He did so stipulate, and secured his [1] discharge by complying with that portion of the order, and after having done that, it was too late for him to complain that this condition had been imposed upon him. He received the benefit which a compliance with the condition proposed to him, and could not subsequently appeal from this portion of the order. For that reason his appeal should be dismissed. The plaintiffs appeal from the portion of the order directing the defendant Frenkel to be discharged from imprisonment under the order made for his arrest, and this appeal presents the more important point to be determined for the disposition of the case. It appeared by one of the affidavits made on behalf of the plaintiffs that they were engaged in business in the city of New York, and sold and delivered to the defendants goods and merchandise, at prices agreed upon, amounting to the sum of $3,755.90, no part of which has been paid.

This affidavit was carelessly drawn, but still it is to be inferred from it, as the plaintiffs were engaged in carrying on their business in the city of New York, that the sales were made at that place, and defendants' liability was incurred for the payment of the price of the goods, under and in conformity with the laws of this state, and for that reason, when he was found here, there would seem to be no impropriety in subjecting him to all the legal remedies which the law secured to the plaintiffs for the purpose of enabling them to obtain payment of their debt.

The order of arrest was made for the reason that the defendants, after contracting this debt, had disposed of their property, with intent to defraud their creditors. This was done in the city of Mobile, in the State of Alabama, where the defendants carried on their business. And that they did so dispose of their property is a fact left free from dispute in the case. Because this disposition was made by them of their property in another state, it has been urged that it formed no ground of arrest in an action prosecuted in this state, and that their arrest was unauthorized if the defendants did not subject themselves to that remedy, by the fact of the goods being purchased and delivered, to them in this state. But, as the Code has provided the remedy of arrest, it has not made it dependent upon any such distinction. It has, on the other hand, declared in general terms that the defendant may be arrested in an action upon contract, express or implied, other than a promise to marry, where since the making of the contract he had removed or disposed of his [1] property with intent to defraud his creditors (*Code of Civ. Pro.* § 550, subd. 2). This remedy has been provided for in terms so broad as to be subject to no exception. In English, certainly, it includes all actions on contract against a defendant who has removed or disposed of his property, intending thereby to defraud his creditors. The Code itself has not declared this to be a violation of the obligation of the debtor to his creditors, but it arises out of the general principles of law adopted to secure the substantial morality and good faith of persons engaged in trade.

At the common law, and wherever its principles may be observed, the debtor is restrained from making any disposition of his property, intending thereby to defraud his creditors. This obligation is recognized and in some form enforced, wherever the common law prevails, and as that law is presumed to exist in the State of Alabama, it was obligatory upon these debtors carrying on their business there. It fact they were prohibited by its wholesome restraint from making any disposition of their property with the intention thereby of preventing their creditors from collecting their debts. By making such a disposition these defendants violated this restraint of the law and the obligations resting upon them in favor of the plaintiffs as their creditors. And for that violation they became subject to arrest under this provision of the Code whenever either of them placed himself within the reach of the process of this court.

[2] The case of Blason v. Bruno (33 *Barb.* 520) has been cited, and is relied upon as requiring a different construction to be placed upon this provision of the Code. That was an action between parties who were residents of Cuba, where the entire transaction took place, and the court at special term discharged the order which had been made for the arrest of the delinquent party. The case very materially differs in the leading circumstances from that which has now been presented. For in addition to those already mentioned, it was merely made to appear that the defendant had converted his property into money. But it was not shown that he had in any manner disposed of the money. The order for that reason was probably

right, while the principal cause assigned for making it was not in harmony with this general provision of the Code.

A point similar to the one now presented arose in Brown v. Ashbrough (40 *How. Pr.* 226). That was presented under a provision of the same note as [*] that now contained in subd. 4, section 549 of the Code of Civil Procedure. The action was upon a contract where the defendant had been guilty of a fraud in creating or incurring his liability. The parties resided in Hamilton, Canada, where the sale of the property had been fraudulently induced, and for that reason it was claimed that the defendant was not liable to arrest in an action for the recovery of the debt brought in this court. But on a very full consideration of the case by MARVIN, J., a different conclusion was reached and sustained, and it was held that the defendant was liable to arrest under the same provision as was contained in the Code of Civil Procedure, when he was found and proceeded against in this State. The right to arrest him was held to be merely an attribute of the remedy which the laws of this State had provided for the fraudulent contract.

That conclusion was well sustained by the construction given to it by the learned justice (Brown v. Ashbrough, *supra*, 241–243). And the reasons which supported the arrest in that instance would seem to be equally as applicable to a case of the nature of that now before the court. No substantial distinction can be drawn between the right of the creditor to arrest the debtor in a case where the debt itself has been fraudulently contracted, and the present case, where, actuated by a like intent to defraud, the debtor has removed or disposed of his property. In each case the fundamental objection requiring the observing of good faith in the conduct of the debtor is equally vile, and in one no more than it is in the other.

The construction which was acted upon in the case just referred to was substantially the same as that which was adopted in City Bank *v.* Lumley (28 *How. Pr.* 397), and in Johnson *v.* Whitman (10 *Abb. N. S.* 111).

And nothing different was suggested in Moller *v.* Aznar (11 *Abb. Pr. N. S.* 233), which was not consistent with the same view. And that this should be held to be the effect of both these provisions of the law results from the circumstance that the right to arrest the debtor when the facts essential to it are made to appear satisfactorily in the case is a part of the remedy secured to the creditor to enable him to coerce his debtor into the payment of his debt. It has been added to the ordinary course of precedure because of the debtor's positive misconduct in either fraudulently contracting the debt or after it has been contracted placing his property with a fraudulent intent beyond the reach of his creditor. The wrong to the creditor is precisely the same, whether the act may be committed in this or another State. And the enactment of a statute on the subject is not necessary for the admonition or in- [*] formation of the debtor that in his dishonest conduct he has violated his obligation to his creditor. Consciousness of his misconduct will result from his knowledge of the common principles of trading morality. When a debtor secures the property of another by making use of false representations, or deprives the creditor of the means of collecting his debt by making a fraudulent disposition of his property, he requires no statutory provision to impress him with the conviction that his act is wrong, and should be made the subject of punishment. Whenever, therefore, the creditor may be able to present his case in such a form as to bring it within the terms of the remedial provisions of the law, he should be held entitled to the complete remedy which has been provided for the collection of his demand.

This point was very fully considered in Whittemore v. Adams (2 *Cow.* 626). There by a cession of the debtor's property under an act of Congress, in force only in the District of Columbia, his person became exonerated from imprisonment. But, notwithstanding that circumstance, he was still held liable to arrest under the laws of this State in an action prosecuted here for the recovery of the debt. This conclusion was held to be warranted by the circumstance that the arrest was a portion of the remedy which the laws had here provided for the enforcement of the contract (*Id.* 632), and a similar view received the approbation of the court in Hinkley v. Marean (3 *Mass.* 88); Titus v. Hobart (5 *Id.* 378).

Upon the fact of copious citations of English and American authorities this has been declared to be the settled law in section 571 of *Story's Conflict of Laws* (6th ed.). The principle is there broadly stated and maintained that a debtor will be liable to arrest on a demand arising against him in an another country, when the proceeding taken for its collection includes that as a part of the remedy.

This general subject was considered in Don v. Lippman (5 *Clark & Fin.* 1), where it was held that the party entitled to a legal remedy had the right to enforce it, as it was provided in the country where the proceeding should be taken.

Under the principles sustained by these authorities, as well as the very general language employed in the enactment of this subdivision of the Code, the plaintiffs had the right to arrest their creditors and hold them to bail, when they had placed themselves within the reach of the process of this court.

The case that was made out was all that could be required for this purpose. The order of arrest was a lawful proceeding in the action, and the order by which it [*] was set aside should be reversed and an order entered denying the defendants' motion and directing his recommitment to the custody of the sheriff, and for the usual costs and disbursements.

DAVIS, P. J., and MACOMBER, J., concurred.

HAUSELT, APPELLANT, v. GODFREY, RESPONDENT, AND EIGHT OTHER CASES.

N. Y. COURT OF COMMON PLEAS; GENERAL TERM, NOVEMBER, 1882.

§ 3238.

Costs—where it is stipulated that the decision of an appeal in an action, shall determine similar appeals in other actions, the successful party is entitled to costs of each appeal.

Where a stipulation was entered into by the parties to appeals in nine actions that the return in one case should be considered the return in all the other cases, and that the decision in one case should stand as the decision in all the others,—*Held*, that the successful party was entitled to tax costs for argument in each of the cases, although there was but one argument.

(*Decided December* 2, 1882.)

Appeal by plaintiff from order allowing the taxation of a bill of costs in each of the nine cases in favor of defendant.

The defendant was originally arrested in each of the nine actions. He moved to vacate each order of arrest, and his motions were denied. He appealed from the orders denying his motions, and they were affirmed. He appealed to the court of appeals, and the orders of the general and special term were reversed and the motion to vacate the order of arrest was granted, with costs. When the motions were originally made at special term, it was stipulated between the parties that but one set of papers be handed up in all the cases. On appeal to the general term, but one set of papers were printed for all the cases. The plaintiffs nevertheless entered orders for costs in each case, both at special and general term. On defendant's appeal to the court of appeals, it was stipulated that the return in one of the cases be considered as the return in all the other cases, and that the decision and judgment of the court of appeals in either of said cases on appeal should stand as the decision and judgment of said court on the appeals in all the other cases.

The defendant, having prevailed on those appeals, taxed full costs of the court of appeals in each of the nine cases. This court at special term on appeal by plaintiff from the taxation, allowed defendant to tax costs for argument in the court of appeals, viz.: $60 in each of the nine cases, and plaintiff now appeals from that decision.

William B. Tullis, for appellant.

Samuel C. Mount, for respondent.

J. F. DALY, J.—I think the defendant was entitled to tax his costs in each of the nine cases, for these reasons: 1st. The stipulation between the attorneys provided that the decision and judgment of the court of appeals in one of the cases, should stand as the decision and judgment of said court in all the cases.

The decision of the court of appeals in the case of Hauselt *v.* Godfrey, was that the orders appealed from be reversed and the motion to vacate order of arrest be granted, with costs. The decision awarding costs in that cause became, under the stipulation, the decision in each of the other cases, and therefore, upon the record in each case that plaintiffs had stipulated for, defendants were entitled to costs.

The original motions and the appeals to the general term had been submitted to the court on one set of papers only, yet the plaintiff, when he succeeded, took orders granting costs in all the cases. This is very satisfactory evidence of the intention (if an inquiry into the intention of the parties be deemed important) that in making the stipulation, costs were to be taxed in all the cases if allowed by the court in the case actually argued.

The practice is to allow costs in each case under such stipulation (Minturn v. Main, 2 *Sand.* 737. See also 5 *N. J. Law Jl.* 226, cases of Green v. French, U. S. C. C. N. J., and Jerman v. Stewart, U. S. C. C. Tennessee).

The order should be affirmed, with $10 costs and disbursements.

HOYT AND ANO., RESPONDENTS, v. GODFREY, APPELLANT.

N. Y. COURT OF COMMON PLEAS; GENERAL TERM, NOVEMBER, 1882.

§ 779.

Set-off.—When interlocutory costs set off against judgment.

The court has power to set off interlocutory costs against the judgment finally rendered in an action, although the party to whom such costs were awarded agreed that his attorney should have such costs

as might be awarded him. The fact that the order granting the costs was made after the judgment was entered, does not affect the question.

(*Decided December* 4, 1882.)

Appeal from order directing that certain interlocutory costs be set off against a judgment.

Judgment was entered in favor of the plaintiffs January 17, 1881. On August 25, 1882, an order of arrest granted in the action was vacated and costs of motion awarded the defendant. The plaintiff moved to have the costs set off against the judgment. The attorney for the defendant opposed the motion, claiming that the defendant had agreed, at the beginning of the action, that he should have the costs recovered in the action, and that by reason thereof, and of an assignment of the costs to him, they belonged to him personally. It appeared that an execution upon the judgment was duly issued and returned unsatisfied, and that defendant had been insolvent for more than three years. The motion was granted, and the defendant thereupon took this appeal therefrom.

Samuel C. Mount, for appellant.

William B. Tullis, for respondent.

The right of a judgment creditor to have set off against his judgment interlocutory costs or costs of a non suit awarded to his adversary is recognized at common law. Howell *v.* Harding, 8 *East*, 362; Lang *v.* Webber, 1 *Price*, 375; Figes *v.* Adams, 4 *Taunt.* 632; Spence *v.* White, 1 *Johns. Cas.* 102; Willet *v.* Starr, 8 *Johns.* 123; Porter *v.* Lane, *Id.* 357; Hurd *v.* Fogg, 2 *Fost.* (*N. H.*) 98.

The right of a court of law to set off a judgment for the costs of an action against a judgment upon the main issue in the same action, even where the latter judgment was assigned to the attorney for his compensation may be exercised upon a motion. Crocker *v.* Claughley, 2 *Duer*, 684; Saunders *v.* Gillett, 8 *Daly*, 183; Garner *v.* Gladwin, 30 *N. Y.* 343; Porter *v.* Lane, *supra;* Purchase *v.* Bellows, 16 *Abb. Pr.*, 105; Gay *v.* Gay, 10 *Paige*, 369.

In the following cases the right of set-off was held to override the lien of an attorney: De Figaniere *v.* Young, 2 *Robt.* 670; Martin *v.* Kanouse, 17 *How.* 146; S. C., 9 *Abb.* 370, note; Hayden *v.* McDermott, *Id.* 14; Nicoll *v.* Nicoll, 16 *Wend.* 446; Ross *v.* Dole, 13 *Johns.* 306.

VAN HOESEN, J.—If this were an application to set off the judgment in one action against the judgment in another, we should feel obliged to apply the law as laid down in Ely *v.* Cook, 28 *N. Y.* 372; Perry *v.* Chester, 53 *N. Y.* 240, and Zogbaum *v.* Parker, 66 *Barb.* 341, and hold that where an attorney had purchased one of the judgments, and paid for it in services rendered in good faith, he should be treated like any other *bona fide* purchaser for value, and that he should not be deprived of his judgment because his assignor was indebted upon the other judgment to the person who applied for the offset.

This, however, is not such a case. The judgment here, is in favor of the plaintiff, but certain costs were allowed to the defendant upon a motion made in the action. These costs are claimed by the defendant's attorney, and it is insisted by him, that the court can not deduct them from the judgment, because the defendant promised him, at the beginning of the action, that he should have whatever costs were recovered against the plaintiff. Interlocutory costs have frequently been offset (*Graham's Practice*,. 349). It is eminently proper that the power to order an offset, should be lodged with the court, otherwise a defendant, who may not care if his proceedings are stayed, may collect costs of the plaintiff without being compellable to pay such costs as may be awarded against himself. On the other hand, it may happen that a defendant, unjustly sued, succeeds in the action, though interlocutory costs may have been awarded to the plaintiff, and the only chance he may have of getting any part of the final costs adjudged against the plaintiff, is by having the interlocutory costs deducted. Ought the law to be so construed as to allow the plaintiff's attorney to collect those costs from the defendant, though the defendant can not recover a dollar from the plaintiff?

If the defendant's theory be correct, a party can, by promising the costs to his attorney, deprive the court of the power of ordering the costs to be deducted. The understanding between the defendant and his attorney must have been—I say must have been, for what the agreement was there is nothing to show, inasmuch as Mr. Mount's affidavit contains his conclusions without the statement of a single fact—The understanding must have been, that the attorney should have such costs as, at the termination of the litigation, might be coming to the defendant. If interlocutory costs had been paid, they could not be recovered. If they were, at the close of the litigation, payable, they were subject to the right of the court to order an offset in a proper case. If the court thought proper to deduct the interlocutory costs, awarded to the defendant from the amount that the plaintiff was entitled to recover, the defendant's attorney ought to have foreseen that such a contingency might arise. In this case, owing to the delays incident to legal proceedings, judgment was entered in favor of the plaintiff before the defendant succeeded in getting a vacatur of the order of arrest, and the other order giving the defendant interlocutory costs was made after the entry of judgment. This circumstance ought not to affect the question, which is simply this, may the court, where an insolvent client agrees that his attorney shall have such costs as may be awarded, order that interlocutory costs allowed to the client shall be deducted from the judgment rendered against him?

I think the order appealed from should be affirmed, with costs and disbursements.

ESTATE OF ROBERT BERNEY, DECEASED.

SURROGATE'S COURT, NEW YORK COUNTY; FEBRUARY, 1883.

§§ 2514, subd. 11, 2685.

Letters testamentary.—Debtor cannot apply for revocation thereof.

Where parties sued in the U. S. circuit court by an executrix, for the conversion of certain bonds alleged to have belonged to her decedent, sought to maintain that the letters testamentary issued to her were illegal and void, and it was held that her appointment as executrix could not be attacked in the U. S. court, and they thereupon petitioned the surrogate for the revocation of the letters testamentary,—*Held*, that they had no such relation to the estate as would empower them to maintain such a proceeding, and their petition must therefore be denied. [1,6]

The authority of the surrogate's court to revoke testamentary letters, is solely derived from section 2685 of the Code. [2] Leave to file a petition for the revocation of letters testamentary, is conferred upon "a creditor or person interested in the estate of the decedent," and upon nobody else. [3] A debtor is not "a person interested," as defined by subdivision 11 of section 2514 of the Code, [4] nor within the meaning of section 2685, [5,6] and a surrogate cannot revoke letters testamentary on his petition. [1,6]

(*Decided February* 20, 1883.)

Petition for the revocation of letters testamentary.

Tracy, Olmstead & Tracy, for petitioners.

Lord, Day & Lord, for executrix.

ROLLINS, S.—This is a petition for the revocation of letters testamentary issued out of this court to decedent's widow, Louisa Berney, on the 25th of May, 1881. The testator died at Paris, France, in the year 1874, leaving a will and codicil, wherein he appointed as his executors his brother James Berney and others, and, as his executrix, Louisa Berney, his wife.

In February, 1875, certain proceedings were had in a probate court in the State of Alabama, whereby the will and codicil were there admitted to probate. James Berney was subsequently granted ancillary letters testamentary by this court. In July, 1880, he died. In May, 1881, letters testamentary were issued by the surrogate of this county to Louisa Berney, under circumstances disclosed in the moving papers. On the 22d of June, 1875, Drexel, Morgan & Co., bankers, of this city, received from Cazade, Crooks & Reynaud, claiming to be the lawful attorneys of James Berney, executor, certain United States bonds, of the face value of $200,000, which were registered in the name of Robert Berney, the decedent. Louisa Berney, as executrix, lately commenced in the United States circuit court of this district, a suit against Drexel, Morgan & Co. and others, for the conversion of the bonds in question. The defendants in that action sought to maintain that the letters testamentary of Louisa Berney were illegal and void upon certain grounds which are among those alleged in the present proceeding as a cause for the revocation of such letters. It was, however, held that the validity of Mrs. Berney's appointment could not be attacked in the United States court, and it was intimated that, if the parties desired relief of that nature, they must seek it in this tribunal. The affidavits and papers which have been submitted upon the present motion are very voluminous, and raise many interesting and important issues as to the validity of the original probate in Alabama, the effect of certain proceedings in the English courts and in French tribunals, the validity of the letters issued to the executrix, &c.

In the view, however, which I am compelled to take of this case, it is necessary to pass upon only one of the questions submitted for my determination. The claim of the counsel for Mrs. Berney, that the petitioners have no such relation to this estate as empowers them to maintain a proceeding for the revocation of her letters, seems to me to be well founded. I feel compelled to hold that within the limitations of
the Code of Procedure, *debtors* of an estate (and it
[1] is only as *debtors* or as *possible debtors* that these
petitioners apply) have no right to make themselves parties to such a proceeding as the present.

The authority of the surrogate's court to revoke testamentary letters is solely derived from section 2685.
That section empowers such a court from which
[2] letters testamentary have been issued to revoke
the same for certain specified causes; and it also establishes the procedure by which in such cases the action of the court must be invoked. It requires that at the outset there shall be filed a petition praying for revocation and stating the grounds upon which it is sought. Leave to file such petition is conferred by the statute upon "*a creditor or person interested in the estate* of the decedent," and upon nobody else.

Now, who is "a person interested in the estate" within the meaning of section 2685.

Whatever might be deemed the fair interpreta-
[3] tion of this expression, if it stood alone, its associa-
tion with the term "creditor" seems to demand for it a narrower construction than that for which

these petitioners contend, and a construction which must exclude them in the present controversy from obtaining the relief which they ask; for, as has been already intimated, the status of the petitioners is in effect that of debtors, or possible debtors, to this estate. Now, nobody would contend that a debtor could with any greater propriety than a creditor be classed in the category of "persons interested." If that term, therefore, is broad enough of itself to include debtors, it is certainly broad enough to include creditors; and the fact that the latter class are expressly mentioned in the statute is a forcible argument in favor of the view that neither they nor debtors were designed to be embraced in the term "persons interested in the estate."

This view is confirmed by an examination of other parts of the Code.

Section 2514 is entitled "Definitions of expressions used in this chapter." "The expression person interested," says subdivision 11, "when it is used in [*] connection with an estate or fund, includes every person *entitled, either absolutely or contingently, to share in the estate* or the proceeds thereof, or in the fund, as husband, wife, legatee, next of kin, heir, devisee, assignee, grantee or otherwise, except as creditor."

It seems obvious that the phraseology of section 2685 was chosen with direct reference to this definition, and that it was deemed necessary, in order to extend to creditors the benefit of that section, to name them [*] expressly in the statute. But debtors are neither named expressly in section 2685 nor are they included within the category of "persons interested," as defined in section 2514.

The petitioners in the present case are not "entitled to share, either absolutely or contingently, in the estate" of this decedent.

An examination of other sections of the Code confirms the views which have been declared already.

For example:

(*a*) Section 2636 provides that after a will has been admitted to probate, the person named therein as executor . . . . is entitled to letters testamentary thereupon, unless before the letters are granted "a creditor of the decedent, or a person interested in the estate," makes objection in the manner specified in the section.

(*b*) In regard to intestate estates, the Code, after prescribing who shall be cited in a proceeding for the grant of letters of administration, provides (section 2665) that any "person interested," though not cited, may make himself a party.

(*c*) Section 2698 declares that upon a petition for ancillary letters, creditors resident within the State shall be cited, and that "any such person" (that is, any creditor) may appear and contest the application.

There is no statutory provision under which persons whose relation to a decedent's estate is like that of these petitioners can be recognized as entitled to be heard in opposition to the grant of either original or ancillary letters testamentary or letters of administration.

And no good reason can be urged why claims for the revocation of such letters should receive more favorable consideration than would have been accorded them if they had been interposed in opposition to the original issue of such letters.

The arguments by which petitioner's counsel seeks to maintain his contention would be almost equally effective to support a debtor's claim to become a party in a proceeding for probate of his creditor's will.

It is doubtful whether any persons by reason of their being indebted to a decedent's estate ever claimed the right to contest the will of such decedent. But claims of that sort have been made by creditors, and

so far as I have discovered, have been uniformly rejected by the courts (Menzies v. Pulbrook, 2 *Curteis*, 845; Taff v. Hosmer, 14 *Mich.* 249; Heilman v.
[*] Jones, 5 *Redf.* 400; Elme v. Da Costa, 1 *Phil.* 173. See Fosdick v. Delafield, 2 *Redf.* 404; Fisher v. Bassett, 9 *Leigh* [*Va.*] 133).

This petition must be denied.

SMITH, AS RECEIVER OF THE CO-OPERATIVE DRESS ASSOCIATION, LIMITED, v. DANZIG, ET AL.

COLE v. CO-OPERATIVE DRESS ASSOCIATION LIMITED.

EDDY v. THE SAME.

SUPREME COURT, SECOND DEPARTMENT; KINGS COUNTY SPECIAL TERM, JANUARY, 1883.

§§ 769, 984, 1788, 1789, 1806, 1810.

Corporation.—Directors of, where their motives and purposes are proper may resign, and their resignation takes effect without any act of the corporation.—Venue of action for sequestration of property of, where laid.—Motions for receiver, &c., where made in such action.—Rule 81 *of the general rules of practice invalid—Appointment of receiver.—Injunction in receiver's action to restrain actions.—When court will order sale of property of insolvent corporation.—Attaching creditor bound by injunction granted under section* 1806 *of the Code.*

Where a corporation had become insolvent, and numerous suits were pending against it to which there was no meritorious defense, and the company was under very heavy expenses for employes, and was doing a losing business, and this exigency was presented to the board of directors, that judgments would be recovered and the property would be sold under executions satisfying but a small portion of the liabilities of the company, and leaving all the other creditors without any remedy except, possibly, a suit against the stockholders for the satisfaction of their claims, and the directors for the purpose of securing an equal distribution of all the property of the corporation, resigned,—*Held*, that such directors could lawfully resign, and that their resignation became effective to vacate their respective offices without any affirmative act on the part of the corporation. [1]

An action by a judgment debtor for the sequestration of the property of a corporation, belongs to the class of actions specified in section 984 of the Code, and, subject to the power of the court to change the venue, "must be tried in the county in which one of the parties resided at the time of the commencement thereof." [2] If such an action is properly located in the county of Kings, a motion for a receiver or any other relief can not be made in the first judicial district. [3]

A rule of the court, to be valid, must be consistant with the Code. Rule 81,—which provides that all motions for the appointment of receivers of corporations "must be made in the judicial district in which the principal place of business of" the corporation is situated,—is not in harmony with the statutory right of a party to locate the venue of his action in the county where he resides, and is invalid. [4] Whenever a suitor, in pursuance of a statutory right, invokes the powers of the supreme court, it is bound to perform its duty, and if the appointment of a receiver be a part of its duty it is not the office of a mere rule to abridge its powers or work a denial of justice. [5]

A receiver of a corporation having its principal place of business in the city of New York, is regularly and validly appointed in Kings county, in an action properly brought therein. [6]

If the validity of the appointment of a receiver is to be questioned, it should be done in the action and district in which he was appointed. [7]

Where the receiver of a corporation, appointed in an action by a stockholder for a receiver thereof, on the ground that no officer remained qualified to take possession of the property of the corporation, and also in an action by a judgment creditor for sequestration of such property, was sued by certain judgment creditors, in behalf of themselves and others in like situation, who alleged that his appointment was collusive, irregular and void, and constituted an obstruction to their execution, and asked for the appointment of a receiver of the property of the corporation, and he, under instruction of the court, brought an action to restrain that suit,—*Held*, that an injunction granted in the receiver's action restraining the prosecution of the judgment creditor's action should be continued until final judgment in the action. [9]

A court of equity will protect the interests of the general creditors and stockholders of an insolvent corporation, if it can be done without injury to judgment creditors having liens on its property, by an immediate sale thereof, and where it appears that the quicker a sale of the property can be made the more it will bring, the property should be sold and the fund resulting from such sale substituted for the property itself. [8]

The supreme court has power to order a sale of the property of a corporation by a receiver thereof, appointed in an action by a stockholder for a receiver on the ground that no officer remained qualified to take possession of the property of the corporation, and again appointed in an action by a judgment creditor for the sequestration of such property. [10] Independent of any statute, a court of equity has inherent power to direct such a disposition of the fund as it shall deem wisest and best for the interests of all concerned. But under sections 1788 and 1789 of the Code the power is clear, for although it may be fairly argued that the statute does not in terms apply to the stockholder's action, it certainly does apply to the action for sequestration. [10]

In such a case, an attachment levied on a part of the property of the corporation prior to the appointment of the receiver in an action on a debt of the corporation which, it asserts, was not then due, does not present any serious difficulty. [11] The order may provide that the receiver procure sufficient advances on the goods which have not been attached to meet any exigency of the case, and out of those amounts he may make special deposits, or otherwise exercise the rights and privileges of the corporation as defendant in the attachment suit. [12]

An action by a stockholder of a corporation for a receiver thereof, and another by a judgment creditor for the sequestration of its property, is for the benefit of all concerned, and an attaching creditor, although not strictly a party on the record, is nevertheless and in fact a party, because he is a creditor so that he is enjoined by a general injunction granted under section 1806 of the Code. [11]

(*Decided January* 10, 1883.)

Motion by receiver of insolvent corporation to continue injunction restraining prosecution of suits against such corporation, granted in action for that relief, and for instructions and leave to sell the property of the corporation.

John L. Hill & L. W. Emerson, for receiver and motion.

John J. Adams, for defendant, Danzig, opposed.

John L. Hill (*Redfield & Hill*, attorneys), for plaintiff, Cole.

Charles E. Lydecker, for plaintiff, Eddy.

S. F. Prentiss (*C. C. & S. F. Prentiss*, attorneys), for Co-operative Dress Association, Limited.

Alexander Blumenstiel (*Blumenstiel & Hirsh*, attorneys), for attaching creditor, Schuloff.

Benjamin F. Tracy, *E. W. Bloomingdale*, *S. F. Kneeland*, *William Ives Washburn*, *Isaac L. Miller*, *Frederick G. Anderson* and *M. H. Ellis*, for creditors of the Co-operative Dress Association, Limited.

Rastus S. Ransom & Edward S. Clinch, for certain stockholders.

PRATT, J.—In order to arrive at a clear understanding of the matters involved in this motion, it is necessary to make a somewhat extended statement of the facts.

On the 26th of December, 1882, the plaintiff was appointed receiver of the Co-operative Dress Association, a domestic corporation of the limited liability class, under an act of 1875,* located in the city of New York, in an action brought by one Coles, a stockholder, on the ground that no officer remained empowered to hold

* Laws of 1875, chap. 611. "An act to provide for the organization and regulation of certain business corporations."

or preserve its property.* The plaintiff qualified and took possession of the property of the company, which consists of a large stock of dry goods, dresses, suits, &c., a very large proportion of which depends upon style and season for the realization of any fair approximation of their cost or value. The corporation is insolvent, and its property must in some way be taken by its creditors. Hence, it is obvious that the goods cannot be sold at retail, as the company intended when it purchased them, and they must therefore be sold to the best advantage consistent with the preservation of the rights of all concerned. On the twenty-third of December, one Schuloff obtained an attachment, in each of two actions, in this court, to secure an aggregate sum of about $5,000, and caused the same to be levied on the silks and velvets in said stock, which cost and were inventoried at some $21,000. A motion is now pending in the first district to vacate that attachment, the corporation denying any liability to Schuloff, except for immature indebtedness.

On the twenty-seventh of December the defendants, Nicholas, Myers, Danzig, Eddy and others, recovered judgments against the company for various sums, which were duly docketed in New York county, and upon which executions were duly issued to the sheriff. Eddy's execution was returned the twenty-eighth day of December, and he thereupon instituted a suit for the sequestration of the said property, pursuant to the statute.† On the thirtieth of December the plaintiff was appointed receiver in that action, and duly qualified. On that date the Danzigs, upon leave granted by this court in the first district, commenced an action as judgment creditors, in that district, in behalf of them-

* The Code, § 1810, subd. 3, provides for the appointment of a receiver in such cases.

† Code of Civil Procedure, § 1784.

selves and others in like situation, alleging that the plaintiff's appointment in the Cole action was collusive, irregular and void, constituted an obstruction to their execution, and asked for the appointment of a receiver of the property. They also obtained a temporary injunction restraining the plaintiff from any interference with the said property, except to preserve the same.

It is evident that this injunction was obtained under at least this misapprehension, viz.: that the plaintiff intended to make some disposition of the property beyond its mere preservation. It now appears, too plainly to admit of controversy, that no such thing had ever been attempted, and had not even been considered, except as a matter to be recommended to the court for its action. The said action in the first district, if meritorious at all, must therefore be justified on some other ground. On the third day of January the plaintiff presented the fact of the Danzig suit to this court in the Cole and Eddy actions, and was instructed to bring an action to enjoin the prosecution of the Danzig suit, and in pursuance of such instructions he has commenced an action, and the court has restrained Danzig and the other judgment creditors who may join therein, and the present application is to continue that injunction.

On the 3d of January, on the application in the respective suits of Cole and Eddy, a general injunction was granted against suits for the recovery of money and other actions. On the 6th of January the plaintiff applied to this court in the three actions named, the Cole, Eddy and receiver's action against the judgment creditors, for instructions, and upon notice to the Danzigs in these actions, asked for leave to sell the merchandise, &c., on the ground that the property is liable to rapid deterioration, and that its preservation involves great expense. It is apparent that the danger from this cause is very great, and that such selves and others in like situation, alleging that the plaintiff's appointment in the Cole action was collusive, irregular and void, constituted an obstruction to their execution, and asked for the appointment of a receiver of the property. They also obtained a temporary injunction restraining the plaintiff from any interference with the said property, except to preserve the same.

It is evident that this injunction was obtained under at least this misapprehension, viz.: that the plaintiff intended to make some disposition of the property beyond its mere preservation. It now appears, too plainly to admit of controversy, that no such thing had ever been attempted, and had not even been considered, except as a matter to be recommended to the court for its action. The said action in the first district, if meritorious at all, must therefore be justified on some other ground. On the third day of January the plaintiff presented the fact of the Danzig suit to this court in the Cole and Eddy actions, and was instructed to bring an action to enjoin the prosecution of the Danzig suit, and in pursuance of such instructions he has commenced an action, and the court has restrained Danzig and the other judgment creditors who may join therein, and the present application is to continue that injunction.

On the 3d of January, on the application in the respective suits of Cole and Eddy, a general injunction was granted against suits for the recovery of money and other actions. On the 6th of January the plaintiff applied to this court in the three actions named, the Cole, Eddy and receiver's action against the judgment creditors, for instructions, and upon notice to the Danzigs in these actions, asked for leave to sell the merchandise, &c., on the ground that the property is liable to rapid deterioration, and that its preservation involves great expense. It is apparent that the danger from this cause is very great, and that such individuals, insolvent corporations are forbidden by law to grant preferences to any creditors. They are forbidden from making assignments, partly for that reason, and in part because that involves the selection of their own trustee, and so working out indirectly that which they are forbidden to do directly (15 *Barb.* 62;* 33 *N. Y.* 95†).

But strangely enough, while this general policy is perfectly clear, the provisions of the new Code are somewhat obscure as to the means by which this general object is to be accomplished. For example, so long as corporate property remains in the hands of its officers it is liable to levies under attachment or execution. Thus creditors whose debts happen to be due may take all the property. Fortunate or favored parties, through the useless sacrifices and delays which usually and necessarily attend a sheriff's sale, may wholly defeat the general creditors and subject them to needless loss. Even in cases where the application is made by the directors for voluntary dissolution under section 2419, any creditor who recovers a judgment without the assent of the corporation (§ 2430) will take the property because this court has held that in such a proceeding a temporary receiver cannot be appointed (*Ex parte* French Manfg. Co., 12 *Hun*, 488; see case of Open Board of Brokers, per LAWRENCE, J., N. Y. sp. term, April‡); and that the only receivership authorized by law was by final judgment, which "must be not less than three months after the commencement of the proceeding" (§§ 2423, 2429). It is needless to add, that under the peculiar circumstances of this case, as disclosed by the papers in the Coles suit, there being nearly $40,000 of suits pending against

* Harris v. Thompson.

† Sibell v. Remsen.

‡ 3 *Law Bulletin*, 57.

the corporation, any such effort to obtain a receivership would have been useless. The corporation would have been stripped so that the receivership would have been a meaningless formality.

To have remained in office if they could have legally resigned in the face of such consequences, as were impending on the day the directors resigned, would have been a responsibility which they might justly seek to avoid.

It being clearly established that the motive and purpose of the resignations in question were proper, it seems to me that under the authorities the direc-
[1] tors could lawfully resign, and that such resignation became effective to vacate the respective offices without any affirmative act of the corporation (2 *Hun*, 613;* affirmed, 63 *N. Y.* 624; 14 *Hun*, 615;† 81 *N. Y.* 46‡ and 49‖).

The Eddy action stands upon quite a different basis. The latter is an action clearly within the provisions of the statute, and under which the fund may certainly be distributed among the creditors of the corporation, unless the appointment of the plaintiff in this suit is invalid by reason of rule eighty-one.

This rule, in my view, presents no difficulty or even embarrassment.

This action belongs to the class specified in section 984 of the Code, which, subject to the power of
[2] the court to change the venue, "must be tried in the county in which one of the parties resided at the time of the commencement thereof."

The plaintiffs, Cole and Eddy, resided in Brooklyn at the commencement of each of these actions, and therefore had a *statutory right* to bring the actions in Kings county.

It was a proper venue, and the court cannot, under

* Chandler *v.* Hoag. † Wade *v.* Baker.
‡ Duckworth *v.* Roach. ‖ Van Amburgh *v.* Baker.

the statute, compel any change of venue for any cause that now appears.

In such an action, thus properly located in [3] Kings county, a motion for a receiver or any other relief could not have been made in the first judicial district (*Code Civ. Pro.* § 769.)

A rule of court, in order to be valid, must be [4] consistent with the Code, and it seems to be clear that rule eighty-one is not in harmony with the statutory right of a party to locate the venue of his action in the county where he resides. A bare statement of the proposition is sufficient to show the invalidity of the rule (55 *N. Y.* 524 ;* 14 *Abb. Pr. N. S.* 124 ;† 64 *N. Y.* 120‡).

It should not be forgotten that this matter relates to mere venue; that the supreme court is an entire tribunal, and that whenever a suitor, in pursuance [5] of a statutory right, invokes its powers, it is bound to perform its duty, and if the appointment of a receiver happen to be a part of its duty, it is not the office of a mere rule to abridge its powers or work a denial of justice in the premises.

If these views are correct, it follows that the [6] plaintiff's appointment was regular and valid, and that he took such rights as the statute conferred upon him under such appointment. It seemed to me that the plaintiff took title to the property and that the corporation ceased to own it.

He was appointed to protect and preserve the property at the suit of a stockholder (subd. 3, § 1810 of Code), and he holds the title until a court of equity in that action shall determine the question touching the funds, and make a final order in the premises (Mickles *v.* Rochester City Bank, 11 *Paige*, 118).

* Rice *v.* Ehele.

† Winston *v.* English.

‡ Glenney *v.* Stedwell.

It is not necessary to discuss the question raised by the plaintiff's counsel, whether the allegations in the suit of Danzig *v.* Smith are sufficient to give a standing in a court of equity, the Cole action having been first commenced. A just and proper administration of affairs will not favor actions instituted in other districts wherever it may suit the caprice or interest of a disappointed creditor to test the validity of the appointment of the present receiver.

[']
If any complaint is to be made it should be in the action and district in which he was appointed (Rinn *v.* Astor Fire Ins. Co., 59 *N. Y.* 143; *In re* Atty.-Gen. *v.* Guardian Ins. Co., 77 *N. Y.* 272; and opinion of general term, fourth dep., in same case;* see, also Att.-Gen. *v.* North America Life Ins Co., per WESTBROOK, J., Ulster special term, 1878†).

But assuming that the contention of the defendant Danzig and the other judgment creditors is sound, and that he having issued an execution prior to plaintiff's appointment in the Eddy suit, he thereby has an absolute lien and is entitled to a preference over all other creditors, and assume, further, that all the judgments obtained prior to the plaintiff's appointment in the Eddy suit, together with the attachments of Schuloff, constitute liens upon the property, does that furnish any argument why the temporary injunction issued herein should be dissolved?

The case would then be that a few creditors representing a small proportion of the indebtedness of the corporation claiming the right to sacrifice all this property to the detriment of the interests of the other creditors and stockholders. A court of equity
[*]
should protect the interests of the general creditors and stockholders, if it can be done without injury to the judgment creditors (assuming that they have

* 8 *Weekly Digest*, 65.
† 56 *How. Pr.* 160; S. C., 6 *Abb. N. C.* 293.

such lien) by an immediate sale of the property and a stoppage of the running expenses, thus obtaining a large fund for general distribution.

It is for the interest of all creditors that the property should bring as much as possible, and the proof is abundant and conclusive that the quicker a sale can be made the more the property will bring.

It is therefore proper that the property should be immediately sold, the fund which it shall bring upon such sale should be substituted for the property itself, and if Danzig, Schuloff and others should have any valid lien thereon, it can be established and settled in the present action. It follows from these views [*] that the injunction should be continued until final judgment in this action.

The next question to be considered is that relating to the plaintiff's application for instructions upon notice to the Danzigs in this action and in the Eddy and Cole actions as well.

The power of the court to make a sale of the property is undoubted. Independent of any statute, a [''] court of equity has inherent power to direct such a disposition of the fund as it shall deem wisest and best for the interests of all concerned. But under the statute the power is clear (§§ 1788, 1789 of the Code); for although it may be fairly argued that the statute does not in terms apply to the Cole case, it certainly applies to the Eddy case, which is strictly within article 3 of title 2 of chapter 15.

It will be noted that the exercise of the power of sale in the Eddy action does no harm to any judgment creditor whose execution was issued before the plaintiff's appointment in the Eddy suit, because, by reason of the plaintiff's title in the Cole suit, a fund was brought into court in Cole's suit and sold. No lien or titled was acquired by or through the sheriff under execution. But, even if Danzig has a lien, it can be proved, as I have before indicated.

The order of sale should be entitled and entered in all the actions, and the receiver should have power to sell upon such terms as he shall deem best.

It seems that he is aided by a committee of experienced merchants, each of whom is interested to secure the very best price for the property, and any limit upon his power of sale, whether it be exercised through or in consequence of bids under his advertisements, or at auction through some reputable auctioneer or commission house, can only embarrass and tend to defeat the end in view.

If, however, the receiver should refuse to comply with the just demands of the creditors having any considerable claim against the said corporation, in regard to the form or terms of sale, a special application may be made to the court upon one day's notice to the receiver. The proceeds of the sale should be immediately deposited in some trust company, which will pay the best interest on the deposit, to the credit of the receiver, to be drawn upon the order of the court in the Cole and Eddy actions. The sale should be absolutely without prejudice to the creditor, and the order should provide that each creditor should have the same rights in the fund which he now has in the property.

The matter of Schuloff's attachments can scarcely present any serious difficulty. The Eddy and Cole
[11] suits are brought for the benefit of all concerned ;
and Schuloff, even although not strictly a party on the record, is nevertheless and in fact a party, because he is a creditor (Attorney-General *v.* Guardian Ins. Co., 77 *N. Y.* 272, 277), so that he is enjoined by the general injunction which has been entered under section 1806, and it appears that he has appeared in these action and made a motion to modify that injunction. It is scarcely conceivable that any real difficulty can

arise between the receiver and parties who simply desire the protection of Schuloff's rights under the attachment; but as against that contingency the order may provide that the receiver may, if necessary, [12] procure sufficient advances on the goods which have not been attached, to meet any exigency of the case, and, out of those amounts he may make special deposits or otherwise exercise the rights and privileges of the corporation, as defendant in the attachment suit, to procure the discharge of the attachment, and so realize and procure the sale of those goods.

The receiver should also commence proceedings to vacate and discharge the attachment, and for that purpose and to that extent the general injunction against suits, &c., may be modified so that either party to that suit may present their proofs touching the attachments; but in all other respects the injunctions should remain.

The order should also provide that the receiver, upon a copy of the papers in this action, and a copy of the order to be entered herein, shall make special application to this court in the Danzig action, in the first district, for the purpose of permitting a sale and disposition of the property herein directed to be sold, so that the proceedings in these actions may be harmonious, and the rights of all parties be protected and preserved.

Now, in considering the questions involved herein, I have given the subject all the care that my limited time and other pressing duties would permit, and I am deeply impressed with the idea that if it shall be determined that the directors of a corporation, when they find that the corporation is insolvent; that its affairs are growing worse every day; that the danger is imminent; that the remaining property will be wasted, leaving the bulk of its creditors unpaid—if they cannot under these circumstances resign for the purpose of securing a fair and equal distribution of the corporate property among its creditors, then the subject imperatively calls for legislative action. But, even should it be held, as I think it must be, that they can resign under such circumstances, yet one or more stubborn or dishonest directors might defeat this action.

The decision of these motions, however, does not depend upon the power of the trustees to resign, as the receiver is in possession of the property under his appointment in the Eddy action as well as in the suit of Cole, and the whole controversy turns upon the question as to the right of the judgment, attaching and general creditors, and these questions can and should be all determined in the action now pending in this district.

DIMICK, Appellant, v. COOLEY, Impleaded, &c., Appellant. DECKER, Respondent.

SAME v. SAME.

Supreme Court, Fourth Department; General Term, October, 1882.

§ 66.

Attorney's lien.—At common law.—Under the Code.—Mode of enforcing it.—When should not attorney be allowed to enforce it.—Court no power to adjust amount of attorney's fees in summary way on his application.

At common law, as between attorney and client, the former had a lien for his costs and charges upon the papers, deeds or written evidences of debt in his hands belonging to his client, received in the course of his employment. He also had a like lien upon moneys which he may have collected at his client's request.[1] He had no lien on or interest in his client's cause of action, but upon a judgment recovered by him, he had a lien for his costs and for the

compensation his client had agreed to pay him.[2] Before judgment, the parties could settle the matter in dispute without consulting the attorneys to the record, provided they acted in good faith. If the settlement was instigated wlth a view to prevent the attorney from receiving his costs and to cheat him out of them, the court had the power to set the same aside so far as to allow the suit to proceed for the purpose of collecting the attorney's costs.[3]*

Th effect of section 66 of the Code is to change the rule of the common law, and give to the attorney a lien on the cause of action from the time the suit is commenced, which cannot be displaced by any action of the parties, by settlement or discontinuance, without his consent, until his costs are paid.[4]

Before the Code gave an attorney a lien upon his client's cause of action for his costs, the proper practice, where the parties settled the action without paying him his costs, was for him to apply to the court for an order modifying the terms of settlement so as to allow him to proceed in the action for the purpose of collecting his costs. This application could only be made upon notice to the plaintiff and defendant, and the court examined fully into the facts and circumstances connected with the settlement and its effect upon the attorney, and if it was a fraud upon him, he was allowed to proceed with the action, or upon the judgment, if one had been entered, and to collect his costs out of the defendant. But without such permission, he was not allowed to move in the action for any purpose.[5] The Code has not changed the practice in this particular, and it is still necessary for the attorney to procure the consent of the court, before he can proceed in the action after the parties have settled it.[6]

Where an attorney's own client has released the defendant from the costs of an action settled between them without the assent of the attorney, he should not be permitted to proceed against her and charge her with costs, unless it is first made to appear that such permission is necessary to secure his costs, and enable him to enforce the lien which he has upon the cause of action.[7] In equity, he should be required to proceed against the plaintiff, his debtor, and the lien which he has upon the papers, &c., in his hands belonging to her, before he is permitted to proceed against the defendant for the purpose of enforcing his lien.[8]

As between attorney and client, the supreme court has no jurisdicture to adjust the amount of the attorney's fees in a summary way on the attorney's application.[9]

(*Decided November*, 1882.)

---

* See In re Wilson & Greig, 2 *N. Y. Civ. Pro.* 343.

Appeal from an order made at the Munroe county special term, granted on the application of plaintiff's attorney, ordering a reference to fix the compensation of the plaintiff's attorney, and to report the facts, and his opinion, to the court, with the evidence.

These actions were commenced in October, 1881, on the same day, to foreclose two mortgages, owned by the plaintiff, in which she is mortgagee, the respondent J. D. Decker, acting as her attorney. In one of the actions the mortgage was given to secure the sum of $1,500, and it was claimed that at the time of the commencement of the action, there was due the sum of $600, and to become due thereafter the further sum of $1,050. Upon the other it is alleged that the bond and mortgage were for the sum of $2,500, and that there was due and unpaid at the time of the commencement of the action, the sum of $1,000, and to become due, the sum of $1,750.

After the summons and complaint were served upon the defendant, Elizabeth M. Cooley, and before the time to answer had expired, and on the 11th day of October, 1881, the mortgagor paid to the plaintiff in person, the sum of $900, on account of the mortgages, without any mention how much should be applied on the mortgages respectively, and the plaintiff gave a stipulation in writing, to the defendant, Mrs. Cooley, withdrawing the actions at her own cost. Subsequently, and on the 24th of October, and before the time to answer had expired, Mrs. Cooley appeared in the action, by Mr. Bacon, her attorney, and served a notice of retainer, and also a copy of the receipt, and the stipulation discontinuing the actions. This settlement was effected without the knowledge or consent of the plaintiff's attorney. Immediately following the settlement, the plaintiff and her attorney, Mr. Decker, had interviews and negotiations, with a view of fixing and determining the amount of his costs.

The attorney made out, and served upon the plaintiff, a bill of his costs and charges, amounting in the aggregate to $294.98. This the plaintiff declined to pay, but acknowledged her obligation to pay a less sum, and offered to pay him $91 as his costs, which he declined to receive. In December, 1881, after the respondent had failed to agree with his client as to the amount of his costs, he made a motion at a special term held in Monroe county, in her name and as her attorney, for a decree of foreclosure, asking for a reference to ascertain the amount due upon the bonds and mortgages, and serving the same on Mr. Bacon, Mrs. Cooley's attorney, giving no notice to the plaintiff. This motion was denied, with $10 costs in each action. The decretal part of the order was in these words. "It is hereby ordered, that the said motions, be, and they are hereby denied, with $10 costs of opposing the same in each action, to be paid by the said Jonah D. Decker, personally."

In opposition to the motion, among the other papers read by the defendant, was the affidavit of the plaintiff, in which she stated in substance, that in consideration of the payment of $900, she withdrew the actions, and gave a stipulation, and that she was willing to pay her attorney all his just costs, and that she was worth the sum of $5,000 over and above all debts and liabilities.

In January, 1882, the plaintiff's attorney made a motion in his own behalf for leave to renew the prior motion, which had been denied, and that the prior rules and orders be vacated, and that a reference be had in the actions, to ascertain the value of his services as attorney, and if the plaintiff or defendant fails to pay such amount so determined, that then the plaintiff may be at liberty to proceed in the actions, to satisfy the amount so ascertained and determined.

The defendant, Mrs. Cooley, appeared, and opposed the motion.

It does not appear that notice of this motion was served upon the plaintiff. Nor is it recited in the order, that she did appear. But among the papers upon which the motion was opposed, was the affidavit of the plaintiff, in which she sets up the history of her negotiations with Mr. Decker, with a view of ascertaining the amount of his costs, and concluded her affidavit with a prayer, that the court do not vacate the prior order, but that it deny the application to proceed in the actions, and asking the court to make such order as shall be just, and will be a protection to her rights.

An order was made, granting leave for the renewal of the prior motions, and that they then be heard, and that it be referred to a referee, "to fix the compensation of the plaintiff's attorney and to report the facts, and his opinion to the court, with the evidence; further directions to stand until the coming in of the referee's report, the two actions to remain in the present situation until that time."

From this order the plaintiff, and the defendant, Elizabeth M. Cooley, both appeal.

Theodore Bacon, for the appellants.

J. D. Decker, respondent in person.

BARKER, J.—The defendant's appeal has the most merit, involves the most examination, and will be first considered.

[1] At common law, as between attorney and client, the former had a lien for his costs and charges, upon the papers, deeds, or written evidences of debt in his hands, belonging to his client, received in the course of his employment. He also had a like lien, upon moneys, which he may have collected, at

his client's request (Matter of application of Knapp, 85 *N. Y.* 285).

[*] He had, however, no lien or interest whatever, in the cause of action, by reason of his employment, to prosecute the same in the courts. After judgment the attorney who prosecuted the same, has a lien thereon to the extent of his costs, and for such further sum, as by agreement, his client has promised to pay him out of the judgment, as compensation for his services (Coughlin *v.* N. Y. C. & H. R. R. R. Co., 71 *N. Y.* 443; Wright *v.* Wright, 70 *N. Y.* 96).

[*] After action was commenced, and before judgment, the parties had a right to settle the matter in dispute, on such terms as they might agree upon, without consulting with the attorney to the record, provided they acted in good faith, and not with the intent to cheat and defraud the attorney out of his costs. But if the settlement was instigated with a view to prevent the attorney from receiving his costs from his client, and to cheat him out of the same, then the court, on the application of the attorney, has power and will interfere to make inquiry into the circumstances of the settlement, and if found to be fraudulent, will set the same aside, so far as to allow the suit to proceed for the purpose of collecting the attorney's costs (Talcott *v.* Bronson, 4 *Paige*, 501; Coughlin *v.* N. Y. C. & H. R. R. R. Co., 71 *N. Y.* 443).

These familiar and unquestioned rules are here stated, that they may be in mind in considering the statute, which, in some particulars, has changed the common law upon this subject.

Section 66 of the Code of Civil Procedure enacts, "The compensation of an attorney or counselor for his services is governed by agreement, express or implied, which is not restrained by law. From the commencement of an action or the service of an answer containtaining a counter-claim, the attorney who appears for a party, has a lien upon his client's cause of action or counter-claim, which attaches to a verdict, report, decision or judgment in his client's favor, and the proceeds thereof, in whosoever hands they may come; and cannot be affected by any settlement between the parties before or after judgment."

[1] The effect of this statute is to change the rule of the common law, and gives to the attorney for the plaintiff, a lien on the cause of action, from the time the suit is commenced, which cannot be displaced by any action of the parties, by settlement or discontinuance, without his consent, until his costs are paid. The extent of the lien is not declared by the statute—whether it shall be in the amount of the taxable costs, which the law gives in the recovery of judgment, or in the sum which the attorney and his client, may have agreed upon as his compensation. The statute is not specific on this question. It is not necessary for us to solve this doubt now.

It is manifest, that under this statute, the plaintiff's attorney, Mr. Decker, had a lien for his costs, on the cause of action, for which the suits were prosecuted,—that is, on the moneys secured and agreed to be paid by the bonds and mortgages, and as the settlement was made after the actions were commenced, and without his consent, such lien is not yet displaced; for the statute in express terms, declares, that the same shall not be disturbed by any settlement between the parties.

In view of all the facts set forth in the papers upon which the order appealed from is founded, we concur in that part of the order, permitting the former motion to be renewed, although, upon the facts presented to the court, when that order was made, it was just and proper. It was made in the name of the plaintiff, and she had no right to proceed, after her consent to a discontinuance. After such settlement, the action could not proceed for any other purpose than to allow the plaintiff's attorney to secure and collect his costs.

The first order being now open and vacated, the plaintiff's attorney was free and at liberty to make a proper application to the court, with a view of enforcing the lien which the statute gives him, upon the cause of action, which he prosecuted, and which the parties have settled.

The only provision in the order appealed from, which affects the defendant, is the provision directing a reference to ascertain the amount of the attorney's fees. And the single question for us to examine, at this time, is, whether that is a just and proper order to make, in this state of the proceedings.

Before the statute, the usual and ordinary practice was for the attorney to apply to the court, and ask for an order modifying the terms of the settlement,
[5] so as to allow him to proceed in the action, for the purpose of collecting his costs. The application could only be heard on notice to the plaintiff and defendant, and the court examined fully into the facts and circumstances connected with the settlement, and the effect it had upon the attorney's claim, and if the same was a fraud upon the attorney, he was allowed to proceed with the action, or upon the judgment, if one had been entered, and to collect his costs out of the defendant. But without such permission from the court, he was not at liberty to move in the action for any purpose (Marshall *v.* Meech, 51 *N. Y.* 141; Talcott *v.* Bronson, 4 *Paige*, 501; Murray *v.* Jibson, 22 *Hun*, 387; Pickard *v.* Yencer, 21 *Id.* 403; Goddard *v.* Trenbath, 24 *Id.* 182).

[6] We are of the opinion, that the statute has not changed the practice in this particular, and that it is necessary for the attorney to procure the consent of the court, before he can proceed with the actions. The statute creates the lien upon the cause of action, and declares that a settlement shall not disturb the lien of the attorney.

As there had been no verdict, report, decision, nor judgment in favor of the plaintiff, at the time of the settlement, the lien is still confined to the original cause of action, which was placed in his hands for collection.

It would be an unwise and dangerous practice, extremely hazardous to the rights of both parties, to allow an attorney to continue the action, after settlement by the parties, for the purpose of collecting his costs, without first obtaining the consent of the court, that he may proceed for that purpose. When such permission is given, it is the duty of the court to direct as to the time and manner, and watch the proceedings and doings of the attorney, so as fully to protect the rights of both parties, and not unnecessarily annoy and embarrass either.

[1] The facts disclosed upon this hearing are such that we are inclined to the opinion, that the attorney should not be permitted to proceed against the defendant, and charge her with the costs of these actions, as his own client has released her from that obligation, without it being first made to appear, that such permission is necessary to secure his costs and enable him to enforce the lien which he has upon the cause of action, in his hands for collection.

If the defendant has in fact conspired with the plaintiff, with the view of cheating and defrauding the attorney out of his costs, or to embarrass him in the enforcement of the lien which he has, then it would be the duty of this court to grant, and it would readily grant, a permit to prosecute the action.

The attorney has a full and complete lien upon that part of the cause of action arising on the bonds and mortgages which have not yet been paid and satisfied. Those papers are yet in his hands and under his control.

It seems to be conceded, at least the contrary does

not appear, that there is a sum due upon the bonds and mortgages, more than sufficient to pay the attorney's fees, and that it is amply secured by lien upon real estate. If the defendant, Mrs. Cooley, is free from fraud and intent to embarrass the attorney in the collection of his costs, it would be a great wrong and injustice to her to compel her to litigate the question, as to the amount of his costs, and to pay them after she had in good faith, contracted with the plaintiff, to be released from that obligation.

In a sense the attorney has two liens as his security, one upon the unpaid portion of the bonds and mortgages, due the plaintiff, and the other against the defendant and the lands covered by the bonds and mortgages, which can be enforced by means of the mortgages to be used for that purpose.

In equity he should be required to proceed against the plaintiff, his debtor, and the lien which he [*] has upon her property, before he is permitted to prosecute this action against the defendant, for the purpose of enforcing his lien.

As the court has not yet given its consent that he may prosecute this action further, for the purpose desired, and the hearing before the referee, which has been ordered, will necessarily be expensive to the defendant, we are of the opinion, that that part of the order was improvidently granted and should be reversed.

As the defendant has not been called upon specifically to meet the charge of an attempt to defraud the attorney and deprive him of the benefit of his lien, the order may be modified, allowing a reference to inquire whether she had such intent and purpose in making the settlement and procuring a discontinuance of the actions. And on the coming in of that report, the court will then finally decide, whether the attorney may then proceed in these actions or not.

We are also of the opinion, that in view of the reversal of this part of the order, as to the defendant, it should also be reversed as to the plaintiff; for, as against her, the reference will be entirely unavailing to the attorney, if he is not given permission hereafter to proceed with the action against the defendant.

If he is permitted, on the coming in of the report, and on the further order of the court, to proceed in this action, then it will be unavailing to him, because it must then be determined in the further prosecution of the actions, whether the defendant is liable to pay costs or not.

This a suit in equity, and the costs are in the discretion of the court, and all the merits of the original controversy will need be inquired into and considered by the court, before it can be decided that the defendant is liable for the costs of these actions.

This question was up and directly decided by this court in this department, in the case of Pickard v. Yencer (21 *Hun*, 403).

[*] As between attorney and client, this court has no jurisdiction to adjust the amount of the attorney's fees, in a summary way, on the attorney's application (Lorillard v. Robinson, 2 *Paige*, 276).

The attorney has a perfect remedy in an action at law, or to proceed in equity to enforce such lien as the law gives him on the papers and causes of action belonging to his client in his possession.

The rule is different where the client applies to the court for relief, by reason of the action of his attorney, in withholding the papers or money, and it becomes necessary to adjust the attorney's costs, as one of the matters to be determined, in disposing of the controversy. And such is the case in the matter of Knapp (85 *N. Y.* 297), referred to in the opinion of the learned judge at special term.

So much of the order as directs a reference, is reversed, and in all other particulars affirmed.

No costs awarded.

SMITH, P. J., and HARDIN, J., concurred.

MELA ET AL. *v.* GEIS.

N. Y. MARINE COURT; TRIAL TERM, FEBRUARY, 1883.

§ 733.

Tender.—Amount of, paid into court belongs to plaintiff.—One party or the other must pay costs, where tender made.—When defendant entitled to costs on plaintiff's acceptance of his tender.

Money paid into court under a plea of tender, belongs of right to the plaintiff, in fact is his money the moment it is in the custody of the court; and he can take it at any time he elects. [1]

One party or the other must pay costs in all cases where a tender has been made and the money brought into court. [2]

Where a defendant pleaded a tender before suit brought, and paid the money into court, and the plaintiff took the money and thereby accepted the tender,—*Held*, that his acceptance was a virtual confession that there was no good cause of action, [4] and he was clearly chargeable with costs. [3, 5]

Where in such a case the plaintiff gave the defendant no notice of the acceptance of the tender until the case was called for trial, and the defendant thereupon moved to dismiss the complaint, —*Held*, that while the plaintiff was not compelled to give the defendant notice of his acceptance, he should have given notice of his intention to abandon the litigation, and pay the accrued costs. Not having done so, the defendant was correct in his practice in prosecuting his defense, and the complaint should be dismissed with costs. [6]

(*Decided March* 3, 1883.)

Motion by defendant to dismiss the plaintiff's complaint.

The opinion states the facts.

Blumenstiel & Hirsch, for plaintiff.

Jacob Neu, for defendant.

HAWES, J.—The action herein is brought to recover for goods sold and delivered. The answer is a plea of tender in full of the amount claimed before suit brought. It further alleges that defendant has always been ready and willing to pay the same, and now brings it into court. On the 16th of October, 1882, the answer was served, the money was placed in the hands of the clerk of the court, and on the same day the money so brought in was accepted by the plaintiff and paid over to him by the clerk under an order made by Mr. Justice McADAM. No notice of acceptance or of withdrawal was given by plaintiff. When the case was duly reached on the calendar these facts were submitted, and defendant, on the one hand, asks that the complaint be dismissed, and on the other, the plaintiff moves to strike the case from the calendar, as being settled and discontinued by reason of the acceptance of the tender, and both parties consented that the matter should be finally disposed of under these admitted facts.

Under the old practice the money was brought into court, and there remained until the action was tried and judgment rendered. If defendant succeeded in establishing the fact of tender, he obtained judgment for costs, the money then in court being transferred to plaintiff (Becker *v.* Boon, 61 *N. Y.* 322).

Section 732 of the new Code as amended in 1877 provides for the payment of money into court, and also permits the plaintiff to take the money out of court, and declares such an act to be an acceptance of the tender. It is clear, therefore, that the money thus paid in belongs of right to the plaintiff—in fact, is his [1] money the moment it is in the custody of the court—and if so, he can take it at any time he elects (See Johnson *v.* Covert, 3 *Law Bulletin*, 91). There would seem to be no reason for his waiting until the action was tried, nor any necessity to give notice of his application to withdraw it under the provision of rule 70 of Supreme Court Rules, notice of payment into court on the behalf of defendant having been given by the answer.

The only question which remains, therefore, is one of costs. Section 733 of the Code provides that in case the sum tendered was sufficient to pay plaintiff's demand and costs, then the plaintiff cannot recover costs, but must pay defendant's costs. This section has reference of course to section 731, which relates to tender after suit brought, but it clearly determines the elementary question, that one party or the other must pay costs in all cases where a tender has been made
[2] and money brought into court. The defendant owed the plaintiff the amount set forth in the complaint, and it must be assumed for the purpose of this motion that he duly tendered it to him before the commencement of the action. He did all that the law
[3] required of him. If the plaintiff elected not to accept it, but to bring an action, he did so at his peril and is clearly chargeable with costs.

Defendant had a right to defend, and plaintiff cannot avail himself of his tardy acceptance to deprive defendant of his accrued costs, as this acceptance was
[4] a virtual confession that there was no good cause of action. It is clear that there was an issuable question, viz., whether the tender alleged by defendant to have been made before suit brought was so made or not, and upon its determination depended the liability for costs. The plaintiff could have proceeded and tried that issue, and it was a right which the defendant was equally entitled to. The defendant accordingly appeared in court upon the trial day, ready to proceed, when he was informed for the first time by the plaintiff

that he had accepted the tender and has abandoned the litigation. Under the provisions of section 733 I have no doubt that plaintiff had the right to accept the tender and withdraw the money, and I know of no provision of the statute which required him to give notice of his acceptance; but does this acceptance of itself terminate the litigation? Clearly not. The defendant had admittedly tendered the money prior to the [*] commencement of the suit, and from the very nature of things he became entitled to costs from the commencement of the action down to and including the date of acceptance. Of this there can be no reasonable doubt.

The only embarrassing question is whether defendant is entitled to costs to date. When plaintiff elected to accept the tender, he could have terminated the litigation upon payment of accrued costs, and it was clearly his duty to have tendered it to the defendant. It is true that he was not compelled to give defendant notice of his acceptance, but that fact does not relieve him from giving notice of his intention to abandon the litigation and pay the accrued costs. This he did not do, and the defendant is correct in his practice in prosecuting his defense. He has an interest in this litigation to the extent of his costs, and the plaintiff [*] has as yet done nothing to deprive him of that vested right. The complaint is therefore dismissed, with costs to be taxed.

I do not think that the case is one which comes within the provisions of section 3253, and no additional allowance will be granted, although I have no question as to my power in that regard.

ROBITZEK *v.* HECT.

N. Y. SUPERIOR COURT; SPECIAL TERM, FEBRUARY, 1883.

§ 3267.

Taxation of costs.—When clerk should take proof of necessity for subpœnaing witnesses.

Where upon the adjustment of the costs of an action an affidavit was presented showing that certain witnesses for whom fees were charged were not called at the trial,—*Held*, that the clerk should require proof of what was expected to be proved by such witnesses, and why they were not called.

(*Decided February* 14, 1883.)

Motion for new taxation of costs.

Upon the taxation of defendant's costs, the plaintiff presented an affidavit showing that certain witnesses for whom fees were charged had not been called on the trial. There was no proof that such witnesses were necessary, nor why they were not called. The clerk allowed the witness fees claimed, and the plaintiff thereupon made this motion.

Thomas C. Campbell, for motion.

Kurzman & Seaman, opposed.

FREEDMAN, J.—Upon the presentation of within affidavit the clerk should have required proof of what was expected to be proved by the witnesses not called, and why they were not called (see cases cited in 2d vol. of Bliss' Code, p. 998). The taxation must there fore be reopened and referred back to the clerk with the instruction to take and pass upon such proof, and if not made, to disallow the items objected to.

MATTHEWS v. MATSON.

N. Y. MARINE COURT; SPECIAL TERM, FEBRUARY, 1883.

§§ 3264, 3265.

Taxation of costs.—When court will not review or order new taxation of costs.—Court has no power to tax costs.

Where a bill of costs, containing an item of $41.41, "allowance by the court of five per cent." on the amount of the recovery, was taxed in favor of plaintiff upon notice to the defendant, and both parties were represented before the clerk at the taxation, and no exception or objection was taken, and the plaintiff afterwards moved for a new taxation, on the ground that he had omitted, through "manifest inadvertence," to claim an allowance on defendant's counter-claim,—*Held*, that he had failed to bring himself within the rules of practice, requiring or permitting the court to interfere with the clerk's taxation, [2] and his motion should be denied. [4]

The court has no power to tax a bill of costs; by law, the clerk alone possesses this power subject to review upon motion. [3]

Where costs have been taxed by default, and the default is properly excused, relief is granted by sending the matter back to the clerk *de novo*. [1]

(*Decided February* 8, 1883.)

Motion for a new taxation of costs.

The facts are stated in the opinion.

Kelly & MacRea, for motion.

T. D. Hodge, opposed.

HYATT, J.—The plaintiff moves for a new taxation of costs; having recovered a judgment, he serves a bill of costs with notice of adjustment containing the item "allowance by court of five per cent. on $828.34—

$41.41," said sum being the amount of his recovery. The parties attend before the clerk when no claim is made for an allowance upon the amount of the defendant's counter-claim, or for any greater allowance than the sum set forth in the bill, and no formal or specific objection to any of the items of the bill was made before the clerk. When the taxation has been made
[1] by default, properly excused, relief is granted by sending the matter back to the clerk, *de novo.* There was no default in this case, but, to adopt the plaintiff's words, there was "manifest inadvertence" on his part to claim an allowance upon the amount of the defendant's counter-claim. His manifest intention in the matter was to take an allowance based upon his recovery, as evidenced by his service of a notice to that effect and his presentation of a bill of costs for adjustment particularly specifying his only claim for an allowance. Both parties were represented before the clerk; no objection or exception was taken. The plaintiff
[2] has failed to bring himself within the rules of practice requiring or permitting the court to interfere with the clerk's taxation. The court has no
[3] power to tax a bill of costs; by law the clerk alone possesses this power, subject to review upon motion. The moving party has made his election and failed to entitle himself, under the rules, to a review
[4] of the clerk's taxation or a new taxation. The motion must therefore be denied, but without costs.

FEIG, AS ADMINISTRATOR, AT ETC., v. WRAY.

SUPREME COURT, FIRST DEPARTMENT; SPECIAL TERM, JANUARY, 1883.

§ 3246.

Administrator—when personally liable for costs.—When judgment therefor may be entered against him personally, without an order of the court.

Where, in an action by an administrator upon a cause of action for conversion, which arose after the death of his intestate, judgment was rendered in favor of the defendant,—*Held*, that the administrator was personally liable for costs, and the defendant had the right to enter judgment against him without an order of the court.

(*Decided January* 5, 1883.)

Motion by plaintiff to amend the postea of a judgment entered against him.

The facts are stated in the opinion.

Jonas H. Goodman, for motion.

Koones & Goldman, opposed.

LAWRENCE, J.—This action was brought by the plaintiff, as administrator of the goods and credits of William Brusle, deceased, to recover the value of certain goods which were alleged in the complaint to have belonged to the deceased. The complaint avers that the intestate died on the 4th of September, 1879, and that, on the 24th of September, 1879, the plaintiff was appointed the administrator of the estate, and that he duly qualified and entered upon the discharge of his duties as such administrator. It is then alleged that the testator was the owner, at the time of his death, of the goods, to recover the value of which this action is brought, and that, subsequent to his death, prior to the appointment of the plaintiff as administrator, the defendant unlawfully took possession of the same and converted them to his own use.

It also alleged that prior to the commencement of this action, after his appointment, the plaintiff, as such administrator, demanded the possession of such goods, &c., from the defendant, who refused to deliver up the same.

The cause was referred to Mr. Abbott, as referee, who found in favor of the defendant, and that he was entitled to judgment with costs. Subsequently judgment was entered dismissing the complaint with costs. The postea is entitled Isaac Feig *v.* Thomas Wray, there being no description of the plaintiff as an administrator in the title. This motion is made to amend the postea, "by adding to the name of the plaintiff in the title thereof the words, as administrator of the goods, chattels, and credits of William T. Brusle, dedeceased," the object being of course to exempt the plaintiff from the payment of costs individually.

The plaintiff's counsel relies upon section 3246 of the Code of Civil Procedure in support of his motion, and of the proposition that it not having been found by the referee that his client has been guilty of bad faith in the prosecution of the action, costs under that section cannot be imposed upon him personally. To this it is replied, on the part of the defendant, that section 3246 of the Code of Civil Procedure is the same as section 317 of the old Code, and that under the old Code it was frequently held that in a case of this nature the unsuccessful plaintiff, executor or administrator, was liable for costs personally, and that, too, without an express order of the court to that effect. It will be observed by a reference to the complaint that the alleged wrongful taking of the goods occurred after the death of Brusle, and that the conversion became complete when, on a subsequent demand by the plaintiff as administrator, the defendant refused to deliver possession of the goods. In Holdridge v. Scott (1 *Lans.* 303) it was held that where the record shows that the cause of action (if any) arose after the death of the testator or intestate, such right of action vests in the executor or administrator in his private right, and that he cannot escape the penalty of costs, by suing in form in his representative capacity, unnecessarily, if he fails to obtain judgment. The case arose under section 317 of the Code of Procedure, and Justice LAMONT, in delivering the opinion of the court, which was concurred in by Justices DANIELS and MARVIN, reviews all the cases and reaches the result above stated. To the same effect is the case of Fox v. Fox (5 *Hun*, 53, 54), decided by the general term of the fourth department, opinion per GILBERT, J.

The doubt which I entertained on the argument of this motion was chiefly as to the right of the defendant to enter judgment against the plaintiff in this case without an order of the court permitting him to do so. An examination of the authorities conclusively shows that he has such right (see Bostwick v. Brown, 15 *Hun*, 308; Holdridge v. Scott, 1 *Lans.* 303; Lyon v. Marshall, 11 *Barb.* 242, and the cases cited per EDWARDS, J., at p. 248; Smith v. Patten, 9 *Abb. N. S.* 205).

This motion will therefore be denied, with costs.

DOLZ, Respondent, v. ATLANTIC AND GULF STREAM TRANSPORTATION COMPANY, Impeaded, &c., Appellant.

Supreme Court, First Department; General Term, Octobre, 1882.

§ 636.

Attachment.—Affidavit upon which granted, must show amount of claim. If amount of claim is alleged on information and belief, the grounds of the belief must be set forth, and the reasons given why a positive affidavit to that effect is not presented.

An allegation, in an affidavit to procure an attachment, that the plaintiff is entitled to recover the sum of $390.64, with interest, etc., is not sufficient to show the amount the plaintiff is entitled to recover. It must be substantiated by statements from which the court may adjudge the fact established for the purposes of the motion, and such statements must be positive, or if on information and belief, the source of the information and the grounds of the belief must be set forth and reasons given why a positive affidavit to that effect is not presented.[1] The statement of the claim is a material part of the affidavit, and its amount must be established by proof; it must not rest on mere allegation.[2]

(*Decided January* 17, 1883.)

Appeal from order of special term denying defendant's motion to vacate an attachment.

The attachment was granted upon an affidavit, made by the plaintiff, in which he states that he is entitled to recover of the defendant $390.64, with interest from November 22, 1881, over and above all counterclaims known to him; that he and one Mudgett were jointly employed as brokers by the defendant to obtain a charter for one of defendant's steamers, and that the defendant agreed to pay to plaintiff and said Mudgett jointly, for their services "a commission of five per cent. upon the gross amount of said charter upon the signing thereof," that they obtained a charter for the steamer which was accepted November 22, 1881; that, as plaintiff "is informed and believes, the gross amount of said charter was the sum of $18,000;" "that said company refused, and still refuses, to pay the plaintiff and said Mudgett, the said commissions . . . or to pay plaintiff for his said services, to his damage $390.64;" that the said Mudgett refused to join with plaintiff in his suit, and "that the commissions, for the recovery of which this action is brought, are jointly due, . . . and said Mudgett is therefore a necessary party to this action."

On this affidavit an attachment was granted and levied upon personal property of the defendant, who moved upon the attachment and the papers on which it was issued to set it aside. The motion was denied, and this appeal taken from the order thereupon entered.

Henry D. Hotchkiss, for appellant.

The plaintiff is required to make out a clear *prima facie* case, and so that the judge can act judicially upon legal proof. Woodhouse *v.* Todd, 10 *Weekly Dig.* 28; *Ex parte* Haynes, 18 *Wend.* 611. . . .

John A. Deady (*Goodrich, Deady & Platt*, attorneys), for respondent.

Cited, in support of contention, that it was sufficient to prove the amount of the claim *to the satisfaction of the judge* granting the attachment: *Ex parte* Haynes, 18 *Wend.* 611; *Ex parte* Fitch, 2 *Id.* 298; Allen *v.* Meyer, 7 *Daly*, 230; affirmed, 73 *N. Y.* 2; Kinner *v.* Kelly, 18, *N. Y.* 355; Schoonmaker *v.* Spencer, 54 *N. Y.*, 366; Van Alstyn *v.* Erwine, 11 *N. Y.* 340;

In re Faulkner, 4 *Hill*, 598; Niles *v.* Vanderzee, 14 *How.* 547; Easton *v.* Malavazi, 7 *Daly*, 146.

DWIGHT, J.—The motion was made on the papers alone on which the warrant was granted. The objection is that the affidavit did not show, as required by the statute, "that the plaintiff is entitled to recover a sum stated therein." The affidavit contains the allegation in the words of the statute, that the plaintiff is entitled to recover the sum of $390.64, with interest, &c., but this
[1] was not sufficient; it must substantiate the allegation by statements from which the court may adjudge the fact established for the purposes of the motion, and such statements must be positive, or, if on information and belief, the source of the information or the grounds of the belief must be set forth and reasons given why a positive affidavit to that effect is not presented (Woodhouse *v.* Todd, 10 *Weekly Dig.* 28; Steuben County Bank *v.* Alberger, 78 *N. Y.* 252; Ruppert *v.* Haug, 13 *Weekly Dig.* 411).

Here is an allegation that the cause of action arises on an agreement to pay, for services of the plaintiff and another, five per cent. of the amount of a certain charter of the defendant's steamer; hence the amount of the plaintiff's claim depends upon the amount of the charter. That amount is stated only on information and belief. So far as legal evidence is afforded by the affidavit, the charter may have been for $100, and the percentage under the agreement the sum of $5, instead of $390.64, as claimed.

The statement of the claim is a material part of the affidavit in these cases, because it determines the amount of the defendant's property upon which
[2] the attachment shall be levied. It prevents the oppression of the seizure of a large amount of property to satisfy a small claim. The amount of the

claim must, therefore, be established by proof: it must not rest on mere allegations.

In this respect, the affidavit seems to have been defective, and the motion to set aside the attachment improperly denied.

BRADY, P. J., and DANIELS, J., concurred.

HESSBERG, APPELLANT, v. RILEY, SHERIFF, &c. WHITE ET AL., RESPONDNETS.

COURT OF APPEALS; JANUARY, 1883.

§§ 1421, 1422, 1423, 1426.

Sheriff.—Substitution of indemnitors for, in action against sheriff

To entitle the sureties to an undertaking given to indemnify the sheriff against loss by reason of making a levy under an attachment or execution to be substituted in the place of the sheriff in an action against him for damages resulting from such levy, it is not necessary that the undertaking should have been given before the levy was made.[1] It would seem to be sufficient if the bond was executed before the action was commenced.[1]

The plaintiff in such an action cannot object that no notice of the application was given the sheriff.[2] The motion being for the benefit of the sheriff, the presumption is that he has knowledge and notice of the fact, and, as he does not object, that he assents and approves of the proceeding.[2]

The Code of Civil Procedure makes the sureties to an undertaking to indemnify the sheriff for loss resulting from a levy liable as parties when substituted in his place in an action against him for damages arising therefrom, and it cannot be maintained that there is no cause of action against them because they were the sheriff's bondsmen.[3] There is no question as to the power of the legislature to make such provision.[4] The levy made by the sheriff includes the consequences which followed it, and where he ejected and kept the plaintiff out of his premises, that act is included.[5]

Where the damages asked in an action against the sheriff for wrongfully levying upon and seizing personal property were $2,000, and the sureties on an indemnity bond for $1,000 moved to be substituted in his place,—*Held*, the requiring of additional security was discretionary with the court ordering the substitution.[6]

(*Decided February* 9, 1883.)

Appeal from an order of the general term of the supreme court, second department, affirming an order substituting the sureties on an indemnity bond in place of the sheriff.

John H. Clayton, for appellant.

Rudolph Sampter, for respondent.

It is well settled that the plaintiff could elect to sue the sheriff alone, or jointly with the indemnitors, or the indemnitors alone. This is on the theory that they are joint tortfeasors with the sheriff, who acts under their direction by virtue of the bond, and consequently the petitioners are originally liable for the full amount of any alleged damage. See Herring *v.* Hoppock, 15 *N. Y.* 409; Weber *v.* Ferris, 37 *How. Pr.* 102.

MILLER, J.—This action was brought against defendant, the sheriff of Kings county, for entering plaintiff's store and wrongfully taking away and converting certain personal property, and also for closing said store, interrupting plaintiff's business, and injuring his credit, and damages are claimed in the sum of $2,000. The property in question was levied upon by the sheriff under an attachment issued in favor of Gustave White and Simon Oberfelder, against one Emanuel Seichert, and thereupon a bond was executed, on behalf of the plaintiffs in the attachment suit, to indemnify the sheriff against any loss he might sustain by reason of the levy under said attachment, which bond was in the sum of $1,000. The indemnitors on said bond made a motion to be substituted in the place and stead of the sheriff, under section 1421 of the Code of Civil Procedure, which motion was granted, and on appeal the general term affirmed the order, and the plaintiff herein appeals to this court.

The provision of the Code referred to is as follows: "Where an action to recover a chattel, hereafter levied upon by virtue of an execution, or a warrant of attachment, or to recover damages by reason of a levy upon, detention, or sale of personal property hereafter made, by virtue of an execution, or a warrant of attachment, is brought against an officer, or against a person who acted by his command, or in his aid, if a bond or written undertaking idemnifying the officer against the levy or other act was given, in behalf of the judgment creditor, or the plaintiff in the warrant, before the action was commenced, the person or persons who gave it, or the survivors, if one or more are dead, may apply to the court for an order to substitute the applicants as defendants in the action, in place of the officer or of the person so acting by his command or in his aid." The appellant claims the proceedings were defective on various grounds, which we will consider. It is insisted that the section of the Code referred to requires that the undertaking should be given before the levy. There is nothing in the section cited that requires this specifically, and it would seem to be sufficient if the bond
[1] was executed before the action was commenced.

The affidavit of the attorney for the plaintiffs in the attachment suit shows that the bond was given upon a claim being made by the plaintift in this action, to the property levied upon, and we think that this was sufficient to cover the sheriff's seizure, as the bond was given specially to indemnify him against loss by reason of such act.

The objection, that notice of the motion was not given to the sheriff personally is not available to the

appellant, who does not represent the sheriff, and
[2] has no right to object that notice was not served on
him. The motion being made for the benefit of the sheriff, the presumption is, he has knowledge and notice of the fact, and as he does not object, that he assents and approves of the proceeding. We see no objections to the forms of the acknowledgments to the consent of the petitioners, and we think they are in compliance with section 1422 of the Code. We think
it cannot be maintained that there is no cause of ac-
[3] tion against the signers of the bond, because they
have become the bondsmen of the sheriff and seek the to be substituted in his place by this motion. The section of Code referred to makes them liable as parties
when substituted in his place. There is no ques-
[4] tion, we think, as to the power of the legislature to
make such a provision. There is no force in the position that the provision of the Code does not include
the act of the sheriff which is complained of, in
[5] ejecting the plaintiff from the premises in question,
and keeping him out of the same. The levy made by the sheriff includes the consequences which follow it. There was but a single act of the sheriff in levying upon the goods, and the results which followed it were a part of that act, and hence it was but one transaction. It is also insisted that the indemnitors are only bound in the sum of $1,000; while the action is to recover the sum of $2,000, and hence the bond is insufficient, and they should be compelled to furnish additional security. This was a matter in the discretion of the
[6] court below, and as they have failed to require ad-
ditional security, the presumption is, it was not deemed essential. It may be added that it does not distinctly appear that the sum named in the bond was stated so specifically as to be entirely controlling.

The order should be affirmed, with costs.

All concurred.

GAY *v.* SEIBOLD.

SUPERIOR COURT OF BUFFALO; SPECIAL TERM, OCTOBER, 1882.

§ 3251, subd. 3.

Costs.—Successful party not entitled to term fees of term when trial was postponed at his request.

A party at whose request a case was postponed cannot subsequently, on recovering a verdict, tax a term fee for the term it was so postponed. The general rule is that a successful party is entitled to his term fees when he attended the circuit, prepared for trial, and the case, through no fault of his, was not tried.

(*Decided November* 26, 1882.)

Motion for a new taxation of costs.

The defendant, having recovered a verdict on the trial of this action, after notice to plaintiff, presented a bill of costs to the clerk for taxation. The plaintiff objected to two term fees,—those for September and November, 1881,—and in support of his objection presented an affidavit, made by his attorney, in which it was alleged that the action "was at issue and was first noticed for trial at the September trial term, 1881, of this court; that on the first day of first term the defendant's attorney requested" the plaintiff's attorney "to let the said action go over the term, as the defendant could not be ready for trial thereat," and the plaintiff's "attorney consenting thereto, the said action was continued by consent of counsel, and at the request and instance of defendant's attorney as aforesaid; that at the November trial term of this court the said defendant's attorney, through his clerk, applied to" the plaintiff's attorney "to let the said action go over the term because of the absence of one of the defendant's witnesses, Jas. S. Seibold, and the" plaintiff's attorney "consented thereto, provided the said witness should not be present before the end of the term, stipulating only that the action should remain where it was, near the end of a very long day calendar, but not be tried unless the said witness should be in the city in season for trial; and the said action went over the term for that reason and because of the absence of the said witness."

The clerk allowed the term fees objected to, and the plaintiff thereupon made this motion.

Joseph P. Carr, for motion.

W. L. Jones, opposed.

SHELDON, Ch. J.—The notice of motion is specific only as to the term fees of September and November, 1881, and which were allowed by the clerk on the adjustment. The motion presents itself as it did before the clerk, and the question is whether, upon the affidavits and papers read before him upon the adjustment, the term fees were properly allowed.

The rule is that where a party at his own request postpones a cause, he cannot, on subsequently recovering a verdict in his favor, tax a term fee for that term (Hanna *v.* Dexter, 15 *Abb. Pr.* 135; Hinman *v.* Bergen, 5 *How. Pr.* 245).

The rule is general that a successful party is entitled to his term fees when he attended the circuit, prepared for trial, and the cause, through no default of his, was not tried (15 *How. Pr.* 156;* 13 *Id.* 139;† 2 *Sandf.* 737.)‡

* Fisher *v.* Hunter.

† Williams *v.* Horgan.

‡ Minturn *v.* Main.

Now in this case it appeared before the clerk that the defendant's counsel requested the plaintiff to allow the case to go over each of the terms for reasons stated in the affidavit of the plaintiff's attorney used on the taxation, and the plaintiff's counsel granted the favor. It would be a hard case to say that his client must now be mulcted in a penalty because the defendant's request was granted. The question of the cause being necessarily on the calendar has nothing to do with it. The defendant must have been prepared and the case not tried, without fault or delay made by him, or he should not be allowed the term fees.

The allowance of the term fees must be stricken out, and costs readjusted as above.

Motion granted, with $10 costs.

MEAD, as Administratrix, &c., Respondent, v. SMITH, Personally and as Executrix, &c. Appellant.

Supreme Court, First Department; General Term, March, 1882.

§§ 992, 993.

Exceptions.—None necessary to authorize review of finding on controverted question of fact.—Finding without evidence to sustain it is a ruling upon a question of law.

No exception to a finding upon a controverted question of fact is necessary to be taken in order to justify a review of the evidence by the supreme court for the purpose of determining whether the finding was against its weight.[6] Section 992 of the Code was intended to abrogate the practice of excepting to findings of questions of fact upon conflicting evidence; the section is a general one and applies to trial by juries, by the court and by referees.[4]

A finding without any evidence whatever tending to sustain it, is a ruling upon a question of law within the meaning of section 992 of the Code, and on such a finding an exception would seem to be necessary.[5]

In an action brought by M. as administratrix with the will annexed of McG. for an accounting of the property of McG. which had come into the hands of defendant's testator as executor of the will of McG.,—*Held*, that proof of a formal statutory character to show that the defendant had advertised for claims against her testator's estate pursuant to an order of the surrogate, was clearly admissible,[1] but, that while findings to that effect and that no claim on behalf of any person interested under the will of said McG. was presented, were justified by the evidence, a conclusion of law that the defendant was entitled to a dismissal of plaintiff's complaint, so far as it was predicated upon them, was erroneous because it was not also shown that the defendant had distributed the estate of her decedent and that no portion of it remained in her hands.[3]

It is questionable whether an exception to the admission of evidence properly admissible for one purpose can be upheld because it appears that in the final disposition of the case the court has probably used it for another and illegitimate purpose.[2]

(*Decided January*, 1883.)

Appeal from judgment of special term dismissing complaint with costs.

James M. Lyddy, for appellant.

J. Wessell Smith, for respondent.

DAVIS, P. J.—This action was brought by the plaintiff, as administratrix with the will annexed of one Catherine McGuire, for an accounting of the property of the deceased which came to the hands of Charles H. Smith as executor of the will of said Catherine McGuire.

It was shown on the trial that the testatrix died in May, 1864; that her will was proved and admitted to probate in July, 1864, and letters testamentary thereon were granted by the surrogate of the county of New

York to Charles H. Smith as sole executor; that Smith duly qualified as such executor, and afterwards, in September, 1864, filed an inventory duly verified by himself, in which the estate of his testatrix was appraised at the sum of $2,907.15.

By the second clause of the will the testatrix bequeathed to her executors the sum of $500 in trust, to apply the net income thereof to the education, support and maintenance of Mary Augusta, child of Samuel and Hannah Mead, until she should become of age, upon which event the testatrix gave the principal sum and all arrears and accumulations of interest to the said Mary Augusta to her own use forever; and after a few small specific legacies, she gave and bequeathed to her mother, Catherine McGuire, of Knocknoishanon county, Fermanagh, Ireland, if living at the time of testatrix's decease, or if dead, to her brothers and sisters who might then be living, and the lawful issue of such as should have died, all the residue of her estate; that Smith continued to act as executor of the estate until his death, which took place in December, 1873; that no account of his proceedings as executor was ever rendered or settled before the surrogate, as required by the statute; that by the last will and testament of said Smith, the defendant, Lucretia C. Smith, was appointed sole executrix of his estate; that on September 15, 1880, letters testamentary were issued to her; that the plaintiff, Hannah Mead, mother of the legatee, Mary Augusta Mead, was appointed by the surrogate administratrix with the will annexed, of said Catherine McGuire, deceased; and that no account of the estate of said Catherine McGuire had been filed by the defendant. Evidence was given tending to show that before the commencement of this action a demand for an accounting was made by and on behalf of the plaintiff of the said defendant. Evidence was also given tending to show that no such demand had been made. It was also shown that Mary Augusta Mead, the legatee, was, at the time of the decease of Catherine McGuire, an infant under the age of fourteen years ; that her legacy had not been paid, and that letters of guardianship of her person and estate were granted by the surrogate to the said Hannah Mead on July 29, 1880.

Evidence was given on the part of the defendant tending to show that an accounting had been had between the executor, Charles H. Smith, and the residuary and specific legatees acting through an attorney in fact, and that the balance, after reserving a part or the whole of the legacy to Mary Augusta Mead, had been paid over by Smith to such attorney in fact. It was also shown that the defendant as executrix of the will of said Smith, pursuant to an order of the surrogate of Queens county by whom she was appointed such executrix, duly advertised for the presentation of claims against the estate of said Smith, for the period prescribed by law and specified in such advertisement which period expired before the commencement of this action ; and that no claim on behalf of any person interested in the will of said Catherine McGuire was presented to said defendant as executrix of said Smith, within the period specified in the advertisement.

Upon this evidence the court found, as matters of fact, amongst other things :

"5th. That before the commencement of this action said executor, C. H. Smith, duly accounted for and paid over the funds and assets of said McGuire estate in his possession to the parties in interest therein.

"6th. That none of the funds or assets of said McGuire estate have come into the possession or control of the defendant.

"7th. That no demand was, before the commencement of this action, made by plaintiff as administratrix, etc., of the McGuire estate on defendant for an accounting of the funds and assets thereof.

"8th. That as executrix of said Smith estate, pursuant to an order of the surrogate of Queens county, New York, having jurisdistion thereof, by whom defendant was appointed as such executrix, defendant duly advertised for the presentation of claims against said Smith estate, within a period prescribed by law, specified in said order and advertisement, which period, so specified, expired before the commencement of this action, to wit, December 15, 1874.

"9th. That no claim on behalf of any person interested under said will of said McGuire, was presented to said defendant as executrix of said Smith estate.

"10th. That the cause of action alleged in the complaint did not accrue within three years before the commencement of this action.

"11th. That the cause of action alleged in the complaint did not accrue within six years before the commencement of the action."

And, as a conclusion of law, that the defendant was entitled to judgment, dismissing the plaintiff's complaint with costs, and judgmant was accordingly entered.

No exceptions whatever appear to have been taken to the findings of fact or to the conclusions of law.

Exceptions were taken in the progress of the trial to the admission of evidence offered to show that the defendant had advertised for claims against her
[1] testator's estate under and pursuant to the order of the surrogate. But the exception was not well taken. The proof offered was of a formal statutory character, and we think was clearly admissible. An exception was also taken to the admission of the evidence showing an accounting and settlement between the attorney in fact of the other legatees of the will of Catherine McGuire, and her executor. This evidence consisted of documents in which the executor stated an account in the form of debtor and creditor,

showing the disposition made by him of the assets, and of the balance stated to be due to the residuary legatees and that such balance was duly paid to them. The authenticity of the papers was properly shown by the subscribing witnesses to them. It does not appear that they were received for the purpose of showing that any disposition of the legacy to Mary A. Mead had been made, but as tending to show that the claims of other legatees under the will had been disposed of by mutual settlement and payment by Smith prior to her death.

We do not see that their admission could have legitimately had any prejudicial effect against the plaintiff as affecting her right to an accounting from the defendant, if no greater effect had been given to them by the court than simply to show that an accounting had been had so far as related to any claim of the legatees with whom the mutual accounting and settlement had been made. Their admission for such a purpose was, therefore, not improper. But they seem to have been the sole basis for the fifth finding of fact, to wit, "That before the commencement of this action the said executor, Charles H. Smith, accounted for and paid over the funds and assets of said Catherine McGuire to the parties in interest." They certainly did not justify any such finding, because on their face they show that a portion of the estate remained in the hands of Smith to satisfy in whole or in part the legacy to Mary A. Mead.

But no exception was taken to this finding, and it is questionable whether an exception to the admission of evidence properly admissible for one purpose [2] can be upheld because it appears that in the final disposition of the case the court has probably used it for another and illegitimate purpose.

In strictness none of the exceptions taken in the course of the trial justify us in interfering with the judgment.

The conclusion of law is simply that the defendant is entitled to judgment dismissing the complaint with costs. That conclusion is quite well founded if the facts found in the case upon which it is based were properly found. But it seems to us that material parts of those facts were unsustained by evidence. The fifth finding, already alluded to, would undoubtedly, if true, be fatal to an action in equity for a further accounting, but as against the plaintiff it was clearly not well founded, for the same evidence which showed an accounting and settlement with the other legatees strongly tended to show that no such accounting had been had as to the legacy due to Mary A. Mead. With respect, therefore, to her claim upon the estate, there cannot be said to have been evidence justifying this finding. The seventh finding, that no demand was made for an accounting, was disposed of upon conflicting evidence, and while we think that the finding might more properly have been that a demand had been made, yet we should not feel justified in interfering with the judgment on that ground.

The eighth and ninth findings relate to the advertisement for claims against the estate of Smith under the order of the surrogate, and that no claim on behalf of any person interested under the will of Catherine McGuire was presented.

The evidence fully justified these findings. But so far as the conclusion of law is predicated upon them
[3] it is erroneous, because it was not also shown that the defendant had distributed the estate of Smith and that no portion of it remained in her hands.

The tenth and eleventh findings are to the effect that the cause of action did not accrue within three years nor within six years before the commencement of the action. These findings were erroneous as bases for a dismissal of the complaint on the ground that the action was barred by statute. The cause of action in favor of the infant legatee was certainly not barred at the time of the decease of the defendant's testatrix. She was then an infant, and remained under that disability up to about the time of the bringing of this action, for letters of guardianship of her estate and person appear to have been issued on the 29th of July, 1880; and the case states that it was conceded on the trial that the plaintiff is her sole guardian, and that a cause of action in favor of the plaintiff as representative of the estate of Catherine McGuire did not accrue until her appointment as administratrix with the will annexed, on the 14th of September, 1880. In the interval between the death of Smith and her appointment as administratrix with the will annexed, there seems to have been no person whose default in taking steps to enforce an accounting could set in operation the statute of limitations. The findings were, therefore, not correct, and yet, for aught that appears, they may have been regarded by the court as justifying the conclusions of law.

The question presented, therefore, is whether we are at liberty, without any exceptions to the findings of fact or the conclusions of law, to look into the evidence and determine that material facts which would uphold that conclusion were unsupported by evidence Section 992 of the Code provides, among other things, that "except as prescribed by section 1180 of this act an exception cannot be taken to a ruling upon a question of fact." Section 1180 relates only to the trial of challenges to jurors, and it provides that on such trials, exceptions may be taken to determinations upon questions of fact. The provision of section 992 is a general one, and applies to trials by juries, by the
[*] court, and by referees; and the note to this section shows that it was intended to abrogate the

practice of excepting to findings of questions of fact upon conflicting evidence.

Section 993 declares that a finding without any evidence whatever tending to sustain it, in a ruling [*] upon a question of law within the meaning of section 992, and on such a finding an exception would seem to be necessary (Sections 992, 994, 995, 996). The language of section 993 is not applicable to a case where there is evidence tending to sustain the finding, and the court or referee reaches a conclusion upon conflicting evidence.

The several provisions of the Code are by no means clear and satisfactory, but we think it safe to say that their effect is to provide that no exceptions to a finding upon a controverted question of fact is nec- [*] essary to be taken in order to justify a review of the evidence by this court for the purpose of determining whether the finding was against its weight. We are at liberty, therefore, in this case, to reverse the judgment if we come to the conclusion that the referee erred in his finding of material facts, because his conclusions were against the weight of evidence in the case. And upon this ground we think the judgment must be reversed, and a new trial granted, with costs to abide the event.

BRADY, J., concurred.

THE PEOPLE *ex rel.* BYRNE *v.* FRENCH ET AL.

SUPREME COURT, FIRST DEPARTMENT; SPECIAL TERM, APRIL, 1883.

§§ 383, 414, 1991.

Mandamus.—Limitation of time within which it may be resorted to, the same as that within which action may be brought.—Is a legal remedy.—Salary of member of N. Y. City police force is fixed by statute, and the liability of the commissioners of police therefore is statutory, and of a strictly legal character.

The time within which a mandamus must be resorted to, is now the same as that within which an action must be brought.[1]

The salary of a member of the police force in the city of New York is fixed by statute, and the liability of the commissioners of police of that city, therefore, springs entirely from the statute; and, therefore, in a proceeding by a member of the police force to recover his salary, he is not entitled to recover for any salary which accrued more than six years before the commencement of the proceeding.[2]

The liability of the commissioners of police of the city of New York, for the salary of a member of the police force, is of a strictly legal character, and enforceable by the appropriate legal remedies.[3]

The writ of mandamus is a legal writ, and the forms of procedure, and the rules which governed in the court of chancery, have no application to it.[4]

(*Decided April* 8, 1883.)

Application for a peremptory writ of mandamus requiring the defendants, commissioners of police in the city of New York, to pay the relator a part of his salary as member of the police force of that city, retained by defendants.

The opinion states the facts.

Ambrose H. Purdy, for relator.

George P. Andrews, for defendants.

LAWRENCE, J.—It was held in the case of The People *v.* Supervisors of Westchester Co. (12 *Barb.* 446), that as there was at that time no statutory limitation of the time within which writs of mandamus could be obtained in this State, that where a party seeks the enforcement of a substantial right by means of a mandamus, he could be allowed the time given by the statute to obtain a remedy for injuries essentially of a similar character in the ordinary way, if that could be pursued. That case was decided in 1852, and the provisions of the present Code have materially altered the law since that time time. Instead of resting upon analogy, the time within which a man-
['] damus must be resorted to is now, by statute, the same as that within which an action must be brought.

It is not necessary, in disposing of this question, to determine whether, under the Code, the proceeding to obtain a mandamus is to be regarded as an action or a special proceeding. Whether that proceeding falls under the definition of an action contained in section 3333, or of a special proceeding under section 3334 of the Code, so far as the limitation of the time within which it must be brought is concerned, the result is the same.

By section 414 of the Code, it is expressly declared that the provisions of this chapter apply, and constitute the only rules of limitation applicable to a civil action or special proceeding, except in one of the following cases: then follows an enumeration of the excepted cases, within which this case does not fall. By section 383 of the Code, it is provided that an action to recover upon a liability created by statute, except a penalty, must be brought within six years. Now in this case, the salary is fixed by statute, and the
[*] liability of the respondent to pay it, springs entirely from the statute. I am of the opinion, therefore, that the relator is not entitled to recover for any

salary which accrued more than six years before the commencement of these proceedings. The cases referred to by the learned counsel for the relators, relating to trusts, do not appear to me to be in point. The liability of the respondents was of a strictly legal [3] character, and enforceable by the appropriate legal remedies. Nor can I accede to the position that these proceedings have an equitable character. The writ of mandamus is a legal writ, and the forms of [4] procedure and the rules which governed in the court of chancery have no application to it.

The relator, therefore, can only claim, as it seems to me, for that portion of his salary which was withheld during the period of six years anterior to the commencement of this proceeding. Let an order be entered that a mandamus issue in accordance with these views, the respondents to be allowed ten days within which to comply with the same.

PLIMPTON AND ANOTHER, APPELLANTS, v. BIGELOW, RESPONDENT.

SUPREME COURT, FIRST DEPARTMENT; GENERAL TERM, JANUARY, 1883.

§§ 413, 647, 649.

Foreign corporation.—Shares of stock of, having its office, factory, etc., in the State of New York, owned by non-resident, may be attached in this State.

Ordinarily, when neither the owner of certain shares of the stock of a corporation, nor the corporation itself, can be found within this State, an attempt to attach the shares would be entirely ineffectual, for the reason that the shares themselves would not be within the county in which the attachment might be issued, and the sheriff, in executing the attachment, could only seize the property of the debtor, which might be found in that county.[1]

Where one of the objects of a corporation, formed under the laws of the State of Pennsylvania, was to transact business in the city and county of New York, and its chief place of business was located there, and it manufactured its goods, made its business arrangements, paid its bills, and carried on its general business there, and two of its three directors were residents of the city of New York,—*Held*, that it placed itself by its operations, in the county of New York,[2] and its stock was, therefore, actually within this State, and as such, subject to the satisfaction of the owner's obligations to his creditors,[3] and might be lawfully seized under an attachment.[10]

The provision of the Code allowing the shares of the stock of an association or corporation, to be levied upon under an attachment, has in no manner been confined in its effect to corporations formed under the laws of this State,[4] and the shares may be attached whenever the requirements of the Code can be complied with.[6, 10]

Where the office, factory, business and affairs of a corporation, organized under the laws of the State of Pennsylvania, are located and conducted here, its stock may be properly deemed to be in this State, so that it may be attached here by a creditor of its owner.[12]

The fact that the time limited for the commencement of an action for the collection of a debt appears to have expired before the action was commenced, will not justify an order vacating an attachment issued in it. The objection can only be taken by answer.[11]

Southern Life Insurance Co. *v.* Packer (17 *N. Y.* 51), followed ;[5] Moore *v.* Gennett (2 *Tenn. Ch.* 375),[7] Steel *v.* Smith (7 *Watts & S.* 448), [8] Danforth *v.* Penny (3 *Metc.* 564), [9] distinguished.

(*Decided March* 19, 1883.)

Appeal from an order of the special term, discharging a levy upon certain shares of the stock of the Hat Sweat Manufacturing Company.

The plaintiffs and the defendant are non-residents of this State. The plaintiff procured a warrant of attachment to be issued in this action, and the sheriff served it upon an officer of the Hat Sweat Manufacturing Company, a corporation organized under the laws of the State of Pennsylvania, at an office kept by it for the sale of goods in the city of New York, and gave the company notice that he attached the defendant's shares of stock in the company and required the secretary to furnish him with a certificate of the number of shares of stock owned by the defendant.

The defendant moved to vacate this levy, and the motion was granted, and from the order thereupon entered, this appeal was taken.

Further facts are stated in the opinion.

Edward D. Bettens (*Bettens & Lilienthal*, attorneys), for appellants.

Simon Sterne (*Sterne & Thompson*), for respondent.

DANIELS, J.—The plaintiffs, who resided in the State of Massachusetts, brought this action to recover the amount unpaid upon promissory notes made by the defendant. The demands were such as were the proper subject of an attachment under the provisions of the Code, and the plaintiffs were entitled to institute their suit for the recovery of the amounts claimed in this court. And for the purpose of obtaining satisfaction they could lawfully avail themselves of all the legal remedies provided by the Code for that purpose (Hibernia National Bank *v.* Lacombe, 84 *N. Y.* 367, 385). Under this authority they had a right to seize whatever property or interests the law of this State rendered the subject of attachment. And by virtue of its provisions the sheriff in form levied upon the shares owned by the defendant in a corporation formed under the laws of the State of Pennsylvania, and known as the Hat Sweat Manufacturing Company. This seizure was set aside, on motion of the defendant, for the reason that the shares were not deemed subject to the power or operation of the attachment. Whether this decision was correct is the chief point in controversy upon this appeal. Ordinarily, when neither the owner of the shares nor the corporation itself can be found within this State, the attempt to make a seizure [ ] of this nature would be entirely ineffectual. For the sheriff, in executing an attachment, can only seize the property of the debtor which may be found in this county, and where the owner of the shares, as well as the corporation issuing them resides and is located in another State, the shares themselves would not be within the county in which the attachment might be issued, and for that reason would be incapable of being levied upon by means of it. But this was not a case of that description. For while the corporation was formed under the laws of the State of Pennsylvania, one of its objects was to transact business in the city of New York, and as a matter of fact its chief place of business was there located, where it manufactured goods, made its business arrangements, paid its bills and carried on its general business and two of its three directors were residents of the city of New York. For this purpose its capital to a very considerable extent certainly must have been brought to this State and invested in such business, and the profits to be derived by it and from which the dividends would be made upon its stock would in that manner be obtained from this State. To that extent it enjoyed all the rights and privileges of a domestic corporation, and ['] placed itself by its operations within the county in which the plaintiff's attachment was afterwards issued. So far as defendant was the owner of the shares of the corporation he himself was interested through them in its capital and the business carried on by it (Burrall *v.* Bushwick R. R. Co., 75 *N. Y.* 211). His stock, of which the certificates held by him were evidence of his title, was actually, therefore, within this State, and as such should be subjected to the satisfaction of his obligations ['] to his creditors. There could be no more reason for exempting his shares from late obligations than there would be if the corporation itself had been organized and existed under the laws of this State. For its business pursuits were carried on substantially the same as if this particular corporation had been created under its laws. There was clearly no substantial difference upon which the owner of such shares could claim immunity. The purpose and object of the corporation was the manufacture and sale of its fabrics, and that business is shown to have been confined to the city of New York. It was here carried on by the corporation through its officers and agents. To that extent, it located itself in this city, as it was contemplated it might under its articles of incorporation, and it was consequently a corporation within this county.

The law has provided in general language that the "rights or shares which the defendant has in the stock of an association or corporation, together with the interests and profits thereon, may be levied upon" under an attachment (*Code Civil Pro.* § 647). This section has in no manner been confined in its effect to corporations formed under the laws of this State. It is of course [4] to be construed with section 644, requiring the property to be levied upon to be within the county, and that is the only restraint to which this general enactment has been subjected. And the association or corporation whose shares may be so levied upon, may as well under this language be one formed under the laws of another State as though it was formed under the laws of this State. And that this section was intended to be so construed is evinced by the circumstance that when a discrimination is intended to be made, the Code by its provisions has designated the particular corporation as either domestic or foreign corporations.

And care has been taken to preserve this distinction by a definition to that effect given in the Code itself

(*Code Civ. Pro.* § 3343, subd. 18). By this definition what shall be known as a domestic corporation has been declared, and every other is denominated a foreign corporation. Where no such discrimination as that has been made and the language is appropriate for that purpose, it is therefore to be presumed that it was intended to include all corporations, and that employed in the section already referred to is of that character. A provision of a like general nature was considered in Southern Life Insurance Co. *v.* Packer (17 *N. Y.* 51), [*] and it was held to include corporations formed in other States as well as those created under the laws of this State, and no reason appears for distinguishing the present case from the principle of construction established by that authority.

The Code has prescribed the particular manner by which the shares of the defendant in a corporation may be seized under an attachment, and that is the only qualification to which the exercise of this authority has been subjected. To make such a seizure, a copy of the attachment, with notice showing the property attached, is to be left with the president or other head of the association or corporation, or secretary, cashier or managing agent thereof (*Code Civ. Pro.* § 649, subd. 3).

Whenever the corporation, by means of its operations in business, may be within the county in which the attachment has been issued, and these requirements [*] can be observed there, the Code has provided for the seizure of the shares owned in it by the defendant. This is all that has been provided for to constitute a literal compliance with all the provisions made on this subject by the statute. When that may be done it was clearly the intention of the law that such shares might be effectually levied upon by means of the attachment.

It has been stated generally, in a recent work upon this subject, that the right to attach the shares of a

defendant in a corporation is restricted to those corporations existing under the laws of the State in which the attachment may be issued (*Drake on Attach-*
[7] *ments*, 5th ed. § 244). This general statement of
the law was made upon the authority of Moore *v.* Gennett (2 *Tenn. Ch.* 375), and it was so generally considered in the opinion of the court; but the case was not determined upon that point, for it appeared that the interest of the defendant in the shares themselves was neither in fact nor in form levied upon under the attachment.

No lien upon or title to the shares could therefore be maintained, and for that reason principally the right and claim of the creditor was rejected. The inability of the creditor to attach the debtor's shares in a corporation created under the laws of another State was maintained, so far as it was considered, substantially upon the authority of Steel *v.* Smith (7 *Watts & S.* 448).
[8] But that is in no sense an authority upon this point.
It was an action upon a judgment recovered in the State of Louisiana, where the suit was commenced by a seizure of the debtor's property; and this was held to create no personal liability against the debtor upon which the action could be maintained. These authorities, consequently, do not maintain the general statement of the law made by this authority. It undoubtedly would be a correct statement of it where neither the debtor himself nor the corporation by which the stock was issued to him should be within the State when the attachment was issued. But such were not the facts of this case as they have been presented by the affidavits; for here the corporation had voluntarily placed itself within this State, where its active and principal
[9] business operations were contracted. The case of
Danforth *v.* Penny (3 *Metc.* 564), is entitled to no broader application. For the statute under which it arose was so construed as to be intended to place cor-

porations on the same footing as to liablity as that of individuals, which had previously been held not to include the residents and inhabitants of any other State. It is no authority for limiting the provisons of the Code so far as to exclude a case of the nature of that now before the court.

What the law may be upon this subject is necessary for the legislature to declare, and when that declaration has been plainly made, it is the duty of the courts to follow and enforce it, even though it may not be in strict accord with the views expressed upon the same subject by the courts of a neighboring State. The legislative purpose as to attachment proceedings has been clearly defined by the provisions which have been made in this State, and by them the shares of a defendant in a corporation have been rendered the subject of seizure by virtue of an attachment whenever the proceeding particularly specified can be taken and followed. This was a case of that description, for one of the resident directors of the corporation, whose shares were owned by the defendant, was its treasurer and secretary, and in the seizure of the shares a copy of the attachment, together with a notice that those shares were levied upon, was served upon this officer, and to promote the proceedings, as he was required by the law to do, that he made his certificate stating the number of shares owned by the defendant in this corporation. The terms, as well as the
spirit of the statute, were fully complied with;
[10] and as the corporation carried on its business, and
had the bulk of its property in this county, that
was all which could be required for the lawful seizure of the shares under the attachment.

The fact that by the provisions of the statute prescribing the time within which an action for the
[11] collection of a debt may be instituted, may appear
to have expired before this suit was commenced,
will not justify the order from which the appeal has

been taken; for, by section 413 of the Code of the Civil Procedure, this objection can only be taken by answer. This section is clearly imperative, and renders an examination of the authorities relied upon by the respondent on this subject unnecessary at this time.

The case is an important one, and it is known as a matter of fact that the learned judge by whom the order was directed from which the appeal has been taken entertained grave doubts as to its propriety. If it should be sustained in this instance, then every creditor, whether a resident or not a resident of the state, would be deprived, in cases of this description, of the power, through the intervention of its tribunals, to obtain satisfaction of their debts simply because the corporation prosecuting its business enterprises within this State had elected to organize itself under the laws of another State. The distinction between this corporation and a corporation formed under the laws of this state, in view of the other facts made to appear, was simply nominal, and the consequence should be held legally to follow that the debtor, profiting in the same manner by the operations of the corporation as he would if it had been formed under the laws of this State, should not be exempt from the compulsory means provided by law for satisfying his debt. Such a distinction should not be made without some provision in the law indicating the necessity of its adoption. No such provision has been inserted in the Code as it now exists. But those which have been enacted plainly require a different view to be taken of their effect.

The order, for these reasons, should be reversed, and an order entered denying the motion made by defendant, but without costs.

Davis, P. J.—[Concurring.]—I concur on the ground that for all practical purposes the Hat Sweat Manufacturing Company may be treated in this case as though it were a domestic corporation. Though organized under the laws of Pennsylvania, yet its office, factory, business and affairs are located and [11] conducted in this State. Its stock may be properly deemed to be in this State. So that it may be attached here by a creditor of its owner. The question is not free from doubt, but it seems to me proper to solve the doubt in favor of the plaintiff.

ADAMS & ANOTHER v. BOWE, AS SHERIFF, ETC.

N. Y. MARINE COURT; SPECIAL TERM, MARCH, 1883.

§ 1266.

Sheriff.—Must at once execute writ placed in his hands.—Return of execution and payment of money made on it substantially one and the same thing.—When to make return of satisfaction.—Action against, for money had and received, when maintainable.—Cannot take collateral security.

The sheriff must execute every writ placed in his hands with the utmost expedition and without favor, refraining from undue force or violence.[1] In the case of an execution, it is his duty upon its receipt by him to indorse upon it the year, month, day and hour when he received it, and then execute its mandates immediately and in every particular.[1]

The return of an execution and the payment of the money made on it are substantially one and the same thing, and the sheriff can not claim to hold the money after he has made his return.[2] In contemplation of law, the money is paid when the return is made.[3]

It is the duty of the sheriff to make his return of the satisfaction of an execution immediately upon the payment of the amount due.[4] The sheriff is *functus officio* the moment the execution has been satisfied.[5]

Where an execution was paid on August 5, and the judgment

creditor brought an action on August 7, against the sheriff, for money had and received to his use,—*Held*, that it must be assumed that the sheriff had complied with the law and immediately indorsed a return of satisfaction;[6] that his duties being performed, the money became payable without demand, and the plaintiff having made a demand, his action could not be deemed premature.[6] *Held*, also, that whether the sheriff had made his return or not was unimportant in view of the character of the action, and that the action was unquestionably maintainable.[7]

Where a sheriff levied upon certain personal property of a judgment debtor under an execution and subsequently released it upon receiving from the judgment debtor a certified check, accompanied by a letter stating that the check was to be deemed a security to him and to be held by him for sixty days,—*Held*, that the taking of any such collateral security by the sheriff was wholly beyond his power and authority.[9,11,13] The sheriff cannot be a stakeholder, neither can he be the agent of the judgment debtor in any phase.[9,11] The certified check so given was clearly tantamount to money,[8,12] and came within the grasp of the execution and was the property of the plaintiff [12,13] and was held by the sheriff for his use and benefit, and the plaintiff had a clear right of action to recover it as such.[13]

(*Decided March* 7, 1883.)

Action against sheriff for money had and received by him to plaintiff's use.

The opinion states the facts.

William W. Badger, for plaintiff.

Charles McLean, for defendant.

Hawes, J.— There is no substantial dispute as to the facts of this case. The plaintiff recovered a judgment for costs against the New York, West-shore and Buffalo R. R. Co., issued execution thereon, and, on August 5, 1882, delivered the same to the sheriff, the defendant herein. On August 5, the defendant made a levy upon the office furniture of the company, and the company, not willing to have their office furniture removed, and desiring to take some legal steps looking to a modification or reversal of the judgment, gave a certified check to the defendant or his deputy for the full amount of the execution; but it appears that when this payment was made a letter was sent by the company to the sheriff to the effect that this check was to be deemed a security for him, and to be held by him for sixty days; and it must be assumed, I think, that the sheriff assented to this arrangement.

On the 7th, and also on the 8th of August, plaintiffs demanded payment of the sheriff, which was refused. This action was commenced on the 9th of August, 1882, and is brought to recover the amount of the execution, as money had and received by the defendant for the plaintiff's use. The defendant claims that no right of action existed on the 9th of August, and that, under provisions of section 1366 of the Code he has sixty days in which to make his return, and pay the money; and further, that the plaintiffs have no claim upon the money thus paid, inasmuch as it was not to be applied upon the execution, but was held by the sheriff as collateral security only, and to procure the release from actual custody of the property levied upon, and it was not the intention of the judgment debtor or the sheriff that the money so paid should be applied upon the execution. The counsel of the sheriff states that this has always been the custom of the office.

And in a case where some error has been committed as to the judgment or the execution, or where ready relief from any cause could not be procured from the court, such an act on the part of the sheriff would certainly seem to be both benevolent and justifiable, provided he had the power under the statute to exercise such a discretion. Under the early English law, the sheriff represented the earl or court in the administration

of the county government, and had all the authority for the administration and exercise of justice which the earl had. Deriving his authority directly from the king, he was not only an officer of great antiquity, "the government of the county being committed to his charge and care," but he was necessarily clothed with certain discretionary and judicial functions. The wide authority once exercised by the sheriff, however, has been seriously modified, and he is now a mere ministerial officer, whose duties are clearly defined by statute, and whose functions are restricted by the court, whose
[1] officer he is. He must execute every writ placed in his hands with the utmost expedition, and without favor, refraining from undue force or violence. In the case of an execution, it is his duty upon its receipt by him to indorse upon it, the year, month, day and hour, when he received it, and then to execute its mandates immediately and in every particular, and with faithful but prudent energy, and if he thus performs his duty the law protects him, even though the execution be irregular (assuming, of course, that it has been issued by a court of competent jurisdiction). But while the law protects him, it exacts, in turn, the most implicit obedience on his part. The statute provides, that the sheriff shall make a return of the execution within sixty days, which must contain a statement of the proceedings taken on the execution. Now it is quite clear that this return, under the old practice, brought in the result of the sheriff's effort as well as its history, and that the payment of the money into court, if it had been made, was an inherent part of the "return." The ancient writ commanded the sheriff "to have the money before our justices on the return day." In *Bacon's Abridgment* (title Execution), it is said that the sheriff cannot deliver the goods to the plaintiff in satisfaction of his debt, but the goods are to

be sold, and the money, in strictness, is to be brought into court." This rule has long since been relaxed, and by acquiescence or permission of the court, rather than by strict force of law, the sheriff is permitted to pay the money directly to the plaintiff. It is clear, therefore, from this brief reference, that the re-
[*] turn and payment are substantially one and the same thing; and that the sheriff can no longer claim the right to hold the money after he has made his return, whoever may be entitled to first receive it. This point being necessarily conceded, we can next inquire, when is the sheriff compelled to make his return. The mandate states that it must be "within sixty days after its receipt by you." The elementary writers all state that no action against the sheriff will lie until the expiration of the sixty days (*Crocker on Sheriffs*, 375; *Freeman on Executions*, 448), and the case of Cassidy v. Meacham, 3 *Paige*, 311, declares that "although a sheriff might lawfully return an execution before the return day, yet such return did not take effect until after the return day had passed, and then was good by relation, and that no bill could be filed until after the return day in such a case (see also Williams v. Hogeboom, 8 *Paige*, 469, and Spencer v. Cuyler, 9 *Abb. Pr.* 382 ; Renaud v. O'Brien, 35 *N. Y.* 29 ; Tyler v. Willis, 33 *Barb.* 327, to the same effect). Since the adoption of the Code, I have been unable to find any case where the doctrine set forth in Cassidy v. Meacham is held. Supplementary proceedings, as well as creditors' bills in equity, are all founded upon returns which have been made by the sheriff within the sixty days, and they cannot now be questioned collaterally, and the return can only be attacked for fraud or collusion. A claim that there was any statutory prohibition as affecting the sheriff, or the vitality of the return would not be seriously considered, and the sheriff having the right to return the execution within

the sixty days, the money which had been realized
[3] upon the execution, would then be clearly due
and payable. Chapter 6 of the Laws of 1860 provides that upon receipt by the sheriff of the amount due upon the execution, he shall, on demand, deliver a copy of such execution, and of his indorsement of satisfaction thereon, and that upon the filing of such execution, so endorsed, the clerk shall enter satisfaction of such judgment. This statute is substantially embodied in section 1266 of the Code. It is clear
[4] that it is the duty of the sheriff to make this return of satisfaction immediately upon the payment of the amount due, and it would not be seriously claimed that he could hold the money after the execution was satisfied, for it has been repeatedly held
[5] that the sheriff is *functus officio* the moment the
execution is satisfied. The word "immediately," in section 1266 of the Code is tantamount to the words "on demand" in the statute of 1860, and cannot be misunderstood. In the case at bar, the money was paid on August 5, and it must be assumed that the sheriff complied with the law, and immediately indorsed a return of satisfaction. His duties were performed,
[6] and the money became payable without demand
(Nelson v. Kerr, 59 *N. Y.* 224). In contemplation of law the money is paid when the return is made. The plaintiffs, however, demanded the amount from the sheriff on August 7, and the action cannot be deemed premature.

In this connection I may say, further, that, in my opinion, the right of action accrued at that time, without regard to the provision of the Code or the statute above cited; for if the execution was in fact satisfied, the money so held by him was not his, but belonged, in equity and good conscience, to the plaintiff, and he could at once maintain an action against the sheriff for money had and received to his use. Whether the

[*] sheriff had made his return or not, is unimportant in view of the character of the action here brought, and no question can be raised that such an action is not maintainable (Armstrong *v.* Garrow, 6 *Cow.* 465). But it is claimed by defendant that the execution was never satisfied, but that the check or money was received by him from the judgment debtor, as collateral security merely, and that it was paid by the judgment debtor under a written notice that it was to be so held, and was not to be applied on the execution.

It does not affirmatively appear that the sheriff assented to this arrangement, or that any such contract was entered into; but even if it had been, and I have assumed that such was the fact, yet, I fail to discover what authority the sheriff had to so deal with the execution. The levy in this case was made and perfected, and presumably upon sufficient property to satisfy the execution. There was no claim of a third party, and no legal reason is suggested for his delay in enforcing the execution. It is not claimed that the property was placed in the hands of a "receiptor" under the well settled rules which would warrant such an act on the part of the sheriff. Every intendment must be assumed that a public officer performs his duty. Now what is the fact in this case? The sheriff voluntarily relinquishes the levy, and accepts the defendant's check for the amount of the execution. The pleadings would seem to imply that the sheriff held money and
[*] not a check, but in my view of the case it is quite unimportant whether the judgment debtor gave a *check or money*, both being assumed upon the argument to be collateral security. It is clear that he has relinquished the levy and accepted the check. Now if the sheriff had the legal authority to receive this money as collateral security merely, then the plaintiff is remediless in this action; for the execution would have been operative at the time action was brought, and the

defendant could not have pleaded the levy as a satisfaction. Upon a careful examination, I think it will [*] be found that the sheriff has no power to make such a contract, and if he did make such a contract as a matter of fact, I am of the opinion that the law will deem it invalid. The sheriff cannot be a stakeholder, neither can he be the agent of the judgment debtor in any phase (See Wright *v.* Child, 1 *Ex.* 358). The duties and powers of the sheriff are often discussed in the early reports. In Codwise *v.* Field (9 *Johns.* 263), the coroner gave a *receipt in full*, agreeing to pay the plaintiff in consideration of a debt due from the coroner to the judgment debtor. Held, no satisfaction, as beyond the power of the coroner; otherwise if the coroner had received the money. In Hoyt *v.* Hudson (12 *Johns.* 207), the officer took security for the debt,—Held, that it constituted payment, and the execution was satisfied. This case is quite conclusive upon the point at issue, in so far as the reason of the rule would tend to establish it (See Clark *v.* Wiltus, 2 *Ld. Raym.* 1072; 1 *Salk.* 322;* Ladd *v.* Blunt, 4 *Mass.* 403; Reed *v.* Pruyn, 7 *Johns.* 428; Sherman *v.* Boyce, 15 *Johns.* 443). It can be well said that all these cases have arisen after the return had been made, and the sheriff is necessarily estopped by his return. There is no case which I have been able to find in the English or American decisions where this question has arisen before the return, and we are therefore compelled to consider it a new question in so far as the want of precedent would make it such. I think, however, that there are general principles underlying the powers and duties of a sheriff, which will be equally conclusive as decided cases, and I am disposed to consider these principles as elementary. The sheriff has the undoubted right to extend favors to the judgment debtor, in case he does not come within the inhi-

* Perkins *v.* Woolaston.

bitions of the statute, and he may, in his discretion, refrain for a reasonable time before selling the property, provided, always, that he grants no such delay as would preclude him from making a final return, on or before the expiration of the sixty days. And the court has no power to compel such sale, nor will the court instruct the sheriff (Bowie *v.* Brahe, 4 *Duer*, 676; Morange *v.* Edwards, 1 *E. D. Smith*, 415). But while this is true, it will be found that the reason of the rule lies in the fact, that the duty of the sheriff is defined and circumscribed in the very writ itself. The law has determined his duty, and the court, therefore, neither instructs nor interferes.

The duty of the officer is to make the levy upon the property of the judgment debtor within his county, but if he has once made a levy sufficient to satisfy
["] the execution, he cannot make a second levy, and if the levy has been made upon sufficient property the debtor is forever discharged, and can plead the levy as a bar, and the proof of such a fact will constitute a good and sufficient defense to any subsequent action in that behalf. Moreover, all the property of the defendant within the bailiwick, whatever its character, is subject to the execution, and whenever defendant's property comes within the insatiable grasp of the execution it is at once absorbed. This arises from the inherent character of the process, for by operation of law property so seized ceases to be the property of defendant, and is transmuted into the property of the plaintiff, subject only to the power of sale, on the part of the sheriff. The sheriff cannot in any sense
["] whatever act as the agent of the debtor, for his authority is measured by the power lodged in the writ, and that is clear and well defined. Applying these principles to the case at bar, it will be seen that the sheriff received a certified check from the defendant, claimed by the sheriff to have been given to him only

as collateral security. By what right, or by whose authority can he receive such a check upon these conditions? His authority is restricted to taking defendant's property for the purpose of satisfying the execution. If he yielded his levy upon the office furniture, he clearly elected to take the check, and resorted to that for the satisfaction of the execution. A certified check is
[12] clearly tantamount to money, and it was the plaintiff's money at that moment. The case of Reed *v.* Pryne, *supra*, holds in substance that a sheriff cannot take a security and still hold the execution, although other questions were involved in that case. It seems to me, that in the very nature of things, the security so-called ceases to be security the moment it comes within the operative power of the execution. The theory of "forthcoming bonds" which are provided for in some statutes is not inconsistent with this view, for they derive their life from the statute; they are eqnal in dignity to any other process, and are not in any sense an outgrowth or incident to the execution. But were it otherwise, it will not be claimed that the rules governing "receiptors" or forthcoming bonds are applicable to the case at bar. It may be further added, that if the position of the sheriff is correct, then this check was given for his (the sheriff's) protection, and being so taken the sheriff would, presumably, have some implied authority in law to enforce the obligation, in case of failure on the part of the judgment debtor. Every wrong has a remedy, and this presumption of law that the sheriff must in the nature of things have power to realize upon his collateral security can arise only upon the assumption that the sheriff whose powers are circumscribed by the writ, could use the writ already in his hands to enforce payment upon his own collateral; but the law will not tolerate that an officer shall wield the process of the courts in his own favor in order to exact such a measure of justice as he may think due to himself.

A sheriff cannot do execution when he himself is a party, and therefore an extent by him when he is a co-user will be void (*Com. Dig.* Viscount, E, 1). He need not be a party to the record but it is equally fatal if he is beneficially interested (2 *R. S.* 441, § 84).

Judge PLATT, in Sherman *v.* Boyce, *supra*, declares "that it would not only lead to oppression and abuse but would tend to subvert the foundation of private rights and of civil liberty." It is clear, therefore, that the sheriff holding this check as collateral security in his own behalf could not enforce it by virtue of the execution, or in fact, in any way as sheriff. But if the right is not enforceable it can safely be said by the simplest syllogistic reasoning that such a right does not exist, and that the sheriff, while acting as such, never received any money for his own protection, and he clearly had no authority to receive it in behalf of any one else.

From every phase of this case, so far as I have been able to examine it in the absence of any precedent or authority, I am convinced that the taking by the sheriff of any such collateral security as was testified to in this case was wholly beyond his power or ["] authority, and that by operation of law the money so paid came within the grasp of the execution and was the property of the plaintiff, and was held by the sheriff for his use and benefit, and that the plaintiff had a clear right of action to recover it as such.

Judgment for plaintiff, with costs.

VELIE *v.* THE NEWARK CITY INSURANCE CO. AND ANOTHER.

SUPREME COURT, THIRD DEPARTMENT; ULSTER COUNTY SPECIAL TERM, FEBRUARY, 1883.

§§ 481, 546.

Complaint.—Several grounds or reasons for the relief demanded may be set up in complaint.—When plaintiff will not be required to make complaint more definite and certain.

When a plaintiff has two or more distinct and separate reasons for the obtainment of the relief he asks, or when there is some uncertainty as to the grounds of recovery, the complaint may set forth a single claim in several distinct counts or statements, and an election should not be compelled.[1, 2, 3, 4, 5, 6,]

The complaint in an action to recovery on a contract of insurance for loss by fire alleged that one C., plaintiff's assignor, was the owner of the property insured and destroyed, at the time of its insurance and destruction, subject "to a mortgage owned by the defendant Thompson to secure the payment of $2,250." *Held*, on a motion by the defendant, who insured, that the complaint be made more definite and certain as to the interest of Thompson in the insured property, that the allegation was definite, certain and clear, and could not be made more so by additional averments.[7]

Talcott *v.* Van Vechten, (25 *Hun*, 565);[6] Jones *v.* Palmer (1 *Abb. Pr.* 442), [6] followed.

Motion by defendant, the Newark City Insurance Company, to compel the plaintiff to elect between two separate statements of a single cause of action, and also to make the complaint more definite and certain.

The facts are stated in the opinion.

G. A. Clement, for motion.

John J. Levison, opposed.

WESTBROOK, J.—The plaintiff, John W. Velie, as the assignee of Giles W. Cowley, seeks to recover of the defendant, the Newark City Insurance Company, the sum of $1,250, with interest from January 4, 1882, that being a portion of the loss which Cowley is alleged to have sustained in the destruction by fire, of certain property of which he was then the owner.

The complaint states separately two grounds, or reasons, for the liability of the insurance company: first, that such defendant in consideration of $25 paid to it by said Cowley, issued to him its policy of insurance, by which it agreed to insure him for the term of one year from December 24, 1881, against loss or damage by fire, upon certain property described in the policy, and fully set out in the complaint, to the amount of $1,250; and, second, That the said insurance company, by its duly authorized agents, Messrs. Ogden and Little, of Middletown, Orange county, N. Y., on or about December 24, 1881, for a consideration agreed to be paid by the said Cowley, promised and contracted to insure the said Cowley against loss or damage by fire to the same property, to the extent of $1,250, for the period of one year, and to issue its policy therefor.

The complaint also avers that by the policy of insurance, the loss, if any, was "first payable to John A. Thompson, mortagee, as interest may appear;" that Cowley was the sole owner of the property insured and destroyed, both at the time of its insurance and of its destruction by fire on January 4, 1882, subject, however, to a mortgage thereon owned by the defendant, Thompson, to secure the payment of $2,250; and that the insurance company has not paid the amount of the insurance to Thompson, nor has Thompson brought any suit to recover the same, and that the company refuses and neglects to make such payment.

The insurance company by this motion asks: first,

that the plaintiff shall be compelled to elect and decide whether he will rely for a recovery upon the written policy of insurance, or upon the agreement to insure and to issue a policy; and second, that the complaint should state more definitely and certainly the interest of Thompson in the insured property. Should the relief asked, or any part thereof, be granted?

The question, which the application to compel the plaintiff to elect between the two grounds of recovery stated in the complaint, presents, is this: When a plaintiff has really two distinct and separate reasons for the obtainment of the relief demanded in the complaint, and states each one therein separately and plainly, or where, as is probably the case in this instance, the plaintiff and his attorney are somewhat uncertain as to the exact ground of recovery the proof may afford, and therefore frame a complaint for the recovery of a single claim in several distinct counts or statements, so as to meet the proof, should an election be compelled?

In the discussion of this question, it must be admitted that the defendant has several reported cases which support his proposition (Gardner *v.* Locke, 2 *N. Y. Civ. Pro.* 252; Comstock *v.* Hoeft, 1 *N. Y. Law Bulletin*, 43; Dickens *v.* N. Y. Central & Hudson R. R. R. Co., 13 *How. Pr.* 228).* Some of the reported cases were rightly decided upon other grounds than that which holds that a party plaintiff must be limited to a single statement of facts giving him a right to the relief demanded, when in truth there are other facts also entitling him to such relief, or when more than one statement is necessary to meet any contingency of the trial. The soundness of the rule compelling an election has never favorably impressed me,

* See also Dorr *v.* Mills, *ante*, 7; Churchill *v.* Churchill, 9 *How. Pr.* 552; Walker *v.* Ruskin, 12 *Id.* 28.

['] and reflection upon the present motion has fully confirmed those impressions. In the discussion of a legal problem there generally are several reasons tending to a certain conclusion, all of which counsel in argument would present; and so, in the trial of a cause, there generally are distinct and separate lines of fact tending to give the same one relief asked, which a careful pleader should embody in the complaint. It would seem to be absurd for a judge to limit counsel to the presentation of a single reason upon the argument of a legal proposition, and to me, at least, it seems equally absurd to limit a party to the statement in his complaint of one line of facts establishing his right [*] of recovery, when he has really several, or when the court can plainly see, as it can in this case, that different averments are proper to meet an emergency of the trial, which cannot be foreseen prior to its occurrence. Take, for instance, the case of a party who is heir-at-law of a deceased testator, seeking, under section 1537 of the Code, to partition and to recover property held under an alleged will.

The reason which he assigns in his complaint for a recovery is, that the apparent devise, under which the property is held, is void, because: first, the testator was legally incompetent to make a valid will; second, that the instrument, alleged to be a will, was procured by fraud and undue influence; and, third, that the execution thereof was insufficient and defective. In a case like the one just put, or in one like that before us, in which it is often very difficult to decide whether a policy of insurance has actually been issued, or whether there has been only an agreement for insurance and for a policy, can any good reason be adduced for com- [*] pelling the plaintiff in advance of a trial, or even at the trial, to elect upon what ground he will stand and present his case? If either or both are tried, the proof upon each ground of recovery stated may be close

and conflicting. A jury of twelve men may be divided in opinion as to which one is established, while all may unite, some for one reason, and some for another, in the conclusion that the plaintiff is entitled to recover. If, under such circumstances as have been stated, an election is compelled, justice may fail and wrong succeed. It is no answer to this argument to say, that if the plaintiff is unsuccessful, another action can be brought setting up a ground of recovery not pressed upon the first trial. The right to bring a second action for the same subject matter, though for a different cause, is more than doubtful; but even though the judgment in the first action is no bar to the second, why should a party fail in the relief to which he is in fact entitled, and which he would have obtained on the first trial, if he had been allowed to state his whole case in the complaint, and be subjected to the delay, cost and vexation of a new trial, by the adoption of a rule, which limits the complaint to the statement of a single reason or ground for a recovery. The second trial, too, might fail, if the issue was limited by the court compelling an election, because twelve men could not agree to sustain a recovery upon that single reason or ground. The practical effect of the rule is obvious. A plaintiff may often fail to obtain that which is his due, because he presents his grounds of recovery singly, when he might succeed if they were all presented in one suit; and often, though he may succeed in the end, he has suffered in costs, delay and vexation, which could and should have been avoided. A defendant may present as many defenses as he has to a single claim, though, on the face of the answer, they may seem to be inconsistent, and no good reason can be given, why a plain
tiff may not present by his complaint as many
['] different statements of distinct lines of fact as he
has, or as he supposes himself to have, giving him the right to the relief which he asks. It, undoubtedly,

is the interest of the defendant to limit the plaintiff in every action, as is now sought to be done by this motion, but as in the administration of justice every argument should be weighed and every pertinent fact considered, it cannot be conceded that, on the trial of an issue of fact, a plaintiff should be limited in his facts to a single ground of recovery, any more than upon the discussion of a legal problem, he should be limited to the statement of a single argument.

The point which has been discussed is not new to the judge writing this opinion. In Talcott *v.* Van Vechten, the plaintiff sought to make the defendant liable for a debt due the former from "The Olcott Iron Company." The complaint alleged, in two separate statements, two distinct lines of fact tending to make the defendant liable for that demand. On a motion made at special term to compel the plaintiff to elect between the two, such motion was denied upon the ground (stated in a memorandum) that it was "the right of the plaintiff to set forth all the facts, which made the defendant liable," and that the statement [*] of "two distinct grounds of liability" for "only one cause of action" was proper. On appeal to the general term of the third department, this decision was affirmed (25 *Hun*, 565). In this department the question argued must therefore be deemed settled.

Perhaps one other thought on this point may be separately added, though it has already been suggested. It is impossible for a party or his counsel to know in advance of a trial the exact facts of a case. It is often difficult in an action like the present to determine whether there was an actual insurance, or a simple agreement to insure and deliver a policy. There may be danger in presenting the case upon a single ground, while a recovery may be certain if the plaintiff is allowed to present both. Many other cases of like uncertainty will readily recur to the mind of a practicing

lawyer. Why then, it may well be asked, unless justice is to be hampered, should a party be compelled to do that which may result in his defeat, when justice and right require his success? So to construe and interpret the Code defeats its entire object, which was to simplify and make easy, and not to perplex the administration of justice. Precisely this view of this question was taken many years ago by Judge COWLES, with the concurrence of the judges of the general
[6] term, in Jones *v.* Palmer (1 *Abb. Pr.* 442), and it seems to be so clearly right as to preclude discussion.

But a single word need be added upon the second application—that to compel a more definite statement as to the interest of John A. Thompson in the insured property. It is difficult to see how the complaint could be made more explicit in that particular. It is distinctly stated that he held a mortgage at the time of the fire to secure the payment of $2,250. What effect,
[7] if any, this fact may have upon the rights of the plaintiff is not before me, and is not determined. The allegation is definite, certain and clear, and cannot be made more so by additional averments.

The motion of the defendant must be denied, but without costs, as the moving party is sustained in its practice by several adjudged cases.

HEIDELBACH v. KILPATRICK & ANOTHER.

SUPREME COURT, FIRST DEPARTMENT; SPECIAL TERM FEBRUARY, 1883.

§ 501.

Counter-claim.—Claim for work done upon certain property, for plaintiff cannot set up as, in action for damages for false representations inducing purchase of such property.

In an action for damages resulting from false representations, by which plaintiff was induced to purchase certain real property, a demand arising upon a contract for work done upon the premises so purchased at the request of the plaintiff, has no such connection with the cause of action, as to entitle it to be set up as a counter-claim to defeat or diminish plaintiff's claim.

(*Decided February* 9, 1883.)

Demurrer to counter-claim.

The complaint alleges that the defendants in the month of September, 1880, for the purpose of inducing plaintiff to purchase a dwelling-house in the city of New York, known as No. 48 East Fifty-eighth street then owned by them and in the course of erection falsely stated and represented to her that it "was or would be by them furnished in a complete workmanlike manner with all modern improvements, that the plumbing work was to be made perfect, and that, in connection with said plumbing, the drains in said house were in perfect order and the sewer connections within and without said house were fully protected against the escape of sewer gas in said house." It also avers that the plaintiff, relying upon said representations and believing them to be true, contracted to, and did thereafter, purchase said house for the sum of $38,000; that she would not have purchased it but for said statements and representations; "that after such purchase, and after plaintiff had entered into possession and occupancy of said dwelling-house, she ascertained that said statements and representations were not true and that said drains were not provided with proper appliances, and that said sewer connections were not properly made, but that on the contrary they were either entirely missing or so defective as to cause foul and unhealthy odors to arise and to escape into said house and into the rooms occupied by plaintiff's family, whereby their health and safety were seriously threatened, and in consequence whereof plaintiff's family were compelled to remove from said house until certain alterations and repairs could be made so as to render said house safe and habitable;" and sets forth the damage resulting therefrom.

The answer denies each and every allegation of the complaint and sets up a counter-claim in words following: "For a counter-claim defendants allege that plaintiff is justly indebted to defendants for the sum of $550, moneys paid out and expended by defendants at the request and for the benefit of plaintiff between the 1st day of September, 1880, and the 1st day of January, 1881, which said moneys were expended in reference to the buildings Nos. 48 and 50 East Fifty-eighth street in the city of New York in improvements in the plumbing thereof contracted for in the contract of purchase set forth in the complaint between plaintiff and defendant, and which is the subject of the action herein." To this counter-claim the plaintiff demurred.

Adolph L. Sanger, for the demurrer.

Kelly & MacRae, opposed.

VAN VORST, J.—The complaint sets up a cause of action growing out of certain representations made by the defendants to induce the plaintiff to purchase property, and relying upon the truthfulness of which, and influenced thereby, the plaintiff made the purchase.

The complaint sets up that the representations were false, and that in relying and in acting upon them she claims to have sustained injury and damage.

The action is not upon the contract for the purchase and sale, but is founded upon the defendants' wrongful misrepresentations, extrinsic to the contract.

These observations are rendered necessary, to meet the suggestion made by the learned counsel for the defendants, that the action may be regarded as one for a breach of warranty.

The action, upon the principal facts stated in the complaint, is clearly not founded upon the contract, nor the breach thereof; but the subject of the action is the injury sustained through the defendant's false representations.

To this cause of action the defendants interpose as a counter-claim, a demand arising out of a contract for work done upon the premises, sold by the defendants to the plaintiff, and for moneys paid by the defendants therefor at the plaintiff's request.

This course cannot be approved. The counter-claim authorized by the Code must tend in some way to diminish or defeat the plaintiff's recovery (*Code Civ. Pro.* § 501).

Under that section, a cause of action, arising out of the contract or transaction set forth in the complaint as the foundation of the plaintiff's claim, or connected with the subject of the action, may be interposed by a defendant.

The transaction of which complaint is made in the plaintiff's pleadings is the making, by the defendant, of false representations, and the subject of the action is the redress to which plaintiff is entitled by acting upon them, in the belief that they were true.

With that matter the alleged counter-claim has no such connection as to entitle it to be here set up, to defeat, or diminish the plantiff's claim for damages (Lehman *v.* Griswold, 40 *N. Y.* 100; Berrian *v.* Mayor, &c., 15 *Abb. Pr. N. S.* 297; People *v.* Dennison, 84 *N. Y.* 272, 279).

Conceding that the defendant did the work to the amount claimed, it is no answer to, and in no manner diminishes, the plaintiff's claim for her peculiar injury and damage sustained through the cause, and in the manner alleged.

There must be judgment for the plaintiff on the demurrer, with liberty to the defendants to withdraw their counter-claim on payment of costs.

NOTE ON COUNTER-CLAIM.

By Montgomery H. Throop.

I. History of the Legislation relating to Counter-claims.

The word "counter-claim" first made its appearance in the statute in 1852, in an amendment to subdivision 2 of section 149 of the Code of Procedure (the former Code). Subdivision 2 of section 128 of the Code of 1848 provided for setting forth in the answer "a statement of any new matter constituting a defense, in ordinary and concise language," &c. This expression was retained in section 149 of the Code of 1849, which took the place of section 128 of the Code of 1849, until 1851, when the words "or set-off" were added after "defense," and in the next year—1852—the word "counter-claim" was substituted for "set-off," and the section, as thus amended, continued unchanged, until it was repealed in 1877, in consequence of the enactment of section 500 of the Code of Civil Procedure—subdivision 2 of which is an exact transcript of the corresponding subdivision of section 149 of the former Code.

In the same year—1852—section 150 of the Code of 1849 (section 129 of the Code of 1848) was also amended, by adding the introductory sentence and subdivisions 1 and 2; which are now represented by section 501 of the Code of Civil Procedure, the original section 150 being represented by section 507 of the present Code. Section 150 also remained unchanged until it was repealed in 1877; and the two sections mentioned constituted the only provisions of the former Code defining a counter-claim. It was said in several cases, that the expression "counter-claim" embraced both set-off and recoupment. Clinton *v.* Eddy, 1 *Lans.* 61; Wilder *v.* Boynton, 63 *Barb.* 547; Vassear *v.* Livingston, 13 *N. Y.* (3 *Kern.*) 248; affirming S. C., 4 *Duer,* 285; Chamboret *v.* Cagney, 32 *N. Y. Super. Ct.* (2 *Sweeney*) 378; and numerous other cases. But nevertheless the distinction between the three was maintained, and has not even yet been entirely abandoned. Crennan *v.* Underhill, 13 *Weekly Dig.* 432; Elwell *v.* Skiddy, 77 *N. Y.* 282. And under the former Code, the provisions of the Revised Statutes relating to set-offs were regarded as applying to counter-claims, as far as they were consistent with the Code itself. But now, by the enactment of sections 502 to 506 of the Code of Civil Procedure, and the repeal of the provisions of the Revised Statutes relating to set-offs, the term set-off in pleading is practically abolished, and the statutory provisions upon that subject relate solely to counter-claims.

II. Analysis of the existing Statutory Provisions relating to Counter-claims, and correspondence thereof to the Provisions of the Revised Statutes relating to Set-offs.

The provisions of the Code of Civil Procedure, defining and regulating counter-claims, are contained in sections 501 to 506. Section 501 corresponds closely to the introductory clause and subdivisions 1 and 2 of section 150 of the former Code, as amended in 1852; except that the words "must tend in some way to diminish or defeat the plaintiff's recovery," and the words "or, in a proper case, against the person whom he represents," were added to the introductory clause. The effect of the latter expression will be subsequently considered. The former was designed to reflect, generally, the ruling of the court in National Fire Ins. Co *v.* McKay, 21 *N. Y.* 191; and the remarks of EARL, Com., in Waddell *v.* Darling, 51 *N. Y.* 327; by embodying the principles thus declared in the statute, so as "to exclude certain causes of action, having no connection whatever with that set forth in the complaint, and which could not in any way affect the judgment upon the latter, although the literal reading of the statute would allow them to be interposed; as, for instance, where, in an action to foreclose a mortgage, the defendant set up as a counter-claim a demand on his part for the foreclosure of a mortgage upon a different piece of property." *Throop's Annotated Code Civ. Proc.* note to § 501. See also Agate *v.* King, 17 *Abb. Pr.* 159.

Section 502 superseded the provisions of the Revised Statutes, defining set-offs, being those contained in 2 R. S. 354, part 3, ch. 6, tit. 2, § 18; which section, and also sections 19 to 28 of the same title of the Revised Statutes, were repealed by the general repealing act of

1877. Of the eleven subdivisions of section 18 of the Revised Statutes, the first six, and part of subdivision 7, were regarded by the framers of the new Code, as having been superseded by section 150 of the Code of Procedure, and as useless under the corresponding provisions of section 501 of the present Code; so that they have no substitutes in the present statutes. The remainder of subdivision 7, and subdivisions 8, 9 and 10, are represented by the section under consideration, it having been the intention of the framers of the new Code to preserve them unaltered in any matter of substance, so far as they were consistent with the existing system of pleading and procedure. Section 502, as reported by the commissioners, and enacted in 1876, also contained a fourth subdivision, which was a substitute for subdivision 11 of section 18 of the Revised Statutes. It provided that in an action by a receiver, or the trustee of an insolvent or imprisoned debtor, a counter-claim could not be allowed, except in cases where it was specially prescribed by law that a set-off might be allowed in such an action; the reference being chiefly to 2 R. S. 47, §§ 36–38, and 2 R. S. 469, §§ 67–74; which were left unrepealed by the general repealing acts of 1877 and 1880, and are still, at least nominally, in force. But subdivision 4 was stricken out by the amendatory act of 1877, so that a grave question arises, whether such of the last cited provisions of the Revised Statutes as relate to set-offs are not repealed by implication, and the cases for which they provide left to be regulated by subdivision 3—a question which must probably be answered in the affirmative.

Sections 19 and 20 of the same title of the Revised Statutes were inconsistent with the present system of pleading, and are consequently not represented in the Code of Civil Procedure. The phraseology of sections 21 and 22 of the Revised Statutes was also not adapted to the new system; but the provisions of those sections affected the rights of the parties, and to that extent they are preserved in sections 503 and 504. The last sentence of section 503 is new; it covers a case which was left doubtful by the authorities under the former statute.

Section 505 of the Code of Civil Procedure represents section 25 of this title of the Revised Statutes, with only such alterations of phraseology as the present system of procedure required; the substance of the original having been preserved.

Section 506 of the Code represents sections 23 and 24 of the Revised Statutes, with similar alterations only. A suggestion made by FOLGER, Ch. J., in Jordan *v.* National S. & L. Bank, 74 *N. Y.* 467, respecting the effect of the alteration of the language of the original is considered subsequently in this note.

III. General Requisites to the validity of a Counter-claim.

(1) To render a counter-claim admissible, it must, by the terms of section 501 of the Code of Civil Procedure, be a cause of action "against the plaintiff, or, in a proper case, against the person whom he represents." The expression "the person whom" the plaintiff "represents" is, in general, intended to apply to the special cases of assignees, executors, &c., for which the statute provides in sections 502, 505 and 506; but it includes also any case where a plaintiff, who sues as the representative of another, is liable to be charged with a counter-claim against the latter. Thus, where a principal sues to recover the price of goods sold for him by a factor in the latter's own name, a counter-claim in favor of the defendant against the factor, which accrued, although by assignment, before the defendant knew that the vendor was a mere factor, is admissible. Judson *v.* Stilwell, 26 *How. Pr.* 213; Pratt *v.* Collins, 20 *Hun*, 126.

A counter-claim, in order to be available to the defendant, must be for a good cause of action; and accordingly section 494 allows the plaintiff to demur to a counter claim, "on the ground that it is insufficient in law, upon the face thereof;" and, if the defendant demands an affirmative judgment upon his counter-claim, section 495 allows a demurrer for the same causes as those for which a demurrer lies to the complaint, having regard to the difference between the character of the pleadings and the situation of the parties. But if the counter-claim is not admissible, the plaintiff is not bound to demur; he may take the objection at the trial. And if he puts in a reply to an inadmissible counter-claim, he is not concluded thereby from objecting to its admissibility as matter of law. Smith *v.* Hall, 67 *N. Y.* 48; overruling Hammond *v.* Terry, 3 *Lans.* 186, and Ayres *v.* O'Farrell, 10 *Bosw.* 147; People *v.* Dennison, 84 *N. Y.* 273; Carpenter *v.* Manhattan L. Ins. Co., 22 *Hun*, 49. And in such a case the record does not preclude the defendant from maintaining a new action upon the counter-claim. People *v.* Dennison, 84 *N. Y.* 272.

As a general rule, the admissibility of a counter-claim, under the provision of section 501 which has been quoted, is to be tested by the question whether, at the time when the action was commenced, an action, legal or equitable (*Code Civ. Proc.* § 507), could have been maintained upon it against the plaintiff; so that the defendant cannot maintain his counter-claim, unless he has a good cause of action which belonged to him, and was payable by or otherwise enforceable against the plaintiff, at the time of the commencement of the action. Heidenheimer *v.* Wilson, 31 Barb 636; Vassear *v.* Livingston, 13 *N. Y.* (3 *Kern.*) 248; affirming S. C., 4 Duer, 285; Merrick *v.* Gordon, 20 *N. Y.* 93; Robinson *v.* Howes, 20 *N. Y.* 84; Myers *v.* Davis, 22 *N.*

Note on Counter-claim.

Y. 489; reversing S. C., 26 *Barb.* 367; Patterson *v.* Patterson, 59 *N. Y.* 574; modifying S. C., 1 *Hun,* 323; Pittman *v.* Mayor, &c., 62 *N. Y.* 637; affirming on opinion below, S. C., 3 *Hun,* 370; Senear *v.* Woods, 74 *N. Y.* 615; Taylor *v.* Mayor, &c., 82 *N. Y.* 10; affirming S. C., 20 *Hun,* 292; Denniston *v.* Trimmer, 27 *Hun,* 393.

But the test, as to ability to maintain an action, relates to the nature or state of the demand, and the sufficiency of the right of action; not to any special regulation suspending or otherwise temporarily affecting the remedy. Thus, where, by the charter of a municipal corporation, an action cannot be maintained against it, until after presentation of the claim and demand of payment from some officer, this does not prevent the defendant, in an action by the corporation, from interposing a counter-claim which has not been thus presented, and payment thereof demanded. Taylor *v.* Mayor, &c., 82 *N. Y.* 10; affirming S. C., 20 *Hun,* 292; and see other illustrations in the opinion of FOLGER, Ch. J., in the same case. See, however, Town of Guilford *v.* Cooley, 58 *N. Y.* 116, apparently contra in part. So it was held that a judgment of a justice of the peace was a proper counter-claim, although an action would not lie upon it under section 71 of the Code of Procedure. Clark *v.* Story, 29 *Barb.* 295. So in an action by the people of the State, the defendant may have a counter-claim allowed to him, although the people cannot be sued; but only to the extent necessary to defeat the people's claim; for an affirmative judgment for the balance cannot be taken against the people. People *v.* Dennison, 84 *N. Y.* 272.

But where the counter-claim is of such a character that our courts would not have jurisdiction of an action upon it, as where it is for damages sustained by waste on land without the State, it cannot be allowed. Cragin *v.* Lovell, 88 *N. Y.* 258; 2 *N. Y. Civ. Proc. Rep.* 128; reversing S. C., 22 *Hun,* 101. In an action against a municipal corporation by the assignee of an officer, to recover his salary, the defendant may have a counter-claim for moneys unlawfully appropriated by the officer, notwithstanding that chapter 49 of the Laws of 1875 (now sections 1969 *et seq.* of the Code of Civil Procedure) vests such a right of action in the people. In an action by the assignee of a banker, the defendant may maintain a counter-claim arising upon a certificate of deposit given by the plaintiff's assignor, although by its terms it is payable only on presentation and demand, which were not made until after the assignment. Seymour *v.* Dunham, 24 *Hun,* 93. See also New Amsterdam Savings Bank *v.* Tartter, 4 *Abb. N. C.* 215 (Sup'm Ct. Sp. T.).

The bar created by the statute of limitations is deemed, for the purposes of this test, to affect the right, and not the remedy. De Lavalette *v.* Wendt, 75 *N. Y.* 579; per FOLGER, Ch. J., in Taylor *v.* Mayor, 82 *N. Y.* 10. But where one of the parties having mutual claims becomes a bankrupt, and the statute has not run against a debt due by him when an assignee is appointed, the other party may insist upon a counter-claim therefor, in an action by the assignee to recover his debt, although the statute has then run. Von Sachs *v.* Kretz, 72 *N. Y.* 548; affirming S. C., 10 *Hun*, 95.

A counter-claim is inadmissible, although it might be the subject of an action between the parties, if in order to maintain such an action it would be necessary to bring in other parties who are not before the court; as for instance where it consists of advances to a copartnership of which the plaintiff, the defendant and a third person were members (Cummings *v.* Morris, 25 *N. Y.* 625; affirming S. C., 3 *Bosw.* 560; Coursen *v.* Hamlin, 2 *Duer*, 513; Goodwin *v.* Conklin, 6 *Weekly Dig.* 131); or a cause of action against a firm of which the plaintiff is a member, even if it arises out of the same transaction (Mynderse *v.* Snook, 1 *Lans.* 488); or a cause of action owned by the defendant and a third person not a party (Kiersted *v.* West, 13 *Week. Dig.* 106, Sup'm Ct. Gen. T.). But where, although a joint action would lie against the plaintiff and a third person, yet the right of action is several, the defendant is entitled to his counter-claim. More *v.* Rand, 60 *N. Y.* 208. And *semble*, that unless the third person's interest appears on the face of the answer, the plaintiff must set it up in a reply. Schubert *v.* Harteau, 34 *Barb.* 447. *Contra*, Mynderse *v.* Snook, 1 *Lans.* 488. And *semble*, that a defendant cannot maintain a counter-claim which is inconsistent with his defense, as where he successfully defends an action to compel him to fulfill a contract on the ground of failure of the other party to fulfill, and then seeks to enforce the contract. Walker *v.* Millard, 29 *N. Y.* 375.

Where the plaintiff is bound to divide the recovery with a third person, not a party, a demand against the latter is not admissible as a counter-claim. Pittman *v.* Mayor, &c., 3 *Hun*, 370; affirmed without opinion, S. C., 62 *N. Y.* 637. Nor is a counter-claim against all the members of a corporation admissible in an action by the corporation. N. Y. Ice Co. *v.* Parker, 8 *Bosw.* 688.

(2) Section 501 also requires that the cause of action must be "in favor of the defendant, or of one or more defendants, between whom and the plaintiff a separate judgment may be had in the action."

Thus, in an action to recover the purchase price, brought by the vendor against the surety for the vendee, the defendant cannot sustain a counter-claim for damages for breach of warranty or fraud on the sale, as the cause of action is not in favor of the defendant, but personal to the vendee. Hendry *v.* Daley, 17 *Hun*, 210. And, in an action between co-sureties for contribution, the defendant cannot have a counter-claim for an indebtedness of the plaintiff to the principal. O'Blenis *v.* Karing, 57 *N. Y.* 649; Davis *v.* Toulmin, 77 *N. Y.* 280.

In an action against principal and sureties, to recover upon an undertaking given upon replevying a chattel, the sureties cannot maintain a counter-claim for a debt due from the plaintiff or his assignor to the principal. Coffin *v.* McLean, 80 *N. Y.* 560. But see Springer *v.* Dwyer, 50 *N. Y.* 19.

This provision is identical in meaning, and almost in language, with the corresponding provision of section 150 of the former Code which effected a material change in the law, for, under subdivision 6 of section 18 of the Revised Statutes, if there were two or more defendants, the demand set off must have been due to all of them jointly. Under this provision, in an action to foreclose a mortgage, where a surety for the mortgagor had executed a joint bond with him for the mortgage debt, and judgment for the deficiency was asked, against both, it was held that both might sustain a counter-claim for a debt due from the plaintiff to the mortgagor, because a several judgment might be taken. Bathgate *v.* Haskin, 59 *N. Y.* 533; reversing S. C., 5 *Daly*, 361.

Where, upon a joint sale of goods to three persons by the plaintiff, each gave a separate note for his share of the purchase money, held, that in an action upon one of the notes, the defendant could not be allowed a counter-claim for breach of warranty and fraud in the sale, as that cause of action belonged to the three jointly. Hopkins *v.* Lane, 87 *N. Y.* 501. See also Newell *v.* Salmons, 22 *Barb.* 247; Peabody *v.* Bloomer, 5 *Duer*, 678; S. C., 6 *Duer*, 53. Hurlbut *v.* Post, 1 *Bosw.* 28; Nat. St. Bk. *v.* Boylan, 2 *Abb. N. C.* 216; Bockover *v.* Harris, 43 *N. Y. Super.* (11 *J. & S.*) 548; Baldwin *v.* Briggs, 53 *How. Pr.* 80; Baldwin *v.* Berrian, 53 *How. Pr.* 81; Clegg *v.* American N. Union, 60 *How. Pr.* 498.

But where an insolvent banking firm had executed to the plaintiff a general assignment in trust for creditors, including their individual and copartnership property, and the individual debts had been paid out of the individual property, it was held, in an action to recover moneys held, under a will, in trust for one of the partners, to which the plaintiff had become entitled by the death, since the assignment, of the person to whom the income was payable during life, that the defendants were entitled to a set-off for moneys deposited by them with the assignors before the assignment. Shipman *v.* Lansing, 25 *Hun*, 290. But this decision was rested, not on the words of the statute, but on general principles of equitable set-off.

Note on Counter-claim.

(3) By subdivision 1 of section 501, a counter-claim may be allowed, where it consists of "a cause of action, arising out of the contract or transaction, set forth in the complaint as the foundation of the plaintiff's claim, or connected with the subject of the action." This subdivision is a literal transcript of subdivision 1 of section 150 of the former Code, added in 1852, which worked a great change in the law, for it allowed counter-claims for torts, and in actions for torts, which were not admissible under the former statute. But the precise meaning of this phrase is yet unsettled. In Glen & Hall Man. Co. *v.* Hall, 61 *N. Y.* 226; reversing S. C., 6 *Lans.* 158, DWIGHT, Com., delivering the opinion of the court, said: "The subject of an action is either property (as illustrated by a real action) or a violated right." And in this case, where an action was brought to restrain the defendant from using a trade-mark, and the defendant set up that it was his own trade-mark, and asked, by way of counter-claim. for a judgment restraining the plaintiff from using it, and for damages for the use already made of it, the court held that this was a good counter-claim, as being "connected with the subject of the action," which was the trade-mark. In Chamboret *v.* Cagney, 32 *N. Y. Super.* (2 *Sweeny*) 378; S. C., 10 *Abb. Pr. N. S.* 31; 41 *How. Pr.* 125; and in Lehmair *v.* Griswold, 40 *N. Y. Super.* (8 *J. & S.*) 100, the court defined "the subject of the action" as "the facts constituting the plaintiff's cause of action;" and in each case, in an action for a tort, disallowed a counter-claim for an independent tort, though it was committed with respect to the property affected by the tort for which the plaintiff sued.

So in People *v.* Dennison, 84 *N. Y.* 272, the allegation in the complaint was that the defendant fraudulently obtained money from the State by false representations, false vouchers, and collusion with certain State officers, in and about the performance of a contract to do certain work on the Erie canal. The defendants set up, as a counter-claim, that the State was indebted to them for work and materials furnished on the same contract. It was held, that the counter-claim was not admissible, as it did not arise out of the transaction set forth in the complaint, nor was it connected with the subject of the action: that the subject of the action was the fraud, which was wholly distinct from the defendants' claim; and the circumstance that the latter arose in the course of the same work with respect to which the fraud was committed, was immaterial.

In an action by a grantee to set aside a junior conveyance as a cloud on the plaintiff's title, it having been recorded before the plaintiff's conveyance, the defendant may ask, by way of counter-claim, that the plaintiff's deed be set aside as fraudulently procured, on the ground that it is a cause of action arising out of the transaction set forth in the complaint. Moody *v.* Moody, 16 *Hun*, 189. Where the action was to recover damages for converting certain cord-wood, and the defendant, by way of counter-claim, alleged that it held a mortgage on the land on which the wood was cut, and the plaintiff, a junior mortgagee in possession, knowing that the land was an inadequate security for the debt, and intending to defraud the defendants, committed waste by cutting the wood, and thereupon claimed a judgment for damages, held, that although ordinarily, in an action to recover damages for a tort, a tort committed by the plaintiff cannot be interposed as a counter-claim, yet in this case the counter-claim was good, as being connected with the subject of the action, which was "the wood converted." Carpenter *v.* Manhattan L. Ins. Co., 22 *Hun*, 49. In this case, the court added: "It is not easy to define what was intended by such a general phrase as 'connected with the subject of the action.' Such language does, however, plainly indicate a design to enlarge the scope of the old rule relating to set-off and recoupment, and to authorize an application of the equitable principle, that cross claims, growing out of the same matter or controversy, should be determined in one action, and that the balance only, found to be due, should be recovered. To that end, the provision cited should receive a liberal interpretation. See Thompson *v.* Kessel, 30 *N. Y.* 389; Fettrech *v.* McKay, 47 *Id.* 427; Isham *v.* Davidson, 52 *Id.* 240."

Under sections 5197, 5198 of the United States Revised Statutes, where usury has been taken by a national bank, the defendant, in an action upon a security discounted for him, may have a counter-claim for the full amount of the interest taken (National Bank *v.* Lewis, 75 *N. Y.* 516); but the penalty of double the usurious interest taken cannot be set up as a counter-claim, but must be recovered in a penal action brought for that purpose. F. & M. Nat. Bk. *v.* Lang, 22 *Hun*, 372; reversed on another point, S. C., 87 *N. Y.* 209.

In an action against the trustee under a will, alleging the invalidity of the trusts of real property created thereby, and praying for a judgment, declaring the title to the real property to be in the plaintiff under the will, the defendant in his answer insisted on the validity of the trusts, and alleged as a counter-claim, that the plaintiff had unlawfully received the rents and profits, and demanded an affirmative judgment for an accounting and the establishment of the trusts. Held, that the subject of the action was the construction of the will and the validity of the trusts, and that the counter-claim was connected therewith, and so allowable. O'Brien *v.* Garniss, 25 *Hun*, 446.

Before the enactment of section 1770 of the Code of Civil Procedure, it was held, that in an action for a divorce, the alleged adultery was the subject of the action, and therefore that the defendant could not set up a counter-claim, either for a separation or for a divorce, by reason of the plaintiff's misconduct. Diddell *v.* Diddell, 3 *Abb. Pr.* 167 (Sup'm. Ct. Sp. T.); R. F. H. *v.* S. H., 40 *Barb.* 9 (Gen. T.). For an illustration of the existing rule under section 1770, see Finn *v.* Finn, 62 *How. Pr.* 83.

In an action to recover for the services of the plaintiff's assignor as attorney and counsel for the defendant, held, that the subject of the action was the contract of employment, and that the defendant might have a counter-claim for malpractice in an action other than that on which the plaintiff counted as the foundation of his claim. Harlock *v.* Le Baron, 1 *N. Y. Civ. Pro. R.* 168 (Sup'm. Ct. Sp. T.).

See also as to the construction of this provision, Kelley *v.* Bernheimer, 3 *T. & C.* 140; Edgerton *v.* Paige, 20 *N. Y.* 281; 10 *Abb. Pr.* 119; Thompson *v.* Kessel, 30 *N. Y.* 383; Sandford *v.* Travers, 40 *Id.* 140; Isham *v.* Davidson, 52 *Id.* 237; Elwell *v.* Skiddy, 77 *Id.* 282; Lazarus *v.* Heilman, 2 *N. Y. Civ. Pro. R.* 204 (N. Y. C. P. Sp. T.).

(4) Subdivision 2 of section 501 provides that a counter-claim is sufficient, if it is "in an action on contract, any other cause of action on contract, existing at the commencement of the action. This is also an almost literal transcript of the corresponding subdivision of section 150 of the former Code, which swept away various nice distinctions as to the nature of admissibility of set-offs in particular cases arising under the provisions of the Revised Statutes. It is now well settled that this subdivision is entirely independent of subdivision 1; so that if a counter-claim arising upon a contract, express or implied, fulfills the conditions of the introductory clause of the section, it is admissible in an action upon a contract, express or implied, subject, of course, to the provisions of sections 502, 505, and 506, although it has no connection with the cause of action, or "subject of the action." Parsons *v.* Sutton, 66 *N. Y.* 92; affirming 39 *N. Y. Super.* (7 *J. & S.*) 544. And this subdivision is exclusive of every action other than an action on contract, and of every counter-claim other than one founded upon a contract. So that in an action for a penalty, there can be no counter-claim. Denniston *v.* Trimmer, 27 *Hun*, 393. And in an action to recover for services, the defendant cannot sustain a counter-claim, founded upon the liability of the plaintiff, as a trustee of a corporation, to the defendant as a creditor of the corporation, by reason of a failure to make and file an annual report; for such a liability does not rest upon contract. Clapp *v.* Wright, 21 *Hun*, 240; Piser *v.* Stearns, 1 *Hilt.* 86. But a judgment is a contract, and, therefore, in an action upon a contract, the defendant may have a

counter-claim for a judgment in tort. Taylor *v.* Root, 4 *Keyes*, 335. Where, however, an appeal is taken from a judgment, the right to set off the same is suspended until the determination of the appeal. Hardt *v.* Shulting, 24 *Hun*, 345. This case, however, arose upon a motion to offset the judgment, and it may be doubted whether the same rule applies to a counter-claim under the statute.

But questions of considerable difficulty, as to which the authorities are not entirely clear and uniform, frequently arise under the present system of pleading, where the cause of action or counter-claim is founded upon a tortious act relating to property, which the party might, at common law, waive, and sue for his damages in assumpsit. In such a case, the weight of authority seems to establish the following rules.

First. That in an action upon contract, the counter-claim is good, if the party interposing it might have brought an action upon it, either in tort or assumpsit, and that he may sustain it as a counter-claim, even upon a statement of the facts, identical with the statement which would be required to render his complaint good in an action to recover damages for the tort. Andrews *v.* Artisan's Bank, 26 *N. Y.* 298; Coit *v.* Stewart, 50 *Id.* 17; Wood *v.* Mayor, &c., 73 *Id.* 556; McDougall *v.* Walling, 48 *Barb.* 364; Brown *v.* Tuttle, 66 *Barb.* 169; Harway *v.* Mayor, &c., 1 *Hun*, 628. *Contra*, Mayor *v.* Parker Vein S. S. Co., 8 *Bosw.* 300; 12 *Abb. Pr.* 300; 21 *How. Pr.* 289; Piser *v.* Stearns, 1 *Hilt.* 86; Berrian *v.* Mayor, &c., 15 *Abb. N. S.* 207. And see Miller *v.* Barber, 66 *N. Y.* 558; affirming S. C., 4 *Hun*, 802.

Secondly. But where the plaintiff sues upon a transaction of the same nature, and his complaint indicates that he relies on its tortious character, and seeks to recover his damages for the tort, the defendant cannot interpose any counter-claim whatever, unless it comes within subdivision 1 of section 501. Fishkill Sav. Institution *v.* National Bank, 80 *N. Y.* 162; affirming S. C., 19 *Hun*, 354; People *v.* Dennison, 84 *N. Y.* 272; Lehmair *v.* Griswold, 40 *N. Y. Super.* (8 *J. & S.*) 100; Smith *v.* Hall, 67 *N. Y.* 48. And see Austin *v.* Rawdon, 44 *N. Y.* 63, therein distinguished; Chambers *v.* Lewis, 11 *Abb. Pr.* 510; 25 *How. Pr.* 293; Henry *v.* Henry, 17 *Abb. Pr.* 411.

(5) Subdivisions 1 and 2 of section 502 regulate the allowance of a counter-claim, in an action by an assignee of a cause of action. They are identical in meaning with 2 R. S. 355, § 18, subd. 8, 9, with such changes of phraseology only in subdivision 1, as were required in order to adapt the statute to the provision allowing the assignee of a contract to maintain an action in his own name. Incidentally, however, the enactment of these subdivisions, in connection with the words "or . . . . the person whom he represents," in section 501,

has apparently abrogated a ruling made in some cases under the former Code, to the effect that a demand against the assignor could not be made the subject of a counter-claim, though it might be set off, and, therefore, that a reply was not necessary where such a set-off was interposed. But in Crennan *v.* Underhill, 13 *Weekly Dig.* 432 (Sup'm. Ct. Gen. T.), decided in 1881, the court seems to have overlooked or disregarded this change in the statute, and the former rule was applied, although it is by no means clear that the supposed former rule was well founded. Von Sachs *v.* Ketz, 10 *Hun*, 95; Isham *v.* Davison, 52 *N. Y.* 237. Under subdivision 1, or under the former statute, in an action by an assignee, the defendant cannot offset a demand against the assignor, which was not payable when the cause of action was assigned. Martin *v.* Kunzmuller, 37 *N. Y.* 396; affirming S. C., 10 *Bosw.* 16; Bailey *v.* Martin, 65 *N. Y.* 558; Myers *v.* Davis, 22 *Id.* 489; Murray *v.* Deyo, 10 *Hun*, 3; Coffin *v.* McLean, 80 *N. Y.* 560.

Where a contract between the plaintiff's assignors and the defendants, for work to be done by the former on a railroad, provided that the defendants might require the contractors to make up and notify them of the amounts due the laborers for each month, whereupon the defendants would pay the laborers, and deduct the money so paid from sums payable to the contractors; but no such requirement had been made; held, that the defendants could not be allowed a counter claim for sums due to the laborers, although paid by them, because they were not liable therefor; but they might have a counter-claim for the laborers' board bills, paid by them at the request of the assignors, though after notice of the assignment; it appearing that such was the custom between them and the contractors, and that by the terms of the assignment the work was to go on as before. Sevear *v.* Woods, 74 *N. Y.* 615. See also Shipman *v.* Lansing, 25 *Hun*, 290, cited in this note. *ante.*

In Stilwell *v.* Carpenter, 62 *N. Y.* 639, better reported in 2 *Abb. N. C.* 238, it was held, that although while a non-negotiable obligation,—*e. g.*, a judgment,—is held under assignment to a third person as collateral security for a debt, the right of a debtor to set off an obligation in his favor subsequently accruing,—*e. g.*, a judgment recovered by him against the judgment creditor,—is suspended, yet, on the satisfaction of the assignee's claim, the right of set-off arises, although the latter judgment was recovered after the assignment.

In an action by the general assignees of a banker who had become insolvent, to recover upon a promissory note, which was past due at the time of the assignment, where the defendant had deposited money with the banker, and received a certificate of deposit therefor, payable on the return of the certificate; it was held, that he might set off the amount of the deposit, although the certificate was not presented until after the assignment. Seymour *v.* Dunham, 24 *Hun*, 93, cited also *supra.*

The right of a bank, holding a protested bill of exchange, to set off the same against an undrawn deposit of the drawer, although suspended while the paper is held by one, to whom the bank has transferred it, and who had a lien thereon, revives when the lien is extinguished, and the bank repossesses itself of the paper, and may be enforced against an assignee of the deposit, where the bank repossessed itself of the paper without notice of the assignment. Robinson *v.* Howes, 20. *N. Y.* 84.

(6) Subdivision 3 of section 502 regulates a counter-claim in an action by a trustee or a nominal plaintiff; it is identical in effect with subdivision 10 of section 18 of the Revised Statutes, except that the words "a demand against the plaintiff shall not be allowed as a counter-claim; but" have been added. These words represent a provision of subdivision 7 of the same section, which has always been regarded as applying to the plaintiff in his personal, as distinguished from his representative, capacity. Thus it was held under the Revised Statutes, that where a person indebted to the estate in a receiver's hands was employed by the receiver to render necessary services for the estate, he might have a counter-claim for the value of his services in an action to recover the debt. Davis *v.* Stover, 58 *N. Y.* 473. So where a debtor to the estate was sued by the executrix upon a demand which accrued after the testator's death, it was held, that he might have a counter-claim for necessary funeral expenses paid by him, though not for a demand due from the testator in his life-time. Patterson *v.* Patterson, 59 *N. Y.* 574; modifying S. C., 1 *Hun*, 323.

Where a person, having a paid-up policy of insurance upon his own life, purchased, after the appointment of a receiver for an insurance company, land mortgaged to the company, and assumed the mortgage, held, that he could not maintain an action to redeem the mortgage upon the payment of the amount due, less the value of his policy. Waring *v.* O'Neill, 15 *Hun*, 105.

(7) Section 503 of the Code of Civil Procedure represents, without any substantial change, sections 21 and 22 of this title of the Revised Statutes, with the addition of the last sentence, which settles a point as to which the authorities under the former statute were not entirely clear. The provision of the Revised Statutes (2 R. S. 236, part 3, ch. 2, tit. 4, § 57) prohibiting a defendant in a justice's court who neglects to interpose a set-off, which might have been allowed in the action against him, from subsequently maintaining an action in

the same demand, was not, nor is its substitute,—section 2947 of the Code of Civil Procedure,—applicable to the defendant in a court of record, who may, in a case within subdivision 2 of section 501, and also in a case within subdivision 1 of the same section, unless the circumstances are such that the record would necessarily conclude him, elect, either to interpose his demand as a counter-claim in the action against him, or to maintain an independent action thereupon. Brown *v.* Gallaudet, 80 *N. Y.* 413. And the rule is not changed by the fact, that in the former action the complaint gave the defendant credit for the counter-claim, and demanded judgment for the balance only, where it appeared that the defendant in that action did not avail himself of the credit, and the verdict therein was for the full amount of the plaintiff's demand. *Ib.*

But if, in the action against him, the defendant relied, in his answer, upon a counter-claim against the plaintiff, exceeding the amount of the plaintiff's demand, but did not demand judgment for the excess, and established the same on the trial, but took judgment only for costs, he cannot afterwards recover the excess; and *semble,* that it makes no difference which action was first commenced. Inslee *v.* Hampton, 11 *Hun,* 156. See also Draper *v.* Stouvenel, 38 *N. Y.* 219; O'Beirne *v.* Lloyd, 43 *Id.* 248.

(8) Section 504 of the Code of Civil Procedure is a substitute for so much of the amendment of 1851 to section 263 of the former Code as relates to equitable actions. This provision had no representative in this title of the Revised Statutes, as the latter did not apply to equitable actions ; but it followed necessarily from the provision of section 150 of the former Code, allowing an equitable counter-claim, which is now represented by section 507 of the Code of Civil Procedure.

In framing section 504 of the Code of Civil Procedure, the corresponding provision of section 263 of the Code of Procedure was qualified by adding the words "demanded in the answer," which were inserted in accordance with section 509; and those words, in connection with section 509, constituted a new statutory provision. But *semble,* that a similar rule was implied from the former statute. Equitable Life Ass. Co. *v.* Cuyler, 75 *N. Y.* 511; affirming S. C., 12 *Hun,* 247. See also Barthet *v.* Elias, 2 *Abb. N. C.* 364 (N. Y. Sup'm. Ct. Sp. T.). Where a counter-claim in an equitable action goes merely to the reduction of the plaintiff's demand, a prayer for affirmative judgment is not necessary. *Ib.;* and Van Brunt *v.* Day, 81 *N. Y.* 251; reversing S. C., 17 *Hun,* 166.

(9) Section 505 of the Code of Civil Procedure regulates counter-claims in actions against executors, administrators, and other persons sued in a representative character. It is substantially identical with

section 25 of the title of the Revised Statutes under consideration. The reason for the special regulations in this section, and those now represented by section 506 of the Code of Civil Procedure, is that the set-off, "if allowed, would alter the course of administration." Per NELSON, Ch. J., Hills *v.* Tallman, 21 *Wend.* 674. It was held that where an administrator, after the rendition of a judgment against him, as administrator, for a debt of the intestate, purchased a judgment against the plaintiff, and took an assignment to himself as administrator, the two judgments could not be set-off against each other on motion. *Ib.* And see Dudley *v.* Griswold, 2 *Bradf.* 24. But where the public administrator of New York had a sum to his credit as such, in a bank, when it failed, and was indebted to the bank in his individual capacity, it was held that, as between him and the receiver, he was entitled to set off the deposit against the debt, and also to set off bills of the bank in his hands; because he could not sue or be sued as public administrator, but only as administrator of the particular estate to which the suit related. Miller *v.* Receiver of Franklin Bank, 1 *Paige*, 444.

(10) Section 506 relates to counter-claims in actions by executors or administrators, and provides that in such a case, the counter-claim may be allowed "as if the action had been brought by the decedent in his lifetime;" and it regulates the judgment and execution if the balance exceeds the plaintiff's demand. It is a substitute for sections 23 and 24 of the same title of the Revised Statutes; and was intended to reproduce those provisions without substantial change. Section 23 of the Revised Statutes provided, that in such cases a set-off might be allowed "in the same manner as if the action had been brought by and in the name of the deceased." And in Jordan *v.* National Shoe & Leather Bank, 74 *N. Y.* 467, affirming S. C., 12 *Hun*, 512, a doubt was suggested by FOLGER, Ch. J., whether section 506 of the Code requires, as it was there ruled that section 23 of the Revised Statutes required, that in an action by an executor or administrator, a demand against the decedent cannot be set off unless it was due and payable in the decedent's lifetime.

But it is believed that the question must be answered in the affirmative, whenever it is presented in such a form as to require an answer; not only upon consideration of the general policy of the two sections, and their substantial correspondence with those of the Revised Statutes, but also upon the literal reading of section 506 of the Code; for if "the action had been brought by the decedent in his lifetime," the executor or administrator, instead of being the original plaintiff, would have become the plaintiff by a substitution under section 757; and by the terms of subdivision 2 of section 501, the defendant's demand, when it matured, could not have been interposed as a counter-claim. The section was drawn in anticipation of section 1814 of the Code of Civil Procedure, which had not been enacted when Jordan v. National Shoe and Leather Bank was decided, which fact, doubtless, gave rise to the doubt suggested.

In an action by an executrix upon a debt due to the testator, but payable after his decease, it was held, under the former statute, that the defendant could not set off a debt due to him from the testator, payable in the latter's lifetime. Patterson v. Patterson, 59 *N. Y.* 574; modifying S. C., 1 *Hun*, 323. This conclusion was reached upon a literal reading of the former statute, as well as upon the principle stated by NELSON, Ch. J., in Hills v. Tallman, 21 *Wend.* 674, cited under the last subdivision.

In an action by an executor, upon a demand which arose after the decedent's death, the defendant cannot set off a demand against the testator, although it existed at the time of his death. Merritt v. Seaman, 6 *N. Y.* (2 *Seld.*) 168; reversing S. C., 6 *Barb.* 330.

One of the next of kin cannot have a counter-claim for his share of the estate of an intestate, in an action against him by the administrator, to recover a debt due to the estate. Woodhouse v. Woodhouse, 11 *Weekly Dig.* 241 (Sup'm Ct. Gen. T.).

LEARY v. BOGGS ET AL.

SUPREME COURT, SECOND DEPARTMENT; KINGS COUNTY SPECIAL TERM, MARCH, 1883.

§ 500.

Answer.—Denial in, whether absolute or of any knowledge or information sufficient to form a belief, must be specific.

An answer must specify distinctly each allegation which defendant intends to deny; and this is true whether the denial is absolute or of any knowledge or information sufficient to form a belief. When, therefore, a defendant admits certain allegations, and specifically denies others, it is not proper pleading to deny all other allegations not before admitted or denied. He must specifically point out the allegation denied.

(*Decided March* 22, 1883.)

Motion by plaintiff to strike out a portion of the defendant's answer as irrelevant and insufficient in law.

Action by a grantee of a sole surviving partner against the widow and children of the deceased partner, who died intestate, to compel them to execute and deliver to the plaintiff quit-claim deeds to certain valuable pier property, which is claimed to have been owned by the two partners as partnership property, and conveyed to the plaintiff in payment of a debt due him from the firm.

The answer, after admitting and denying several allegations in the complaint, contains the following paragraph, which the plaintiff asserts should be stricken out: "III. As to each and every allegation contained in said complaint not hereinbefore specifically admitted or denied, this defendant denies any knowledge or information sufficient to form a belief as to the truth thereof, and therefore denies the same."

Sidney J. Cowen, for the motion.

Timothy Perry, opposed.

Brown, J.—It was decided in Miller *v.* McCloskey (1 *N. Y. Civ. Pro.* 259), that a denial in an answer such as is contained in paragraph III. of the answer in this action, was not authorized by section 500 of the Code.

The section of the Code seems to require a denial of each material allegation of the complaint, and the answer must therefore specify distinctly each allegation which defendant intends to deny ; and this is true whether the denial is absolute, or of any knowledge or information sufficient to form a belief. When, therefore, a defendant admits certain allegations, and specifically denies others, it is not proper pleading to deny all other allegations not before admitted or denied. He must explicitly point out the allegation denied.

Motion granted, with $10 costs, with leave to defendant to serve an amended answer within twenty days.

ESTATE OF WILLIAM E. DUFFY, DECEASED.

SURROGATE'S COURT, NEW YORK COUNTY; APRIL, 1883.

§§ 2472, 2476.

Surrogate not divested of jurisdiction, and administrator not excused from accounting, by proceedings in foreign probate court.

Where decedent, who resided and died in another State, left assets which were in New York county at the time of his decease, or came into that county after his decease, and assets did not come into any other county of this State, the surrogate of New York county had exclusive jurisdiction to grant letters of administration on those assets. [1]

Where letters of administration are regularly issued by a surrogate, he thereby acquires jurisdiction over the administrators, and is empowered to direct and control their conduct and settle their accounts, and to make orders requiring them to attend to be examined touching any personal property owned or held by the decedent at the time of his death. [2] Administrators appointed in another State two years subsequent to the grant of letters here, and long after the taking possession of the property here, cannot be allowed to take it from the State until it has been accounted for here, and there is no question as to the liability of the administrators to account here for that property. [3]

Administrators appointed by the surrogate of New York county of the assets in this State of a decedent who resided and died in Connecticut, were subsequently granted letters of administration by a probate court in Connecticut, and there accounted and were discharged. *Held*, that the probate court of Connecticut was not a court of competent jurisdiction to make any decree discharging administrators appointed by a surrogate of this State from their obligation to account to the court which appointed them for the property of the decedent received by them and made subject by the laws of this State to such surrogate's jurisdiction.[4]

(*Decided April* 11, 1883.)

Motion by an administrator to vacate an order of the surrogate of New York county referring his accounts and the objections thereto to a referee for hearing and determination, and to set aside all proceedings taken in said surrogate's court.

The facts are stated in the opinion.

John Flanagan, for adm'r Duffy, for motion.

M. J. Kelly, for administrator Kelly.

Luther W. Emerson, and *G. F. Langbein*, for objectors.

ROLLINS, Surrogate.—The decedent resided in the State of Connecticut, where he died intestate in August, 1876. Letters of administration upon his estate were, in September, 1876, issued to one Dennis McQuillan out of the probate court of the district in which the decedent had died.

McQuillan was superseded in 1878 by James Duffy and William H. Kelly, who more than a year before had been granted letters of administration by the surrogate of this county. Such letters had been issued upon the application of James Duffy, who swore in his petition that the decedent "died possessed of personal property in the city of New York, not exceeding in value $6,000, or thereabouts."

An inventory, afterward filed in the office of the surrogate, and disclosing assets amounting to $6,000, contained, according to the affidavit of administrator Kelly, a true statement, so far as he knew, of all the personal property of the deceased in the State of New York. Upon citation at the instance of one of the next of kin, Mr. Kelly, in June, 1881, filed his account in this court. It thereby appeared, among other things, that the sum of $7,600 had been collected, and had come to his hands in the State of New York. To this account objections were interposed by nearly all of decedent's next of kin—as also to a similar account subsequently filed by administrator Duffy.

By order of the surrogate, these accounts and objections were submitted to a referee for hearing and determination.

While this reference was pending in September, 1881, a stipulation was entered into before the referee whereby it was in effect agreed that administrator Kelly should render an additional account, including all assets, from whatever source derived, which had at any time come into his possession or under his control. This stipulation was signed by the attorneys for the adult contestants, by the attorney for administrator Duffy, by the special guardian for infant objectors, and by administrator Kelly personally, who appended the following statement to an account which, in pursuance of such stipulation, was subsequently filed in October, 1881:

"The reason for including the Connecticut estate in this account is because of my desire to be discharged upon this accounting, if legal, and to be relieved from any further accounting here or in Connecticut."

He charged himself at this time with:

Amount of Connecticut inventory . . .	$18,512 04
Amount of New York inventory	6,000 00
Increase	2,168 82
	$26,680 86
He credited himself in all with	24,895 48
Leaving an apparent balance in his hands of	$1,785 38

The reference again proceeded. A large amount of testimony was taken, and in July, 1882, was submitted to the surrogate, together with the report of the referee, to the effect that the administrators should be held accountable in excess of the sums wherewith they charged themselves, with various amounts, aggregating about $11,000. Upon application by Mr. Kelly, who claimed that the reference had been brought to an unexpected close, so that he was deprived of opportunity to make full presentation of the evidence in his behalf, the matter was again submitted to the referee in November, 1882.

After several sessions, during which little testimony was taken, counsel for administrator Duffy, in January, 1883, procured from the surrogate an order to show cause why the order of reference should not be vacated and all proceedings in this court be dismissed, on the ground of want of jurisdiction, and on the further ground that the accounts of the admin-
[1] istrators had been settled and adjudicated by a court of competent jurisdiction in the State of Connecticut.

Duffy's affidavit, upon which the order to show cause was based, alleged that late in June, 1882, while the reference was pending here, he and his co-administrator were cited by the probate court of Connecticut, from which they had obtained letters of administration, to appear at Portland, in that State, on July 3, and to show cause why they should not there render an account of their doings; that they attended with counsel in pursuance of such citation, and that the pendency of proceedings before the surrogate of this county was suggested as a sufficient ground for delay in accounting elsewhere: that the court would not heed the suggestion, but directed that the administrators account within three days; that thereupon, on July 6, they filed accounts, disclosing all their proceedings, both in this State and in the State of Connecticut, and that on the day of their presentation such accounts were examined by the probate court and adjudicated to be just and true by a decree, whereof the following is a copy:

"The administrators on said estate, pursuant to the order of this court, filed and exhibited their administration account with said estate, showing debts and charges paid by said administrators and allowances to be, $36,393.75, and assets of personal property $26,392, showing a deficiency over and above personal estate, to be $10,001.55, which said account is allowed by this court."

The following awards to parties and to counsel made by the probate judge constitute a part of this deficiency: To administrator Kelly, $2,000; to administrator Duffy, $750; to Duffy's counsel, $500; to Kelly's counsel, $500.

In view of the delays incident to the New York litigation, the celerity with which the accounts of the administrators were settled in Connecticut, seems almost startling until it is discovered that the order for an accounting, while it directed service upon both the administrators at their several places of abode in New York, made no provision for similar service upon the three brothers of decedent or upon his sister, all of whom reside in this city, and each of whom, as the administrators well knew, was strenuously contesting the accuracy of their accounts.

It is true that the Connecticut court directed that a

copy of the citiation should be posted on a sign-post in the town of Portland, and that there should be publication of its contents in a newspaper printed in the town of Middletown. But as none of the dissatisfied next of kin, so far as it appears, ever saw or were likely to see either the sign-post or the newspaper, the dispatch with which the accounts were discovered to be correct, ceases to be remarkable.

Now, whether the proceedings culminating in this Connecticut judgment were or were not in accordance with the law of that State so as to be legal and binding until they shall be set aside or the judgment reversed, is unnecessary to be here determined. The validity and effect of that judgment may be the subject of consideration hereafter. But unless the surrogate lacked authority to pass upon these administrators' accounts when he first assumed jurisdiction, I am convinced that he possesses that authority now, in spite of the proceedings in Connecticut. Now, if the statements of the administrators themselves, in the various papers on the files of this court, are to be taken as true, the surrogate's jurisdiction originally is not open to dispute.

Section 2476 of the Code of Civil Procedure provides that "the surrogate's court of each county has jurisdiction exclusive of every other surrogate's court . . . . to grant letters of administration . . . ." (subd. 3). "When the decedent, not being a resident of this State, died without the State leaving personal property within that county and no other, or leaving personal property, which has, since his death, come into that county, and no other and remains unadministered."

That the decedent left assets which were in this county at the time of his death seems to be now disputed, though it was one of the allegations of the petition for letters of administration. But that he left assets which have since his death come into this county is very clearly established by the motion papers; and there is no claim that any such assets have come into any other county of this State.

By reason of these facts the surrogate acquired jurisdiction over these administrators and was [¹] empowered under the Code* "to direct and control their conduct and settle their accounts" and "to make orders requiring them to attend and be examined touching any personal property owned or held by the decedent at the time of his death."

The Connecticut administrators, appointed nearly two years subsequent to the grant of letters in this county, and long after the taking possession of property here to the amount of at least $7,600, cannot be allowed to take this fund from New York until it [³] has been here accounted for. If there is any question about the obligation to account here for other amounts, certainly none exists as to the amount which, by their petitions, inventory and account is vouched for as by the administrators themselves.

I fully recognize the doctrine that the decision of a court of competent jurisdiction is final and conclusive upon the parties, and that matters therein determined cannot be again contested between the same litigants, either in the same tribunal or another. But the probate court of Connecticut was not a court of competent jurisdiction to make any decree discharging administrators appointed by this court from their [⁴] obligation to account to this court for the property of decedent received by them and made subject, by the laws of this State, to the surrogate's jurisdiction.

This application must therefore be denied.

* § 2472, subd. 3.

EAGAN *v.* LYNCH.

N. Y. SUPERIOR COURT; SPECIAL TERM, APRIL, 1883.

§§ 14, 2285.

Contempt of court.—Perjury is, and may be punished as such.—Proceeding to punish for, in summary manner, is constitutional.

The indictment and conviction of sureties to an undertaking on which an order of arrest was granted for their perjury in falsely swearing that they were worth double the amount of the undertaking, would be a punishment for the offense they committed against the people of the State, but it would not purge their contempt of court.[2] Perjury has always been held to be a great contempt of court,[1] and the court has power to punish such sureties for that offense, by imposing upon them a fine sufficient to indemnify the defendant for the loss and injury he has sustained through their misconduct, and by imprisoning them for six months and until the fine is paid.[3]

Courts of justice have had the power of punishing contempt by summary proceedings, from time immemorial. This power is a branch of the common law which has been adopted and sanctioned by the constitution of this State, and therefore a proceeding to punish for contempt is not one of the cases in which article 1, section 2, of the constitution gives the right to a trial by jury.[4]

A summary proceeding to punish for contempt is a due process of law, and was recognized as such when the constitution of the United States was adopted, and is not within the prohibition of that section of it which provides that "no person shall be deprived of life, liberty or property without due process of law."[5]

(*Decided April* 18, 1883.)

Motion to punish sureties to an undertaking on which an order of arrest had been granted for contempt in swearing falsely as to their pecuniary responsibility.

This action was brought to recover $25,000 damages for an alleged breach of promise to marry. An order of arrest was granted in the action, on which the the defendant was arrested and held in $10,000 bail. This bail was afterwards reduced to $250, and an order granted requiring the sureties, Daniel Peixotto and Horatio M. Sadler, to appear and be examined as to to their pecuniary qualifications. On the examination, it appeared that the sureties were entirely irresponsible. Subsequently, when the case was called for trial, the plaintiff failed to appear, and the complaint was dismissed. The defendant thereupon entered judgment against the plaintiff for $772.52, his costs, including $750 extra allowance.

Abram Kling, for motion.

Vanderpoel, Green & Cuming, opposed.

TRUAX, J.—The examination of the sureties shows that they were not worth the sum in which they justified, and that they knew they were not worth that sum when they justified; that they became sureties for the purpose of enabling the attorney for the plaintiff to obtain the order of arrest, and that their misconduct in so doing defeated and impaired the rights and remedies of the defendant.

The defendant would not have been arrested and held to bail in the sum of $10,000 if Peixotto and Sadler, or some one else, had not acted as sureties for the plaintiff. The defendant was entitled to two responsible sureties upon the undertaking which was given upon obtaining the order sought. He lost this right by the fraudulent acts of this attorney for the plaintiff, and the false swearing of the sureties. No plainer case of an attempt to prevent the course of justice and to impair and defeat the rights and remedies of a party can be shown than the one now presented to this court. Perjury has always been

[1] held to be a great contempt of court (Stackhouse *v.* French, 1 *Bing.* 365).

It is true that the sureties may, and should be, indicted for their perjury. But their indictment and conviction will be a punishment for the offense
[2] that they have committed against the people of this State, but will not purge the contempt. Their offense against the court will still remain unpunished. That offense the court has power to punish by imposing upon them a fine sufficient to indemnify the defendant for the loss and injury he has sustained
[3] through their misconduct, and by imprisoning them for six months, and until the fine is paid (§ 2285).

If they should happen to be indicted and convicted for their perjury, the court before whom they are convicted will, in pronouncing its sentence, take into consideration the previous punishment (§ 2287).

It was suggested on the argument that this application could not be granted, because a commitment to prison would be a violation of that part of the constitution of this State which declares that "the trial by jury in all case in which it has been heretofore used shall remain inviolate forever" (art. 1, § 2). This suggestion is untenable. Courts of justice have had the power of punishing contempt by summary proceedings from time immemorial. The process of attachment for contempt must necessarily be as ancient as the laws themselves—for laws without a competent authority to secure their administration from disobedience and contempt would be vain and nugatory (4 *Black. Comm.* 286). To punish for contempt was part of the common law of England when the constitution of 1777 was adopted. That constitution (art. 35) declared that the common law of England should be and continue the law of this State. The power to punish for a contempt is a branch of the common

[*] law which has been adopted and sanctioned by our State constitution (Yates *v.* Lansing, 9 *Johns.* 416). Therefore, this is not one of the cases in which trial by jury "has been heretofore used."

Nor is this proceeding within the prohibition of that portion of the Constitution of the United States which provides that "no person shall be deprived of life, liberty, or property without due process of law."

This is a due process of law, and was recognized as [*] such when the constitution of the United States was passed. "It is not to be doubted," says Chancellor KENT, "that the constitution and laws of the United States were made with reference to the existence of the common law. In many cases the language of the constitution and laws would be inexplicable without reference to the common law; and the existence of the common law is not only supposed by the constitution, but it is appealed to for the construction and interpretation of its powers" (1 *Kent Comm.* 336).

The actual loss produced by the misconduct of the sureties is the amount of the judgment which the defendant has recovered against the plaintiff, to wit, $772.52. The sureties are fined that amount. They will also be imprisoned for six months, and until the above fine is paid.

PERKINS ET AL., RESPONDENTS, v. KENDALL, IMPLEADED, ETC., APPELLANT.

N. Y. MARINE COURT; GENERAL TERM, JANUARY, 1883.

§§ 2457, 2458.

Supplementary proceedings.—Partner not served with summons may be examined in, as to partnership property, on judgment entered against the partners jointly.

In an action against copartners upon a partnership obligation, where the summons was served upon but one of the partners, and judgment entered thereon against all the partners jointly, and so as to bind the individual property of the party served only, an execution issued against the joint property of all the defendants, and returned unsatisfied, is a sufficient exhaustion of the remedy at law upon that judgment, entitling the judgment creditor to proceed in equity to search for joint property.

Where, in such a case, a partner not served with the summons did not obey an order for his examination, in supplementary proceedings, as to the joint property of the judgment debtors,—*Held*, that an order adjudging him guilty of a contempt of court, and providing for his punishment, should be affirmed.

(*Decided*, *March* 19, 1883.)

Appeal from an order adjudging a judgment debtor guilty of a contempt of court, and fining him the amount of the judgment, for not obeying an order for his examination in supplementary proceedings.

On December 1, 1882, the plaintiffs recovered judgment against Charles B. Kendall and Hugh F. Kendall, composing the firm of Kendall Brothers, for the sum of $1,173.24. It was recovered upon personal service of the summons on Charles B. Kendall, no summons having been served on Hugh F. Kendall, and he not having appeared in the action. Execution was duly issued upon the judgment, to the sheriff of New York county, against the property of the defendant Charles B. Kendall, owned solely, and also against the joint property of the defendants. This execution was returned wholly unsatisfied, and on December 4, 1882, an order was granted in proceedings supplementary to execution, requiring the defendants to appear before a referee therein named, to "make discovery on oath concerning their joint property, and Charles B. Kendall, as to his sole property."

On the return day of the order, December 7, 1882, Hugh F. Kendall attended before the referee, was duly sworn, and his examination commenced, and adjourned to December 9.

On the adjourned day, Hugh F. Kendall did not appear, but a person claiming to represent his attorneys appeared and requested an adjournment of the examination, and an adjournment was then had to December 13, when the defendant Hugh F. Kendall again failed to appear. An order requiring said Hugh F. Kendall to show cause why he should not be punished for contempt was thereupon granted and served on his attorneys.

On the return day, after hearing counsel for both parties, an order was entered adjudging said defendant guilty of contempt, and that he pay to the clerk of the "court the sum of $1,173.24, with interest thereon from the 1st day of December, 1882, being the amount of the judgment in this action, and thirty dollars the costs of this proceeding, as a fine for the judgment creditors herein, and that he stand committed to the common jail of the city and county of New York, until said fine be paid, unless he appears before said referee on the 4th day of January, 1883, at two o'clock in the forenoon, and submits to the required examination, and pays ten dollars costs of this motion."

From that order this appeal was taken.

John Yard, and *Charles W. Gould* (*Vanderpoel, Green & Cuming*, attorneys), for appellant.

Franklin A. Paddock, and *Russell Benedict*, for respondents.

Supplementary proceedings may be taken in any case where a judgment creditor's action would lie. Produce Bank *v.* Morton, 67 *N. Y.* 199; Bilhofer *v.* Heubach, 15 *Abb. Pr.* 143.

BY THE COURT.—Order appealed from affirmed, except it be modified in this particular: that a provision be added to the order, to the further effect that the defendant be discharged on payment of the judgment, or on submitting to the examination required by the original order, and on payment of $10 costs.

In an action against copartners, upon a partnership obligation, where the summons was served upon but one of the partners, and the judgment entered thereupon against all the partners jointly, and so as to bind the individual property of the party served only, an execution issued against the joint property of all the defendants, and returned unsatisfied, is a sufficient exhaustion of the remedy at law, upon that judgment, entitling the judgment creditor to proceed in equity, to search for joint property (Produce Bank of New York *v.* Morton, 67 *N. Y.* 199; Commercial Bank of Lake Erie *v.* Meach, 7 *Paige*, 448).

NOTE ON SUPPLEMENTARY PROCEEDINGS.

BY DANIEL S. RIDDLE.

Nature of.—These proceedings are now special proceedings, instituted before a judge out of court. *Code Civ. Pro.* § 2433. This is contrary to the current of decisions under the former Code, which held them to be proceedings in the original action. See West Side Bank *v.* Pugsley, 47 *N. Y.* 368; Seeley *v.* Black, 35 *How. Pr.* 369. As special proceedings, they should be brought in the name of the real owner of the judgment as plaintiff against the party proceeded against as defendant. See § 1909.

Any judge of a court of record, out of which an execution against property may issue to a sheriff, except a surrogate, can entertain these proceedings upon a judgment of his own court, provided the requisite facts exist and are proved. A county judge, or special county judge, may in like case entertain the proceedings upon any judgment of any court, if the execution thereon was issued out of a court of record, and to the sheriff of his county. A judge of the court of common pleas, for the city and county of New York, may in like case entertain the proceedings upon an execution issued to said city and county from an inferior court other than the marine court of that city. A county, or common pleas judge may also entertain proceedings upon a surrogate's decree, when the execution was issued to his county, the same as if it were a judgment of his own court. § 2554. And likewise upon the return of a collector of taxes of his county, certifying that a tax exceeding $10 is uncollected for want of goods and chattels. *Laws* 1867, ch. 361; *Laws* 1879, ch. 446; *Laws* 1881, ch. 610.

A supreme court justice may grant the order for these proceedings in any part of the State, upon any judgment of his court, no matter from what county, or to what county the execution was issued; and all proceedings may be had before him, except the examination of the party. See Crouse *v.* Wheeler, 33 *How. Pr.* 337. When the execution was issued out of a local court, and it is shown by affidavit that each of the judges before whom the proceedings might be instituted is unable to act, etc., a justice of the supreme court may entertain proceedings in such case, and if he does not reside in the judicial district embracing the county to which the execution was issued, he must make the order or warrant returnable to a supreme court justice of that district, or to a county judge, etc., of the county to which it was issued, or of an adjoining county, and make this direction in the order or warrant. § 2434.

In what cases proceedings may be taken.—1st. Any judicial determination of a tribunal, or officer of this State, which adjudges a sum of money of twenty-five dollars, or upwards, to be due and payable from one party, not a corporation, to another, and upon which an execution against property has been issued to a sheriff, may form the basis of a proceeding, provided the judgment was rendered upon the judgment debtor's appearance, or personal service of the summons, or process upon him, and the execution is issued out of a court of record. § 2458: Bartlett *v.* McNiel, 60 *N. Y.* 53; affirming S. C., 49 *How. Pr.* 55. But if the judgment is against the plaintiff, the provision about the debtor's appearance, etc., does not apply, because he has brought himself voluntarily within the jurisdiction of the court. Bean *v.* Tonnelle, 1 *N. Y. Civ. Pro. Rep.* 33.

2nd. A tax exceeding $10, levied by the board of supervisors of a county, and returned by a collector as uncollected, for want of personal property, may also form the basis of a proceeding as above stated.

3rd. Proceedings may be instituted before a federal judge, upon a judgment of his court. See *Ex parte* Boyd, 105 *U. S.* 647. But no proceeding can be instituted by a State judge or justice upon a judgment of a Federal court. Tompkins *v.* Piercell, 12 *Hun*, 662; Davis *v.* Breens, 11 *N. Y. Weekly Dig.* 436. Nor upon an order for costs of motion; because the execution in such case goes only against personal property. § 779, as amended in 1882. And this seems to be so, although such costs exceed twenty-five dollars, as they well may, when there are disbursements. The execution must be issued to the county where the judgment debtor then resides. Bingham *v.* Disbrow, 37 *Barb.* 24; S. C. affirmed, 5 *Trans. App.* 198; Jesup *v.* Jones, 32 *How. Pr.* 91. Or to the county where he has, at the time of the commencement of the proceeding, a place for the regular transaction of business in person. § 2458; Brown *v.* Gump, 59 *How. Pr.* 507. If he does not reside or have a place of business in this State, it must be issued to the county where the judgment roll, etc., is filed.

Who may take proceedings.—Any person who is entitled to a judgment in his own right, or as trustee, may institute the proceeding. He is a judgment creditor. *Code Civ. Pro.* § 3343, subd. 13; Crill *v.* Koenmayer, 56 *How. Pr.* 276; Collier *v.* De Revere, 7 *Hun*, 61; Pardee *v.* Tilton, 20 *Hun*, 76; S. C., 58 *How. Pr.* 476; Walker *v.* Donavan, 6 *Daly*, 552; S. C., 53 *How. Pr.* 3.

An attorney may take proceeding to enforce the payment to the extent of his lien. Russell *v.* Summerville, 4 *N. Y. Mo. Law Bull.* 3.

Against whom.—They may be taken against any judgment debtor, including an infant, against whom a money judgment may be enforced by execution, except a domestic corporation, or a foreign corporation doing business, or having an agency in this State. §§ 2463, 1820; Lederer *v.* Ehrenefeld, 49 *How. Pr.* 403. As to third parties, the proceedings may be taken against any person or corporation, company, or association that has personal property of the judgment debtor exceeding $10, or is indebted to him exceeding $10, provided proceedings would lie against the latter. §§ 2441, 1919. Except against the depository of the United States bankruptcy court. Havens *v.* National City Bank of Brooklyn, 4 *Hun*, 131. But no proceedings can be instituted when the judgment debtor is deceased.

His death carries all his property into a surrogate's court, where equality among claimants of the same class is the rule. If the judgment debtor, however, dies after proceedings are regularly instituted, his death does not extinguish the lien acquired thereby. The proceeding may go on and work out the lien upon the property, the same as where an execution against property is issued to a sheriff in the lifetime of the judgment debtor. Becker *v.* Becker, 47 *Barb.* 497.

Proof to obtain the order or warrant instituting the proceedings must be by affidavit, or other competent written evidence. §§ 2435, 2436, 2437, 2441; Driggs *v.* Smith, 47 *How. Pr.* 215; Baker *v.* Stephens, 10 *Abb. Pr. N. S.* 1, 27; Kennedy *v.* Thorp, 3 *Id.* 131; S. C., 2 *Daly*, 258; Hawes *v.* Barr, 7 *Robt.* 452. The omission of the averment, that no previous application has been made, held to be simply an irregularity. Bean *v.* Tonnelle, 1 *N. Y. Civ. Pro. Rep.* 33; S. C., 24 *Hun*, 353; see Diossy *v.* West, 1 *N. Y. Mo. Law Bull.* 23. It must appear by the proof, that the judgment was rendered upon the judgment debtor's appearance, or personal service of the summons upon him unless he was the plaintiff in the action, or the right to institute the proceeding had accrued while the former Code was in force. Bean *v.* Tonnelle, *supra.*

For order after return of execution, must prove a judgment and issue of execution to proper county, and the return thereof within ten years next preceding. Wyman *v.* Childs, 44 *Barb.* 403; People, &c. *v.* Oliver 66 *Id.* 570; Bingham *v.* Disbrow, 3 *Trans. App.* 199. But the sheriff is presumed to have returned execution after expiration of 60 days. Bean *v.* Tonnelle, *supra.* And in what county the judgment debtor resided at the time of issuing the execution, or in what county he has a place of business, at the time of commencing the proceeding; or if he has neither residence, or place of business in the State, where the judgment-roll, &c., is filed. Under the former Code, some cases held, there was no need of proving the facts on application for the order; it was only necessary that they existed, in order to confer jurisdiction on the judge. Collier *v.* De Revere, 7 *Hun*, 61; Rugg *v.* Spinner, 59 *Barb.* 383; Scott *v.* Durfie, 59 *Id.* 390, marg. note; Hart *v.* Stevens, 4 *N. Y. Weekly Dig.* 540. The new Code has superseded these decisions.

For order before return of execution. See First National Bank of Rome *v.* Wilson, 13 *Hun*, 232; Sackett *v.* Newton, 10 *How. Pr.* 560; Owen *v.* Dupignac, 17 *Id.* 512.

For warrant, the facts must be positively averred. Netzel *v.* Mulford, 59 *How. Pr.* 452; Mosher *v.* People, &c., 5 *Barb.* 575. It is the alternative of an order. Andrews *v.* Wilson, 9 *How. Pr.* 39. An assignee of judgment may have it. King *v.* Kirby, 28 *Barb.* 49. If concealment is the ground for the warrant, that must appear to be within the State. Rohshand *v.* Waring, 1 *Abb. N. C.* 311.

For order against a third party. The fact of the party having property of the judgment debtor, &c., if stated on information and belief, will confer jurisdiction on the judge. Miller *v.* Adams, 52 *N. Y.* 409, affirming 9 S. C., 7 *Lans.* 131. But see People *v.* Jones, 1 *Abb. N. C.* 172; S. C., as Day *v.* Lee, 52 *How. Pr.* 95, Sp. T. Com. Pleas.

The Order.—Recital of the requisite proof, is not necessary. People *v.* Oliver, 66 *Barb.* 570. But see Day *v.* Brosnan, 6 *Abb. N. C.* 312, as to judgments from inferior courts. See Bank for Savings *v.* Pope, 8 *Daly*, 316, as to what is surplusage in an order. It must require the party to appear for examination in the county of his residence, or place of business. § 2459. Or in the county where the judgment-roll, &c., is filed, if he is not a resident, and has no place of business within the State. Anway *v.* Davies, 9 *Hun*, 296.

Service of order, &c., provided for, by § 2452. See Banker *v.* Johnson, 4 *Abb. Pr.* 435; Bingham *v.* Disbrow, 14 *Id.* 25; S. C., 39 *Barb.* 24; Billings *v.* Carver, 54 *Barb.* 40; Newell *v.* Cutter, 19 *Hun*, 74.

Where Served.—An order made by a supreme court justice, may be served anywhere in the state. Bingham *v.* Disbrow, *supra.* But when made by any other judge, must be served within his territorial jurisdiction.

Referee may be appointed at any stage of the proceeding, to take and report the evidence, or to report the facts. The judge may remove one referee, and appoint another. §§ 2442, 2443; Green *v.* Ballard, Pardee *v.* Tilton, 11 *N. Y. Weekly Dig.* 445; Lewis *v.* Penfield, 39 *How Pr.* 490.

The order of reference may be two-fold. Sickles *v.* Henley, 4 *Abb. N. C.* 231.

Objection to the referee, must be made to the judge who appointed him. Tremain *v.* Richardson, 68 *N. Y.* 617.

Referee has the power to adjourn the proceeding before him. § 2444; Kaufman *v.* Thrasher, 10 *Hun*, 438. May fix the time and place of attendance for examination, where the judge has not done so, and may require the parties to appear accordingly. Redmond *v.* Goldsmith, 2 *N. Y. Mo. Law Bull.* 19. May issue subpœnas for the attendance of witnesses. §§ 854–858. Must be sworn, unless the oath is expressly waived. § 2445; Browning *v.* Marvin, 5 *Abb. N. C.* 285; Mason *v.* Luddington, 56 *How. Pr.* 172, affirming S. C., 55 *Id.* 342. His duty is to take, not make the examination. People *v.*

Liepzig, 52 *How. Pr.* 410. Must make his report, or certify the examination, in name to the judge who appointed him, or to the officer to whom the order supplementary is returnable. Kennedy *v.* Norcott, 54 *How. Pr.* 87; Smith *v.* Johnson, 7 *Id.* 39; Ball *v.* Goodenough, 37 *Id.* 479.

Witnesses.—Are required to attend and produce books and papers upon subpœnas issued by the judge or referee. §§ 854–858, 866–869, 2008, 2009; People *v.* Marston. How served. See § 852; Davis *v.* Turner. 4 *How.* 190.

His privilege.—From arrest and proceeding while going to, remaining at, and returning from the place. §§ 860–861; Person *v.* Grier, 66 *N. Y.* 124; Person *v.* Pardee, 14 *Abb. L. J.* 13; affirming S. C., 6 *Hun.* 477; Mackay *v.* Lewis, 7 *Id.* 83. But may lose this privilege. Schultz *v.* Andrews, 54 *How. Pr.* 380.

His privilege on the witness stand.—Peck *v.* Williams. 13 *Abb. Pr.* 68; Mitchell's case, 12 *Id.* 449; Forbes *v.* Millard, 54 *Barb.* 520.

No examination of witness under commission. Graham *v.* Colburn, 14 *How. Pr.* 52; Morrell *a.* Hoey, 24 *Id.* 48; S. C., 15 *Abb. Pr.* 430.

Adjournments. § 2444; Squires *v.* Young, 1 *Bosw.* 690; People *v.* Oliver, 66 *Barb.* 570; Contra, Meyers *v.* Jones, 3 *Abb. Pr.* 301. Service of order of adjournment. Johnson *v.* Tuttle, 17 *Abb. Pr.* 315; Ammiden *v.* Walcott, 15 *Id.* 314; Parker *v.* Hunt, 15 *Id.* 410, note.

Examination.—Must be under oath. § 2444. When a person may refuse to subscribe the deposition. Sherwood *v.* Dolan, 14 *Hun*, 191. See Corning *v.* Tooker, 5 *How.* 16.

Extent of Inquiry.—The proceedings are eminently inquisitorial. They were meant to be so by the Legislature; and the courts have of late fairly interpreted this legislative intent. It is but just to the creditor class, that they should have this cheap and summary remedy for the collection of their dues; especially so, since the non-imprisonment act has been repealed. The examination is therefore allowed to take a wide and searching range, both as to the parties to the proceedings, and to the witnesses Lathrop *v.* Clapp, 40 *N. Y.* 328; affirming S. C., as Clapp *v.* Lathrop, 23 *How. Pr.* 423; Forbes *v.* Willard, 54 *Barb.* 520; S. C., 37 *How Pr.* 193; Mechanics and Traders' Bank *v.* Healy, 14 *N. Y. Weekly Dig.* 120; Sandford *v.* Carr, 2 *Abb. Pr.* 462; Contra, Barculow *v.* Protection Co., 2 *C. R.* 72; Van Wyck *v.* Bradley, 3 *C. R.* 157; Town *v.* Lafeguard Ins. Co., 4 *Bosw.* 683.

How proceedings discontinued. Can only be discontinued like an action. § 2454. See Underwood *v.* Sutcliffe, 10 *Hun*, 453; Stanley *v.* Lovett, 14 *Id.* 402; Allen *v.* Starring, 26 *How.* 57; Contra, Ballou *v.* Boland, 14 *Hun*, 355; Gaylord *v.* Jones, 7 *Id.* 480; Bennett *v.* McGuire, 58 *Barb.* 625; and others, which are superseded by § 2454.

Injunctions out may be granted at any time, and even against a person not a party. § 2451; Seeley *v.* Garrison, 10 *Abb. Pr.* 460; Green *v.* Bullard, 8 *How. Pr.* 313.

Nature, continuance, and extent thereof. Green *v.* Bullard, *supra;* Wilson *v.* Andrews, 9 *How. Pr.* 39; Reynolds *v.* McElhone, 20 *Id.* 454; Allen *v.* Starring, 26 *Id.* 57; People *v.* Randall, 73 *N. Y.* 416; Glenville Woolen Co. *v.* Ripley, 43 *Id.* 206; Morris *v.* First Nat. Bank of N. Y., 68 *Id.* 362; People *v.* Kingsland, 5 *Abb. Pr. N. S.* 90; S. C., 3 *Keyes*, 325; 3 *Abb. Ct. App. Dec.* 526; Tinkey *v.* Langdon, 60 *How.* 180; Butler *v.* Niles, 35 *Id.* 329; Deposit Nat. Bank *v.* Wickham, 44 *Id.* 421; Ross *v.* Chessman, 3 *Sandf.* 676; McRedie *v.* Senior, 4 *Paige*, 378; Lansing *v.* Easton, 7 *Id.* 364; Fenner *v.* Sanborn, 37 *Barb.* 610; Newell *v.* Cutter, 19 *Hun*, 74; Wolf *v.* Jacobs, 4 *J. & S.* 408.

What act is no violation. Parker *v.* Wakeman, 10 *Paige*, 485; Hudson *v.* Plets, 4 *Id.* 180; Richardson *v.* Reest, 9 *Id.* 243; Ireland *v.* Smith, 1 *Barb.* 419.

Costs.—When allowed to the judgment creditor, may be made payable out of property discovered, and in proceeding against a third person, the latter may be ordered to pay them personally. § 2455. What disbursements not taxable. Provost *v.* Farrell, 13 *Hun*, 303; Colton *v.* Simmons, 14 *Id.* 75.

A judgment debtor, or third party, must be examined before he is entitled to costs. § 2456; Engle *v.* Bonneau, 3 *Sandf.* 679; Simms *v.* Fries, 2 *N. Y. Mo. Law Bull.* 97; Anonymous, 11 *Abb. Pr.* 108; Anonymous, 3 *Sandf.* 725.

Witness not entitled to costs. Davis *v.* Turner, 4 *How. Pr.* 90; Anonymous, 11 *Abb. Pr.* 108; Contra *dictum* in Webber *v.* Hobbie, 13 *How. Pr.* 382.

Disobedience to orders—What may be punished. § 2457; Lothrop *v.* Clapp, 48 *N. Y.* 328; S. C., 23 *How. Pr.* 23; People *v.* Marston, 18 *Abb. Pr.* 257; Keanney's Case, 13 *Id.* 459; S. C., 22 *How. Pr.* 309; Wicker *v.* Dresser, 14 *Id.* 465; Brush *v.* Lee, 1 *Abb. Ct. App. Dec.* 238; S. C., 6 *Abb. Pr. N. S.* 50; Schultz *v.* Andrews, 54 *How. Pr.* 378; Livingston *v.* Swift, 23 *Id.* 1; Taggart *v.* Talcott, 2 *Edw.* 628; West Side Bank *v.* Pugsley, 47 *N. Y.* 374; *Re* Smithurst, 2 *Sandf.* 724.

What is not punishable.—Disregarding an order made without jurisdiction not punishable. Reed *v.* Champagne, 5 *N. Y. Weekly Dig.* 227; Tinker *v.* Crooks, 22 *Hun*, 579; West Side Bank *v.* Pugsley, 47 *N. Y.* 368; Griswold *v.* Tompkins, 7 *Daly*, 214; Tucker *v.* Langdon, 13 *N. Y. Weekly Dig.* 384; Wicker *v.* Dresser, 14 *How. Pr.* 465; People *v.* Ring, 9 *Id.* 97; Watson *v.* Fitzsimmons, 5 *Duer*, 629; Parker *v.* Hunt. 15 *Abb. Pr.* 410, note; Kennedy *v.* Weed, 10 *Id.* 62; Perkins *v.* Taylor, 19 *Id.* 146; Myers *v.* Trimble, 3 *E. D. Smith*, 607; 1 *Barb. Ch. Pr.* 671.

The procedure to punish as for contempt is regulated by the Code. See title III. of chapter 17.

What property may be reached.—Any property or right of property which is transferable or survives the owner, and is not exempt by law, may be reached by supplementary proceedings, unless it belongs to a domestic corporation, or a foreign corporation doing business or having an agency within the State as prescribed in section 1812 of Code, or is held under a trust created by a person other than the judgment debtor. See § 2463; Eamston *v.* Lyde, 1 *Paige*, 637. There may be reached, a watch when unnecessary. Deposit Nat. Bank *v.* Wickham, 44 *How. Pr.* 421. A United States patent. Barnes *v.* Morgan, 3 *Hun*, 703; S. C., 6 *N. Y. Supreme Ct.* (*T. & C.*) 105; Thorne *v.* Thomas, 1 *N. Y. Mo. Law Bull.* 53. An interest in an estate as next of kin. McArthur *v.* Hoysrod, 11 *Paige*, 495. An interest in a partnership or business. Webb *v.* Overmann, 6 *Abb. Pr.* 92; Taylor *v.* Perkins, 26 *Wend.* 124. Uses, rents and profits of real estate. Farnham *v.* Campbell, 10 *Paige*, 598; 9 *Id.* 372. Right to redeem real estate. 2 *R. S.* p. 371, 372, § 51, 55; Van Rensselaer *v.* Sheriff of Onondaga, 1 *Cow.* 443; Phyfe *v.* Riley, 15 *Wend.* 251; Chatauque Co. Bank *v.* Risly, 19 *N. Y.* 369. Inchoate interest as tenant by the courtesy. Ellsworth *v.* Cook, 8 *Paige*, 643; Beamish *v.* Hoyt, 2 *Robt.* 307. Right of dower. Tompkins *v.* Fonda, 4 *Paige*, 448. Stewart *v.* McMartin, 5 *Barb.* 438; Moak *v.* Coats, 33 *Id.* 498. An annuity. Degraw *v.* Closon, 11 *Paige*, 136; Ten Broeck *v.* Sloo, 2 *Abb. Pr.* 234; S. C., 13 *How. Pr.* 280. An interest in contract for real estate. Ellsworth *v.* Cuyler, 9 *Paige*, 418; Fenner *v.* Sanborn, 37 *Barb.* 610. Choses in action. People *v.* Tioga C. P., 19 *Wend.* 73; McKee *v.* Judd, 12 *N. Y.* 622; Zabriskie *v.* Smith, 13 *Id.* 332; Butler *v.* N. Y. and Erie R. R. Co., 22 *Barb.* 110; Gould *v.* Gould, 36 *Id.* 275; 6 *How. Pr.* 161 (Thurman *v.* Wells, 18 *Barb.* 500, overruled); Hudson *v.* Plets, 11 *Paige*, 180; Dwight *v.* Curtiss, 8 *How. Pr.* 56; Gillett *v.* Fairchild, 4 *Denio*, 80; Browner *v.* Hill, 1 *Sandf.* 629; Levy *v.* Cavanaugh, 2 *Bosw.* 100; Campbell *v.* Fish, 8 *Daly*, 62. A seat or membership in a board. Powell *v.* Waldron, 89 *N. Y.* 328; Ritterband *v.* Baggett, 10 *J. & Sp.* (42 *N. Y. Super. Ct.*) 556; 4 *Abb. N. C.* 67; Grocers' Bank *v.* Murphy, 11 *N. Y. Weekly Dig.* 538. Permit to occupy market, held not to be property. Barry *v.* Kennedy, 11 *Abb. Pr. N. S.* 421.

What property can not be reached.—§ 2463. Exempt property cannot. Brown *v.* Fonda, 2 *Code R.* 70; Finnin *v.* Malloy, 1 *J. & Sp.* (33 *N. Y. Super. Ct.*) 382. Nor the proceeds, etc., of such property. Andrews *v.* Rowan, 28 *How. Pr.* 126; Tillotson *v.* Walcott, 48 *N. Y.* 188. Nor watch of ordinary value. Merriam *v.* Hill, 1 *N. Y. Weekly Dig.* 260. Nor necessary wearing apparel. Bumpus *v.* Maynard, 38 *Barb.* 626. Nor debtor's earnings for sixty preceding days. Bush *v.* White, 12 *Abb. Pr.* 21; Martin *v.* Sheridon, 2 *Hilt.* 586; Miller *v.* Hooper, 19 *Hun* 394, Cummings *v.* Timberman, 49 *How. Pr.* 236; Von Vichten *v.* Hall, 14 *Id.* 436. All other earnings may be reached. Tripp *v.* Child, 14 *Barb.* 85; Thompson *v.* Nixon, 3 *Edw. Ch.* 457. Nor can future earnings or acquisitions be reached. Du Bois *v.* Cassidy, 8 *N. Y. Weekly Dig.* 132; affirming S. C., 5 *Id.* 210; Woodman *v.* Goodenough, 18 *Abb. Pr.* 26; Sands *v.* Roberts, 8 *Id.* 343; Coton *v.* Southwell, 13 *Barb.* 335; Potter *v.* Law, 16 *How. Pr.* 549; Campbell *v.* Foster, 16 *Id.* 275; Browning *v.* Bettis, 8 *Paige,* 568; McCoren *v.* Dorsheimer, 1 *Clark,* 144. Nor a *jus precarium.* Smith *v.* Kearney, 2 *Barb. Ch.* 533; Munsell *v.* Servis, 4 *Hill,* 642; McCormick *v.* Kehoe, 9 *N. Y. Leg. Obs.* 184. Nor property held under a valid assignment. Watrous *v.* Lothrop, 4 *Sand.* 700; 9 *Cow.* 728. Nor trust property, real or personal. 1 *R. S.* p. 730, § 63, p. 773, § 21; Williams *v.* Thorn, 70 *N. Y.* 270; Campbell *v.* Foster, 35 *Id.* 361; Graff *v.* Bennett, 31 *Id.* 9; Sackett *v.* Mabbitt, 2 *Keyes,* 457; Manning *v.* Evans, 19 *Hun,* 500; McEwen *v.* Brewster, 17 *Id.* 223; Morgan *v.* Kohnstammer, 60 *How. Pr.* 161; Genet *v.* Foster, 18 *Id.* 50; Campbell *v.* Foster, 16 *Id.* 275; Scott *v.* Nevins, 6 *Duer,* 672; Stewart *v.* Foster, 1 *Hilt.* 505; Hallett *v.* Thompson, 5 *Paige,* 583; Clute *v.* Bool, 8 *Id.* 83; Rider *v.* Mason, 4 *Sandf. Ch.* 351; Lamoureaux *v.* Van Rensselaer, 1 *Barb. Ch.* 34; Hawley *v.* James, 16 *Wend.* 118, 165, 262; Craig *v.* Hone, 2 *Edw.* 554. Nor property equitably appropriated. Ireland *v.* Smith, 1 *Barb.* 419; S. C., 3 *How. Pr.* 244. Nor money in hands of disbursing officer. Waldmon *v.* O'Donnell, 57 *How. Pr.* 215; Remmey *v.* Gedney, *Id.* 217; Waldman *v.* O'Connell, 1 *N. Y. Mo. Law Bull.* 47; Nagle *v.* Stagg, 15 *Abb. Pr. N. S.* 348; Havens *v.* National City Bank of Brooklyn, 4 *Hun,* 131. Nor unassigned dower. Payne *v.* Becker, 22 *Hun,* 28. Nor real property standing in debtor's name. Bunn *v.* Daly, 24 *Hun,* 526; Tinkey *v.* Langdon, 13 *N. Y. Weekly Dig.* 384. Nor money in hands of a receiver of a corporation. Smith *v.* McNamara, 15 *Hun,* 447. Nor right of action for a personal wrong. Zabriskie *v.* Smith, 13 *N. Y.* 332; Davenport *v.* Ludlow, 3 *Code R.* 66; Crouch *v.* Gridley, 6 *Hill,* 250.

How property may be reached.—By permissive order. **§ 2446.**

Effect of order. Gibson *v.* Haggerty, 37 *N. Y.* 555; Lynch *v.* Johnson, 48 *Id.* 27; Adams *v.* Walsh, 43 *N. Y. Super. Ct.* 52; State of Michigan *v.* Phenix Bank, 33 *N. Y.* 25; Fowler *v.* Lowenstein, 7 *Lans.* 167; Mallony *v.* Norton, 21 *Barb.* 424.

As to the proof. Calkin *v.* Becker, 21 *Barb.* 275; Hadley *v.* Greene, 15 *Id.* 601; Beebe *v.* Kenyon, 3 *Hun*, 73. A sheriff cannot have this order. Baker *v.* Kenworthy, 41 *N. Y.* 215.

By compulsory order. The property subject to this order must consist of money, or other personal property, belonging to the judgment debtor, whose right to the possession thereof is not substantially disputed, and it must be capable of delivery. § 2447; West Side Bank *v.* Pugsley, 47 *N. Y.* 368; Tinker *v.* Crooks, 22 *Hun*, 579. It is irregular to make this order in any other case. Bailey *v.* Buel, 50 *N. Y.* 662; Drake *v.* Shurtliff, 24 *Hun*, 422; Winters *v.* McCarthy, 2 *Abb. N. C.* 357; Locke *v.* Mabbett, 3 *Abb. Ct. App. Dec.* 68; Bernard *v.* Kobbe, 54 *N. Y.* 516; affirming S. C., 3 *Daly*, 373; Durand *v.* Hankerson, 39 *N. Y.* 296; Rodman *v.* Henry, 17 *Id.* 482; Dickinson *v.* Onderdonk, 18 *Hun*, 479; Teller *v.* Randall, 40 *Barb.* 242; S. C., 26 *How. Pr.* 155; Crounse *v.* Whipple, 34 *Id.* 333; Sherwood *v.* Buffalo & N. Y. City R. R. Co., 12 *Id.* 136; Alexander *v.* Richardson, 7 *Robt.* 63; Town *v.* Safeguard Ins. Co. of N. Y. & Penn., 4 *Bosw.* 683; Grossmuch *v.* Richards, 2 *Abb. N. C.* 59; Hentz *v.* McGehie, 1 *N. Y. Mo. Law Bull.* 3; Griswold *v.* Tompkins, 7 *Daly*, 214; People *v.* King, 9 *How.* 97; Goodyear *v.* Betts, 7 *Id.* 187; Corning *v.* Tooker, 5 *How.* 16; Gosper *v.* Burnett, 12 *Id.* 307; Sandford *v.* Moshier, 13 *Id.* 137; Joyce *v.* Holbrook, 2 *Hilt.* 95; Hall *v.* McMahon, 10 *Abb. Pr.* 103. But a mere claim of title to, or interest in the property, adverse to the judgment debtor, is not sufficient. Facts must be adduced to show that a substantial question exists for determination by an action. Mosier *v.* Lees, *Daily Register*, Aug. 24, 1878; 2 *Bliss N. Y. Ann. Code*, 534. Through a receiver. In any case where property of the judgment debtor has been discovered, or it appears that he has some rights or interest in property applicable to the payment of the judgment, and the same cannot be reached by order, a receiver may be appointed. But when the only property discovered is real estate standing in the judgment debtor's name, no receiver should be appointed. Bann *v.* Daly, 24 *Hun*, 526; S. C., 12 *N. Y. Weekly Dig.* 395; Tinkey *v.* Langdon, 13 *Id.* 384; Petition of Englehart, 1 *Sheldon*, 514. See §§ 2464–2467, as to appointing receivers; also Barraclough *v.* Poolman, 3 *Daly*; De Bemer *v.* Drew, 59 *Barb.* 438; S. C., 39 *How. Pr.* 466; Tyler *v.* Willis, 33 *Barb.* 327; Union Bank of Troy *v.* Sargent, 53 *Barb.* 422; S. C., 35 *How. Pr.* 87; Geary *v.* Geary, 66 *N. Y.* 252; McCartney *v.* Bostwick, 32 *Id.* 53, Bingham *v.*

Disbrow, 14 *Abb. Pr.* 251; Miller *v.* Miller, 7 *Hun*, 209; Hanson *v.* Tripler, 3 *Sandf.* 733. All the cases which hold that a receiver could only be appointed in proceedings against the debtor after execution returned are superseded by §2464. He is appointed on notice. Morgan *v.* Von Kohnstamm, 60 *How. Pr.* 161; Whitney *v.* Welch, 2 *Abb. N. C.* 242; Andrews *v.* Glenville Woolen Co., 11 *Abb. Pr. N. S.* 78; Clark *v.* Savage, 5 *N. Y. Weekly Dig.* 193; Ashley *v.* Turner, 22 *Hun*, 226; People *v.* Norton, 1 *Paige*, 17; 2 *Id.* 438; 8 *Id.* 373; Lattimer *v.* Lord, 4 *E. D. Smith*, 183. Third person cannot object to regularity of appointment. Tyler *v.* Willis, 33 *Barb.* 327; S. C., 12 *Abb. Pr.* 465; Underwood *v.* Sutcliffe, 10 *Hun*, 453; Maguire *v.* Potter, 17 *Id.* 403; Hobert *v.* Frost, 5 *Duer*, 672.

Who may be. Chamberlain *v.* Greenleaf, 4 *Abb. N. C.* 92, and *Code*, § 90.

His bond. See Morgan *v.* Potter, 17 *Hun*, 403; Underwood *v.* Sutcliffe, 10 *Id.* 453; Tyler *v.* Willis, *supra;* Johnson *v.* Martin, 1 *N. Y. Supreme Ct.* (*T. & C.*) 504; Conger *v.* Sands, 19 *How. Pr.* 8; Banks *v.* Potter, 21 *Id.* 469; Voorhees *v.* Seymour, 26 *Barb.* 569.

No conveyance or assignment to receiver necessary. Porter *v.* Williams, 9 *N. Y.* 142; Manning *v.* Evans, 19 *Hun*, 500; Wing *v.* Disse, 15 *Id.* 190; Cooney *v.* Cooney, 65 *Barb.* 524; Hayes *v.* Buckley, 53 *How. Pr.* 173; West *v.* Frazier, 5 *Sandf.* 653; Contra, Scott *v.* Elmore, 10 *Hun*, 68. Judge may order assignment. Fenner *v.* Sanborn, 37 *Barb.* 610; Sickles *v.* Hanly, 14 *Abb. N. C.* 231; Bunn *v.* Fonda, 2 *Code R.* 70; Contra, People *v.* Hurburt, 3 *How. Pr.* 446; Tinkey *v.* Langdon, 60 *Id.* 180; Ten Broeck *v.* Sloo, 13 *Id.* 28. Receiver is not vested with exempt property. Finnin *v.* Malley, 1 *J. & Sp.* (33 *N. Y. Super. Ct.*) 382; Cooney *v.* Cooney, 65 *Barb.* 524; Tillotson *v.* Walcott, 48 *N. Y.* 188. Nor with after-acquired property. Thom *v.* Fellows, 5 *N. Y. Weekly Dig.* 473; Merritt *v.* Sawyer, 6 *N. Y. Supreme Ct.* (*T. & C*) 160; Graff *v.* Barnett, 25 *How. Pr.* 470; Dubois *v.* Cassidy, 75 *N. Y.* 298. Nor with trust estate. Manning *v.* Evans, 9 *N. Y. Weekly Dig.* 311; Campbell *v.* Foster, 35 *N. Y.* 361; Underwood *v.* Sutcliffe, 77 *Id.* 58; Graff *v.* Barnett, 31 *Id.* 9; affirming 2 *Robt.* 54; Scott *v.* Nevins, 6 *Duer*, 672.

Liens.—A proceeding regularly instituted creates a lien on the judgment debtor's reachable personal property from the time of the service of the order. See §2469; Albany City Bank *v.* Schermerhorn, *Clarke*, 297; Boynton *v.* Rawson, *Id.* 584; Eameston *v.* Lyde, 1 *Paige*, 637; Corning *v.* White, 2 *Id.* 567; Jeffers *v.* Cochrane, 47 *Barb.* 557; Davenport *v.* Kelly, 42 *N. Y.* 193; Brown *v.* Nichols, *Id.* 26; Lynch *v.* Johnson, 48 *Id.* 27; affirming out S. C., 46 *Barb.* 56; Dubois *v.* Cassidy, 75 *N. Y.* 298; Corning *v.* Glenville Woolen Co., 14 *Abb. Pr.*

339; Jay v. De Groot, 2 *Hun*, 205; Hazewell v. Penmore, 13 *How. Pr.* 114; Deposit Nat. Bank v. Wickham, 44 *Id.* 421. But no lien is acquired on property already transferred. Field v. Sands, 8 *Bosw.* 685; Conger v. Sands, 19 *How. Pr.* 8.

Priorities.—Different proceedings against the same judgment debtor, or in pursuit of the same property, take preference according to the respective dates of their commencement, provided no laches occur. Becker v. Torrance, 31 *N. Y.* 631; Van Alstyne v. Cook, 25 *Id.* 489; Voorhies v. Seymour, 26 *Barb.* 569.

MOLOUGHNEY, RESPONDENT, v. KAVANAGH, APPELLANT.

SUPREME COURT, FIRST DEPARTMENT; GENERAL TERM, OCTOBER, 1882.

§ 66.

Set-off.—Not ordered until judgment perfected.—Attorney's lien exists before entry of judgment.—Where costs only are awarded, attorney need not give notice of lien.

The right to set off judgments does not accrue until judgment has been perfected, and a motion to set off costs to be thereafter taxed, against a judgment for costs recovered in another action is premature.[2]

An attorney has a lien upon the costs awarded in an action before the entry of judgment, and where costs only are awarded to protec- his rights he is not bound to give notice of lien.[3]

Armstrong v. Cummings (22 *Hun*, 570), distinguished.[1]

(*Decided January* 17, 1883.)

Appeal from order of the special term, setting off costs of this action to be hereafter taxed by the defendant, against costs recovered by the plaintiff, in a former action, brought against the plaintiff by the defendant herein, and another.

Denis A. Spellissy, for appellant.

H. H. Morange, for respondent.

DAVIS, P. J.—It appears by the memorandum of the learned judge at special term, that the motion was granted by him upon the authority of the decision
[1] of the general term in Armstrong *v.* Cummings (decided October, 1880, MS. opinion per CURIAM).*
It appears from the opinion that that case was disposed of altogether, upon a question of assignment. Interlocutory costs of demurrer, were awarded to the plaintiff and taxed. The defendant then moved to have them set off against the judgment recovered by him against the plaintiff. The plaintiff resisted the motion on the ground, that the interlocutory costs, had been assigned by her, to a stranger, previous to the making of the motion. The case was disposed of altogether, upon the ground that the costs of the demurrer were not capable of assignment at the time when they were shown to have been assigned.

The question decided by Armstrong *v.* Cummings, does not seem to us, to have any bearing upon the question presented on this appeal.

There are two reasons why the motion for set-off in this case should have been denied: First. That the motion was premature. Costs had not ripened into judgment; and it was held by the court, in Prouty *v.* Swift (10 *Hun*, 234), that the right to set off judg-
[2] ments, does not accrue until judgment has been perfected, the court citing, Perry *v.* Chester (53

* 22 *Hun.* 570.

N. Y. 243), Mackey *v.* Mackey (43 *Barb.* 58), and Roberts *v.* Carter (38 *N. Y.* 107). Second. Because no right of set-off had accrued, superior to the attorney's lien, on the costs in the action, at that stage of the proceedings, under section 66 of the Code of Civil
[*] Procedure (Ennis *v.* Curry, 22 *Hun*, 584; Hovey *v.* Rubber Type Co., 14 *Abb. Pr.* 66).

The attorney's lien existed upon the costs awarded, before the entry of the judgment, and as the order awarded costs only, to protect his rights, he was not bound to give notice of the lien.

The order of the court below, must therefore be reversed, with the costs, besides disbursements.

DANIELS and BRADY, JJ., concurred.

DENNY, APPELLANT, v. HORTON, RESPONDENT.

N. Y. COURT OF COMMON PLEAS; GENERAL TERM, JANUARY, 1883.

§§ 501, 910, 911, 2986.

Commission—Provisions of Code relative to suppression of, apply to justice's court—Too late to make motion for suppression on day of trial, or after trial began—Mistake in affidavit on which commission was granted as to Christian name of person to be examined, is mere irregularity—A cause of action for breach of contract, to employ is properly set up as a counter-claim in an action on contract.

The provisions of the Code, which confer upon the district courts the authority to issue commissions for the examination of witnesses not within the county, contemplates that in those courts, the commission may be suppressed when it appears by affidavit that it has been improperly or irregularly taken, or for the other causes specified in section 910, and confers upon the court, authority to make an order for its suppression on the application of the party aggrieved upon notice to the adverse party.[1] Sections 2986 and 911 of the Code, taken together, indicate that such remedy for the suppression of a commission is equally available when one is issued in a justice's court.[2]

When a statutory provision gives a court authority to issue a commission it impliedly gives what is necessarily incident thereto, to carry out the purpose of the statute, and what is necessarily incident thereto, such as suppressing a commission when it is irregularly issued or executed, is to be judged by preceding or collateral statutory provisions on the subject of the examination of witnesses by commission or by the practice established in relation thereto, when the statute was enacted.[3]

Where a commission to take the testimony of one Frank C. Fox, was issued, in a district court of the city of New York, on the application of the defendant, on an affidavit in which the person to be examined was described as George C. Fox,—*Held*, that this was a mere irregularity;[6] that the plaintiff having had notice or abundant opportunity, to know of the defect, and as he could have applied with reasonable dilligence to suppress the commission it was too late to do so on the adjourned day when the cause was called on for trial,[4] or after the trial had been commenced.[5]

VAN BRUNT, J. (concurring in result), *Held*, that the plaintiff should have moved, at least at the opening of the trial, to suppress the commission, and not have waited until the trial had so far progressed that the defendant could not remedy the defect.[11]

Where, in such a case, the commission was granted by a judge other than the one before whom the case was tried, and the defendant offered to read the deposition on the trial. *Held*, that neither the irregularity nor the justice, who granted the commission was before the court on the trial, and therefore the objection to the defect or irregularity in the issuing of the commission, was not in any way before the court, and the justice having only before him, a duly executed commission, properly allowed it to be read, and it would have been error, for him to have excluded it.[7]

Where it did not appear and the plaintiff did not offer to show that the defendant knew that a witness, examined under a commission at his instance was in the city, and the defendant's attention was not called to the fact until the plaintiff was through with his case, and the defendant's own examination, as a witness for the defense had been completed, he was not then required to consent that the trial be suspended, and the cause adjourned to a future day that the witness might be subpœnaed to attend, because the plaintiff was willing or offered to consent that that be done.[8]

A cause of action for damages for breach of an agreement to employ, is on contract, and may be properly set up as a counter-claim in an action founded on contract.[9]

Pease v. Sterns (1 *Hill*, 86), distinguished.[10]

(*Decided, March* 15, 1883).

Appeal from judgment of the district court in the city of New York for the sixth judicial district, in favor of the defendant.

This action was brought to recover the sum of $83, and interest, from July 1, 1880, for two suits of clothes alleged to have been made for the defendant, at his request, and delivered to him by one George C. Miller, who assigned his claim therefor to the plaintiff. The answer alleged that the defendant had no knowledge or information sufficient to form a belief as to the assignment to the plaintiff, and denied the other allegations of the complaint. It also set up as counter-claims (1) that on or about August 1, 1880, one Frank C. Fox made and entered into an agreement with said "George C. Miller whereby said Fox undertook to render his services as a cutter, and the said Miller undertook and agreed to so employ the said Fox for the term of one year, namely, from September 1, 1880, to September 1, 1881, and said Miller agreed to pay said Fox for his services as cutter the sum of $50 per week, during said term; that the said Fox duly entered upon his employment and duly discharged all the duties thereof until about" August 1, 1881, "when the said Miller discharged him from his employ without cause, although the said Fox was then and always remained ready and willing to perform all the conditions of said agreement on his part; that said Miller then refused and always refused to allow said Fox to do so or to pay him therefor to the damage of said Fox to the amount of $160," and that said Fox had assigned his said claim to the plaintiff for value, and (2) a demand of $100 due upon an account for commissions upon sales made by said Fox for said Miller, assigned by said Fox to defendant. The plaintiff asserted that the first claim sounded in tort, and hence could not be set up as a counter-claim in this action. The second counter-claim was abandoned on the trial.

On March 2, 1882, the day issue was joined, the defendant's counsel presented to the justice then presiding in the sixth district court an affidavit setting forth that one George C. Fox was a necessary and material witness for the defendant to prove "that no clothes were ever sold and delivered to said defendant by George C. Miller," and to establish the counter-claims set up in the answer, and asking for a commission to take the testimony of said Fox, on the ground that he then resided in Washington, D. C. This affidavit was filed with the clerk and a commission subsequently issued on it to take the testimony of Frank C. Fox, was duly executed and returned.

On the trial the justice, overruling plaintiff's objection, allowed the testimony taken under the commission to be read as evidence.

The defendant recovered judgment, and the plaintiff thereupon took this appeal.

Further facts are stated in the opinion.

William H. Gibson (*James O. Clark*, attorney), for appellant.

A waiver of a defect in the commission would not be binding unless in writing. Mason & Hamlin Organ Co. v. Pugsby, 19 *Hun*, 282. The defendant is supposed to know the defects of his commission upon its return, and can apply to the court to have them corrected. If he carry his defective commission into court he subjects it to judicial scrutiny. Terry v. McNiel, 58 *Barb.* 244. The statute must be strictly complied with. *Ib.* The commission was extra-judicial. For mistake in Christian name of witness examined under a commission, see Brown v. Southworth, 9 *Paige*, 351.

Malcolm R. Lawrence (*Swain & Lawrence*, attorneys), for respondent.

DALY, Ch. J.—The provisions of the Code, which confer upon the district courts the authority to issue commissions for the examination of witnesses not within the county contemplate that in those
[1] courts (§§ 910 911, and 2986) the commission
may be suppressed where it appears by affidavit that it has been improperly or irregularly taken, or for the other causes specified in section 910, and confers upon the court authority to make an order for its suppression on the application of the party aggrieved, upon notice to the adverse party. Sections 910 and 911 of the Code provide for the suppression of commissions in the cases therein stated, and the section
[2] 2986 declares that the deposition shall have the
effect specified in section 911. These sections, taken together, indicate, I think, that the remedy for the suppression of a commission provided for in sections 910 and 911 is equally available when one is issued in the justice's court; but even if this is not clear, it is sufficient to say that when a statutory provision gives a court authority to issue a commission, it impliedly gives what is necessarily incident thereto, to carry
[3] out the purpose of the statute; and what is neces-
sarily incident, such as suppressing a commission where it is irregularly issued or executed, is to be

judged by preceding or collateral statutory provisions on the subject of the examination of witnesses by commission, or the practice established in relation thereto, when the statute was enacted.

The commission was issued for the examination of Frank C. Fox, and the person so named was the witness whose deposition was taken. The fact that in the affidavit upon which the commission was granted he was named George C. Fox showed simply that there was an irregularity between the application as made and the commission as issued and executed. It does not appear by the return whether or not any order was made by the justice for the granting of the commission. The commission upon its face was tested in the name of WILLIAM H. KELLY, justice of the district court for the sixth judicial district, and it was signed by JAMES R. ANGEL, justice of the tenth judicial district, acting in the absence of Justice KELLY. It bears date the 23d of March. Issue was joined on the 2d March, so that the commission could not have been granted under the statute without six days' written notice of the application having been served upon the plaintiff. He was therefore advised that an application would be made for it, and that after it was executed it would, in conformity with the statute, be transmitted to the justice and remain on file with him until the trial (§ 2985). He had the opportunity, therefore, before the time of trial, of examining it and moving to suppress it for any irregularity that called for such a remedy. In addition to this, the interrogatories have, by the statute, to be settled by the justice, of which, we may assume, the plaintiff had notice and knew, or could have known, if he attended upon the settlement, that they were for the examination, not of George C. Fox, as in the affidavit, but of Frank C. Fox; and it was incumbent upon him, then, to raise the objection, as the defendant could then, before the commission was issued, have

removed the objection by making his application upon the proper affidavit. If the plaintiff was not present at the granting of the application and settlement of the interrogatories, and therefore ignorant of the irregularity, he could, after the return and filing of the
[4] commission with the justice, have applied with reasonable diligence to suppress the deposition, and it was too late to do so at the adjourned day when the cause was called on for trial (Jackson *v.* Hobby, 20 *Johns.* 362).

He did not even do this, but went to trial, and
[5] having examined his own witnesses and rested he raised the objection, for the first time, when the defendant, to establish his defense, undertook to read the deposition. If the commission upon its face had been, together with the interrogatories, for the examination of George C. Fox, and Frank C. Fox's deposition had been taken under it, the deposition could not have been read, as the person examined would have been of a different name from the one named in the commission. Such a deposition would be extra judicial, the commissioner having no authority to examine a person of a different name from that in the commission (Brown *v.* Southworth, 9 *Paige*, 351). But the defect was not of this grave character. It was
[6] a mere irregularity between the name in the affidavit presented to the justice and the name in the commission as issued by him. The witness examined was the one provided for in the commission—the one whose deposition the commissioner was authorized to take. Whatever irregularity may have existed in the proceedings on or between the application for and the issuing of the commission, all that the defendant had to do was to present the commission as executed and filed, and it appearing upon the face of it that the witness examined under it was the one named in it, defendant was entitled to read his deposition, as properly

taken under it. The irregularity was not before
[7] the court on the trial; nor was the justice who
granted the commission. The objection, therefore, to this defect or irregularity in the issuing of the commission was in no way before the court, upon the trial, and the justice having only before him a commission granted by a justice who, at the time was presiding in his place, and which was duly executed, as provided for in the commission, was right in allowing it to be read, and it would have been error for him to have excluded it.

It did not appear, nor did the plaintiff offer to show,
that the defendant knew before the trial that the
[8] witness examined under the commission was in this
city, so as to make it obligatory upon the defendant to have subpœnaed him to appear upon the trial, and the defendant's attention not being called to the fact until the plantiff was through with his case and the defendant's own examination as a witness for the defense had been completed, the defendant was not then required to consent that the trial might be suspended and the cause adjourned to a future day, that the witness might be subpœnaed to attend, because the plaintiff was willing or offered to consent that that might be done.

The justice was of the opinion that, having entered upon the trial, he had no authority then to suspend it and resume the trial on a day when the witness's attendance could be compelled by subpœna, and it was not error that what the justice had not authority to do, the defendant refused to consent to.

The assignment of Frank C. Fox to the defendant, of his claim against George C. Miller, the plaintiff's assignor, for breach of contract of hiring, was a good counterclaim under the Code.

The plaintiff's action was founded upon contract,
[9] and the counterclaim was for a cause of action

also arising upon contract—the breach of an agreement on the part of the plaintiff to employ the assignor Fox for a year.

In the case relied upon (Pease *v.* Sterns, 1 *Hill*, 86)
[10] the action was brought to recover for goods bought at a stipulated price; and what the defendant sought to counter-claim was damages for the conversion of a chattel, which was a very different case from the present one, where both the cause of action and the counter-claim arose out of contracts.

The judgment should be affirmed.

VAN BRUNT, J.—I concur in the result of the foregoing opinion. The plaintiff should have moved at
[11] least at the opening of the trial to have suppressed the commission, and not have waited until the trial had so far progressed that the defendant could not remedy the defect.

BENGTSON *v.* THINGVALLA STEAMSHIP COMPANY.

SUPREME COURT, SECOND DEPARTMENT; KINGS COUNTY SPECIAL TERM, APRIL, 1883.

§ 1776.

Incorporation of defendant need not to be proven unless the answer contains an affirmative allegation that the defendant is not a corporation.—If on information and belief, the allegation is not sufficient.—Meaning of affirm.

A plaintiff is not bound to prove the incorporation of a defendant unless a verified answer was served containing an affirmative allegation that the defendant is not a corporation.

An allegation in an answer upon information and belief that a defendant is not and never was a corporation, does not put in issue the incorporation of the defendant. It is not an affirmative allegation. To affirm is to assert positively; to declare the existence of something. An affirmative allegation is a positive allegation.

East River Bank *v.* Rogers (7 *Bosw.* 493), followed.

(*Decided April* 30, 1883.)

Motion on behalf of defendant to set aside verdict in favor of the plaintiff, and for a new trial, on the ground that plaintiff failed to prove upon the trial that defendant was incorporated.

The action was brought against defendant, a common carrier, to recover for the loss of plaintiff's baggage.

The complaint alleged that defendant was a foreign corporation existing under the laws of Denmark.

The answer denied this, and alleged on information and belief that defendant was not a corporation.

The plaintiff claimed on the trial that this answer was not sufficient under section 1776 of the Code, to compel proof of defendant's incorporation. Plaintiff recovered a verdict, and subsequently this motion was made for a new trial.

Hill, Wing & Shoudy, for motion.

J. Edward Swanstrom, opposed.

BROWN, J.—The plaintiff was not bound to prove the incorporation of the defendant unless a verified answer was served containing an affirmative allegation that the defendant is not a corporation. The answer contains an allegation as follows: "For a second and separate defense the defendant alleges on information and belief that it is not and never was a corporation." I do not think this allegation puts in issue the incorporation of the defendant. It is not affirmative allegation. To affirm is to assert positively; to declare the existence of something. An affirmative allegation is a positive allegation. The allegation in the answer is nothing. It neither affirms nor denies. Of all persons the defendant's officers should know whether it is a corporation or not. In the case of the East River Bank v. Rogers (7 *Bosw.* 493), an answer by the defendant, "that he is informed and believes the plaintiff is not a corporation," was held not to amount to a plea "that the plaintiff is not a corporation." The reasoning of that case applies with greater force to an answer by the corporation itself. The rule of pleading is a salutary one, and the party intending to raise the issue as to the corporation should be held to a positive allegation to that effect; at the least such should be the rule where a company holding itself out to the world as a corporation denies its own existence.

Motion for a new trial denied, with costs.

MURTHA, Appellant, *v.* CURLEY, Respondent.

Court of Appeals; April, 1883.

§ 3238.

Costs of appeal.—When plaintiff entitled to, of course.—When the court of appeals affirms a judgment of the special term with costs, "with costs" means all costs subsequent to the entry of judgment.—When costs are discretionary, upon an appeal to the court of appeals all costs subsequent to the judgment are subject to its control.

Where a plaintiff was entitled to costs of course, under section 3228 of the Code, upon the entry of a final judgment in his favor, and his judgment was finally affirmed in the court of appeals,—*Held*, that he was entitled to his costs of the appeals to the general term, aud to the court of appeals.[1]

Where the court of appeals reversed an order of the general term directing a new trial, and affirmed the judgment of the special term, with costs,—*Held*, that "with costs" meant all the taxable costs subsequent to the judgment affirmed, consequent upon the appeals both to the general term and to the court of appeals.[2]

Where the costs of an action are in the discretion of the court, the whole subject of costs, both in the court in which the judgment was originally recovered subsequent to the judgment, and in the court of appeals, are subject to the control of the latter court upon an appeal to it.[3]

Murtha *v.* Curley (3 *N. Y. Civ. Pro.* 86), reversed.
(*Decided May* 1, 1883).

Appeal from an order of the N. Y. superior court, general term, reversing an order of the special term.

The facts are stated in the opinion.

Adolphus D. Pape, for appellant.

Starr & Hooker, for respondent.

The first appeal to the general term being from a final judgment the costs thereof were in the discretion of the general term under section 3238 of the Code of Civil Procedure, because that a new trial was directed. See subd. 1, last clause of § 3238. Also because the action was in equity. § 3238, subd. 2; Black v. O'Brien, 23 *Hun*, 82; Taylor v. Root, 48 *N. Y.* 678; Palmer v. Ranken, 56 *How. Pr.* 354. So in every stage of the action. Chipman v. Montgomery, 63 *N. Y.* 222. The court of appeals has heretofore declined to interpose to overrule the discretion of the general term as to costs where such discretionary power plainly existed. *In re* Protestant Episcopal School, 86 *N. Y.* 397. And where, as in the present case, there was a reversal by the court of appeals, "with costs," the costs of the court of appeals only are intended. Sisters of Charity v. Kelly, 68 *N. Y.* 628; Post v. Doremus, 60 *N. Y.* 372.

EARL, J.—In this action a money judgment was recovered against the defendant. From that judgment he appealed to the general term of New York superior court, where the judgment was reversed and a new trial granted, "*with costs to the appellant to abide the event of such new trial.*" From the order of the general term the plaintiff appealed to the court of appeals, which reversed the order of the general term and affirmed the judgment of the special term, "*with costs.*" Upon the taxation of costs, plaintiff sought to tax the costs of the appeal to the general term. Upon objection on behalf of defendant, the clerk disallowed such costs, and plaintiff then appealed to the special term, which reversed the ruling of the clerk and directed him to tax the costs of the appeal to the general term. The defendant then appealed from the order of the special term to the general term, which reversed the order of the special term and affirmed the ruling of the clerk,* and this appeal is from that order of the general term.

Section 3228 of the Code provides for the cases in which a plaintiff is entitled to costs of course, and subdivisions 1, 2 and 3 of that section provide for costs in what are commonly called actions at law. Subdivision 4 gives costs to the plaintiff in "an action, other than one of those specified in the foregoing subdivisions of this section in which the complaint demands judgment for a sum of money only." Under this subdivision it does not matter whether the action be legal or equitable; the sole condition being that the judgment demanded must be for money only.

Section 3229 provides that the defendant shall have costs of course in the same actions specified in the preceding section, unless the plaintiff is entitled to costs as therein prescribed. Section 3230 provides that, except as prescribed in the preceding section, the court may in its discretion award costs to any party upon the rendering of a final judgment. Section 3237 provides that the preceding sections "do not affect the recovery of costs upon an appeal," and then section 3238 provides that, "Upon an appeal from the final judgment in an action the recovery of costs is regulated as follows: 1st. In an action specified in section 3228 of this act the respondent is entitled to costs upon the affirmance, and the appellant upon the reversal, of the judgment appealed from; except that, where a new trial is directed, costs may be awarded to either party, absolutely or to abide the event, in the discretion of the court. 2d. In every other action, and also where the final judgment appealed from is affirmed in part and reversed in part, costs may be awarded in like manner, in the discretion of the court."

* The opinion of the general term is reported, *ante*, p. 86.

It does not appear on the record before us what judgment was demanded in the complaint. From the fact a money judgment was rendered we may infer that a money judgment only was demanded in the complaint; and such from records in our possession we know to be the fact (90 *N. Y.* 372).* Therefore this is a case where the plaintiff was entitled to costs of course under section 3228, upon the entry of the judg-
[1] ment in his favor; and as his judgment was finally
affirmed in this court he was of course entitled to his costs of the appeals to the general term and to this court under section 3238, but if we assume that this is an equitable action, that the costs are not controlled by subdivision 4 of section 3228, and that they rest in the discretion of the court, *the result is yet the same.* Then while the cause was pending in the superior court, the costs were in the discretion of that court; and when it came here the costs were in the discretion of this court.

The order of the general term would have governed as to the costs if a new trial had been had. But the plaintiff was not satisfied with that order; he did not take the new trial, but appealed to this court. That order was reversed, and thus its entire effect was wiped out, and this court exercised its discretion upon the costs by affirming the judgment of the special term, "with costs." *That means all the taxable costs*
[2] *subsequent to the judgment affirmed consequent*
upon the appeals, both to the general term and to this court. The whole subject of costs, both in the superior court, subsequent to the judgment there, and in
[3] this court, was then subject to the control of this
court, and it exercised its discretion by granting them to the plaintiff.

It follows from these views that the order of the

* See Murtha v. Curley, *ante*, p. 1.

general term should be reversed and that of the special term affirmed, with costs, and when we say "*with costs," we mean the costs of the appeal to the general term and to this court.*

All concurred.

IN THE MATTER OF THE VOLUNTARY DISSOLUTION OF THE PYROLUSITE MANGANESE COMPANY.

SUPREME COURT, FIRST DEPARTMENT; GENERAL TERM, MARCH, 1883.

§§ 2419, 2420, 2421, 2423, 2426.

Dissolution of corporation.—Petition for voluntary, must show that it will be to the interest of the stockholders.—Nature, and contents of order to show cause why corporation should not be dissolved.—Report of referee in proceeding for dissolution of corporation.—Statutory proceedings must conform to the requirements of the statute providing for them, and when they fail to do so, the court does not acquire jurisdiction.

The petition for the voluntary dissolution of a corporation must show that such dissolution would be beneficial to the interest of the stockholders. [1]

In a proceeding for the voluntary dissolution of a corporation, the order prescribed by section 2423 of the Code, that the persons interested in the corporation, show cause why it should not be dissolved, is in the nature of process for bringing the persons interested in contesting and resisting the application before the court. [2] Where the order did not require those interested in the corporation to show cause why it should not be dissolved, but contained the requirement that they show cause "why the prayer of the petitioners should not be granted." *Held*, that it was neither in substance nor effect what the law prescribed it should be;[3] that the code clearly intended that every person receiving a copy of the order should be informed by its contents that the proceeding was taken to dissolve the corporation itself, and as the order contained no such information, and in that respect entirely failed to comply with what the statute had required, the proceeding was not legally commenced.[4]

Where, in such a case, the creditors of the corporation did not appear or in any way waive their right to be served with precisely such an order as the code prescribes, no jurisdiction was acquired over them, and as this was an indispensable step in the proceeding, the omission to take it could be insisted upon at any time by either of the other parties[7,8] and although the objection was not taken on their motion to vacate the order, or in their answers.[6]

The report of the referee in a proceeding for the voluntary dissolution of a corporation, must contain "a statement of the effects, credits and other property, and of the debts and other engagements of the corporation, and of all other matters appertaining to its affairs," and where it contained no statement of the debts of the corporation, but stated, generally, that the schedules annexed to the petition were correct, *Held*, that this was not a compliance with what the Code demands.[9]

The rule in all statutory proceedings is that they must conform to the requirements made by the statute providing for them, and if they fail to do so, then the court does not acquire jurisdiction over the proceedings, and it will have no authority to make any adjudication affecting the rights of the parties designed to be controlled by it.[6]

(*Decided March* 30, 1883.)

Appeal from an order dissolving a corporation and appointing a receiver of it.

This proceeding was initiated by a petition of which the following is a copy:

"To the Supreme Court of the State of New York:

"The petition of Charles C. Dodge and Anson Phelps Pond, as trustees of the Pyrolusite Manganese Company, respectfully shows:

"I. That the said Pyrolusite Manganese Company

is a corporation created under the laws of the State of New York, having been incorporated under the provisions of the Laws of 1848, chap. 40, and the Acts amendatory thereto, and its principal office is located at No 76 Pine street, in the city of New York, county of New York and State of New York.

"II. That your petitioners are one-half in number of the trustees of the said Pyrolusite Manganese Company, the remaining two trustees being Edward H. Woodward, residing at Plainfield, New Jersey, and Arthur T. Woodward, residing at Brooklyn, Kings county, New York.

"III. That the business of said Pyrolusite Manganese Company is the mining, purifying and selling of ores.

"IV. That the said company has a capital of $100,000, divided into 2000 shares. That your petitioner Charles C. Dodge is the owner and holder of 995 shares thereof, and your petitioner, Anson Phelps Pond is the owner and holder of 5 shares thereof; that the said Edward H. Woodward was, and to the best of your petitioner's knowledge, information and belief still is, the owner and holder of 995 shares thereof, except such number of the said 995 shares as the said Edward H. Woodward may have transferred to his wife Pauline Woodward, who resides at Plainfield, New Jersey; these petitioners having been informed that a transfer of a certain number of his shares had been made by him to his wife, the said Pauline Woodward, but what number of shares, these petitioners are wholly unable to allege, and state; and that the said Arthur T. Woodward was, and to the best of your petitioners knowledge, information, and belief still is the owner and holder of 5 shares thereof.

"V. That the schedules hereto annexed state, so far as your petitioners know or have the means of knowing, 1st, a full and true account of all creditors of the corporation and of all unsatisfied engagements entered into by and subsisting against the said corporation; 2d, a statement of the name and place of residence of each creditor and of each person with whom such engagement was made, and to whom it is to be performed if known, or, if either is not known a statement of that fact; 3rd, a statement of the sum owing to each creditor or other person specified in the last subdivision and the nature of each debt demanded or other engagement; 4th, a statement of the true cause and consideration of the indebtedness of each creditor; 5th, a full, just and true inventory of all property of the corporation and of all books, vouchers and securities relating thereto; 6th, a statement of each incumbrance upon the property of the corporation by judgment, mortgage, pledge or otherwise; 7th, a full just and true account of the capital stock of the corporation specifying the name of each stockholder, his residence, if it is known, or, if it is not known stating that fact; the number of shares belonging to him; the amount paid in upon his shares, the amount still due thereupon.

"VI. That your petitioners, as trustees of said corporation on the one side, and said Edward H. Woodward and Arthur T. Woodward, as trustees of said corporation on the other side, are wholly, irreconcilably and materially at variance as to the manner and mode in which the affairs of said Pyrolusite Manganese Company should be and are managed and your petitioners believe and are fully convinced that should the course, methods and plans advocated and pursued by the said Edward H. Woodward and Arthur T. Woodward in relation to the management of said corporation be carried out the result wiil be the financial ruin of the said corporation.

"Wherefore your petitioners pray for a final order dissolving said corporation and appointimg one or more receivers of its property, and for such other relief as may be just. Dated June 3, 1882.

"CHARLES C. DODGE,
"ANSON P. POND."

Annexed to this petition were the schedules referred to in its fifth paragraph, and an affidavit by each of the petitioners that the matters of fact stated in the "petition and the schedules thereto annexed are just and true so far as he knows or has means of knowing."

On these papers an order was granted "that all persons interested in said corporation show cause before Horace H. Chittenden, Esq., who is hereby appointed referee for that purpose at his office," etc., "why the prayer of the petitioners should not be granted."

On the return day mentioned in the order, the Pyrolusite Manganese Company, Edward H. Woodward, Arthur T. Woodward and Pauline Woodward, appeared and answered. Poor & Freeborn and Ernest G. Stedman, creditors of the corporation, also appeared, but did not answer.

Subsequently, on September 29, 1882, Pauline Woodward, Edward H. Woodward and Arthur T. Woodward, moved at special term to vacate and set aside the order to show cause and of reference "on the ground of want of jurisdiction of the court to make the same, and on the ground that the petition herein does not show that the case is one of those specified in sections 2419 and 2420 of the Code of Civil Procedure or either of them, and that the statute has not been complied with and on the ground that said application and schedules is not in compliance with section 2421 of the Code of Civil Procedure." This motion was denied.

The referee, after hearing the proof offered by the

several parties, filed his report, January 27, 1883, on which an order was granted by the court at special term, February 13, 1883, dissolving the corporation and appointing a receiver of it.

From that order and the order denying the motion to vacate and set aside the order to show cause, &c., the Pyrolusite Manganese Company, Edward H. Woodward, Arthur T. Woodward and Pauline Woodward, took this appeal.

Edward C. James and *James B. Dill* (*Dill & Chandler*, attorneys), for appellants.

A corporation can only effect its voluntary dissolution in the manner prescribed in sections 2419 to 2432 of the Code. Lake Ontario Bank *v.* Onondaga Co. Bank, 7 *Hun*, 549 . . . . The law is well settled that proceedings for the voluntary dissolution of a corporation must conform to the statute strictly. Chamberlain *v.* Rochester Seamless Paper Vessel Co., 7 *Hun*, 557; Matter of Dubois, 15 *How. Pr.* 7; S. C., 6 *Abb. Pr.* 386 note. The court cannot acquire jurisdiction of the proceedings for any purpose unless the petition shows a case within the statute, and complies strictly with the statutory requirements. *Ib.* The same rule obtains in all statutory proceedings. *In re* Valentine, 72 *N. Y.* 184; Battell *v.* Torrey, 65 *Id.* 294; People *v.* Hulburt, 46 *Id.* 110; Onderdonk *v.* Mott, 34 *Barb.* 106; Ackley *v.* Dygert, 33 *Id.* 176; Corwin *v.* Merrit, 3 *Id.* 343; *In re* Pettit, 2 *Paige*, 596; Atkins *v.* Kinnan, 20 *Wend.* 241; Ford *v.* Walsworth, 15 *Id.* 449; Van Nostrand *v.* Wright, *Hill & Denio Sup.* 260; Sharp *v.* Spier, 4 *Hill*, 76. If the statute is not complied with the decision is a nullity. Stilwell *v.* Swarthout, 81 *N. Y.* 109; Brown *v.* Mayor, 3 *Hun*, 686; People *v.* Police Board, 6 *Abb. Pr.* 164; Cock *v.* Ferren, 34 *Barb.* 95. There is no distinction between superior and inferior courts in this regard. Bloom *v.*

Burdick, 1 *Hill*, 130; Bangs *v.* McIntosh, 23 *Barb.* 591; Chamberlain *v.* Rochester, &c. Co., *supra;* Striker *v.* Kelly, 2 *Denio*, 323; Castellanus *v.* Jones, 5 *N. Y.* 164. . . . . The appearance by these appellants could not confer jurisdiction of the subject matter herein, or cure the defects of the petition. Jurisdiction of the subject matter cannot be conferred by consent. Dudley *v.* Mayhew, 3 *N. Y.* 9; Beach *v.* Nixon, 9 *N. Y.* 36 . . . . Where a petition is sufficient to give the court jurisdiction to proceed, the only jurisdiction conferred is to proceed, not according to the discretion of the court, but in accordance with the statute. It gives a special statutory jurisdiction which can only be exercised as the statute directs. *In re* Valentine, 72 *N. Y.* 184; Battell *v.* Torrey, 65 *Id.* 294; Agricultural Ins. Co. *v.* Barnard, 26 *Hun*, 320, Chamberlain *v.* Rochester, &c. Co., *supra; In re* French M'fg. Co., 12 *Hun*, 488 . . . . The court could not get jurisdiction by deciding that it had it. Sibley *v.* Waffle, 16 *N. Y.* 180.

John E. Ward, for respondents, Charles E. Dodge and Anson P. Pond.

E. G. Stedman, respondent in person.

Walter S. Poor, for respondents Poor and Freeborn.

DANIELS, J.—The proceedings were taken under the authority of title 2, chapter 17 of the Code of Civil Procedure. By the petition it was stated, and the proof taken established the fact, that one-half the shares of the corporate stock was owned by the petitioners, who were two of the trustee of the company proceeded against, and the other one-half was owned by the individual appellants. And it was for the reason, as it was stated, that these parties differed concerning the management of the affairs of the

company, that the proceedings for its dissolution were instituted. But why the corporation should be dissolved because of that difference was not clearly stated in the petition. The statement upon that subject was that the petitioners were convinced that if the "methods and plans" advocated and pursued by the said "Edward H. Woodward and Arthur T. Woodward in relation to the management of said corporation be carried out, the result would be the financial ruin of the said corporation." What these plans and methods were, was in no manner stated in the petition; neither was it shown, on account of this disagreement or for any other reason, that it would be deemed beneficial to the interests of the stockholders that
[1] the corporation should be dissolved. And at least as much as that has been required by section 2419 of the Code of Civil Procedure to justify and support this proceeding. In this respect the petition was quite defective, and it was objected to as such by the appellants in the answers which they filed before the referee.

An equally serious, if not a more fatal defect, was contained in the order required to be and which was actually published and served upon the creditors and stockholders of the corporation. This order was in the nature of process provided for bringing the
[2] persons interested in contesting and resisting the application before the court, and its form and contents were specially prescribed by the provision directing it to be made and served. By the terms of this provision, where the court entertains the application, or the case is one of those mentioned in section 2419, it has been directed that it "must make an order requiring all persons interested in the corporation to show cause before it, or before a referee designated in the order, at a time and place therein specified, not less than three months after the granting

of the order, why the corporation should not be dissolved" (*Code Civ. Pro.* § 2423). And this order has been required not only to be published once in each week of the three weeks immediately preceding the time fixed therein for showing cause, but it also has been directed that a copy of it must be served upon each of the persons specified in the schedule annexed to the petition, as a creditor or stockholder of the corporation (*Id.* § 2425).

The order, which was in fact made, published and served, was neither in form nor effect what section 2423 directed it should be, for it did not require the persons interested in the corporation to show cause why it should not be dissolved, but the require-
[3] ment contained in it was that they should show cause "why the prayer of the petitioners should not be granted," which was neither in substance nor effect what the law had prescribed the order should be. No service of the petition itself was directed to be made by the statute or by the order, and it was not in fact served on either of the persons to whom the order was sent. For that reason, neither of the persons proceeded against as interested in the corporation could understand, from anything contained in the order, that the proceeding was one to dissolve the corporation. No intimation whatever, that this was intended to be its character, was in any form contained in the order. This was a radical as well as material defect, for it wholly omitted to give the notice which the law had prescribed the creditors and stockholders should have as the foundation of the proceeding.

It was clearly intended by this portion of the Code, that every person receiving a copy of the order should be informed by its contents, that the proceeding was taken to dissolve the corporation itself. But this
[4] order contained no such information, and in that respect it entirely failed to comply with what the

statute had required, and for that reason the proceeding was not legally commenced. The rule in all statutory proceedings is, that they must conform to the requirements made by the statute providing for them, and if they fail to do that, then the court
[*] does not acquire jurisdiction over the proceeding,
and it will have no authority to make any adjudication affecting the rights of the parties designed to be controlled by it (Sharp *v.* Spier, 4 *Hill*, 76; Matter of Haff, 72 *N. Y.* 134).

The fact that the parties appealing did not themselves take this objection to the proceeding, either
[*] on their motion to vacate the order or by their
answers, does not remove the difficulty in the case. For they are not the only persons upon whom the order was required to be served, or who had the right to contest the proceeding itself. By section 2421 of the Code, a schedule was required to be annexed to the petition containing a full and true account of the creditors of the corporation and of all its unsatisfied engagements; and each of these persons are required to be served with the order before the hearing, provided for could take place, or the corporation could be dissolved. Neither of these creditors, and the schedule to the petition named a considerable number of them, appeared in the proceeding, and they in no manner waived their right to be served with precisely such an order as was prescribed by the statute. By the service of the order upon them, which was in fact made, no jurisdiction was acquired over them,
['] and as this was an indispensable step in the
progress of the proceeding, the omission to take it could be insisted upon at any time by either of the other parties. For while they might waive the direction to make and serve such an order upon themselves, they could not do that for either of these creditors, whom they do not appear to have had any

authority whatever to represent. And they did not in fact attempt to appear for them. This omission in the order was a substantial jurisdictional defect in the proceeding, which prevented the court from obtaining complete jurisdiction over it, or over these creditors who were required to be made parties to it. The provisions of the statute are peremptory, that the order shall be in the prescribed form, and that a copy of it must be served upon each of the specified persons in the schedule as a creditor or stockholder of the corporation. And as it was not in this form and could [*] not be so served, every party to the proceeding was at liberty to resist it because of these omissions.

The law has also declared that the report of the referee must contain "a statement of the effects, credits and other property, and of the debts and other engagements of the corporation and of all other matters appertaining to its affairs."* That which was made by the referee contained no statement of the debts of the corporation, but it stated generally that the schedules annexed to the petition were correct.

This was not a compliance with what this [°] section of the Code demanded, and so far as the amounts owing to the creditors were involved, no obstacle stood in the way of a literal compliance with this provision, even if the effects, credits and property of the corporation could not be set forth because of the abstraction of the books and papers by the contestants.

Other objections have been taken to the regularity of the proceedings which, even though well founded, are by no means of so serious a character as those which have already been considered. For the disposition of the appeal, it is not requisite that they should

---

* *Code Civ. Pro.* § 2426.

receive specific attention. The objections made to the substance of the petition and to the form of the order are fundamental, and as they have neither been removed nor obviated by anything afterwards transpiring in the proceeding, it cannot be sustained. These failures to comply with what the law has explicitly required to institute and maintain such a proceeding are so important as to render it incapable of being supported.

The order from which the appeal has been taken should be reversed, with costs, and the proceeding itself should be dismissed, but without prejudice to the commencement of another proceeding for the dissolution of the corporation in the form prescribed by the Code of Civil Procedure.

DAVIS, P. J., and BRADY, J., concurred.

SHERWOOD ET AL. v. THE TRAVELERS' INSURANCE COMPANY OF HARTFORD, RESPONDENTS.

CHARLES C. BIGELOW, APPELLANT.

N. Y. COURT OF COMMON PLEAS; GENERAL TERM, MARCH, 1883.

§§ 3047, 3060.

District court in the city of New York.—Costs paid to perfect appeal from, should be paid to successful party in district court.

The costs paid to a justice or his clerk to perfect an appeal from a district court in the city of New York, are to be paid to the successful party in the district court. The appellant, if costs are awarded to him on the appeal, may tax, among other items, the costs and fees so paid. The authority to do so seems to contemplate a prior disposition by the justice or his clerk, and as they do not belong to either of them, the only one possible is a payment to the successful party.

Sherwood *v.* Traveler's Insurance Co. (2 *N. Y. Civ. Pro.* 67), reversed.

(*Decided May* 18, 1883.)

Appeal from an order requiring the clerk of a district court in the city of New York to return to a successful appellant the costs paid to perfect the appeal. (Reversing 2 *N. Y. Civ. Pro.* 67.)

On January 5, 1882, the plaintiffs recovered a judgment in the district court in the city of New York for the tenth judicial district, against the defendant, for $60 damages and $17.50 costs. The defendant thereafter, January 19, 1882, appealed to the general term of this court, serving notice of appeal, and at the same time, to perfect its appeal, it paid to the clerk of the district court the fees of the justice for a return, and $17.50 costs of the action. It also, to stay execution, gave an undertaking, which was duly approved by the justice and filed with the clerk. The judgment was reversed with costs. The defendant thereafter, on March 11, 1882, served a certified copy of the judgment of reversal on the clerk and demanded the $17.50 costs, which had been paid to him when the appeal was taken. He had paid the amount to plaintiff's attorney January 28, 1882, and refused now to pay it to the defendant, who thereupon moved this court at special term for an order directing the clerk to pay the money. The court below granted the motion, with $10 costs, and the clerk took this appeal.

Charles C. Bigelow, appellant, in person.

F. E. Mather (*Thomas C. Ennever*, attorney), for respondent.

BEACH, J.—I have been unable to find any adjudication bearing upon the question. In Ex parte Stephen *v.* The Saratoga Common Pleas (1 *Wend.* 282), the court go no further than to decide that the method of appeal must be strictly followed, and payment of costs to the party instead of the justice was not a compliance with the statute. The appellant, if costs are awarded him on the appeal, may tax, among other items, the costs and fee paid to the justice upon taking the appeal (*Code Civil Pro.* § 3060). The authority to include these costs among the disbursements on appeal seems to contemplate a prior disposition of them by the justice or his clerk.

The only one possible is a payment to the successful party in the district court, as they certainly do not belong to either of those officials, and if to rest on deposit, no necessity existed for such a provision. I do not think the giving of an undertaking affects the question, for its purpose does not reach beyond a stay of execution (*Code Civ. Pro.* § 3050). Neither can these costs fall within section 3058. They are not property lost by means of the erroneous judgment, because not taken from the party under the judgment, but paid as one of the steps needful to perfect his appeal.

The order should be reversed, with costs and disbursements.

CANADA STEAMSHIP COMPANY, LIMITED, RESPONDENT, v. SINCLAIR AND ANOTHER, APPELLANTS.

N. Y. SUPERIOR COURT; GENERAL TERM, MAY, 1883.

§§ 837, 870, *et seq.*, 880.

Examination of party before trial.—Order for, should not be set aside on ground that it will tend to criminate him, unless the evidence sought to be obtained relates exclusively to facts which, if proven, would show that the witness was guilty of a crime.—The right of a witness to refuse to answer a question on that ground, is a personal privilege.—Possession of stolen goods, received without knowledge that they were stolen, is not a crime.

The right of a witness to refuse to answer a question which would tend to convict him of a crime is a personal privilege, and should be urged when he is asked the questions having such a tendency. It is not sufficient ground for setting aside an order for his examination before trial, unless it appears that the testimony which is sought to be obtained relates exclusively to facts which, if proven, would show that the witness was guilty of a crime.[2]

The possession of goods that have been stolen, is not of itself a crime. The crime is only committed when a person buys or receives property stolen from another, knowing the same to have been stolen.[1]

Where certain bales of rubber were stolen from a common carrier, having a special property in them, and it brought an action against a person alleged to have become possessed of a part of them to recover possession thereof, and an order for the examination of the defendant to enable plaintiff to frame its complaint was granted on an affidavit setting forth that it was impossible for plaintiff to allege the number of bales that came into possession of the defendant, or the weight of the rubber, or to properly frame the complaint without such examination,—*Held,* that the order should not be set aside on the ground that the testimony to be given would make the defendant liable to indictment for receiving stolen goods;[3, 4] that as the defendant's possession of the stolen goods is consistent with his innocence, the objection should be left to be passed on upon the examination itself.[5]

(*Decided May* 10, 1883.)

Appeal from order denying motion to vacate order for examination of defendants to enable plaintiff to frame its complaint.

The facts are sufficiently stated in the opinion.

Richard S. Newcombe, for appellant.

C. Stewart Davison (*Ullo & Davison*, attorneys), for respondent.

INGRAHAM, J.—From the affidavit on which the order for the examination of the defendants was granted, it appears that plaintiff had, as common carrier, a special property in thirty-one bales of rubber which were stolen from the plaintiffs about January 10, 1883, and some portion of which was thereafter in possession of defendants. That the action was commenced to recover the return of the property or the value thereof from the defendants, and that it was impossible for plaintiff to allege the number of the bales that came into possession of the defendants or the weight of the rubber, or to properly frame the complaint, without the examination of defendants. On the affidavit the defendants moved to vacate the order for the examination of the defendants, which motion was denied, and from that order denying such motion the defendants appeal.

The ground upon which it is claimed that the order should be reversed is "that the testimony to be given would make the defendants liable to indictment for receiving stolen goods."

The possession of goods that have been stolen is
[1] not of itself a crime. The crime is only committed where a person buys or receives property stolen from another, knowing the same to have been stolen (2 *Edm. Rev. Stat.* 700, § 71). The right of a wit-
[2] ness to object to answer a question which would tend to convict him of a crime is a personal privilege and should be urged when he is asked the questions having such a tendency. It is not sufficient ground for setting aside an order for his examination unless it should appear that the testimony which the party seeks to obtain relates exclusively to facts which, if proven, would show that the witness was guilty of a crime.*

In this case the object of the examination is to identify the goods stolen from the plaintiff, which, it is claimed, came into the possession of the defendant. That of itself would not be a crime, it would
[3] undoubtedly be one of the facts which it would be necessary to prove to convict of the crime of receiving stolen goods; but, as the fact is consistent with the innocence of the defendant, I am of the opinion that the objection should be left to be passed on upon the examination itself (Patterson v. Sandford, 45 *N. Y. Super.* 127).

The order should be affirmed, but without costs.

TRUAX, J. [Concurring.]—I concur in this result,
[4] because I think that in this particular case the defendant should be left to take the objection upon the examination.

SEDGWICK, Ch. J., concurred.

* See Russ v. Campbell, 1 *N. Y. Civ. Pro.* 41; Tenney v. Mautner, *Id.* 64, and cases there cited.

LANG, ET AL., RESPONDENTS, v. MARKS, APPELLANT.

N. Y. COURT OF COMMON PLEAS; GENERAL TERM, JANUARY, 1883.

§§ 2917, 3211.

Attachment.—Practice as to granting, etc., of, in district court of the city of New York not changed by Code.—Motion to vacate, issued out of district court, may be reviewed on appeal.—Must be allowed by justice and signed by clerk.

On appeal from a district court in the city of New York, all the proceedings before the justice are brought up,[4] and the appellate court can review a decision of the justice denying a motion to vacate an attachment issued in the action.[1,3]* The Code of Civil Procedure has made no change in the manner of applying for, granting or executing attachments in district courts, except that the action must always be commenced by summons.[2]

An attachment issued out of a district court of the city of New York must be allowed by the justice and signed by the clerk. An attachment signed by the justice as if issued under the Code is fatally defective.[5]

(*Decided March* 15, 1883.)

Appeal from judgment of the district court in the city of New York for the seventh judicial district.

An attachment was granted against the defendant's property and served upon him, and at the same time he

* The issuing of an attachment upon insufficient affidavits by a justice of the peace is an error of law, affecting the substantial rights of the defendant, for which the judgment may be reversed. Fritze v. Pultz, 2 *N. Y. Civ. Pro.* 142.

was personally served with the summons and thereafter appeared generally in the action.

The defendant moved to vacate the attachment, upon the ground that the warrant was signed by the justice alone, instead of being indorsed by him as "allowed," and then signed by the clerk. The motion was denied, and the defendant thereupon answered, and the action was tried and resulted in a judgment for the plaintiffs. From that judgment this appeal was taken.

Aaron Levy, for appellant.

John L. Lindsay (*Lindsay & Flammer*, attorneys), for respondent.

VAN BRUNT, J.—The main question which it is necessary to decide in disposing of this appeal seems to be this: Upon an appeal to this court from a district court in the city of New York, can this court review the decision of the justice denying a motion to vacate an attachment issued against property which had been previously issued in the action? Unless it can, then, no matter how erroneous the proceeding of a justice may have been in the issuing or sustaining an attachment, the defendant is wholly without remedy. Under the practice prior to the new Code it was well settled that upon an appeal from a judgment the
[1] proceedings of an attachment so issued could be reviewed upon an appeal from the judgment.

It is urged, and there is great force in the suggestion, that under the practice before the new Code, where an attachment was issued, it was the process by which the action was commenced, and therefore properly came before the appellate court as part of the record showing how the court acquired jurisdiction;

but that under the new Code the court does not acquire jurisdiction by the attachment but by the service of the summons, and even though the attachment be vacated the court may proceed to judgment in case of a general appearance of the defendant or a personal service of a summons upon him (section 2917), thus making the attachment simply a provisional remedy, as in courts of record. But when we consider that section 3211 of the new Code especially provides that no change in the manner of applying for, granting and executing a warrant of attachment, and the proceedings thereupon, is intended to be made, unless the statute under
[2] which those proceedings are regulated is expressly repealed, it is clear that no change whatever in any respect was made in the old statute, except that an action must always be commenced by summons. Under the practice existing at the time of the adoption of the Code, under the then existing statutes the proceedings upon attachment could be reviewed
[3] upon appeal, and the language above shows a manifest intent not to disturb the practice in any respect by implication.

It would appear, therefore, that on appeal from
[4] the judgment, all the proceedings before the justice are brought up as before. The objection that the attachment was not allowed by the justice and signed by the clerk seems to be fatal. The attachment is signed by the justice as if it was issued under the Code, but as the Code has made no change in
[5] the manner of granting an attachment, it should have been allowed by the justice, and signed by the clerk.

Judgment must be reversed.

Daly, Ch. J., and Beach, J., concurred.

PARSONS AND ANOTHER, RESPONDENTS, v. SPRAGUE, IMPLEADED, &c., APPELLANT.

SUPREME COURT, FIRST DEPARTMENT; GENERAL TERM, MARCH, 1883.

§ 682.

Attachment.—Motion to vacate for irregularities may be made after judgment and the issuing of execution, and at any time before the actual application of the attached property.

A motion to vacate an attachment, under section 682 of the Code, may be made after judgment, and notwithstanding an execution has been issued, unless there has been an actual application of the attached property which would necessarily involve a sale.[1]

Where an attachment was issued and levied in December, 1879, and the defendant in March, 1882, after judgment had been entered in the action in favor of plaintiffs and an execution issued thereon and the attached property levied upon thereunder, moved to vacate the attachment for irregularities in papers on which it was granted,—*Held*, that it was not too late to make such motion, and it should be heard on its merits.[2]

(*Decided May* 11, 1883.)

Appeal from order of special term denying motion to vacate attachment against the property of the appellant.

The action was brought to enforce against the defendant, as one of the trustees of the McKillop and Sprague Company, a manufacturing corporation, the statutory liability for a debt of the corporation for not filing the annual report required by law.

The action was commenced in June, 1879. On December 8, 1879, the plaintiff procured an attachment to be issued against the property of the defendant as a non-resident of the State.

The cause was tried on March 13, 1882, and resulted in a verdict for the plaintiff.

On March 14, 1882, before judgment had been entered, the defendant moved to vacate attachment on the ground that the affidavit on which it was granted was insufficient.

It appeared from the moving papers that the defendant's attorney had been unable to find the affidavit on file in the clerk's office; but it had been found and was read on the argument of the motion.

The judge who heard the motion evidently understood that it was made for irregularity on the part of the plaintiffs in not filing their affidavit, and holding that this should have been specified in the moving papers, he denied it March 17, 1882. On March 18, 1882, the defendant moved on affidavits showing that the motion had not been made for irregularity, but for jurisdictional defects, for the rehearing of the first motion on an order to show cause, dated that day, containing a stay of proceedings on the part of the plaintiffs until the decision of the motion. This order was served on the plaintiff's attorney, the same day, the 18th of March, and the motion argued on March 21 (although additional affidavits were handed in as late as June 20), but was decided December 30, 1882. In the mean time, on March 22, the plaintiff's attorney obtained an *ex parte* order from Judge BARRETT, who tried the case, modifying his former stay so as to allow execution to issue on the judgment, sufficient to reach and levy on the property attached. An execution was so issued, and the property attached levied upon thereunder, but none of the attached property or its proceeds has ever been actually applied to the payment of the judgment, which is wholly unpaid and is secured on appeal.

The order, as entered on December 30, 1882, ordered

a rehearing of the first motion, vacated the order made upon it, and then denied the motion to vacate the attachment, on the sole ground that a judgment had been entered and an execution issued.

This appeal is taken from so much of that order as denies the motion to vacate the attachment.

W. L. Larned (*Larned, Warren & Elhridge*, attorneys), for appellant.

The order affects substantial rights of the defendant; the court below erred in supposing that because an execution had been issued there was no necessity for vacating the attachment; that is, the rights of the parties would not be affected by his decision. (1) Under this illegal warrant the plaintiffs have seized the defendant's property, and put him to great expense and damage thereby. Vose *v.* Woods, 26 *Hun*, 486. (2) They have carried into their judgment the additional costs and disbursements authorized in case of an attachment properly issued. (3) Until set aside this void attachment protects the sheriff, and he still holds the defendant's property by virtue of the attachment and execution, for while under section 1311 the court may, after appeal and security, on application, make an order discharging the levy under the execution, it is not authorized to discharge the levy under the attachment.

Gilbert R. Hawes, for respondents.

Brady, J.—Daniel J. Sprague, the appellant and one of the defendants, applied at the special term for an order vacating the attachment issued herein. The application was not made, however, until after final judgment and execution had been issued thereupon. For that reason the learned justice who presided at the time the motion was made denied it. He says: "The motion to vacate the attachment is denied in this case for the reason that judgment has been entered and execution has been issued."

No other question, therefore, was considered by him, and the merits of the application were not passed upon.

The views of the learned justice would seem erroneous. By section 682 of the Code of Civil Procedure, it is provided that the defendant or a person who has acquired a lien upon or interest in his property after it was attached, may at any time before the actual application of the attached property or the proceeds thereof to the payment of a judgment recovered in the action, apply to vacate or modify the warrant or to increase the security given by the plaintiff, or for one or more of these forms of relief, together or in the alternative; and section 683 provides for the manner in which the application may be made, namely, upon the papers on which the warrant was granted, or upon proof by affidavit on the part of the defendant.

It appears, therefore, clearly, that the legislature intended to give the defendant all opportunity of
[1] moving to vacate the attachment, notwithstanding an execution had been issued, unless there has been an actual application of the attached property, which would necessarily involve the sale. This view is confirmed by reference to section 687, which provides that the defendant may, at any time after he has appeared in the action, and before final judgment, apply to the judge who granted the warrant or to the court for an order to discharge the attachment as to the whole or a part of the property attached. But by section 688, upon such application, the defendant must give an undertaking.

There are, therefore, two remedies provided for the defendant for relief from the presence of an attachment; one of these being by motion, which may be made at any time before the actual application of the attached property or the proceeds thereof to the payment of the judgment, and the other by application before final judgment, which must rest upon an undertaking, as we have already seen.

The right of the defendant to move after final judgment and execution issued seems to be an anomaly and would not be sustained except upon imperative necessity, demanded by the absolute construction of the provisions of the Code, for the reason that upon the issuing of the execution and the levy of the attached property under it the attachment itself for all purposes ceased to exist. Its office has been performed and the property was *in custodia legis*, under another process which was altogether distinct from the attachment itself and founded upon an entirely different result. But there seems to be no doubt about the intention of the legislature to extend the remedy down to the period named, "before the actual application of the attached property or the proceeds thereof to the payment of the judgment recovered in the action." What the particular object of this was cannot be well divined. It may have had some connection with the right of the defendant to appeal to have his property surrendered to him during the pendency of this appeal. If that were the object it was a good one, doubtless, but we are not called upon to furnish reasons why an act of the legislature was passed. It is our duty to declare what is accomplished by it, and nothing more.

For these reasons the order below must be reversed, with $10 costs and disbursements of this appeal, [2] and the motion to vacate to be heard upon its merits.

DAVIS, P. J., and DANIELS, J., concurred.

RICHARDSON v. CASE.

SUPREME COURT, SECOND DEPARTMENT; GENERAL TERM, MARCH, 1883.

§§ 1933, 1939.

Joint debtor, has same defenses in action to charge him with judgment entered against him, not summoned, and his co-debtor as he would have had if served in the original action, and the judgment is not conclusive evidence of the amount of the debt.—Instance of an agreement which made the parties thereto partners as to third persons.

K. and C. entered into an agreement, whereby it was agreed that K. should furnish all the money and materials necessary to complete the construction of an elevated railway which he had contracted to build, and pay all bills on account thereof, and keep C. supplied at all times with the sum of $100 to meet expenses, of which C. was to render an accurate account; that if any of the private property of either party was used, he was to be paid for the use thereof at the rate designated in a schedule accompanying the agreement; that C. should give all his time, skill and energy to the completion of the work under the contract, and should receive therefor one-half of all profits arising therefrom, and that all moneys advanced by K. to C. and not accounted for, were to be charged to him and the same made good. *Held*, that if the agreement had stopped here, it would not have made the parties partners or made C. liable to third parties for debts contracted by K;[1] but as the agreement also provided that the accounts should be balanced on the last day of each month, and the profits then appearing be divided, the said K. and C. "to be responsible mutually for all bills contracted the same in profit or loss," and that any property purchased under the agreement and remaining on the completion of the work, be owned in equal shares by the parties thereto, and be equally divided, it contained all the elements which go to make a partnership, at least as far as third parties are concerned, [2,3] and there was no question of fact upon this point to submit to the jury.[4]

In an action to charge a partner with the amount remaining unpaid on a judgment recovered against his firm, on service on his copartner alone,—*Held*, that he can make the same defenses or counter-claim which he might have made in the original action, if the summons had been served upon him therein, and that it was error to hold that the former judgment was conclusive as to the amount.[4]

(*Decided May* 22, 1883.)

Motion for a new trial upon exceptions ordered to be heard in first instance at general term.

In 1880 the firm of E. L. Richardson & Co., of which the plaintiff is the surviving partner, sold and delivered lumber to one Daniel R. Kelly, and charged it to him individually.

On September 8, 1882, the plaintiff commenced an action in the marine court of the city of New York against said Kelly, and the defendant, in this action to recover the amount of his bill for said lumber alleging in his complaint that Kelly and the defendant herein were copartners, under the name of D. R. Kelly. The defendant herein was not served, and did not appear in that action. Kelly was served, but did not appear and judgment was entered against him and the defendant herein, "not summoned," September 21, 1882 for $620.99.

No part of that judgment has been paid. On September 29, 1882, this action was brought to charge the property of the defendant with the amount of that judgment. The lumber in suit was used in the erection of the Coney Island Elevated Railway, and on the trial, the plaintiff to prove that the defendant and Kelly were partners in that work, put in evidence an agreement between them of which the following is a copy:

"Articles of agreement made this 23d day of April, 1880, between Daniel R. Kelly, of the city of New

York, and Henry Case, of the city of Brooklyn, witnesseth as follows:

"Whereas the said Daniel R. Kelly, has contracted with the Coney Island Elevated Railroad Co. to construct an Elevated Railway at Coney Island, Kings Co., New York, as will more fully appear by reference to the contract between said Kelly and said company, know therefore the parties hereto agree:

"First. That the said Kelly should furnish the money and materials necessary to complete the said contract, as the progress of the work thereunder shall require, and shall pay all bills for accounts of construction of said work.

"Second. That the said D. R. Kelly, should also keep the said H. Case, supplied with the sum of $100 to meet the minor current expenses of such work, of which moneys and the payment thereof the said Case shall keep an accurate account and render the same 1st and 15th of each month, the said Kelly agrees to keep the amount paid so as the said Case will at all times have $100 on hand.

"Third. The said Case shall give all his time, skill, and energy to the completion of the work under said contract, for which he is to receive one-half of the profits arising therefrom.

"Fourth. Should any of the private property of said Case be used on said work, said Case shall receive for the use thereof one-half the rate per day specified in the schedule hereto attached, the use thereof to be paid for on the completion of said work. This section tc apply to all plant and material furnished in construction by said Daniel R. Kelly also.

"Fifth. The profits arising under said contract, and from any extra work connected therewith, shall be divided equally between the parties hereto, when all debts contracted are paid, the account in respect thereto to be balanced on the last day of each month, and the profits then appearing to be divided as aforesaid. The said D. R. Kelly, and Henry Case to be responsible mutually for all bills contracted the same in profit or loss.

"Sixth. Any property purchased under this agreement and remaining on the completion of said work, shall be owned in equal shares by the parties hereto, and shall be equally divided between them, and if not so divided, shall be sold and the proceeds thereof shall be equally divided between the parties hereto, either party to have the privilege of purchasing at such sale if he shall so elect.

"Seventh. For all moneys advanced by D. R. Kelly to said H. Case, during the work not accounted for by the said H. Case, are to be charged to him, and same to be made good on the completion of said work.

"DANIEL R. KELLY.
"HENRY CASE."

The court, at trial term, held that this agreement made Kelly and the defendant partners; that the marine court judgment was conclusive as to the amount, and directed a verdict for the plaintiff. It also ordered that the exceptions taken by the defendant be heard in the first instance at the general term, and that judgment upon the verdict be suspended in the meantime.

James White, for plaintiff.

Cited, in support of contention that Kelly and the defendant were copartners: Ontario Bank *v.* Hennesy, 48 *N. Y.* 545; Mohawk National Bank *v.* Van Slyck, 16 *N. Y. Weekly Dig.* 167.

Edward S. Clinch, for defendant.

The fact that Case was to be paid for his services by

receiving one half the profits did not necessarily make him a partner . . . . Richardson v. Hughitt, 76 *N. Y.* 55; Smith v. Bodine, 74 *N. Y.* 30 . . . . In construing this contract the facts in view of which it was made must be considered and it must be so construed that it may have effect according to the intention of the parties. Stapenhorst v. Wolf, 35 *N. Y. Super.* 25; affirmed, 65 *N. Y.* 596; Parshall v. Eggart, 54 *N. Y.* 18; 1 *Lindley on Partnership*, 18; . . . . Coyne v. Weaver, 84 *N. Y.* 386. Whether two or more persons associated in business are partners depends upon their intentions.

Under sections 1933 and 1939 of the Code of Civil Procedure, after a judgment has been obtained against one joint debtor, it is not conclusive on the other joint debtor of the amount of the demand against him. Oakley v. Aspinwall, 4 *N. Y.* 513; Denny v. Smith, 18 *N. Y.* 567; Lane v. Salter, 51 *N. Y.* 1; Maples v. Mackey, 89 *N. Y.* 146; Newman v. Marvin, 12 *Hun*, 241; Pratt v. Chase, 44 *N. Y.* 600; Field v. Ashhain, 22 *How. Pr.* 332; Foster v. Wood, 30 *Id.* 284.

McCue, Ch. J.—This case comes before us on exceptions taken by the defendant and ordered to be heard in the first instance at the general term. Two questions are presented for decision: First. Was there a copartnership between the defendant and Kelly who purchased from the plaintiff the goods and materials which were used in the performance of a contract made between Kelly and the Coney Island Elevated Railway Company, so as to make the defendant liable therefor? and second, Was the judgment recovered in the marine court of the city of New York conclusive against the defendant as to the amount?

To sustain the liability of the defendant as a partner, the plaintiff offered in evidence an agreement executed by the defendant and Kelly. By the terms of the agreement, Kelly was to furnish all the money and materials necessary to complete the work, and to pay all bills on account of construction. Kelly was to keep the defendant supplied at all times with the sum of one hundred dollars to meet minor expenses, of which advances the defendant was to render an accurate account. If any of the private property of the defendant was to be used on the work, he was to receive pay for the use thereof, according to the rate designated in a schedule accompanying the agreement, and this provision was also to apply to all plant and materials furnished in construction by said Kelly.

The defendant was to give all his time, skill and energy to the completion of the work under the contract (*i. e.*, the contract between Kelly and the railway company), and was to receive for this one half of the profits arising therefrom, and all moneys advanced by Kelly to the defendant during the progress of the work, and not accounted for were to be charged to him and the same made good on the completion of the work.

If the agreement had stopped here, it would be easy to determine the right of the parties, and to [1] say that as between the defendant and Kelly, the agreement amounted to nothing more than the very usual employment of the services of a party, to be paid for out of the profits of the enterprise by way of price or compensation for such services—such a partnership in the profits would not make the principals partners nor would the one receiving the profits be thus made liable to third persons for debts contracted by the other. The authorities are full upon this point.

Another portion of the agreement, however (§§ 5, 6), provides for the accounts to be balanced on the last day of each month, and the profits then appearing to divided. "The said D. R. Kelly and Henry Case to be responsible mutually for all bills contracted the same in profits or loss" (§ 5). "Any property purchased under this agreement and remaining on the completion of said work to be owned in equal shares by the parties hereto," and to be equally divided and to be eventually sold and the receipts to be divided equally (§ 6).

It is very clear that the provisions contained in sections 5 and 6, meant something more than that
[2] Kelly was to furnish the money and materials necessary, and to pay all bills for account of construction. It was very likely the case, that between themselves, Kelly was the capitalist, and Case the real man of work, because he was to give all his time, skill and energy, while the agreement did not contemplate any participation on the part of Kelly in the actual work itself, but it is equally clear and must have been the intention of the parties that there was to be kept a profit and loss account, and that for all bills contracted they would be responsible mutually (§ 5).

It is evident that also under section 6, it was in contemplation that property would be necessarily required and purchased for the purpose of the work outside of the private property owned by each at the time the work started, which property should be owned in common and distributed after the contract was completed. Sections 5 and 6, therefore, provide for a community of property, for payment of losses as well as the division of profits. All the elements go to make a partnership, at least so far as third parties are
[3] concerned, whatever may be their respective rights as between each other.

We think that the judge at trial term properly construed the agreement, and that there was no question of fact upon this point to submit to the jury.

As to the second question presented on the appeal The plaintiff has sued Kelly for the same merchandise, &c., which is the subject of the present action. **Case** was made defendant as a joint defendant, and was not served with the summons. Kelly was served with the summons and complaint, and made default, and judgment by default was entered against both.

Upon the trial now under review, the court held that the former judgment was conclusive as to the amount, both as to the defendant in this action, and as to Kelly.

We think that the ruling was erroneous, and carefully examining the question, the judge below concurs with us, that under §§ 1933 and 1939 of the Code [4] of Civil Procedure, the defendant on this trial can make the same defenses or counter-claim which he might have made in the original action, if the summons had been served upon him when it was first served upon the defendant indebted with him.

Such were the provisions as to the same subject matter in section 379 of the former Code (Oakley *v.* Aspinwall, 4 *N. Y.* 513; Maples *v.* Mackey, 89 *N. Y.* 151).

There must therefore be a new trial, costs to abide the event.

CLEMENT, J., concurred.

BAKER, APPELLANT, v. HATFIELD AND ANOTHER, RESPONDENTS.

SUPREME COURT, SECOND DEPARTMENT; GENERAL TERM, FEBRUARY, 1883.

§ 1351.

What notice of the entry of an order is sufficient to limit the time to appeal therefrom.

Where the copy of an order served upon the attorney for a party was certified by the clerk, in whose office it was entered, in these words: "Indorsed filed October 11, 1882. A copy, C. A. Hart, Clerk," and indorsed on the back, "Copy order striking out amended complaint, and dismissing cause." *Held*, that this amounted to a written notice that the order had been entered by the clerk; that no particular form of words or notice is prescribed, and if written notice of the entry of the order was served, the statute was complied with, and the time to appeal commenced to run.

(*Decided May* 15, 1883.)

Appeal from order of Kings county special term, denying motion to compel defendants' attorneys to receive notice of appeal from order of the Richmond County special term.

The opinion states the facts.

Henry H. Browne (*Charles H. Adler*, attorney), for appellant.

A motion to compel the acceptance of a paper is entirely proper, and an order denying such motion is appealable. Pattison v. O'Connor, 23 *Hun*, 307; S. C.,

60 *How. Pr.* 141; see also Sherman *v.* Wells, 14 *How. Pr.* 522.

The copy order served on plaintiff did not limit his time to appeal. "There being no power in the court to relieve a party who fails to take an appeal in due time, however meritorious his excuse, the party undertaking to limit the time is held to strict practice," Kelly *v.* Sheehan, 76 *N. Y.* 325, to same effect Matter of N. Y. Central & H. R. R. R. Co., 60 *N. Y.* 116. The Code (§ 1351), allows an appeal within thirty days after the service upon the attorney for the appellant of "a copy of order appealed from and a written notice of the entry thereof." The notice here required must be a formal notice (Fry *v.* Bennett, 16 *How. Pr.* 405; People *ex rel.* Backus *v.* Spalding, 9 *Paige*, 606; Tyler *v.* Simmons, 6 *Paige*, 132), in writing (Whitlock *v.* Joseph, 14 *Abb. Pr.* 345), coming from the opposing party (Fry *v.* Bennett, 16 *How. Pr.* 405), subscribed by him or his attorney (Yorks *v.* Peck, 17 *How. Pr.* 192), and bearing the office address of the party signing it. *Id.*; Kelly *v.* Sheehan, 76 *N. Y.* 325. It must state when the order was entered, and in what clerk's office. Valton *v.* Natl. Fund Life Ass. Soc., 19 *How. Pr.* 515, Matter of N. Y. Cen. & H. R. R. R. Co., *supra.* In this case the memorandum subjoined to the copy order served, does not comply with these requirements. It does not state where or when the order was entered or even that it has been entered. It merely states that the original or some copy thereof, was "indorsed, filed October 11th, 1882." It is not signed by the defendants or their attorneys, and is not even in form a notice. Unless the notice prescribed by the Code is served, the time to appeal is unlimited. Matter of N. Y. Central and H. R. R. R., 60 *N. Y.* 116. Even when the party appealing enters the order himself, the time is not limited unless the prescribed notice is given. *Id.*, and cases cited.

S. F. Rawson (*De Groot, Rawson & Stafford*, attorneys), for respondents.

DYKMAN, J.—This cause was on the calendar for trial at the Richmond Circuit on October 9, 1882, and on that day the defendants moved the court on affidavit, to strike out the plaintiffs amended complaint because it had been interposed only for delay. Thereupon the court decided to allow the amended complaint to remain and directed the defendants to answer the same immediately, the cause to be set down for trial on the ensuing Wednesday on condition that the plaintiffs should then proceed with the trial. The condition was declined by the plaintiff and the motion was granted. The cause then stood for trial and on its regular call on the calendar the plaintiff answered not, and the complaint was dismissed. This order was entered and a certified copy procured with the words. "Indorsed filed October 11, '82." A copy. C. A. HART, clerk. It was also indorsed as follows: "Supreme Court. John Baker *v.* Jacob Hatfield and another. Copy order. De Groot, Rawson & Stafford, Defendants' attorneys, Port Richmond, N. Y." This copy with these words was served on the attorney for the plaintiff on October 7, 1882, by mail with the additional words indorsed on the back of it: "Order striking out amended complaint and dismissing cause."

On December 30, 1882, the attorney for the plaintiff served a notice of appeal from that order, which was returned with a statement of the ground that the same was not served within the time limited by law for that purpose.

Thereupon a motion was made to compel the acceptance of the notice of appeal, which was denied, and from that order comes this appeal.

Under the requirement of the Code of Civil Procedure, section 1351, it was necessary to take the appeal from this order within thirty days after service of a copy of the order and a written notice of its entry.

The claim of the plaintiff is that no written notice of the entry of the order was served, and therefore his time to appeal was not set in motion.

In the first place the clerk certified that it was a copy, and then the defendant's attorneys indorsed on it the words "copy order striking out amended complaint and dismissing cause." This certainly amounted to written notice that the order had been entered by the clerk. No particular form of words or notice is prescribed. If written notice of the entry of the order was served on the plaintiff's attorney, the statute was complied with and the time to appeal commenced to run.

A substantial compliance with the statute was only necessary and that was accomplished.

The order should be affirmed, with costs and disbursements.

BARNARD, P. J., and PRATT, J., concurred.

LORILLARD, Respondent, v. CLYDE, Impleaded, etc., Appellant.

N. Y. Superior Court; General Term, November, 1882.

§ 970.

Findings on issues framed under section 970 of the Code, not conclusive in another action between same parties, unless the issues were raised by the pleadings, and their decision necessary to the determination of the action.—What determinations are an estoppel.—Inferences from testimony in a former proceeding, do not constitute an estoppel in a subsequent case where the same testimony is given.

The findings of the jury on issues framed under section 970 of the Code of Civil Procedure, are not *res adjudicata* in another action between parties to the proceeding or action in which they were made, unless the issues so framed were raised by the pleadings in the first action, and their decision was necessary to its determination.

Where, in a proceeding bv the people to dissolve a corporation, a stockholder of it, at whose instance the proceeding was instituted, was made a party plaintiff after issue had been joined, and it did not appear from the record that any amendment to the pleadings were made to show how or why he was made a party plaintiff, or what was his interest in the litigation, nor was any judgment against him asked. *Held*, that the effect of making him a plaintiff would extend no further at the utmost, than to bind him by the determination made between the people and the defendants of the issues formed by the complaint and answer.[1]

Where, in a proceeding to dissolve a corporation on the grounds that it had forfeited its charter by abuse of its power and the exercise of franchises or privileges not conferred by law, issues were framed under section 970 of the Code, inquiring, among other things, into the validity of the organization of the corporation, and the jury found that its organization was illegal and invalid, and had been effected pursuant to an agreement between certain stock-holders of the corporation, for the purpose of enabling them to carry on a partnership or joint adventure in the guise of a corporation, and thus of using the act of the legislature under which the corporation was organized to evade the personal liability attaching to partnerships or joint adventures. And judgment was rendered, dissolving the corporation on the ground that it had forfeited its charter, and not because it was formed in an unlawful manner,—*Held*, in an action by a stockholder, L., who was joined with the people as plaintiff in such proceeding against certain other stockholders, C. & Co., for dividends guaranteed by them, that the questions framed for the jury went outside of the issues raised by the pleadings;[2] that while the agreement, pursuant to which the company was organized, and under which, L. brought his action for dividends, and its intent might be received in evidence for certain purposes, an adjudication as to them was not called for by a necessity to adjudicate upon the real issues, but was immaterial;[6] that the verdict of the jury did not itself constitute an estoppel;[9] and that the findings in the people's action that the corporation had violated the provisions of the law under which it was organized, and had exercised a franchise not conferred by law, excludes that the first organization of the company was invalid, and therefore, there was no former binding adjudication that the agreement was invalid on its face, or in the intent with which it was made, or that the organization of the company was not at the time lawful and in pursuance of the statute;[10] also *Held*, that as L. could not, in the proceeding to dissolve the corporation, have had an adjudication as to the agreement or its validity, which could have been the foundation of any judgment in his favor as to his rights under the agreement, or be used defensively as to any claim made adversely to him, it would not bind him in his action against C. & Co.[8]

A judgment is conclusive upon the parties thereto, only in respect to the grounds covered by it, and although a decree in express terms purports to affirm a particular fact or rule of law, yet if such fact or rule of law was immaterial to the issue, and the controversy did not turn upon it, the decree will not conclude the parties in reference thereto.[6] To determine whether any issue in an action was decided by a former proceeding, the substance and not the form of the proceeding must be considered.[3]

There is no rule that inferences from testimony in a former proceeding, constitute an estoppel in a subsequent case, wherein the same testimony is given.[4]

(*Decided December* 4, 1882.)

Appeal by defendant, from a judgment in favor of plaintiff, entered on a verdict of a jury, as directed by the court.

The action was upon an agreement between the parties, in which a firm of which appellant was one partner agreed to "guarantee Jacob Lorillard" the plaintiff "a dividend of not less than 7 per cent. per annum for seven years" upon certain stock in an incorporated company, to be taken by plaintiff, under the agreement which provided that the company was to be formed in the future.

The particulars of this agreement, are stated in the opinion of the court of appeals in Lorillard *v.* Clyde, 86 *N. Y.* 387.

The defense was that the agreement was void as against public policy, in that as alleged, it contemplated that the corporation should be formed with less than seven *bona fide* corporators, that the directors other than William P. Clyde and Jacob Lorillard should not be *bona fide* stockholders; that such other persons, should "after its issue to them," transfer their stock to William P. Clyde & Co., that the names of the persons should remain on the stock book as stockholders but their stock and the votes of those who were directors were to be controlled by William P. Clyde & Co.

The evidence to sustain this defense was a record of certain proceedings particularly described in the opinion.

The court directed a verdict in favor of the plaintiff, and the defendant took this appeal.

E. C. Boardman, (*Boardman & Boardman*, attorneys), for appellant.

The plaintiff and defendant in the present action having been respectively plaintiff and defendant in the action brought in the supreme court to dissolve the corporation, every question determined in that action is *res adjudicata* as between them, and the findings of the jury and judgment therein, are conclusive evidence against both as to all matters therein litigated. Doty *v.* Brown, 4 *N. Y.* 71; Gardner *v.* Buckbee, 3 *Cow.* 120; Wood *v.* Jackson 8 *Wend.* 9; Birkhead *v.* Brown, 5 *Sandf.* 134; Kingsland *v.* Spaulding, 3 *Barb. Ch.* 341. The action to dissolve the corporation was one in which the defendants were, under the provisions of the constitution entitled as of right to a trial by jury. Attorney General *v.* Utica Ins. Co., 2 *Johns. Ch.* 370; People *v.* Albany & Susquehanna R. R. Co., 57 *N. Y.* 161. In such actions the answers by the jury to the issues framed are, by express statute, made conclusive on the parties, and binding on the court. They cannot be set aside or disapproved by the court, as can be done when the court, in cases in which the parties are not entitled as of right to a jury trial sends certain issues to a jury in order to have the benefit of the jury's findings on a disputed question of fact.

Horace Barnard, for respondent.

It is a cardinal principle in the orderly administration of justice by courts of law, that a party to one action shall not be bound by the issues and findings in another to which he was a party, which were not properly raised by the pleadings and duly litigated, not even if such issues were found by stipulation of his attorneys appearing for him. Campbell *v.* Consalus, 25 *N. Y.* 613. See also Jarvis *v.* Driggs, 69 *N. Y.* 146.

SEDGWICK, Ch. J.—On the trial, the counsel for defendant claimed that the defense of the illegality of the agreement complained upon was *res adjudicata*, between the parties, in an action formerly determined in the supreme court. The record in the action was produced. The plaintiff was The People of the State of New York against The Philadelphia & New York Steam Navigation Company, William P. Clyde, Benjamin Betts, John A. Leslie, and Amos Rogers.

The complaint alleged that on June 10, 1874, the individual defendants and others, executed articles of association to form a company under the act for the incorporation of companies formed to navigate the ocean, &c., passed April 12, 1852,* and other amendatory acts; that the certificate of incorporation was duly filed; that it provided that the points between which the company was to navigate its vessels were Philadelphia and New York, and also that William P. Clyde, Jacob Lorillard, Benjamin Betts, Amos Rogers and John A. Leslie, should constitute the board of directors for the first year; that at a meeting for the organization of the board of directors the last named persons acted as directors and that the officers of the company were then chosen; that at this meeting William P. Clyde & Co., agents of the company, were made the agents and managers of the company's business, to be paid specified commissions; that at the time of the execution of the articles five of the "said incorporators" were and afterwards continued to be clerks of William P. Clyde & Co.; that each of the said clerks were noted on the subscription book of the company, as having subscribed for one share of its stock, of the par value of $100, "but that soon afterwards" the said William P. Clyde, required the five clerks, to indorse upon the certificates, respectively "an irrevocable assignment and transfer of the stock in blank, as to the assignee, and at the same time took possession of such indorsed certificates, and had for several years retained control

* Chapter 228 of the laws of 1852.

of the certificates; that "by such indorsement and delivery as aforesaid they parted with their legal and equitable title to the said shares of stock by which said Benjamin Betts, &c., the clerks, no longer continued to be either the legal or equitable owners of said five named shares of the par value, &c., within the meaning of the statute, &c.;" "that up to this date, such shares are the only ones standing in the name of such clerks on the book of the company;" that the effect of such transfer was to "knowingly reduce" the number of actual *bona fide* shareholders below the number required by law, to constitute such a company; that such a condition of affairs has privately continued for several years, and that there have not been a sufficient number of lawful stockholders or directors, since such transfer and assignments as before mentioned, to constitute a board of five directors "as required by law; that the effect "purpose and intent of the said transfer and assignment by the persons specified" who held subordinate positions in the hire and employ of William P. Clyde & Co. was to enable William P. Clyde, president of the company, and his father who was a stockholder, to obtain a complete control of the company to the advantage of said Clyde and in fraud of the rights in said company of any other *bona fide* and lawful stockholders; that persons named, being the clerks already specified, had unlawfully combined to manage the affairs of the corporation in the interest of William P. Clyde & Co. "and in fraud of the rights of Jacob Lorillard, the principal stockholder, and in violation of the statute;" that contrary to the statute there had never been an annual or any election held by the stockholders, or stockholders meeting called; that in fraud of the rights of Jacob Lorillard, vice president, director and principal stockholder a directors' meeting was held, and it was then and there resolved that two steamers be taken from the line between Philadelphia and New York, and run between Philadelphia and Boston, or any other ports that might be for the interest of the company; that this resolution was contrary to the articles of the association and of the express objects of its formation; that said William P. Clyde as president, had in other respects specified, used the property of the company, in a manner that was in violation of the articles of association that in violation of the statute, no certificate by the said William P. Clyde as president, and a majority of the directors, stating the amount of the capital stock, and that the same had been paid in, was ever filed; that the company had been for more than a year insolvent.

The complaint further alleged, by way of recapitulation and as they have hereinbefore in substance alleged and complained, "that the private assignment and transfer by the said Betts, &c., of these single shares of stock in said corporation, left said corporation without the number of stockholders requisite under the statute incorporating it, to carry on its business, and that they are not now lawfully directors in said company."

The complaint asked judgment that the charter of the company be vacated, its corporate existence annulled, and the corporation be dissolved, and that a receiver be appointed, &c.

The complaint was verified by Jacob Lorillard, now the plaintiff here.

The defendants, the company, William P. Clyde and John A. Leslie answered. The answer denied many of the allegations of the complaint: it admitted that the indorsement upon the certificates charged in the complaint had been made as charged, but denied "that the intention was that any of such parties should part with their legal title to such shares, until a transfer on the books was so made, or that any of the parties ceased to be shareholders in said company, until and by such transfer on the books of the company, or that they ceased to be the legal owners of said stock until such transfer." The answer alleged that Jacob Lorillard and William P. Clyde & Co. entered into the agreement which is now the subject of this action; that said company was formed pursuant to said agreement, and mainly under the advice of said Lorillard; that all the names of the stockholders and directors were selected by agreement between said Lorillard and said William P. Clyde & Co.; that it was contemplated by the agreement that the vessels of the company should be employed on other routes than between Philadelphia and New York; that it was supposed that the words of the articles would allow such employment; and if there had been any violation of the statute in this regard, it was unintentional and inadvertent; that the action had brought on the relation or information "of the said Jacob Lorillard, who has an interest in the questions involved in this action;" that Lorillard had retained counsel to prosecute the action, and had indemnified the People, as plaintiff, against the costs and expenses of the action. The answer continued: "these defendants aver that there is a defect of parties in this action, in this, that the said Jacob Lorillard has not been joined with the people as a party plaintiff. They further allege, that he is a necessary party to this action either as plaintiff or defendant." The answer was verified June, 1879.

On January 15, 1880, issues were framed for a trial before a jury.* Among these issues were the following. "First. Was the corporation defendant created, organized and conducted in good faith for the legitimate purposes contemplated by the acts of the Legislature, specified in the second section of the complaint?

* These issues were framed under section 970 of the Code of Civil Procedure

Second. Was said corporation defendant created, organized and conducted, with the real design and for the sole purpose of enabling Jacob Lorillard and William P. Clyde & Co., through the forms of law and in the guise of a corporation, to carry on and conduct a private enterprise which was in truth and in fact a partnership or joint adventure between said Lorillard on the one part and the said William P. Clyde & Co. (of the other part), and thus of using the said acts of the Legislature to evade the personal liability attaching to partnerships or joint adventures. Third. Were there seven *bona fide* corporators and five *bona fide* directors of said corporation defendant, as required by law? Fourth. Were the directors of said corporation defendant other than William P. Clyde and Jacob Lorillard *bona fide* stockholders therein as required by law. Fifth. Was the share of stock of said corporation which was issued to each of the . . . . five corporators and three directors (other than William P. Clyde and Jacob Lorillard) so issued, and was the power of attorney in blank authorizing a transfer and signed by said persons . . . . and by them delivered to William P. Clyde with the real design and for the purpose in part of giving said persons the appearance of owning a share of said stock, when in truth each of said shares was well understood by them to be and in reality was, the property of William P. Clyde or William P. Clyde & Company, and thus of apparently complying with, but actually evading, the provisions of said act of the Legislature specified in the second section of the complaint? And was it also in execution of the purpose specified in the second question? Seventh. Was the appointment of William P. Clyde & Co. as the agents of said corporation, &c., so made in execution and fulfillment of the contract . . . . referred to in the pleadings, &c., and was the corporation pursuant to said contract &c., thereafter exclusively managed by said William P. Clyde

& Co., and was such appointment and exclusive management . . . . part and parcel of the methods adopted, to enable said Lorillard and William P. Clyde & Co. to effect the purpose specified in the second question and in execution thereof?"

There are many other issues framed, but such as have been stated, will present the question that is to be answered.

On the 24th of February, 1880, an order was allowed "that Jacob Lorillard be made a party plaintiff in this action with the People, the defendants, except Amos Rogers, hereby stipulating in open court, that upon said Lorillard being made a party to consent to a summary amendment of all the proceedings herein by inserting the name of said Lorillard as a party plaintiff, and every issue and proceeding to remain unaltered except in said amendment and without prejudice to the proceedings already had."

The present plaintiff Lorillard was not a party to this order. The record does not show, that any amendments to the pleadings were made to show how or why, he was party plaintiff, or what was his interest in the litigation, nor was any judgment against him asked. He did not take part in any proceeding until June 2, 1880. In the judgment-roll appears a certificate of the judge before whom the framed issues were tried by the jury. Before the certificate begins is a statement as follows: "Entered that Jacob Lorillard appeared and was made a party plaintiff, under the order of the court, and moves with the people the litigation on." Then by the certificate it appears, that to the first issue as framed, the jury answered No; to the second Yes; to the third and fourth No; to the fifth Yes; and to the seventh Yes. Upon the verdict the judgment was entered which recited, "it having been established in this action, first, that the defendant corporation, The Philadelphia and New York Steam Navigation

Company has offended against the provision of the act creating it. Second. That it has violated the provisions of law, to wit, the third and seventh sections of chapter 228 of the act entitled an act for the incorporation of companies formed to navigate the ocean by steamships, passed April 12, 1852, by which said defendant corporation has forfeited its charter by abuse of its powers. Third. That it has exercised a franchise or privilege not conferred by law," and after hearing counsel for the defendants, and counsel for the people, and on motion of the attorney general, "It is ordered, adjudged and decreed that the defendant corporation . . . . be and hereby is dissolved."

In considering whether this judgment was conclusive as to any issue in the present case, it is first to be [1] noticed, that the effect of making the present plaintiff a plaintiff in that action, would extend no further at the utmost than to bind him by the determination to be made between the people and the defendants of the issues formed by the complaint and answer. A scrutiny of those issues will show that the people did not claim that the corporation was formed in an unlawful manner, or anything in respect to an alleged cause of forfeiture, which rested upon the illegality of the agreement, or the intent with which it was made, or upon anything being done in pursuance of the agreement. The complaint did not claim, that the clerks of Clyde & Co. were not owners of the stock that had been issued to them, and which made them shareholders and qualified to become directors, but only claimed that some time afterwards the certificates of stock were delivered to William P. Clyde & Co. with a power of attorney in blank indorsed, and that from that time they ceased to be shareholders or qualified to be or remain directors.

The complaint did not rest upon the illegality of the agreement. It is not to be intended that Lorillard, when made a plaintiff, meant to allege that the agreement was unlawful, or that, as the defendants claimed, there was no cause of forfeiture; they proffered an issue to maintain that the agreement which they averred led to the formation of the corporation was illegal.

[*] The conclusion seems to be irresistible that the questions framed for the jury went outside of the issues formed by the pleadings. The pleadings formed no issue as to whether the corporation was created in good faith, as asked in the first framed issue. Nor did they, as to whether the corporation was created, organized or conducted with the sole purpose of enabling Lorillard and William P. Clyde & Co., through the forms of law and in the guise of a corporation, to carry on what was in fact a private enterprise in the nature of a partnership or joint adventure, as was asked in the second framed issue. The third and fourth framed issues, asked whether there were seven *bona fide* corporators and five *bona fide* directors as required by law, and whether the directors who were the clerks of Clyde & Co. were *bona fide* stockholders. The time referred to is indefinite, and it must be presumed, that it referred to the time when the complaint, as part of its cause of action, stated they ceased to be shareholders, which we have seen was after the formation of the company. So also the 5th framed issue asked whether the shares had been delivered or issued to the directors who were clerks, with the real design and for the purpose in part of giving an appearance of ownership in the stock, when in truth the stock remained the property of W. P. Clyde & Co., and whether it was in execution of the purpose specified in the second question. The com plaint, as has been already pointed out, made no claim that the directors referred to, were not the owners of the shares, upon the certificate being issued to them, nor that the transfer was in execution of the purpose

referred to. It must also be said that the seventh question as to whether the appointment of William P. Clyde as agent of the corporation, was made in fulfillment of the agreement, responded to an allegation of the answer made for the purpose of showing that the charter was not to be forfeited, but did not refer to any issue made, as to the illegality of the agreement. And again, no issue was made by the pleadings as to whether or not the agreement was made with the intent of consummating or executing it, in violation of the statute.

To determine whether any issue in this case was determined by the former proceeding, the sub-
[3] stance and not the form of the proceeding must be considered (Palmer v. Hussey, 87 *N. Y.* 303). It must have been that in the case by the people, on the issues actually framed, there was no purpose of determining as to whether the agreement was void on its face or by its actual intent. It would be another question as to whether the agreement was not a piece of evidence relative to the intent with which the things complained of were done. But in that case, the agreement and its quality, would only be looked at as circumstantial evidence. There is no rule, that inferences from testimony in a former proceeding, con-
[4] stitute an estoppel in a subsequent case, where the same testimony is given. In substance, then, the matters referred to in the framed issued that have been examined, were at the best pieces of evidence as to the issue actually framed.

It further appears from the issues framed by the pleadings, that it was an immaterial matter, whether the agreement was valid and with valid intent or the reverse. As we have seen, the parties made no issue but that, in its original formation, the corporation had a lawful origin. The matters that were complained of as happening subsequent to the formation were

impeached for the existence of certain things, and the doing and intent of certain acts, at this subsequent time. Evidently, although the agreement and
[5] intent of the agreement might be received in evidence for certain purposes, an adjudication as to them was not called for by a necessity to adjudicate upon the real issue, but would be immaterial whether found one way or the other. "A judgment is
[6] conclusive upon the parties thereto, only in respect to the grounds covered by it; and although a decree in express terms, purports to affirm a particular fact or rule of law, yet if such fact or rule of law was immaterial to the issue and the controversy did not turn upon it, the decree will not conclude the parties in reference thereto" (Woodgate *v.* Fleet, 44 *N. Y.* 14, citing People *v.* Johnson, 38 *N. Y.* 63; Remington Paper Co. *v.* O'Dougherty, 81 *N. Y.* 474).

Again, it appears that in the former proceeding, the plaintiff in this action would not have had an
[7] adjudication, as to the agreement or its validity or intent, which could have been the foundation of any judgment in his favor, as to his rights under the agreement. He could not have claimed as to it, that he should have judgment for an amount due upon it. An adjudication that the agreement was valid, would not have been any bar to the defense in the former proceeding. It would if it possessed any influence have tended to show, that the people, and its co-plaintiff, who is plaintiff here, had no cause of action. As the former proceeding could not have given the plaintiff a favorable adjudication either in his own favor,
[8] upon its terms, or have been used defensively, as to any claim made adversely to him, it would not bind him in this action (Dawley *v.* Brown, 79 *N. Y.* 390, citing Stowell *v.* Chamberlain, 60 *Id.* 272; Perry *v.* Dickerson, 85 *Id.* 346).

The verdict of the jury, did not itself constitute an

estoppel. It is the adjudication upon the verdict ['] which concludes the party,—*e. g.*, notwithstanding the facts, found by a jury, a party in whose favor the verdict is, may not be entitled to judgment. The adjudication in this case, or the judgment, did not make any determination as to or upon the matters, we have noticed as outside of the issues in the former proceeding. Webb *v.* Buckelew, 82 *N. Y.* 559. The judgment that the corporation be dissolved was placed upon a recital, that certain things had been established in the action. The first was that the corporation had offended against the provisions of the act creating it. This refers necessarily to a corporate act, after the formation of the company. The second, that it has violated the provisions of law, to wit, the 3rd and 7th section of the act, as to the number of shareholders and directors, and the qualification of the latter, "by which said corporation has forfeited its charter by abuse of its power," examined in the light of the complaint, excludes that it was established that the first organizing of the company was invalid. The same is true of the third, which recited that it had been established, that the corporation has exercised a franchise not conferred by law.

In brief, there had been no former binding adjudication, that the agreement was invalid on its face [''] or in the intent with which it was made, or that the organization of the company was not at the time lawful and in pursuance of the statute.

The plaintiff, on this trial, gave sufficient proof that the company was duly organized. In Lorillard *v.* Clyde, 86 *N. Y.* 384, it had been held that the agreement was not invalid on its face. On this trial, the only evidence to establish that there was an actual unlawful intent, or that the subsequent action upon it, in respect to the formation and conduct of the corporation, showed that there was such an actual unlawful intent, was the proceeding in the supreme court, that has been examined and passed upon.

One particular objection to the agreement may be noticed now. It is, that one of its clauses provides for vesting the exclusive management of the corporation in William P. Clyde & Co., and if it were valid would bind the directors of the corporation to be formed, to keep the management of the corporation in the hands of William P. Clyde & Co., no matter how prejudicial to the interests of the company such management might be. The court of appeals held that the agreement to do so was not invalid, because it contemplated, by proper construction, only a proper management beneficial to the company. Even if the former proceedings be considered on this point, although the findings, but not the judgment, declare that the appointment of William P. Clyde & Co. as managers, was in pursuance and in execution of the agreement, there is no finding that this execution of the agreement, was prejudicial to the company. The pleadings did not allege any improper notice in the appointment but improper action as managers. The defendants in the present action did not set up as a defense, that William P. Clyde & Co. were ousted from the management, in consequence of the action of the plaintiff, nor was there any recovery of an amount equal to dividends at 7 per cent. for any time after they ceased to be managers by the dissolution of the corporation.

The agreement being valid, the corporation at its organization having been formed in a lawful manner, and it having carried on business, for the time covered by the recovery in this case, entitled the plaintiff to the verdict that was directed. It was sufficient for the purposes of this action, that in the time referred, to the corporation existed *de facto*, although there existed cause for its subsequent dissolution.

Judgment affirmed, with costs.

FREEDMAN, J., concurred.

ESTATE OF GEORGE G. SCOFIELD, DECEASED.

SURROGATE'S COURT; NEW YORK COUNTY, APRIL, 1883.

§§ 2607, 2608, 2609.

Action on administrator's bond.—When cannot be maintained.—When leave of surrogate not necessary.

Where an administratrix died without having fully executed her trust, and letters of administration *de bonis non* were thereafter issued to J. S., and he in a petition, alleging that his predecessor at the time of her death was in possession of certain money and other property belonging to the estate for which she was bound to account, and that he had ineffectually demanded from the sureties upon her bond payment and delivery thereof, prayed for leave of the surrogate to commence an action against such sureties for recovering of them the value of the property in the hands of their principal at her death. *Held*, that in the present situation of affairs, the petition ought not to be granted;[1] that whatever authority the surrogate has in the premises is solely derived from statute, and none of the statutory provisions relating to actions upon administrators' bonds, are broad enough to include such a case as the present.[2] *Held*, also, that even if the situation was ripe for prosecuting the sureties on the administratrix's bond, the case is one wherewith the surrogate has no concern,[3] and his leave need not be procured before the commencement of the proceedings against the sureties.[3, 4, 6]

After the death of one holding testamentary letters or letters of administration, if there has been issued against him no execution which has been returned wholly or partly unsatisfied, and if he has not failed to obey some order or decree of the surrogate, the prosecution of his bond is a matter quite outside of that officer's jurisdiction.[6]

(*Decided April* 9, 1883.)

Application by administrator *de bonis non* for leave of surrogate to sue on his predecessor's bond.

The facts are stated in the opinion.

Frederick Hemming, for petitioner.

ROLLINS, Surrogate.—In January, 1879, letters were issued out of this court to Catherine A. Scofield, as administratrix of decedent's estate. Upon the granting of such leters she made and filed her bond in the customary form. She died in August last without having fully executed her trust, and letters of administration *de bonis non* have since been issued to Jesse Scofield, who is the petitioner in this proceeding. He alleges that his predecessor, at the time of her death, was in possession of certain money and other property belonging to the estate, for which she was bound to account, and that he has ineffectually demanded from the sureties upon her bond, payment and delivery thereof. He prays therefore for leave of the surrogate to commence an action against such sureties, for recovering of them the value of the property in the hands of their principal at her death.

First. Assuming for the present that the permission of the surrogate is a necessary preliminary to [1] the commencement of such an action, I am satisfied that in the present situation of affairs it ought not to be granted.

The circumstances under which the prosecution will lie against the sureties on an executor's, administrator's or guardian's bond are distinctly specified in the statutes. Section 2607 of the Code of Procedure provides that such suit can be maintained where an execution issued upon a surrogate's decree against the property of any such officer has been returned wholly or partly unsatisfied.

Section 2608 and 2609 declare that where by a decree of the surrogate's court the letters of such an officer have been revoked, an action upon his bond may be maintained by his successor, or, if no successor has been appointed, by any person aggrieved who has previously obtained leave from the surrogate.

None of the statutory provisions bearing upon this subject are broad enough to include such a case as [*] the present, and it is from the statutes, it is scarcely necessary to say, that whatever authority the surrogate has in the premises is solely derived. While the Code of Civil Procedure has made certain changes in the law by which proceedings against sureties are regulated, it has rather restricted than enlarged the jurisdiction of this court; and judicial decisions rendered before the Code became operative and under the statutes theretofore in force are accordingly pertinent and instructive. The limitations upon proceedings against sureties on executors', administrators' and guardians' bonds are clearly set forth in Stillwell *v.* Mills (19 *Johns.* 304), People *v.* Barnes (12 *Wend.* 492), Salisbury *v.* Van Hoesen (3 *Hill*, 77), People *v.* Corlies (1 *Sandf.* 228), Annett *v.* Kerr (28 *How. Pr.* 324).

The most recent and most authoritative exposition of the law upon this subject as it stood before the enactment of the Code is reported in the recent case (1881) of Hood *v.* Hood (85 *N. Y.* 561). It is there held that the default of an executor must be established in a proper proceeding against him before the sureties on his bond can be prosecuted, and that, as the statutes have prescribed the steps necessary to be taken, the right of action against the sureties only arises upon compliance with those requirements. No action at law, the case holds, can be maintained on an executor's bond, save in case of disobedience to some order of the surrogate, nor can the requirement of the statute be disregarded even in an equitable action where the statutory remedies can be pursued. In the language of the court: "The statute having provided for the cases in which actions may be brought upon the bond of an executor or administrator and having regulated the prior steps for such action, the mere fact of so prescribing would seem to deny the right, except upon compliance with the statutory regulations. The bond was taken by an officer of limited jurisdiction in pursuance of special statutory provisions, and it would seem to follow that where the same statutes prescribe the mode of its enforcement no other can be pursued."

[3] Second. Even if the situation is ripe for prosecuting the sureties upon the bond of the former administratrix of this estate, I cannot discover that the interference of the surrogate is either necessary or proper. In respect to the procedure for such prosecutions the Code seems to have made wide departures from the methods formerly in vogue. For example: 1. Sections 63, 64 and 65 of chapter 460 of the Laws of 1837 as amended by chapter 104 of the Laws of 1844,* established the practice for the issuance of executions upon surrogates' decrees directing the payment of moneys by executors, administrators and guardians. The sixty-fifth section of the act of 1837 provided that if such an execution should be returned unsatisfied the surrogate upon due application should assign the bond given by such delinquent officer to the person in whose favor the decree was made, upon which the execution was founded.

These acts of 1837 and 1844, were both repealed by chapter 245 of the Laws of 1880†. In their place have appeared sections 2553, 2545 and 2607 of the Code. The last named section makes unnecessary an assignment of the bond such as has been hitherto requisite. It provides that "where an execution issued upon a surrogate's decree against the property of an executor, &c., has been returned wholly or partly unsatisfied, an

* Section 1.

† Section 1, subds. 14 and 21.

action to recover the sum remaining uncollected may be maintained upon his official bond, by and in the name of the person in whose favor the decree was made."

Leave of the surrogate need not, it would seem, be procured before the commencement, under this
[*] section, of proceedings against sureties.

By section 21, title 3, chapter 6, part 2 of the revised statutes (3 Banks' 6th ed. 95,)* it was provided as follows: "In every case of revocation of testamentary letters or of letters of administration for neglect or refusal to return an inventory, and whenever directed by the surrogate, the bond given by such former executor or administrator shall be prosecuted and a recovery shall be had thereon . . . . and the moneys collected thereon shall be deemed assets in the hands of the person to whom such subsequent letters shall have been issued."

This provision was abrogated by the repealing act of 1880,† and there appear in its place sections 2608 and 2609 of the Code. The former section declares that "where letters have been revoked by a decree of the surrogate's court, the successor of the executor, administrator or guardian whose letters are so revoked may maintain an action upon his predecessor's official bond, &c."

The statute is silent as to the necessity of preliminarily obtaining the surrogate's leave, and purposely so it would seem; for the very next section (§ 2609) declares that if no successor to the removed officer has been appointed, such leave must be procured before a "person aggrieved" may maintain an action upon such officer's bond.

The foregoing are believed to be all the existing provisions of law upon the subject under discussion

* 2 R. S. 86.

† Chap. 245, § 1, subd. 2 (3).

[5] and serve to show that the case at bar is one wherewith the surrogate has no concern. After the death of one holding testamentary letters, or letters of administration, if there has been issued against him no execution which has been returned wholly or
[6] partly unsatisfied, and if he has not failed to obey some lawful order or decree of the surrogate, the prosecution of his bond is a matter quite outside of that officer's jurisdiction.

From the foregoing considerations it is equally apparent that I could not grant this petition if I would and that I ought not to do so if I could. For both these reasons it must, therefore, be denied.

BRISTOL AND ANOTHER, RESPONDENTS, v. SEARS, APPELLANT.

SUPREME COURT, THIRD DEPARTMENT; GENERAL TERM, NOVEMBER, 1882.

§ 829.

In action against a surviving partner, a general question concerning transaction with the firm which will permit plaintiff to testify to transactions with the deceased partner, should not be allowed when special objection is made.

Where, on the trial of an action against one S. as surviving partner of McC. & S., McC. being dead, one of the plaintiffs was asked, "Did you have business transactions with McC. & S. in 1872?" and the defendant objected to the question on the ground that the testimony should be confined to transactions with the living partner. *Held*, that it was error to overrule such objection; that it was not proper by such a general question, when special objection was

made, to permit the plaintiff to give an answer which might include objectionable evidence.
(*Decided January*, 1883.)

Appeal from a judgment in favor of the plaintiffs entered in Rensselaer county upon the report of a referee.

The plaintiffs assert that between February 1, and June 28, 1872, they sold and delivered to the firm of McCarthy & Sears, goods, wares and merchandise of the value of $100.20, on account of which only $20 has been paid.

In 1874, the firm of McCarthy & Sears was dissolved, and subsequently, before the commencement of this action McCarthy died. This action is brought against the defendant as surviving partner of the firm of McCarthy & Sears for the amount remaining unpaid for the goods so sold.

Further facts are stated in the opinion.

John H. Colby, for appellant.

The plaintiff was examined as a witness in his own behalf against the survivor. (defendant Sears) of a deceased person, (McCarthy) concerning a personal transaction and communication between witness and the deceased. This was error, and within the prohibition of section 829 of the Code. Green *v.* Edick, 56 *N. Y.* 613; Pellett *v.* Geesler, 58 *How. Pr.* 195; Kale *v.* Elliot, 18 *Hun*, 198; Conway *v.* Moulton, 6 *Id.* 650.

James Lansing (*Martin L. Townsend*, attorney), for respondents.

LEARNED, P. J.—The plaintiff Church was a witness in his own behalf. He testified that of his own knowledge he could say that his firm sold and delivered some of the goods in question to the firm of McCarthy & Sears. The defendant was the surviving partner of that firm. On cross-examination he testified that such sale and delivery was made to McCarthy. Thereupon, the defendant moved to strike out the former testimony above mentioned under section 829, Code of Civil Procedure. The referee denied the motion, and defendant excepted.

It may be urged that this testimony might have meant only that the witness saw a sale and delivery which was made by some other person.* But other testimony of the witness forbids that construction. We are obliged to consider it testimony therefore to a personal transaction, and so inadmissible. Afterwards, the plaintiff consented to the striking out of any such transaction which had been shown. But it does not appear how the referee acted on such consent.

Again a general question was put: Did you have business transactions with McCarthy and Sears in 1872? Objection was made that the transactions must be confined to transactions referred to with the living partner, and must exclude a personal transaction with McCarthy, deceased. The objection was overruled. We think this error. Green *v.* Edick, 56 *N. Y.* 613. It was not proper by such a general question (when special objection was made†), to permit the plaintiff to

* A party may testify to a transaction or conversation between a third party and the deceased. Hildebrandt *v.* Crawford, 65 *N. Y.* 107; Patterson *v.* Copeland, 52 *How. Pr.* 460; but not where he took part in the conversation. Brague *v.* Lord, 67 *N. Y.* 495; S. C., 2 *Abb. N. C.* 1; Moyer *v.* Moyer, 21 *Hun*, 67; Kranshaar *v.* Meyer, 72 *N. Y.* 602; Smith *v.* Ulman, 26 *Hun*, 386; Ross *v.* Harden, 42 *N. Y. Supr.* 427.

† It is not sufficient to object to the testimony as incompetent and irrelevant. The objection must be specific. Sanford *v.* Ellithorpe, 14 *Weekly Dig.* 154.

give an answer which might include objectionable evidence. Under some circumstances, such as the presence of the surviving partner, conversations with the deceased have been admitted. Kale *v.* Elliot, 18 *Hun*, 198.* But when a party fairly presents the objection arising under the aforesaid section of the Code, the question should be so modified as to call only for testimony not objectionable.

Again: in like manner, against objection, the plaintiff testified that he presented the account to McCarthy & Sears. On cross-examination he testified that he could not swear whether he ever presented it to Sears. Here again the same difficulty arises of improper evidence brought in by a general question duly objected to. There are other exceptions which we need not examine.

The judgment should be reversed, and a new trial granted. Referee discharged. Costs to abide event.

BOARDMAN and BOCKES, JJ., concurred.

* See also Comstock *v.* Hier, 73 *N. Y.* 269; Comins *v.* Hetfield, 80 *N. Y.* 261.

COOKE, AN INFANT, BY COOKE, HIS GUARDIAN AD LITEM, RESPONDENT, *v.* THE LALANCE GROSJEAN MANUFACTURING COMPANY, APPELLANT.

SUPREME COURT, SECOND DEPARTMENT; GENERAL TERM, FEBRUARY, 1883.

§ 870 *et seq.*

Court has no power in action for personal injuries to order inspection of machine by which plaintiff was injured.—Such inspection cannot be required as a condition to an examination of plaintiff before trial, which is a matter of right.

Where, in an action for personal injuries, an order for the examination of the plaintiff before trial was obtained by defendant, and the plaintiff's attorney thereupon, on his affidavit that he could not cross-examine his client on the examination before trial, or comprehend such examination without an inspection of a certain machine, while working on which, plaintiff received the injuries for which he sues, and after notice to the defendants' attorney, procured an order that the defendant allow the plaintiff's attorneys to inspect said machine before an examination of the plaintiff is had,—*Held*, that there was neither power nor discretion in the court to assist the plaintiff's attorneys by ordering such inspection; that such an exercise of power would be an usurpation of authority to search and inspect the private premises of a citizen in a manner and for a purpose untolerated by our law. Nor can the order for inspection be upheld as a condition to the examination of the plaintiff, which was granted as a right secured by law, and did not proceed from the favor of the court.

(*Decided May* 15, 1883.)

Appeal from an order requiring the defendant to allow plaintiff's attorney to inspect a certain machine, before the plaintiff is examined as a party before trial, pursuant to an order theretofore made.

This is an action for damages for injuries alleged to have been received by the plaintiff, from a machine belonging to the defendant, while the plaintiff was in the employ of the defendant, and working upon said machine. The defendant, after the joinder of issue herein, made application to this court at chambers upon proper affidavit for an order requiring the plaintiff to submit to an examination before trial in order to ascertain: (1) His method of working at said machinery; (2) As to the instructions given him; (3) As to the manner of managing the machine; (4) As to the nature of said machine; (5) To ascertain plaintiff's age; (6) As to how his injuries were sustained; (7) The particular work plaintiff was engaged in at the time he was injured. Plaintiff's attorney then procured an order from a justice of this court, requiring the defendant to show cause "why the defendant should not be compelled to allow the plaintiff's attorney to inspect the machine on which the plaintiff was working when injured, as alleged in complaint, before any examination of the plaintiff is had" and staying the examination of the plaintiff until hearing of said motion. Subsequently, on January 26, 1883, the motion was heard and granted, and the examination of the plaintiff was stayed until the plaintiff should be allowed to examine said machine. The defendant appeals from the order thereupon entered.

Morris & Pearsall, for appellant.

The examination of a party to an action before trial under section 870 of the Code of Civil Procedure, is a matter of absolute right, and does not rest in the discretion of the court. *Code Civ. Pro.* § 873; Ludgewig *v.* Pariser, 54 *How. Pr.* 498; Corbet *v.* De Comeau, 54 *Id.* 506; reversing S. C., 4 *Abb. N. C.* 252; Webster *v.* Stockwell, 3 *Abb. N. C.* 115; Hynes *v.* McDermott,

7 *Daly*, 513; reversing S. C., 55 *How. Pr.* 259; Harrold *v.* N. Y. El. R. R. Co., 21 *Hun*, 268.

In the marine court of the city of New York, it was held at the general term thereof, in Huerstel *v.* Tilman, *McAdam's Marine Ct. Pr.* 1st appendix, p. 61 (cited in 1 *Civ. Pro. R.* 83), "that the right of a party to examine his adversary before trial was a matter of strict right which no court had power by rules or otherwise to abridge."

Charles J. Patterson, for respondent.

The court had undoubted power to compel the defendants to permit plaintiff to inspect and examine the machinery in their possession, when it became necessary for the ends of justice in the progress of the case. *Curtis on Patents*, § 435, and cases; United Co., &c. *v.* Kynaston, 3 *Bligh*, 153; Russel *v.* Cowley, 1 *Webs'. Patent Cases*, 457; Morgan *v.* Seaward, *Id.* 168; Patent Type Foundry Company *v.* Walter, *Johnson's Eng. R.* 727; Jones *v.* Lee, 36 *Eng. L. & Eq.* 558.

The power is of the same nature as that which the court exercises to compel a plaintiff in an action for physical injuries, to submit his person to examination by a physician, selected by his adversary (Supm. Ct., Iowa) Schroeder *v.* C. R. I. & P. R. R., 19 *Alb. L. J.* 234.

The power to compel a party to submit a piece of evidence in his possession, to the inspection of his adversary, existed at common law, prior to the statutes relating to discovery and inspection. Lawrence *v.* Ocean Ins. Co., 11 *Johns.* 246; Wallace *v.* Murray, 4 *Cow.* 399; Jackson *v.* Jones, 3 *Id.* 17.

The several statutes respecting the inspection and discovery of books and papers, regulate classes of cases. They were not intended to limit or abridge the power of inspection such as is involved here. That power was preserved by section 469 of the old Code and section 4 of the new Code. Tilton *v.* Beecher, 59 *N. Y.* 176.

The view of the order taken in the argument of the appellants' counsel is that it is an obstacle tending to prevent them from examining plaintiff, and is thus an abridgment of their right in that respect. This is an error. The court had the power to direct the inspection of the machinery, and having made an order requiring the defendants to permit it, the presumption is that they will obey, and thus the order will prove no obstacle to their proceeding.

It is only in the event of defendant's disobedience to the lawful command of the court that the order will operate as a barrier against them. This is not an unlawful or improper consummation, for the court has the right to require from the defendants, an obedience to its lawful mandate, and in case of their refusal to obey, can decline to hear them for any purpose in the cause. Walker *v.* Walker, 82 *N. Y.* 260. Much is said in the defendants' points about the right to examine before trial being absolute. So is the right to put in a defense absolute, but it may be forfeited by failure to comply with the order of the court. Gould *v.* McCarty, 11 *N. Y.* 580.

Dykman, J.—The defendant procured an order for the examination of the plaintiff before trial. Then the plaintiff on motion obtained an order, directing the defendant to allow the plaintiff's attorney to inspect the machine, on which the plaintiff was working at the time he sustained the injury for which the action is brought.

This order contained a stay of the examination of the plaintiff, until his attorney should be allowed to examine the machine. From this last order we have this appeal.

We find neither precedent nor authority for this order. Under the common law, the revised statutes and the Code of Civil Procedure, courts of record possessed jurisdiction and power to compel a party to an action to produce and discover books of account, papers and documents, or to permit an inspection and copy thereof. This same right is now continued by our Code of Civil Procedure.* We find no law, and have been referred to none, carrying the right of discovery or inspection to the private personal property of an adverse party in a civil action. This order is founded on an affidavit of the plaintiff's attorney that he cannot cross-examine his client on the preliminary examination before trial, or comprehend such examination without an inspection of the machine previous thereto. There is neither power nor discretion in this court to assist him in that respect. Such an exercise of power would be an usurpation of authority to search and inspect the private premises of a citizen, in a manner and for a purpose untolerated by our law. Even the power vested in the courts to order discovery and inspection of books of account and documents is discretionary and not obligatory and is exercised with great caution where the party applying has some right or interests in the accounts, or papers. No discovery or inspection will be ordered, even of account books or documents, which are of strictly private character. The dwellings of our citizens would be of small security to them, if they may be invaded by their enemies and searched for articles of personal property, to be inspected under an order of a court. Such a proceeding would be at war with all our traditions as freemen, and should find justification in some direct mandate of the law at least.

* § 803 *et seq.*

Neither can this order be upheld as a condition to the examination of the plaintiff. That order was granted as a right secured by law, and did not proceed from the favor of the court.

The order should be reversed with costs and disbursements.

BARNARD, P. J., and CULLEN, J., concurred.

MACDONAL, APPELLANT, v. WOODBURY, AS EXECUTRIX, ETC., RESPONDENT.

SUPREME COURT, FIRST DEPARTMENT; GENERAL TERM, MARCH, 1883.

§§ 829, 881.

Where both parties were examined before trial, and one died and his executor was substituted for him, the other's deposition may be read on the trial, although it relates to personal transactions with the deceased.—Stipulation as to reading of such deposition should be enforced.

Where both the plaintiff and defendant in an action were examined before trial under a stipulation between their attorneys, and the defendant thereafter died and the action was continued against his executrix,—*Held*, that the plaintiff's deposition could be read in evidence on the trial although it related to personal transactions with the deceased;[1] that as the examination and cross-examination of the plaintiff was conducted in the presence of the defendant, and he had an opportunity to respond upon his examination to all the statements made by the plaintiff it must be supposed that he did so.[2]

Where, in such a case, the stipulation also provided that either or both the depositions might be read upon the trial,—*Held*, that substantial justice required that the stipulation be enforced.[3]

Rice v. Motley, 24 *Hun*, 143, followed.[1]

(*Decided May* 11, 1883.)

Appeal from judgment dismissing the complaint.

The action was brought against defendant's testator Henry Woodbury, to recover $611.33 damages for the breach of an alleged contract made in December, 1879, between the plaintiff and the said Henry Woodbury, whereby the latter employed plaintiff to go to Paris and sell a patent syringe. The answer contained a general denial and set up a counter-claim of $30, money loaned plaintiff by said Woodbury.

In May, 1881, the plaintiff and said Henry Woodbury were examined before trial pursuant to a stipulation between their attorneys. The examinations were reduced to writing and signed and sworn to by the respective parties before a justice of this court, and a stipulation was signed by the attorney for the plaintiff and the attorney for the then defendant that the depositions "be read in evidence by either party on the trial."

Subsequently, in December, 1881, Henry Woodbury died leaving a will appointing his widow executrix. She thereafter qualified, and in July, 1882, was by an order of this court substituted as defendant in the action.

On the trial, the plaintiff, being disqualified from testifying concerning his personal transactions with the defendant's testator, offered his own deposition, taken as aforesaid, in evidence. It was excluded, and he duly excepted. He then read the deposition of Henry Woodbury in evidence, and again offered his own deposition in evidence. It was again excluded, and he again excepted.

At the close of plaintiff's case his complaint was dismissed upon the ground that he had not proven an offer to carry out the contract on his part. From the judgment thereupon entered comes this appeal.

Edward C. Graves, for appellant.

By virtue of sections 828 and 870 of the Code the plaintiff stands in the same position as any other witness, and the defense having made him their witness before trial and taken his deposition for their benefit, on general principles cannot now suppress that deposition to their advantage and the plaintiff's disadvantage. Code, section 830 ; 1 *Green. Ev.* §§ 163, 168 ; 3 *Id.* § 326 ; Jackson *v.* Lawson, 15 *Johns.* 539. . . . . The defendant having made the plaintiff his witness and examined him at length . . . . can neither impeach his testimony nor suppress it. . . . . He is subject to the same rules and restrictions as any other witness. Jordan *v.* Jordan, 2 *Sup'r Ct.* 269. A party examines an adversary before trial at his peril and whatever evidence is taken is competent and may be used. Barry *v.* Galvin, 37 *How. Pr.* 310. The deposition of a party may be "read on the trial by either party," *Code*, § 881. . . . . The stipulation at the end of plaintiff's deposition providing that it may be read to the jury by either party would make the deposition admissible. Mills *v.* Thursby, 11 *How. Pr.* 124.

Reuben H. Underhill (*S. A. Underhill* attorney), for respondent.

Cited, as to the construction of section 829 of the Code, Card *v.* Card, 7 *Trans. App.* 147 ; Pinney *v.* Orth, 2 *N. Y. Civ. Pro.* 1.

The offer by plaintiff to read both the defendants' and his own deposition in evidence, cannot make the latter competent. He cannot put in evidence the adverse statement, of a deceased party, and so open the door to his own version of the same transaction. Pott *v.* Mayer, 10 *Abb. N. C.* 63. Neither can plaintiff derive any benefit from the stipulation, entered into at the time the depositions were taken, providing for the reading of the same, &c., as it does not supersede the law applicable to the the case. Miller *v.* Adkins, 9 *Hun*, 9.

BRADY, J.—It appears that this action was originally against Henry Woodbury, who died during its pendency. It also appears that after issue was joined the depositions of plaintiff and of Mr. Woodbury, were both taken under a stipulation between the restrictive attorneys. The examination of the plaintiff was conducted in the nature of a cross-examination by Mr. Underhill, the defendant's counsel, the defendant being personally present. A similar examination of the defendant was also taken, and was signed, acknowledged and sworn to before a justice of this court.

The defendant died, and his executrix was substituted as defendant.

Upon the trial, the plaintiff being disqualified from testifying concering his personal dealings with the deceased, offered in evidence his deposition which was taken as already mentioned, which was excluded by the court. He then offered the deposition of the defendant, although it was against his interest, which was received and read to the jury, after which the plaintiff's deposition was again offered and excluded. The complaint was then dismissed upon the ground that the plaintiff has not offered to carry out the contract on which his claim rests, and which seems to have been an essential prerequisite, and as to which there was testimony contained in his deposition. The question presented on this appeal, therefore, and, indeed, the only question presented, is whether the plaintiff's deposition should have been admitted and read to the jury under the circumstances. The precise question has been decided by the general term of the second department in favor of the plaintiff in the case of
[1] Rice *v.* Motley (24 *Hun*, 143). Although, perhaps, there may be some room to doubt the accuracy of

this, yet nevertheless we think the reasoning by which it is sustained is such as to justify us in concurring.

The examination of the plaintiff, as we have seen, took place in the presence of the defendant, and
[2] the cross-examination was conducted also in his presence, and the defendant had an opportunity to respond upon his examination to all the statements made by the plaintiff, either upon direct or cross-examination, which it must be supposed he did, and thus the respective parties perpetuated their statements in writing and in a formal way. In addition to the provisions of the Code relating to the subject, we have in this case an express stipulation that these depositions,
[3] either or both, might be read upon the trial, and substantial justice would seem to require that the stipulations should be enforced, inasmuch as the plaintiff by the death of the defendant is prevented from giving evidence which is essential to the maintenance of his action, and as to which the deposition is sufficient, and as to which the defendant's evidence is also before this court.

The judgment should therefore be reversed, and a new trial ordered, with costs to abide the event.

Davis, P. J., and Daniels, J., concurred.

MURRAY, RESPONDENT, *v.* HANKIN. RYLE, APPELLANT.

SUPREME COURT, FIRST DEPARTMENT; GENERAL TERM, MARCH, 1883.

§§ 636, 682, 683.

Attachment.—Allegation in affidavit on which, granted, must be in conformity with the statute.—Affidavit, where made by agent, not sufficient when it states that there are no counter-claims, etc., to the knowledge of deponent.—It must state that there are none to knowledge of plaintiff.

Although the Code only requires the facts necessary to the granting of an attachment to be shown to the satisfaction of the judge granting it, and although the affidavit may undoubtedly be made by an agent having the necessary knowledge to make the required allegations; nevertheless, when the allegations are made, they must be in conformity with the statute, particularly in a case where the attachment is granted upon a variety of claims in part originating with the plaintiff and in part acquired by him by assignment.[1]

Where the affidavit on which an attachment was granted was made by an agent of the plaintiff, and he stated therein, that there was a certain amount due over and above all counter-claims etc., in favor of the defendant to the "knowledge of the deponent,"—*Held*, that this allegation was insufficient; that it should have shown that the sum demanded was due over and above all counter-claims, etc., to the knowledge of the plaintiff, notwithstanding the affidavit was made by the plaintiff's agent; [2,4] also *Held*, that this was not an irregularity which might be waived, but a jurisdictional defect.[3]

DAVIS, P. J. (dissenting), *Held*, that the defendant in the action, by not taking the objection, waived it, and that a junior attaching creditor, seeking to vacate the attachment, ought to be required to show that there were counter-claims or off-sets which might be interposed.[4]

(*Decided May* 15, 1883.)

Appeal from order, denying motion to vacate or modify an attachment.

The plaintiff in this action, procured to be granted and issued herein on November 22, 1882, an attachment against the property of the defendant, he being a non-resident of the State. The attachment was granted on the affidavit of Ebenzer K. Rose, an agent of the plaintiff, from which it appeared that the action was brought to recover the sum of $3,324.21, and was founded upon a note for $219.71, made and delivered to plaintiff, by defendant; a claim of $1266.63 for goods, wares and merchandise sold and delivered by plaintiff to defendant, and five other claims for goods wares and merchandise, sold and delivered to defendant by as many persons, and assigned to plaintiff. The allegation as to the amount due the plaintiff was as follows: "That plaintiff is justly entitled to recover therefor from the said defendant, the sum of $3,324.21 over and above all counter-claims, discounts and set-offs existing in favor of the defendant to the knowledge of deponent."

The property of the defendant was duly levied upon under the warrant of attachment so issued and thereafter, one William T. Ryle, a creditor of the defendant, also procured an attachment and had it levied upon the same property. He then moved to vacate the attachment granted herein, and his motion having been denied he took this appeal.

Preston Stevenson, for appellant.

The statute requires that the party (plaintiff) should furnish proof of the non existence of a counter-claim to his knowledge. Here we have only a statement of the agent's knowledge . . . . This is not merely not following the language of the statute; it is a failure to give any evidence on the point required, and is an omission of that which is indispensable to give the court authority to issue the warrant. Trow Printing, etc. Co. *v.* Hart, 1 *N. Y. Civ. Pro.* 240; Lyon *v.* Blakesly,

19 *Hun*, 299; Ruppert *v.* Haug, 1 *N. Y. Civ. Pro.* 411.

Lewis J. Morrison, for respondent.

It is competent for the agent of plaintiff, to make the affidavit upon which warrant of attachment is based. Crandall *v.* McKaye, 6 *Hun*, 483; Lamkin *v.* Douglass, 27 *Hun*, 517. . . . The statute not specifying that the affidavit must be made by any particular person, it follows that any one having knowledge of the jurisdictional facts may make it. *Drake on Attachments* (5 ed.) § 94. . . . The allegation, as to counter-claims, is in accord with the substantial requirement of the statute, and that is sufficient. Ruppert *v.* Haug, 1 *N. Y. Civ. Pro.* 411; Lamkin *v.* Douglass, *supra*. . . . A subsequent attaching creditor who does not allege fraud or collusion in the prior attachment cannot take advantage of any mere irregularity, therein which the defendants have waived. Jacobs *v.* Hogan, 15 *Hun*, 197.

Brady, J.—The affidavit upon which the attachment was granted in this case was made by the agent of the plaintiff, who alleges that he is personally acquainted with the facts and circumstances which he proceeds to set forth. The claim consists of a promissory note, payable to the order of the plaintiff, and a sale of merchandise made at a date subsequent to that of the note, and of merchandise also sold to various persons who have assigned their demands to the plaintiff. The agent then states that the plaintiff is justly entitled to recover for these various claims the sum named "over and above all counter-claims, discounts and set-offs existing in favor of the defendant to the knowledge of deponent."

The subsequent attaching creditor, who made the motion resulting in this appeal, assails the affidavit because it fails to comply with the statute in not averring that the plaintiff is entitled to recover the sum demanded over and above all counter-claims known to him, and this objection seems to be well taken.

Although the Code only requires the necessary facts to be shown by affidavit to the satisfaction of
[1] the judge granting the attachment, and although the affidavit may therefore undoubtedly be made by an agent who has the necessary knowledge to make the required allegations, nevertheless when the allegations are made they must be in conformity to the statute, and particularly in a case where the attachment is granted upon a variety of claims, in part originating with the plaintiff and in part acquired by him by assignment. The statute requires among other things that the plaintiff shall show, either by his own affidavit or by that of somebody in his behalf conversant with the facts, that there are no counter-claims known to him, *i. e.*, known to him the plaintiff.

The asseveration by the agent that there were no counter-claims known to him might be made with
[2] very great propriety, and hence the necessity of the information which is exacted by the statute *non constat*, but that in this case there was a counter-claim to some one or more of the numerous items set forth, of which the plaintiff had knowledge, but of which his agent had no knowledge. If the allegation of the agent in his affidavit had been that the sum demanded was due over all counter-claims, discounts and set-offs existing in favor of the defendant to the knowledge of the plaintiff, the affidavits would have been sufficient. But the allegation is that it was due over and above all counter-claims, discounts and set-offs existing in favor of the defendant to the "knowledge of the deponent,"—*i. e.*, to the knowledge of the agent, as already suggested.

Inasmuch as in this case an attachment was

demanded for a sum of money, which rested partly upon merchandise sold by the plaintiff to the defendant, and partly upon claims assigned to him, the affidavits should perhaps show that, as to each of the items, there was no counter-claim existing in favor of the defendant to the knowledge of the plaintiff, notwithstanding that the affidavit on which the attachment is granted may be made by the plaintiff's agent or attorney in fact.

The objection taken is not to a mere irregularity which the defendant might be regarded as having [3] waived, because he made no objection to it, so far as the court is advised. It is to a jurisdictional objection (Donnell *v.* Williams 21 *Hun*, 216; Ruppert *v.* Haug, 87 *N. Y.* 141*).

For these reasons the order made by the court below must be reversed and the motion granted, with $10 costs and disbursements of this appeal.

DANIELS, J., concurred.

DAVIS, P. J.—[Dissenting.]—I do not think a subsequent attaching creditor ought to be allowed to succeed upon a point of this kind. The defendant in [4] the action, by not taking such an objection, waives it. The junior attaching creditor ought to be required to show that there were counter-claims or offsets which might be interposed. One creditor should not be allowed to trip up the heel of another prior in diligence without being able to assert some more substantial objection than this. The agent evidently had better, or at least as good, knowledge of the condition of things between the plaintiff and the defendant as the plaintiff himself. His affidavit on this point presents facts upon which the judge, in granting the

* More fully reported 1 *N. Y. Civ. Pro.* 411.

attachment, might find the fact asserted to be substantially proved.

I am of opinion that the court below rightfully disposed of the motion.

TIM ET AL., APPELLANTS, v SMITH.
SCHROEDER AND ANOTHER, RESPONDENTS.

BOYD, ET AL., APPELLANTS, v. SAME.
SAME, RESPONDENTS.

N. Y. COURT OF COMMON PLEAS; GENERAL TERM, MARCH, 1883.

§ 683.

Attachment.—Person who has acquired interest in or lien upon attached property, upon moving to vacate attachment must furnish legal proof of such interest or lien.—Party moved against may question its validity.

Where a party claiming to have acquired an interest in or lien upon attached property moves to vacate the attachment, the fact that he has such lien or interest must appear to the court by competent evidence before it can acquire jurisdiction to entertain the motion.[1]

Where junior attaching creditors moved to vacate a prior attachment on an affidavit, made by their attorney, that in an action brought by them an attachment was granted and duly issued to the sheriff, who by virtue thereof attached the property of the defendant, and that said attachment was still in force and said action was pending,—*Held*, that this was insufficient; that the party moved against could insist upon strict legal proof of the subsequent lien, and had the right to question its validity.[2]

Ruppert v. Haug (87 *N. Y.* 141, 1 *N. Y. Civ. Pro.* 411), distinguished.[2]

(*Decided May* 18, 1883.)

Appeal from two orders (one in each action) made at special term, vacating the attachments granted herein.

The proceedings in these cases were simultaneous and identical. On March 9, 1882, the plaintiffs, in each case, procured an attachment which was subsequently levied upon the property of the defendant. Each attachment recited that the action was to recover "damages for injury to personal property of plaintiffs, in consequence of the negligence and fraud of defendant, in fraudulently procuring credit of plaintiffs for goods sold and delivered to defendant, and that the defendant is a natural person, who has assigned, disposed of, and secreted, and is about to assign, dispose of, and secrete, his property with intent to hinder and delay his creditors and plaintiffs."

Subsequently the respondents, upon an affidavit of their attorney stating that, he was the attorney in an action brought in this court, in which the respondents were plaintiffs, and the defendant herein, defendant, and that on March 17, 1882, an attachment was granted in said action, and duly issued to the sheriff, who by virtue thereof attached the property of the defendant, that said attachment was still in force and said action pending, and that the attachment herein constituted a lien upon the defendants' property prior to the respondents' attachment, moved, in each of these actions, to vacate the attachment granted therein, because of the insufficiency of the affidavits upon which it was issued.

These motions were granted, and this appeal was taken from the orders thereupon entered.

Otto Horwitz and *Daniel Clark Briggs*, for appellants.

Cited, in support of contention that the respondents

should have proven that they had a lien upon, or interest in the attached property: Davis *v.* Brooks, 14 *N. Y. Weekly Dig.* 454.

Alexander Blumenstiel (*Samuel Greenbaum,* attorney), for respondents.

VAN BRUNT, J.—One of the questions which was argued upon this appeal, and the only one which I deem it necessary to consider, is that the moving papers in this case did not show that any valid attachment had been obtained by the moving creditors, and that therefore this motion could not be entertained. In order that this motion may be made, the party moving must have acquired a lien or interest in
[1] the property attached. This fact must appear to the court, by competent evidence, before it can acquire jurisdiction to entertain this motion.

The only proof in this action of the subsequent lien of the moving party, is an affidavit by an attorney, that an attachment was granted in an action in which the moving party was plaintiff against the property of the defendants herein: the grounds of the attachment do not appear. Whether the papers upon which it was granted conferred jurisdiction upon the judge granting the attachment, is not disclosed, and for aught that appears upon the record, the attachment of the moving party may have been founded upon the same facts upon which the plaintiffs herein claimed to maintain their attachment: and we may have presented to us, as a result of this motion, the vacation of an attachment by an alleged subsequent lienor, whose alleged lien is acquired by an attachment having less legal foundation than the one sought to be set aside. It seems to me, that in the face of an objection raising the
[2] point, the party moved against has the right to insist upon strict legal proof of the subsequent

lien, so that he can attack the same because of defects therein.

It cannot be, but that the party moved against has the right to question the validity of the subsequent lien, because the papers upon which it was granted do not confer jurisdiction upon the court precisely in the same manner as the alleged subsequent lienor is attempting to set aside the prior attachment.

It is well established that if the sheriff wishes to justify the taking of personal property, under an attachment, he must show that the attachment is regularly issued by the production of the papers upon which it is founded ; so here, if the party claims a lien by virtue of process, he must show that the process was regularly issued.

It is claimed, upon the part of the respondent, that the case of Ruppert *v.* Haug (87 *N. Y.* 141)* is [*] opposed to the view above expressed. Certainly language is used in the opinion of the court, which sustains this claim : but an examination of the case shows that but one question was considered, as to the status of the moving party, and that was that it did not sufficiently appear by the affidavit of the moving party, that two processes were levied upon the same property, which was necessary to appear in order to give the moving party a standing in court. This is the only question in that regard decided by the court ; and when they say that, in all respects, the affidavit of the moving party was sufficient to give him a standing in court, they had in mind only the point which had been raised, as to the sufficiency of the affidavits, viz.: the identity of the property levied upon.

In the case at bar, the objection is raised at once, that there is nothing whatever to show that the court had any jurisdiction to issue the subsequent attach-

* More fully reported, 1 *N. Y. Civ. Pro.* 411.

ment, or that such attachment, when levied, gave the plaintiff therein any lien upon the defendant's property which authorized them to make the motion, to set aside the plaintiff's prior attachment herein.

As far as I have been able to examine the adjudications, the question now presented has never before been raised; but it seems to me that the plaintiffs in the process attacked, have a right to claim that legal evidence of the existence of the subsequent lien shall be furnished before they can be called upon to justify their own proceedings, and that they may insist that the moving lienor shall show to the court, that his process, at least, is regular and has a better foundation than the process attacked.

The order should be reversed with costs and disbursements.

ALMY ET AL., APPELLANTS, v. THURBER ET AL., RESPONDENTS.

N. Y. COURT OF COMMON PLEAS; GENERAL TERM, JANUARY, 1883.

§§ 650, 651.

Certificate of person served with attachment as to the property of the debtor he has in his possession, or the amount he is indebted to the debtor does estop him from showing error therein.—Voluntary statements only are an estoppel.

Where persons, who have property of, or are indebted to, an attachment debtor, upon being served with the attachment make the certificate as to the amount of the property or indebtedness required by section 650 of the Code,—*Held*, that they are not estopped thereby from showing an error in such certificate in an action brought on the faith of their statement; [1] that the certificate is to be used as evidence only, and the sheriff and plaintiff are not justified in using it for any other purpose.[2]

The certificate made by, or the examination of a person served with an attachment as to his indebtedness to, or the property in his possession of the attachment debtor will be *prima facie* evidence against the party giving it in an action by the attaching creditor or by the sheriff, but it is not conclusive.[3]

The doctrine of estoppel applies only to voluntary representations, declarations, admissions and acts, and has not been extended to declarations exacted by statute.[4] A party certifying or testifying under stress of the law has not the option of speaking or holding his tongue, but is required to give testimony and is to be indulged therefore as any other witness, and allowed to correct honest mistakes in his testimony when confronted with it.[5]

(*Decided March* 15, 1883.)

Appeal by plaintiffs from a judgment in their favor, and from an order denying a motion for a new trial made by them.

This action was brought by the plaintiffs to recover from the defendants, the sum of $2,003.43. The cause of action arose as follows: The plaintiffs herein brought an action in May, 1881, in the supreme court of this State, to recover from the firm of John Gomard & Co., who were non-residents, residing and doing business at Curacoa, West Indies, the sum of $2,200, and obtained a warrant of attachment in said action against Gomard & Co. On the 10th day of May, 1881, they served said attachment upon the defendants, and delivered to them a certified copy of the said warrant and the affidavits, and a notice that by said warrant all the property, credits and demands of said Gomard & Co. in hands of the defendants were thereby attached.

The sheriff also demanded a certificate from the defendants of all moneys or property, in their hands, belonging to Gomard & Co., which the defendants promised to give.

This certificate not having been given, the attorney for the plaintiffs, Almy & Co., upon May 23, 1881, wrote a letter to the defendants, requesting them to give to the sheriff a certificate of the moneys in their hands belonging to Gomard & Co., upon May 10, 1881. To this letter the defendants replied in writing, promising to give the certificate, and on the 28th day of May, 1881, they delivered to the sheriff a certificate of which the following is a copy :

"NEW YORK, May 28 1881.

"Messrs. John Gomard & Co., Curacoa, to H. K. and F. B. Thurber & Co. Dr., importers and wholesale grocers, West Broadway, Reade and Hudson Streets, P. O. Box 3895 :

Cr.,	April 26, By cash		$2,003.63
Dr.,	May 10, To cash . . .	20	
	May 13, To mdse. . .	$1,882.48	
			1,882.68
			$120.95

"H. K. & F. B. THURBER & Co."

On January, 13, 1882, the plaintiffs obtained a judgment in the aforesaid action, against the firm of John Gomard & Co., for the sum of $2,179.53 damages and costs. Upon the same day an execution was issued to the said sheriff, who thereafter demanded from the defendants, payment of the sum of $2,003.43, which demand was refused.

Leave of the court being thereafter obtained, this action was brought in the court below, where it was tried before the Hon. CHARLES P. DALY, and a jury, on November 23, 1882.

It was shown, on the trial, that on May 10, 1881, there was but $120.95 in the hands of the defendants to the credit of the debtors, J. Gomard & Co., the merchandise charged at $1,882.48 having been sold and delivered to the debtors by defendants, some time prior to that date.

The plaintiffs claimed that defendants were estopped from showing these facts by their statement, delivered to the sheriff, in which the merchandise was charged on May 13, 1881, because, on receipt of such statement, the sheriff, relying thereon, made no further effort to find property subject to the attachment.

The defendants contended that the statement alleged a balance of $120.95, only, subject to the attachment.

The court left it to the jury, to say if the certificate was given for the purpose of certifying, they had $120.95 in their hands, at the time of the levy, and it rendered a verdict in favor of plaintiff for that sum.

A motion was made upon the minutes by plaintiffs for a new trial, upon the ground that the damages awarded by the jury were insufficient, and upon the exceptions.

The motion was denied, and from the order thereupon entered, and from the judgment upon the verdict this appeal was taken.

Edward B. Merrill and *Henry D. Hotckkiss*, for appellants.

The court below erred in leaving the construction of the certificate to the jury. There was no mixed question of law and fact in the case which required the judgment of the jury. Vedder v. Fellows, 20 *N. Y.* 126; Lewis v. Carstairs, 5 *W. & S.* 209.

No special form of certificate is required by law, and there is no doubt but that the certificate in question was sufficient in form. Defendants having given such a certificate, and the plaintiffs having no reason to doubt the truth of the facts stated in it, they could not have examined defendants as to the property of Gomard & Co. in defendants' hands. *Code*, § 651;

Carroll *v.* Findley, 29 *Barb.* 61; Hoagland *v.* Stodolla, 1 *Code Rep. N. S.* 210.

The plaintiffs herein relied upon the declarations and admissions made by the defendants in the certificate, as to the property of Gomard & Co. in defendants' hands on the day the attachment was served; they were lulled into a sense of security thereby, and made no further efforts to find property in New York city belonging to Gomard & Co. and they were justified in so relying. 6 *Wait Actions and Defenses*, 694, § 6, and cases cited.

The defendants are estopped from now denying the statements so clearly set forth in the certificate which the case shows had such a controlling effect upon the conduct of the plaintiffs. Cornell *v.* Dakin, 38 *N. Y.* 253; Faston *v.* Goodwin, 22 *Minn.* 426; Dezell *v.* Odell, 3 *Hill*, 215.

If a man has willfully made a false assertion calculated to lead others to act upon it, and they have done so to their prejudice, he is forbidden as against them to deny it. Pickard *v.* Sears, 6 *Adol. & Ellis*, 469; Continental Nat'l Bank *v.* Nat'l Bank of Commonwealth, 50 *N. Y.* 575.

"Willfully" in this rule must be understood, if not that the party represented that to be true which he knows to be untrue, at least that he *means* his representation to be acted upon. Freeman *v.* Cooke, 2 *Exch.* 663.

If a party uses language which, in the ordinary course of business, and the general sense in which words are understood, conveys a certain meaning, he cannot afterwards say he is not bound, if another, so understanding it, has acted upon it. Cornish *v.* Abington, 4 *H. & N.* 549; Welland Canal Co. *v.* Hathaway, 8 *Wend.* 480. "When an act produces conduct from which flows injury, it cannot matter whether that conduct be affirmative or negative, active or quiescent." Continental

Nat'l Bank *v.* Nat'l Bank of Commonwealth, *supra.* It was not necessary for plaintiffs to show that had it not been for the certificate they could have found other property of Gomard & Co. which they could have subjected to the attachment; it was enough that their position was altered by the certificate, and a consequent right to abstain from further search for property. Voorhis *v.* Olmstead, 66 *N. Y.* 113.

More, Applington & More, for respondents.

J. F. DALY, J.—If it was shown by evidence that there was an error in the statement delivered to the sheriff by defendants, by which it appeared that the charge for merchandise in their favor against the defendants in the attachment accrued after the levy; whereas, in fact, such charge accrued long prior to the levy, and that at the date of levy, May 10, 1881, there was but $120.95 due John Gomard & Co., the defendants in the attachment, from these defendants.

Defendants were not estopped from showing such error in an action brought on the faith of their statement.

The certificate required of a person, who has
[1] property of the attachment debtor, or is indebted to him, by section 650, is evidently intended as the basis of an action under sections 655 and 677 against such person by the sheriff or the plaintiff in the attachment.

By section 651 it is provided that if such person refuses to give a certificate or gives a false or insufficient certificate, he may be required to submit to an examination under oath concerning the same.

A certificate voluntarily given is of no higher character than the statement under oath made upon such an examination, yet it would not be claimed that a person so examined, if mistaken in his testimony

could not correct it or show the truth when
[2] subsequently sued upon it. The object of the certificate or examination is apparent from the statute; it is to be used as evidence only; and the sheriff and plaintiff are not justified in using it for any other purpose,—*e. g.*, as a representation of fact upon which they may rely in omitting to secure the demand in suit. The certificate or examination will be *prima facie* evidence against the party giving it in an
[3] action by the sheriff or the attaching creditor, but is no more conclusive than is an examination of a party in anticipation of an action under section 870 of the code. The doctrine of estoppel applies only to voluntary representations, declarations, admis-
[4] sions and acts, and has not been extended, as far as I can discover, to declarations exacted by statute. A party certifying or testifying under stress of the law has not the option of speaking or holding his
[5] tongue; he is required to give testimony, and is to be indulged, therefore, as any other witness, and allowed to correct honest mistakes in his testimony when confronted with it.

The judgment should be affirmed with costs.

VALIENTE AND ANOTHER v. BRYAN.

N. Y. MARINE COURT; SPECIAL TERM, APRIL, 1883.

§§ 779, 2455.

Costs.—Motion costs, both in actions and special proceedings, to be collected by execution issued under section 779 of the Code.—Costs, when not collectible by execution.—History of the legislation relating to the collection of costs.

The Code of Civil Procedure makes no distinction between motion costs awarded in an action and those awarded in a special proceeding, and an execution for the collection of the latter may issue under section 779 of the Code.[2]

The $30 costs which may be granted to the judgment creditor in proceedings supplementary to execution are not motion costs, but the final costs of the proceeding, payable out of any money which has or may come into the hands of the receiver, or they may be directed to be paid by the judgment debtor. The establishment of a method of collection impliedly precludes their collection in any other way.[3] They cannot be deemed motion costs, and are not therefore collectible by execution.[4]

The history of the statutory provisions relating to the collection of costs by precept and execution, stated.[1]

(*Decided April* 10, 1883.)

Motion to set aside execution issued for the collection of costs.

The facts are stated in the opinion.

William H. Newman, for motion.

Poultney Bigelow, opposed.

Wherever there is an order of the court, directing the payment of interlocutory costs, a process or precept in the nature of a *fieri facias* may issue against the property of the party directed to pay such costs. 4

Wait's Pr. 208; *Laws of* 1847, ch. 390, § 3; *Laws of* 1840, ch. 386, § 15.

A precept to enforce the payment of costs may issue without any demand or application to the court. 4 *Wait's Pr.* 209; Mitchell *v.* Westervelt, 6 *How. Pr.* 265, 311, note; Lucas *v.* Johnson, *Id.* 121; *Laws* 1847, ch. 390; Weitzel *v.* Schultz, 3 *Abb. Pr.* 468.

HAWES, J.—Supplementary proceedings were instituted upon return of execution in this action, and during the course of the proceeding $10 costs were allowed by the judge, and also the further sum of $30 at the close of the examination, when a receiver was appointed. The plaintiff has issued a precept to the sheriff to recover these costs, and the present
[*] motion is to vacate this precept. Under the provision of the Laws of 1840, chap. 386, and the Laws of 1847, chap. 390, a precept could be issued to collect costs, if based upon an order of the court, but these were strictly motion costs (Wesley *v.* Bennet, 6 *Abb.* 12). The provisions of the act of 1840 allowed an attachment against the person, but this provision was, in the main, repealed by the act of 1847, which allowed a *fieri facias* to issue for their collection, and it may be said in general terms that the one was a substitution of process against property for one against the person. The law of 1847 was repealed by chapter 417 of the Laws of 1877, and not being re-enacted by the Code there was no provision for their collection by execution or precept under the provision of section 779 prior to the enactment of 1882 (McCulloch *v.* Hoffman, 1 *Law Bull.* 24). The amendment of section 779, passed July 1, 1882, re-enacts in substance the provision of the Laws of 1847, and now allows an execution to issue for the collection of motion costs.

The $10 allowed by the court are clearly motion costs and are collectible by execution, and I know

[2] of no rule which would prevent collection by such a remedy in a special proceeding as well as in actions. The Code in that regard makes no distinction that I am aware of. The only possible question is as to the classification which should be given to the $30 costs allowed on the appointment of a receiver. The law of 1847 provided that process in the nature of a *fieri facias* against personal property may be issued for the collection of "costs founded on an order of court." The question of the right to issue a writ for the collection of the $30 costs in supplementary proceedings was fully discussed in the case of Halsaver *v.* Wilas (11 *How. Pr.* 450), and it was there held that, inasmuch as supplementary proceedings were special proceedings, the order then made by the judge was not an "order of court," but was merely an order of the judge, and did not, therefore fall within the provision of the statute. It will be noticed that no such restriction exists in section 779 of the Code, but only refers to "costs of motion directed by an order." It is clear, therefore, that an order of a judge is as good a foundation for such a writ as an order of the court.

The question therefore returns as to whether the $30 costs allowed to plaintiff for costs of this proceeding are to be deemed "costs of a motion directed by an order." The legal history of this provision of the Code is very voluminous, and many nice distinctions have been drawn; but I am inclined to think that the motion costs referred to in this section are confined strictly to the class of motions which were first allowed under the statute 1840, and which statute required the justices of the supreme court to regulate by rule the amount to be allowed upon granting or denying motions. This amount was fixed at that time at $10 to the moving party and $7 to the opposing party if successful, and in peculiar cases the costs to either

party might be allowed to an amount not exceeding $20. The codes of 1848 and 1849 severally modified the rule and provided that costs might be allowed on motions in the discretion of the court not exceeding $10. These provisions of the statute, upon which section 779 is founded, clearly had no reference to statutory or taxable costs, but were special motion costs allowed in the progress of the litigation and collectible at once. If this is the correct view of the intent of the statute, I do not see how the $30 costs can come within the
[3] provisions of section 779, although they are directed by an order to be paid. This allowance of $30 is granted by virtue of the statute, and is the final costs in the proceeding and is payable out any money which has come into the hands of the receiver (§ 2455 of Code), or it may be directed to be paid by the judgment debtor, if so set forth in the order. This would seem to establish a method of collection, and in the nature of things would impliedly preclude its collection in any other way. Specific provision for the collection of final costs which may, perhaps, be deemed tantamount to judgment costs in various special proceedings, are provided for. Section 2250 establishes the costs to be allowed in summary proceedings, and expressly allows their collection by execution.

Section 2556 allows costs in surrogate's court to be collected by execution. In supplementary pro-
[4] ceedings the final costs cannot be deemed motion costs, and are not, therefore collectible by execution. The execution, therefore, will be modified in that respect. The examination was regularly adjourned to February 16, and it appeared from the uncontradicted affidavit of plaintiff's attorney that the application was made on that day, although the order was not entered until the 20th inst. The appointment of the receiver was, therefore, regular. **Motion granted, unless modified as above.**

NEWMAN v. GREIFF ET AL.

N. Y. SUPERIOR COURT; SPECIAL TERM, MAY, 1883.

§ 3251.

Costs.—Where a party was examined before trial under a stipulation and not by order, costs for such examination cannot be taxed.—Clerk to be guided in adjusting costs, by the Code.

The clerk of a court should refuse to tax costs unless strictly in accordance with the Code. It is his only guide.

Where a party to an action was examined before trial pursuant to a stipulation between the parties, and not under an order of the court obtained as provided in sections 870 and 871 of the Code,—*Held*, that $10 costs for such examination could not be taxed.

(*Decided May* 13, 1883.)

Motion for a new taxation of the costs of an action.

The opinion states the facts.

William L. Larned, for motion.

Stern & Meyers, opposed.

O'GORMAN, J.—The clerk is right in refusing to tax costs unless strictly in accordance with the provisions of the Code. It is his only guide.

Section 870 and 871 of the Code prescribe the mode of securing the examination of a witness before trial, viz.: application to a judge of the court on affidavit, service of order, etc. Section 3251, subdivision 3, provides that costs shall be awarded to either party, for taking the deposition of a witness or a party, as prescribed in sections 870, 871 and 893 of the Code, $10. The testimony of the witness here was taken, not under order of the court obtained on affidavit, &c., as prescribed by sections 870 and 871, but by stipulation between the parties and to be read on the trial by either party.

This proceeding thus facilitated for the convenience of the parties, and, though attaining the same result, the procuring of testimony did not involve the trouble to the attorney for which it may be assumed the allowance of $10 was wholly or in part awarded by section 3251. Section 893 refers to the issuing of a commission to examine a witness, and is not in point here.

The action of the clerk must be sustained.

NEHRESHEIMER, RESPONDENT, v. BOWE, AS SHERIFF, ETC., APPELLANT.

N. Y. COURT OF COMMON PLEAS; GENERAL TERM, NOVEMBER, 1882.

§ 600.

Sheriff.—Not granted relief under section 600 *of the Code, where prisoner escaped.*

The provisions of section 600 of the Code, that if a defendant, after his discharge upon bail is imprisoned upon a criminal charge, etc., the court in which an action against the bail is pending may, before the expiration of the time to answer and upon notice to the adverse party, make such an order for the relief of the bail as justice requires, applies only when the defendant was discharged in such a manner upon bail as relieved the sheriff from liability. Accordingly,—*Held*, in a case where a defendant imprisoned under an order of arrest escaped to another State where he was arrested and imprisoned upon conviction of a criminal offense, that a motion for the relief of the sheriff under section 600 was properly denied.
(*Decided December* 4, 1882.)

Appeal from order denying motion, made at special term for an order exonerating the defendant as bail, etc.

The facts are fully stated in the opinion.

E. W. Crittenden (*Charles F. McLean*, attorney), for appellant.

Before the Code, it was customary to exonerate bail in like circumstances. (1) Where a prisoner was arrested on a charge of forgery, and detained in prison. Biggnell *v.* Forrest, 2 *Johns.* 482. (2) Where there was imprisonment for life. Cathcart *v.* Cannon, 1 *Johns. Cas.* 28. (3) Where prisoner had been convicted in Vermont, for passing counterfeit money. The court said: "The defendant has been taken out of the power of his bail, by the judgment of law; he is in this respect as if he were dead. The motion for an exoneration ought, therefore to be granted." Loflin *v.* Fowler, 18 *Johns.* 335. The Code has not changed the ground upon which exoneration may be granted. Bank of Geneva *v.* Reynolds, 12 *Abb. Pr.* 81.

In a case where imprisonment within the state was not deemed good cause of an *exoneratur* the court said time might be given for a surrender. Phœnix Fire Ins. Co. *v.* Mowatt, 6 *Cow.* 599. And see Bank of Geneva *v.* Reynolds, *supra.*

Benjamin F. Bayliss (*Birdseye, Cloyd & Bayliss*, attorneys), for respondent.

Van Brunt, J.—The complaint in this action after alleging the commencement of an action in the marine court, by this plaintiff against one E. Anchise, in which action an order of arrest was issued, directed to the defendant in this action, whereby he was ordered to arrest the said defendant, Anchise, and hold him to bail in the sum of $1,500, and that thereupon this defendant duly arrested the said Anchise, and served upon him the summons and complaint and other papers in said action, and that the defendant Anchise, duly appeared and answered in said action, and such proceedings were thereupon had that on the 12th of

November, 1881, the plaintiff duly recovered a judgment therein against said Anchise: that the judgment roll was duly filed in the office of the clerk of said marine court, and a transcript thereof duly filed, and the judgment duly docketed in the office of the clerk of the city and county of New York, and that afterwards an execution against the property of said Anchise was duly issued upon said judgment, to the defendant, sheriff, which was afterwards duly returned wholly unsatisfied; and that afterwards an execution against the person of said Anchise, upon said judgment was duly issued to said sheriff, and has been duly returned by said sheriff, not found, further alleges upon information and belief, and that after said Anchise was so arrested, as aforesaid by the defendant herein, *and without being discharged upon bail and before bail had been furnished, by said Anchise, he the said Anchise escaped from the said defendant, sheriff; that after said arrest and escape* the defendant herein served upon the attorneys, for plaintiff in said action a paper, purporting to be a copy undertaking upon an order of arrest. That thereupon plaintiff caused due notice to be served upon said defendant sheriff, that he did not accept the bail, so as aforesaid claimed to have been offered by said Anchise, and that said alleged bail did not justify, and no notice of their justification was served upon plaintiff or his attorney, and that by reason of the premises defendant became liable to the plaintiff in the sum of $1,500.

The defendant in this action thereupon made a motion to this court for an order exonerating the defendant as bail, or for such an order for the relief of the defendant as bail as justice required, and for such other or further order as the court might see fit to grant.

The papers upon this motion show, taking the most favorable view of the same for the defendant, that the said Anchise was arrested and that an undertaking on arrest was executed to the sheriff by two sureties, who thereupon discharged the said Anchise from custody, and the said Anchise left the State of New York for the State of California; that the plaintiffs excepted to the sufficiency of the sureties in said undertaking and said sureties did not justify nor did they attempt to do so; that at the city of San Francisco in September 1881, the said Anchise was tried, convicted and sentenced to four years' imprisonment for a felony, and he was at the time of the making of the motion serving out said sentence.

The court denied the motion, and from the order thereupon entered this appeal is taken.

In the above statement of facts I have merely alluded to the conceded facts of the case. The question raised upon the papers as to the manner in which the bail was taken have not been mentioned, the same being immaterial in view of the conclusion which has been arrived at upon the law as applicable to the conceded facts.

It is urged upon the part of the appellant that as the sheriff is liable as bail he has all the rights and privileges of bail and that it was customary to exonerate bail under like circumstances. The provisions of the Code, however, do not seem to contemplate that the sheriff shall be exonerated under circumstances like those above stated. Section 587 of the Code provides that "if after the defendant is arrested he escapes or is rescued, or the bail, if any, given by him do not justify when they are not accepted . . . . the sheriff is liable as bail. But the sheriff may except in an action to recover a chattel, discharge himself from liability, by the giving and justification of bail," &c. The bail attempted to be given by Anchise not having justified under the provisions of the foregoing section the sheriff became liable as bail. Section 595 provides as follows: "When the sheriff is liable as bail he has all the rights and privileges and is subject to all the duties and liabilities of bail; and bail given by him, in order to discharge himself from liability, must be regarded as the bail of the defendant in the action, but this section does not apply to an action to recover a chattel or to a case where a defense arises to an action against the bail in consequence of an act or omission of the sheriff."

By section 600 it is provided: "If the defendant in the original action after his discharge upon bail, is imprisoned either within or without the state, upon a criminal charge or a conviction of a criminal offense, the court, in which an action against the bail is pending, may before the expiration of the time to answer, and upon notice to the adverse party, make such an order for the relief of the bail, as justice requires."

It seems to us that the construction of the words "after his discharge upon bail" means after his discharge in such a manner upon bail as relieves the sheriff from liability.

The provisions of section 587 are that the sheriff is discharged from liability only upon justification of the bail, if it is not accepted.

In the case at bar no bail ever justified, and the sheriff therefore became liable as bail. It is true that by section 595 it is provided that where the sheriff is liable as bail he has all the rights and privileges and is subject to all the duties and liabilities of bail: but section 600 especially limits the right to apply for and obtain the relief provided for by this section to the case where a defendant "after his discharge *upon bail* is imprisoned," &c. Such discharge is a discharge without the consent of the sheriff, and he cannot be surrendered, and relieves the sheriff from all liability.

In the case at bar as has already been said the defendant in the original action was never discharged upon bail, and was never entitled to go at large so as to provide himself with a home in a prison in a foreign state.

We are of the opinion, therefore, that the order appealed from should be affirmed with costs and disbursements, to abide the final event of the action.

BEACH, J., concurred.

NEHRESHEIMER, RESPONDENT, *v.* BOWE, AS SHERIFF, ETC., APPELLANT.

N. Y. COURT OF COMMON PLEAS; GENERAL TERM, NOVEMBER, 1882.

§§ 158, 545, 587.

Complaint.—When not sufficiently definite and certain.—Sheriff has right to know whether action against him is to charge him as bail or to recover damages for an escape.—Order denying motion to strike out portions of complaint, affects a material right of the defendant, and is appealable.

Where, in an action against the sheriff, the complaint, after setting forth the arrest by the sheriff of one A. under an order of arrest issued in an action brought against A. by the plaintiff, alleged that without being discharged upon bail and before bail had been furnished by A., he escaped from the sheriff, and that after the arrest and escape the sheriff served upon the plaintiff's attorneys a bail bond, the sureties to which, upon its being excepted to, failed to justify,—*Held*, that it is impossible to tell from the complaint whether the plaintiff seeks to charge the sheriff as bail or to recover damages for an escape;[1] that if he sought to charge the sheriff as bail, the allegations of the complaint as to the escape are entirely irrelevant and redundant,[2] and that if it is sought to recover of the sheriff damages for an escape, the allegations in respect to the failure of the bail to justify are irrelevant and redundant.[3]

In such a case the sheriff has a right to know whether he is to be charged as bail or whether it is sought to recover damages for an escape, because defenses may be pleaded in an action for an escape which cannot be set up in an action to charge the sheriff as bail.[*]

An order denying a motion to strike out certain portions of a complaint as irrelevant and redundant is appealable.[*] The motion is not one resting absolutely in the discretion of the court, but affects a material right of the defendant.[*]

(*Decided December* 4, 1882.)

Appeal from order made at special term, denying a motion to strike out certain portions of the complaint as irrelevant and redundant.

The facts are stated in the opinion, on appeal from order denying motion to exonerate the sheriff as bail, etc. (*ante*, p. 364), and in the opinion here reported.

Edward W. Crittenden (*Charles F. MacLean*, attorney), for appellant.

The abolition of all distinctions between actions at law and suits in equity, and of all forms of those actions and suits, does not affect the legal rights of the parties, and causes of action remain as they were before. *Pomeroy on Remedies*, p. 133, § 107 *et seq.*, and cases there cited.

Benjamin H. Bayliss (*Birdseye, Cloyd & Bayliss*, attorneys), for respondents.

Even if the words sought to be rejected were irrelevant or redundant, which is not admitted, they nevertheless should not be stricken out. Town of Essex *v.* N. Y. & Canada R. R. Co., 8 *Hun*, 361. If in any aspect of the case the allegation can be material it should not be striken out. Cahill *v.* Palmer, 17 *Abb. Pr.* 196. The true test is to inquire whether the averment tends to constitute a cause of action or defense. If it does, it is not irrelevant. Ingersoll *v.* Ingersoll, 1 *Code R.* 102; Averill *v.* Taylor, 5 *How Pr.* 476; Quintard *v.*

Newton, 5 *Robt.* 72; Devan *v.* Dinsmore, 33 *Barb.* 86.

But this order is not appealable, and for that reason, the appeal should be dismissed. It cannot involve the merits of the action or some part thereof, for the very ground of the motion is that the matter sought to be stricken out is "redundant and irrelevant." Therefore, not involving the merits, it cannot get to this general term by appeal. Bedell *v.* Stickles, 4 *How. Pr.* 432; Whitney *v.* Waterman, 4 *Id.* 315; Tallman *v.* Hinman, 10 *Id.* 90; Field *v.* Stewart, 41 *How. Pr.* 95.

VAN BRUNT, J.—[After stating the allegations contained in the complaint as in the opinion on appeal from order denying motion to exonerate sheriff as bail (*ante*, pp. 364, 365), and *ipsima verba.*]—The defendant in this action thereupon made a motion to have the foregoing underlined words* stricken from said complaint as irrelevant or redundant matter, and in case such motion was denied, he moved that plaintiff be required to separately state and number the several causes of action stated in the complaint. This motion was denied, and from the order denying such motion this appeal is taken.

It is impossible by examination of this complaint
to determine whether the plaintiff in this action
[1] seeks to charge the sheriff as bail, or to recover
damages for an escape. All the allegations of the
complaint, prior to the clause which has been quoted
in the foregoing statement of facts, would be equally
necessary in an action for an escape or in an action to
charge the sheriff as bail. If it is sought to charge
[2] the sheriff as bail, the allegations contained in the
complaint as to his escape are entirely irrelevant

* In italics on p. 365, *ante*.

and redundant; if it is sought to recover damages of the sheriff for an escape, the allegations in the
[3] complaint, in respect to the failure of the bail to justify are irrelevant and redundant.

The defendant in this action has a right to know whether he is to be charged as bail, or whether it
[4] is sought to recover damages of the sheriff, for an escape because defenses may be pleaded to an action for an escape which cannot be set up in an action to charge the sheriff as bail. The objection
[5] that the order denying the motion is not appealable is not well taken, as the motion made is one not resting absolutely in the discretion of the court below but affects a material right of the defendant.

The order appealed from should be reversed, with costs and disbursements to the defendant to abide the final event.

BEACH, J., concurred.

WERTHEIM ET AL. v. THE CONTINENTAL RAILWAY AND TRUST CO.

U. S. CIRCUIT COURT, SOUTHERN DISTRICT OF NEW YORK; FEBRUARY, 1883.

Officers of corporation, not parties to action, may, at common law, be compelled to produce books and papers of the corporation by subpœna duces tecum.—Proceedings in suit in equity in United States circuit court not governed by N. Y. Code of Civil Procedure.

The officers of a corporation may be compelled by a *subpœna duces tecum* to produce books and papers of the corporation in a suit in equity to which it is not a party, upon the application of one of the parties, [1, 2] and where the books, etc., are in the custody of an officer other than the one served with a subpœna, if the latter has the power to produce them he is bound to do so.[6,7]

In a suit in equity in the U. S. circuit court, the proceedings are not affected by the provisions of the Code of Civil Procedure.[4]

Bank of Utica *v.* Hilliard (5 *Cow.* 153);[1] S. C. (*Id.* 419);[2] La Farge *v.* La Farge Fire Ins. Co. (14 *How. Pr.* 26);[3] distinguished; Amey *v.* Long (1 *Campbell* 17);[6] Crowther *v.* Appleby (*L. R.* 9 *C. P.* 27),[7] approved.

(*Decided February* 17, 1883.)

Motion for attachment against Edward F. Winslow and F. E. Worcester, for contempt in failing to produce books and papers of a corporation in which they are officers as required by a *subpœna duces tecum.*

This is a suit in equity brought under a Connecticut statute to wind up the defendant, a corporation. In a proceeding, in the suit, for the taking of testimony *de bene esse* a *subpœna duces tecum* was served upon Edward F. Winslow the president of the North River Construction Company, and another on F. E. Worcester, another officer of the company, requiring them to appear before John A. Shields, a U. S. commissioner, and testify and to produce certain books, papers, &c., in the posession of said company. They both appeared and testified, but failed to produce the books, papers, &c. Thereupon this motion for an attachment was made.

Evarts, Southmayd & Choate, for the motion.

Henry L. Burnett, opposed.

The papers called for must be in the witness's actual possession. Amey *v.* Long, 1 *Camp.* 14. Documents filed in a public office are not in the possession of a witness and cannot be produced under a subpœna *duces tecum.* Austin *v.* Evans, 2 *M. & G.* 430. This rule applies to the servants of a company. Such servant is not required to produce the books and papers.

Crowther v. Appleby, 43 *L. J., C. P.* 7; S. C., *L. R.*, 9 *C. P.* 23. So of the books of a bank, a partner cannot be required to produce them unless the other partner consents. Attorney General v. Wilson, 9 *Sim.* 526.

Also cited in support of contention that an officer of a corporation cannot be compelled to produce books and papers which are in his custody as such officer. Bank of Utica v. Hilliard, 5 *Cow.* 153; S. C., 5 *Id.* 419; 6 *Id.* 62; La Farge v. La Farge Fire Ins. Co., 14 *How. Pr.* 26; S. C., 6 *Duer*, 680; Woods v. De Figaniere, 16 *Abb. Pr.* 159; Opdyke v. Marble, 44 *Barb.* 64; Central National Bank v. White, 37 *N. Y. Supr. Ct.* 297; Morgan v. Morgan, 16 *Abb. Pr. N. S.* 291; United States v. Tilden, 18 *Alb. L. J.* 416.

WALLACE, J.—There are informalities in the record upon which this motion to attach witnesses for contempt has been argued, which lead to a denial of the motion. But counsel have desired that the main question involved should be considered and decided as a guide to their future action in the cause. This question is whether the president and secretary of the North River Construction Company, a corporation, can be compelled by a *subpœna duces tecum* to produce books and papers of the corporation in a suit in equity, to which the corporation is not a party upon the application of one of the parties.

The proceeding is opposed upon the authority of several cases in the State courts of New York which deny the right of a party to compel the officers of a corporation to produce its books as evidence in a cause to which it is not a party. The first of these cases is the President, etc. of Bank of Utica v. Hillard, 5 *Cow.* 153, where a clerk of the bank refused to produce the books. SAVAGE, Ch. J., said: "The obligation of the witnesses to produce the books upon the *duces*

[1] *tecum* depends on the question, whether they were
in his possession or under his control;" and the
obligation was denied, because he was a mere clerk
of the corporation. The same case was before the court
again (5 *Cow.* 419) upon a motion to attach the
[2] cashier of the bank, who had refused to produce
the books under the subpœna, and was denied
because the bank could not be required to produce
evidence against itself, as a party to the action. Both
of these cases, by the strongest implication, concede
the power to compel the production of the books by an
officer when the corporation is not a party. Thirty
years later the point arose again in La Farge *v.* La
[3] Farge Fire Ins. Co., 14 *How.* 26, upon a motion for
an attachment against the president of the defendant for refusing to produce its books, under a *subpœna duces tecum*, and the motion was denied upon the authority of the cases in 5 *Cow.* The precedent thus established was recognized, incidentally or directly, in several subsequent cases, and was assumed to apply whether the corporation was a party or not a party to the suit. The question was never considered by the courts of last resort, and was put at rest by section 869 of the Code of Code Procedure, which expressly conferred the right theretofore denied.

As this suit is in equity, the present motion is not
affected by the provisions of the Code of Civil Pro-
[4] cedure,* and the court is asked to apply the doctrine of the antecedent decisions of the State courts.
No authority is found in any decisions of the federal
courts denying the right to compel corporations to
produce evidence which may be necessary and vital
[5] to the rights of the litigants. On principle it is
impossible to suggest any reason why a corporation should be privileged to withhold evidence which

*§§ 868, 869.

an individual would be required to produce. It may be inconvenient, and sometimes embarrassing, to the managers of a corporation to require its books and papers to be taken from its office, and exhibited to third persons, but it is also inconvenient, and often onerous to individuals, to require them to do the same thing. Considerations of inconvenience must give way to the paramount right of litigants to resort to evidence which it may be in the power of witnesses to produce, and without which grave interests might be jeoparded, and the administration of justice thwarted.

The researches of counsel have been unavailing to find any decisions of the courts of other States which sanction the rule thus maintained by the courts of New York. Notwithstanding these cases, it is believed to have been the common practice in this State to subpœna officers as witnesses to produce the books of their corporations in actions between third persons. In other States, so far as is known, the right to do so has never been controverted. There has been strenuous opposition on the part of corporations to the production of their papers and records in suits to which they were not parties. The effort of telegraph companies to maintain the privacy of their messages is an illustration, (see Henisler *v.* Freedman, 2 *Pars. Select Cas.* 274; United States *v.* Babcock, 3 *Dill.* 566), but immunity has never been claimed upon the ground now taken.

Why should not the officers of a corporation be required to produce the books of the corporation as witnesses when the books are necessary evidence? The corporation can only act through its officers. The suggestion that the books are in the legal custody of the corporation, and not of its officers, may be theoretically correct. If technically true, it is not an objection to compelling the officers to produce them. As said
[*] by Lord ELLENBOROUGH, in Amey *v.* Long, 1 *Campb.* 17: "Although a paper should be in the

legal custody of one man, yet if a *subpœna duces tecum* is served on another, who has the means to produce it, he is bound to do so."

In Crowther *v.* Appleby, *L. R.* 9 *C. P.* 27,
[7] Lord DENMAN asks: "When documents are in the possession of a company, who but the secretary can be subpœnaed to produce them?" Courts of equity have always permitted the officers of corporations to be made parties to bills of discovery, upon the theory that they are the custodians of the books and documents of the corporation, and may be compelled to produce them and answer to the interrogatories propounded.

As has been indicated, the cases in 5 *Cow.* have
[8] been misapplied by the later cases in the courts of New York, and do not sanction the precedent which they are asserted to establish. This court must refuse to follow these later decisions, deeming them to be unsupported by precedent, an innovation upon the rule generally recognized, and opposed to good sense.

RECK, APPELLANT, *v.* THE PHŒNIX INSURANCE COMPANY, RESPONDENT.

SUPREME COURT, FIRST DEPARTMENT; GENERAL TERM, MARCH, 1883.

§ 723.

Complaint.—When court should order it amended.—When sufficiently alleges loss during life of policy in action upon policy of insurance on ship alleged to have been lost at sea.

Where, in an action upon a policy of insurance on a ship alleged to have been lost at sea, which had been pending twelve years, the defendant's counsel, on the trial, made a motion at the opening of the case to dismiss the complaint on the ground that it did not state facts sufficient to constitute a cause of action, and reserved the motion until the close of the evidence, and the plaintiff gave evidence which would have entitled him to go to the jury upon the question of loss within the life of the policy, and at the close of his case, the defendant's counsel renewed his motion to dismiss, on the ground that on the face of the complaint it was not shown or alleged that the vessel could complete the voyage she was, at the time of her loss, making, within the life of the policy, nor that she was lost during the life of the policy by any peril insured against, which objections were there raised for the first time, and the complaint was thereupon dismissed,—*Held*, that if there was anything substantial or meritorious in the motion, the error or defect in the complaint was not one which affected the substantial rights of the defendant;[2] that substantial justice required that the court should order an amendment of its own motion the moment the point was definitely suggested;[7] and that not only simple justice but the Code required that to be done after the proof had been admitted without objection, and the error first pointed out at the close of the plaintiff's case.[7]

In the case of missing vessels never heard from after a definite date, the loss is presumed to have happened immediately after the date of the last news from them.[1]

Where the complaint in an action upon a policy of insurance on a ship alleged to have been lost at sea, averred that on or about May 28, 1866, she sailed from the port of New York for Yokohama, Japan; that she "has not been heard from since the 16th day of October, 1866, on which day she was in the Indian Ocean, beyond Zullabessy in Pits' Passage, steering from Honolulu Passage and pursuing her said voyage, and although a reasonable length of time had elapsed to complete the same prior to the commencement of this action, the said ship never arrived at Yokohama, but was totally lost by and through the perils of the sea," and a copy of the policy was annexed to the complaint, from which it appeared that the vessel was insured from December 29, 1865, to December 29, 1866.—*Held*, that a dismissal of the complaint on the ground that it did not allege that the loss occurred during the life of the policy was error;[9] that the presumption of law that the loss of a vessel is presumed to have occurred immediately after the last news from it makes the averment of the complaint, quoted, equivalent to an allegation that the ship was lost during the life of the policy.[9]

Slack *v.* Lyons (26 *Mass.* (9 *Pick.*) 62);[1] White *v.* Spencer (14 *N. Y.* 247);[4] Bate *v.* Graham (11 *N. Y.* 242);[5] Sealey *v.* Engel (13

N. Y. 542);[5] Wood *v.* Wood (26 *Barb.* 359);[6] approved and followed.

(*Decided May* 11, 1883.)

Appeal by plaintiff from a judgment entered upon a dismissal of his complaint at circuit.

The facts are stated, at length, in the opinion.

Joseph A. Shoudy (*James K. Hill, Wing & Shoudy*, attorneys), for appellant.

There is no substantial defect in the complaint; it contains every allegation essential to constitute a cause of action. The plaintiff is not required to aver any fact not necessary to be proved on the trial. Nat'l Shoe & Leather Bank *v.* Brown, 18 *How. Pr.* 308. In Marie *v.* Garrison (83 *N. Y.* 14), the court of appeals held that a complaint, even on demurrer, is to be deemed to allege what can be implied from the allegations therein by a reasonable and fair intendment, and that facts impliedly averred are traversable in the same manner as though directly averred. It is not necessary that legal inferences should be alleged Glenny *v.* Hitchins, 4 *Abb. Pr.* 98. "It is sufficient that the requisite allegations can be fairly gathered from all the averments in the complaint, though the statement of them may be argumentative and the complaint deficient in technical language." DENIO, J., in Zabriskie *v.* Smith, 15 *N. Y.* 330. If the allegations are uncertain or indefinite the remedy is by motion and not by demurrer even. People *v.* Ryder, 11 *N. Y.* 440; Seeley *v.* Engell, 13 *Id.* 542. The complaint is not defective in substance for omitting to state conclusions which are to be implied from other facts sufficiently stated. Case *v.* Carroll, 35 *N. Y.* 385. The Code requires a pleading to be liberally construed with a view to substantial justice (section 519) and when the complaint may be construed to import a cause of action it is held sufficient although another construction is possible. Olcott *v.* Carroll, 39 *N. Y.* 436.

G. A. Black (*Scudder & Carter*, attorneys), for respondent.

DAVIS, P. J.—This was an action upon a policy of insurance on the ship Elise Ruger alleged to have been lost at sea. On the opening of the case by the plaintiff's attorney a motion was made by defendant's counsel to dismiss the complaint on the ground that it did not state facts sufficient to constitute a cause of action. No particular defect was pointed out, but the objection was reserved until the close of the evidence. The plaintiff gave evidence tending to show that the ship sailed from the port of New York for Yokohama, Japan May 28, 1866, that she had not been heard from since October 16, 1866, on which day she was in the Indian Ocean; that she never reached her port of destination, and was never afterwards heard from. This evidence was received without any suggestion or objection that it was not admissible under the pleadings. The policy on which the suit is brought insured the vessel from December 29 1865, to December 29, 1866. The evidence under the settled rules in such cases therefore tended to show, and standing uncontradicted would require a finding that the ship was lost from the perils of the sea before the expiration of the policy, which had more than two months to run after the ship had last been heard from. In the case of missing vessels never
heard from after a definite date, the loss is pre-
[1] sumed to have happened immediately after the
date of the last news from them (3 *Kent Comm.*
410). So far, therefore, as the question of proof was concerned, there was enough to entitle the plaintiff to go to the jury upon the question of loss within the lifetime of the policy.

At the close of the plaintiff's case the defendant renewed the motion to dismiss, upon the ground that on the face of the complaint it is not shown or alleged that the vessel could complete the voyage within the life of the policy, or that she was lost during the life of the policy by any peril insured against, and on this ground the court dismissed the complaint and ordered judgment for the defendant. If there had been anything substantial or meritorious in the motion, it
[2] is apparent that the error or defect in the pleadings was not one which affected the substantial rights of the adverse party. The complaint had been treated for a period of twelve years, during which the action seems to have been pending, as sufficient in its averments, and the defendant in the answer has distinctly taken issue upon the question whether the vessel was lost during the continuance of the policy, by denying the same.

Section 723 of the Code enacts that in every stage of the action the court must disregard an error or defect in the pleadings which does not affect the substantial rights of the adverse party.

In Slack *v.* Lyons (9 *Pick.*, 26 *Mass.* 62) the court having no statutory provision, held that "when
[3] the defendant chooses to understand the plaintiff's count to contain all the facts essential to his liability, and in his plea sets out and answers those which have been omitted in his count, so that the parties go to trial upon a full knowledge of the charge, and the record contains enough to show the court that all the material facts were in issue, the defendants shall not tread back and trip up the heels of the plaintiff on a defect which he would seem to have thus purposely omitted to notice in the outset of the controversy."

This just and sensible rule is an admirable expression of the intention of the provision of the Code just cited. Our own courts in numerous cases have applied the same rule.

In White *v.* Spencer (14 *N. Y.* 247) the answer [*] omitted an essential averment, viz.: that the possession claimed by the defendant had been exercised adversely. The court held that while the answer would have been bad on demurrer, still, as the plaintiff took issue upon it and went down to trial, it was sufficient to admit evidence of the adverse user. And DENIO, J., after citing various cases, said: "The doctrine established by these cases is, that a defective pleading, though the defect be one of substance, will not warrant the judge at circuit in excluding evidence of the claim or defense thus imperfectly set up" (p. 250).

[*] And in Bate *v.* Graham (11 *N. Y.* 242) the complaint omitted to state a vital fact, but the fact appeared in the answer; it was held that the court would deem the defect in the complaint supplied by amendment (See, also, Lounsbury *v.* Purdy, 18 *N. Y.* 515). In Sealey *v.* Engel (13 *N. Y.* 542) a reply had been put in to an answer which did not sufficiently allege an important fact, and in reversing judgment because evidence of that fact had been excluded, the court held that the plaintiff, by omitting to move to make the answer more definite and certain, and especially by replying as though he understood what was intended to be set up was precluded from objecting to the evidence on trial.

In Wood *v.* Wood (26 *Barb.* 359) the court say: "A plaintiff who expects to recover in a cause where there is a substantial defense to it, solely by reasons [*] of defects in the answer, or a defendant who thinks of succeeding in an action upon errors in the complaint without regard to the merits of his defense, may as well stay out of court as come in under the Code."

To us nothing seems plainer than that substantial

justice required the court below, the moment the point was definitively suggested, and of its own motion, [1] to have ordered the amendment on the spot if it were deemed there were any such substantial defect in the pleadings. And not only simple justice, but the imperative direction of the Code (§ 723), required that to be done after the proof had been admitted without objection and the error first pointed out at the close of the plaintiff's case.

But we are of opinion also that the complaint itself was not defective in substance, although of course it would have been much better in form if it had contained a distinct averment that the vessel was lost within the lifetime of the policy. The averment of the complaint was as follows:

"That at the time said insurance was applied for and said policy issued, the said ship was in the port of Rotterdam. That she afterwards sailed for the port of New York, where she arrived on the 14th day of April 1866, and afterwards, on or about the 28th day May, 1866, sailed from said port of New York for Yokohama in Japan. That the said ship has not been heard from since the 16th day of October, 1866, on which day she was in the Indian Ocean, beyond Zullabessa, in Pit's Passage, steering from Honolulu Passage, and pursuing her said voyage, and although a reasonable length of time had elapsed to complete the same, prior to the commencement of this action, the said ship never arrived Yokohama, but was totally lost by and through the perils of the sea."

A copy of the policy was annexed to the complaint. It was issued on January 23,* and insured the vessel from December 29, 1865, to December 29, 1866, at noon. The complaint also avers the presentation of

* 1866.

due proofs of loss and interest of the plaintiff, &c. These facts aver distinctly the time when the vessel was last heard from—to wit, on October 16, 1866, when she was pursuing her voyage in the Indian Ocean,
[*] more than two months before the expiration of the policy—and a total loss by perils of the sea, it being also averred that she never arrived at Yokohama. The presumption of law above referred to makes this language equivalent to the allegation that she was lost during the life of the policy. These averments were helped by the issues accepted or presented by the answer, and proof having been admitted under them tending to show that the ship was lost during the life of the policy, they were quite sufficient to uphold a recovery.

We are therefore of opinion that the dismissal of the complaint, to which exception was duly taken,
[*] was a fatal error, for which the judgment must be reversed and a new trial ordered, with costs to appellant to abide the event.

DANIELS, J., concurred.

ESTATE OF JAMES STOKES, DECEASED.

SURROGATE'S COURT, NEW YORK COUNTY, JUNE, 1883.

§§ 768, 2556, 2672, 3251.

Counsel fee.—Is an expense of administration which may be a charge upon the estate when incurred in interest of estate.—Surrogate may order its payment.—When paid by administrator, etc., should be charged in account, and if proper, allowed.—Surrogate cannot grant allowance to contestant.

The fees incurred by an administrator for legal services are expenses of administration, and their payment should, in proper cases, and within proper limits, be made a charge upon an estate in whose interest such services were rendered. [2] The power of the surrogate to make an order directing the payment ot such fees is not open to dispute. [1]

When an administrator, temporary administrator or executor has expended sums of money as counsel fees, he may properly assert a claim to be credited therefor in his accounts with the estate, and upon the settlement of such accounts the surrogate will allow such credit if it appear that the expenditure has been necessarily incurred, and is reasonable in amount. [3]

Where a daughter of a decedent who was contesting the probate of an instrument propounded as a codicil to his will, petitioned the surrogate that she be allowed out of the estate a certain amount by way of compensation for the services of her counsel in connection with the appointment of a temporary administrator, and with divers other proceedings which had been instituted before the surrogate, all of which were proceedings for the procurement of orders,—*Held*, that however laudable may be the motives by which the petitioner was actuated, and however meritorious may have been the services of her counsel, her application must be denied; [4] that the svrrogate has only such authority in respect to the award of costs or allowances as is conferred upon him by the Code of Civil Procedure, [6] and in such proceedings ten dollars is the maximum sum which can be allowed as costs. [5]

Estate of St. John (*Daily Register*, May 21, 1883); [3] Estate of Withers (2 *N. Y. Civ. Pro.* 162), [5] followed.

(*Decided June* 27, 1883.)

Application by temporary administrator for an order directing him to pay certain sums to his counsel for legal services. Also, petition by contesting next of kin for an order allowing her certain sums by way of compensation for services rendered by her counsel.

Butler, Stillman & Hubbard, for temporary administrator.

Theron G. Strong, for Mrs. Dora S. Dale.

ROLLINS, Surrogate.—First. The temporary administrator of this estate has applied for an order directing the payment of a certain specified sum as compensation to his counsel for legal services rendered by them in the course of this administration.

[1] The power of the surrogate to make such an order is not open to dispute. By section 2672 of the Code of Civil Procedure, he is authorized to direct a temporary administrator "to pay any expenses of the administration of his trust."

[2] There can be no doubt that fees for legal services are "expenses of administration," and that the payment of such fees should, in proper cases and within proper limits, be made a charge upon an estate in whose interest such services have been rendered.

The situation of the temporary administrator does not essentially differ in this respect from that of any other administrator or from that of any executor. When either of those officers has expended sums of money as counsel fees he may properly assert a claim to be credited therefor in his accounts with the estate, and upon the settlement of such accounts, the surrogate
[3] will allow such credit, if it appears that the expenditure has been necessarily incurred and is reasonable in amount (Estate of St. John, *Daily Register*, May 21, 1883).

In the present case, I will allow the temporary

administrator to withdraw from deposit a sum not exceeding $3,585.32, and to pay thereout a reasonable sum for the services and disbursements of his counsel. The section of the Code to which I have already referred (§ 2672), may, doubtless, be fairly construed as empowering the surrogate, upon such an application as the present, to give absolute and final direction for the payment of the administration expenses. I am not inclined, however, to depart from the practice which I have hitherto pursued in this regard.

Whether the amount which the present applicant may choose to expend by virtue of the authority here given him, shall be allowed in his accounts, as an item of credit, is a matter which will be passed upon when those accounts shall be judicially settled and determined.

At present, I do not direct him to pay the sum above specified, but simply afford him an opportunity to exercise his own discretion in the premises, subject to the final accounting.

Second. Mrs. Dora S. Dale, a daughter of decedent, who is now contesting in this court the probate of an instrument propounded as a codicil to his will, asks that she be allowed out of this estate a certain amount in her petition specified, by way of compensation for the services of her counsel in connection with the appointment of the temporary administrator, and with divers other proceedings which have from time to time been instituted before the surrogate. Her petition describes in some detail, the nature of these proceedings, and declares, in substance, that the efforts of her counsel have been beneficial not only to herself, but to the other parties interested in the probate controversy, and that she and her counsel have been at all times "animated by the desire to protect and care for this estate and to prevent any action which would be likely to produce injury or loss." Several affidavits have been filed answering this application, and denying some of its allegations, particularly those which assert that the petitioner and her counsel have been governed in all that they have done and said in reference to this estate by the regard for what they believed its best interests. Since these answering affidavits were placed on file, I have allowed the respective counsel to present such other evidence for and against the motion, as they have seen fit to submit. This has occasioned an earnest and somewhat bitter controversy over matters which are not, in my judgment, pertinent to the present inquiry, for I am clearly of the opinion that however laudable may be the motives by [*] which the petitioner has been actuated, and however meritorious may have been the services of her counsel, her application must be denied.

The nature of the surrogate's authority respect- [*] ing the award of costs or allowances to parties or their counsel was the subject of careful consideration in the case of Withers' Estate (2 *N. Y. Civ. Pro.* 162). As is there stated, the surrogate had no authority whatever in such matters prior to the adoption of the Revised Statutes, and has now only such limited power as is conferred upon him by the Code of Civil Procedure.

The various proceedings wherein were rendered the services for whose payment the petitioner now asks an allowance were proceedings for the procurement of orders (Code, §§ 2669-2672). By referring to sections 2556, 768 and 3251 (subd. 3), it will appear that ten [*] dollars is the maximum sum which can be allowed as costs in such proceedings. These motion costs would very likely have been awarded in some of the controversies which have arisen in this estate if counsel had thought it worth while to claim them. But such an allowance is all that the surrogate has authority to grant.

Petition denied.

MUSER ET AL. v. MILLER AND ANOTHER.

N. Y. SUPERIOR COURT; SPECIAL TERM, JUNE, 1883.

§§ 450, 553.

Married woman.—Husband need not be joined with, in action for her tort.—May be arrested where arrest of female is authorized in general terms.—What is a willful injury to property within the meaning of section 553 of the Code.

It is settled that a willful injury to property, within the meaning of section 553 of the Code of Civil Procedure, is not an injury merely to the thing itself, but an injury to the owner's right in and to the thing.[1]

The necessity for the joinder of a husband with his wife in an action at common law founded on a tort or contract of the latter, was not, strictly speaking, because the husband was absolutely liable, but it grew out of the fact that a suit could not be maintained against a wife alone during coverture.[2] The reason of this rule has wholly ceased to exist, and the rule itself has been abrogated in all cases of torts as well as contracts, affecting the separate property of a married woman, or connected with, or arising from the management or control of her business,[3] and the exemption of a married woman from arrest which sprang solely from the reason of the rule, has ceased, in all cases where the rule has ceased and the law expressly authorizes the arrest of females in general terms.[3]

(*Decided June* 18, 1883.)

Motion to vacate an order of arrest.

This is an action to recover the value of a large quantity of laces stolen from plaintiffs by one James J. Madden while in their employ, and purchased by the defendant, Mrs. Julia Miller, from one Fannie Lewis, who received them from Madden. The plaintiffs assert that Mrs. Miller bought the laces with the knowledge that they had been stolen, and, upon the ground that she had commited a willful injury to their property, they procured an order for her arrest, which she now seeks to have vacated.* Mrs. Miller's husband is a party defendant with her in this action.

---

* The validity of this order of arrest was again considered in

THE PEOPLE *ex rel.* MILLER *v.* DAVIDSON, SHERIFF, &c.

SUPREME COURT, FIRST DEPARTMENT; SPECIAL TERM, JULY, 1883.

(*Decided July* 5, 1883.)

Motion for the discharge from arrest of relator on return of habeas corpus to inquire into the cause of her detention.

The facts are stated in Muser *v.* Miller, *supra.*

A. R. Dyett, for habeas corpus and motion.

At common law a married woman was liable in a civil action for her torts. Her husband was not liable therefore, but was a necessary party, as she could not be sued alone for her torts. Kowing *v.* Manley, 49 *N. Y.* 192, at page 198, and cases there cited. None of the married woman's acts, so called, affect the present question. They all confer on her power to hold and dispose of property separate and apart from her husband, and give her power to make contracts in relation thereto, and in her separate business and render her liable therefor. *Laws* 1848, chap. 200; *Laws* 1849, chap. 375; *Laws* 1860, chap. 90; *Laws* 1862, chap. 172. They do not change her liability for her torts, nor do they create any liability against her for her torts, which did not exist before. Schaus *v.* Putchers, per BOSWORTH, J., cited in note to Baldwin *v.* Kimmel, 16 *Abb. Pr.* 355. Nor is there anything in the Code of Civil Procedure which creates any liability for her torts on the part of a married woman which did not previously exist. The provision that no female shall be arrested except for a willful injury, etc., (§ 553) simply creates an exception in favor of all females. Without that section females would have been, as they always were, liable to arrest.

The Revised Statutes contained a similar provision as to actions on contract (2 *R. S.* 428, § 8), and yet married women could not be arrested in any case. *Graham's Practice*, 127 (2nd ed.). Before the act of 1831 to abolish imprisonment for debt, etc., and under the Revised Statutes, and before them, all actions were commenced by *capias*, under which the defendant could be arrested and held to bail (*Grah. Pr.*), and females were liable equally with males. But married women were not. The husband alone was liable to arrest. This was the rule of common law, and it was founded not only on the mythical union of husband and wife as one person (*unica persona*), but upon the necessity of preserving and guarding the domestic

Charles S. Spencer, for motion.

D. M. Porter, opposed.

Cited, *Code Civ. Pro.* §§ 450, 553, 1206, 1488· Duncan *v.* Katen, 6 *Hun*, 1; S. C., affirmed, 64 *N. Y.* 625; Solomon *v.* Waas, 2 *Hilton*, 179.

relations, to protect the household, to forbid a wife (and oftimes a mother) being taken from her husband and children and imprisoned, and the danger to a woman's honor was not lost sight of. The language of the Revised Statutes authorizing a bailable capias in all cases is as broad as any language of the Code in regard to persons, and contains no exception as to married women. Yet they are not liable to arrest on the capias. *Grah. Pr.* 2 ed. 127.

The common law rule was not repealed by that general language, nor is by any language of the Code. If section 1206 of the Code is invoked, the answer is that that applies only to judgment and that by section 1488, no execution on a judgment against a married woman can issue, unless after a previous order of arrest; and as none can issue against a married woman, no execution can issue against her.

If it be said here that the relator conducted a separate business and bought and received the goods in question while so doing, and that therefore, she might be sued alone (Code § 450), the answer is, that is of no consequence. (1.) Her exemption from arrest extends to cases where she is sued alone. *Grah. Pr.* 127, *supra.* (2.) Because, as we have shown, the statute conferring on her the power to carry on such a business, confers on her powers to make contracts only, and does not create, affect or change her common law liability for torts. (3.) The action upon which the order of arrest is based in no sense affects her separate property. The theory of that action is that the goods in question never were her property, and she never acquired any interest in or right to them, but that they were the property always of the plaintiff in the action. Neville *v.* Neville, 22 *How. Pr.* 504. As well might it be argued that if she had assaulted some one in her place of business, that that constituted a cause of action against her, growing out of her separate business. In Schaus *v.* Putchers, 25 *How. Pr.* 463, also cited in note to Baldwin *v.* Kimmel, 10 *Abb. Pr.* 355, BOSWORTH, Ch. J., held that a married woman could not be arrested in any case. In that case the order was asked for, for an assault and battery, certainly a willful injury.

FREEDMAN, J.—The plaintiffs have made out a prima facie case against the defendant Julia Miller which has not been overcome by the proofs adduced by her to such a degree that I can determine the merits The testimony of James J. Madden, the thief, and

A precisely similar decision was made by Justice CAMPBELL in Anonymous (1 *Duer*, 613), which was approved on consultation by the other judges. Among them were OAKLEY, SANDFORD, DUER and BOSWORTH. This case is cited with approval in Baldwin *v.* Kimmel, 16 *Abb.* 353. To the same effect is Neville *v.* Neville, 22 *How. Pr.* 504, per W. F. ALLEN, J.

If it be of any consequence to the question now presented, we insist that the rule, that in actions for the torts of a wife, her husband must be joined, still exists. Fitzsimmons *v.* Harrington, 1 *N. Y. Civ. Pro.* 360; Hoffman *v.* Lachman, 1 *Id.* 278 *note;* Kowing *v.* Manley, 49 *N. Y.* 198.

The only case contra is Fitzgerald *v.* Quann, 1 *N. Y. Civ. Pro.* 273, and that case not only stands alone, but is opposed by the numerous cases cited *supra.*

D. M. Porter, opposed.

This question is res adjudicata. See opinion of FREEDMAN, J., in Muser *v.* Miller, *supra.* See also Eypert *v.* Bolenus, 2 *Abb. N. C.* 193.

At common law a married woman can be arrested upon a judgment for her personal tort. McKinstry *v.* Davis, 3 *Cow.* 339; Starr *v.* Kent, 2 *Code R.* 30.

The petitioner has been and is detained by a mandate issued out of the superior court, which court has held that the mandate was properly issued, and that the petitioner was properly taken into custody and detained thereunder. The said superior court has jurisdiction of this matter, and the petitioner's application should be made to that court. Daly *v.* Byrne, 1 *Law Bul.* 58.

W. B. Cockran, for the sheriff

VAN VORST, J.—After consideration, I reach the same conclusion as that to which Justice FREEDMAN arrived when the motion was pending before him in the superior court, to vacate the order of arrest. He denied that motion and accompanied his decision with an opinion in the correctness of which I entirely concur. I can add nothing to it. For the same reasons which led to the denial of the motion, the writ of *habeas corpus* must be dismissed, and the prisoner remanded.

Fannie Lewis, the receiver, is corroborated in several particulars, and especially by the circumstance that some of the stolen goods have been shown beyond controversy to have been in the possession of the defendant. Her statement, by affidavit, that she paid a fair value for the goods she did purchase from the receiver, cannot overcome the case made against her, because from the fact that she was a dealer in laces since 1877, and a purchaser from leading merchants in New York, and had even received goods on consignment from the plaintiffs in this action, the inference may be drawn that her statement is not true, and that she knew at the time that she was getting the goods very much below their intrinsic as well as market value. Without going into particulars, it is sufficient to say that much of what the defendant shows may be true, and yet a *prima facie* case remains against her that she committed at least a willful injury to plaintiffs' property within the meaning of section 553 of the Code of Civil Procedure. By the affirmance of the court of appeals (64 *N. Y.* 625), of Duncan *v.* Katen (6 *Hun*, 1), it is
[1] now settled that in such a case a willful injury to property does not mean an injury merely to the thing itself, but an injury to the owner's right in and to the thing.

The case at bar, therefore, falls within that class of cases in which the rule prevails that the court will not try the merits upon affidavits. This being so the order of arrest cannot be vacated unless the defendant's point is well taken, that because she is a married woman no order of arrest will lie against her under any circumstances.

At common law a married woman could not be held to bail in an action founded upon her personal tort, though the husband might be held and might be compelled to give bail for both (*Grah. Pr.* 127; Anonymous, 1 *Duer*, 613; Schaus *v.* Putchers, 16 *Abb. Pr.* 353, note).

That the Code in force before the Code of Civil Procedure did not change the rule upon this point was distinctly held in Solomon *v.* Wass (2 *Hilt.* 179).

The necessity for holding the husband arose from the legal effect of the marriage relation. At common law the husband and wife by marriage became one person in law, that is, the very being or legal existence of the woman was suspended during the marriage, and incorporated or consolidated into that of the husband. But the necessity for such joinder was not, strictly speaking, because the husband was absolutely [2] liable, but it grew out of the fact that a suit could not be maintained against a wife alone during coverture (*Bishop on Mar. Women*, § 254).

Under the statutes of this State any married woman may take and hold real as well as personal property separate and apart from her husband, and enjoy the same, and the rents, issues and profits thereof, in the same manner as if she were a single female; and she has express authority to bargain, sell, assign and transfer her separate personal property to carry on any trade or business, and perform any labor or services on her sole and separate account. The power thus conferred to carry on a trade or business includes the ability to make bargains and contracts in relation to it in almost any mode known to the law, and in accordance with the practice of the commercial community, and such bargains and contracts have been held valid against her, notwithstanding her coverture, provided they were made in the course of her trade or business and as an incident to it. Upon any such bargain or contract she could, since 1860, sue and be sued in the same manner as if she were sole, and the same may be said generally concerning all matters having relation to her sole and separate property.

It was held, however, that these changes by statute did not alter the common law liability of the husband for the mere personal torts of the wife, but that the rule was changed only in cases of torts committed in the management and control of her separate property (Baum *v.* Mullen, 47 *N. Y.* 578; Kowing *v.* Manley, 49 *N. Y.* 192). But even then the husband was held in some cases to be still a necessary party to the action.

Thus, the rule as to the necessity of the joinder of the husband with the wife, in a case of tort committed by the wife, remained until the enactment of the Code of Civil Procedure. Section 450, as originally enacted, read: "In an action . . . a married woman appears, prosecutes or defends alone . . . as if she was single." In his notes Mr. Throop states that that section was intended to sweep away all distinctions between a feme sole and feme covert, in respect to suing and being sued, and in Janinski *v.* Heidelberg (21 *Hun*, 439), it was held by the general term of the supreme court that the language used was comprehensive enough to do it.

In 1879, section 450 was amended by adding at the end thereof the further express provision that in any action or special proceeding affecting the separate property of a married woman, it is not necessary or proper to join her husband with her as a party.

Since that amendment it was held in Fitzgerald *v.* Quann (1 *N. Y. Civ. Pro.* 273,) that it is now no longer necessary or proper to join the husband as a defendant in an action against the wife for her personal tort, though such tort was wholly unconnected with the wife's separate estate or the management or control of her business, and that the reason of the rule in regard to the joinder had wholly ceased to exist.

For the purpose of determining the motion before me, it is not necessary to go quite as far. It is suf-
[¹] ficient to hold that the reason of the rule in regard to the joinder has wholly ceased to exist, and the rule itself has been abrogated in all cases, of torts as

well as contracts, affecting the separate property of a married woman or connected with or arising from the managment or control of her business. For it is conceded that the wrongful acts complained of in the case at bar were committed in the course of the defendant's business as a dealer in laces. It follows, then, that, if to the extent stated the reason of the rule has ceased to exist and the rule itself has been abrogated, the exemption of a married woman from arrest, which sprang solely from the reason of the rule, must cease, whenever the rule ceases, in all cases in which the law expressly authorizes the arrest of females in general terms. In looking for such authority it will be found that section 553 of the Code of Civil Procedure gives the right of arrest during the pendency of the action against any woman in an action to recover damages for a willful injury to person, character or property.

Having already shown that the case made out against the defendant is one which falls within the class of cases specified in section 553, and it appearing that the wrongful acts charged against the defendant were committed by her in the management of her business, she is not entitled to have the order of arrest vacated for the sole reason that she is a married woman.

From the examination so far made, it appears that no ground whatever exists for the vacation of the order.

As to reducing the bail, I have also failed to discover any ground upon which the defendant can be relieved. According to some of the testimony, the defendant had all the goods which were stolen from the plaintiffs, and if the jury should, under all the circumstances, find such testimony worthy of belief, their verdict will be for an amount which, with interest and costs, will exceed the amount of bail specified in the order. In view of such contingency, the plaintiffs have a right to have the bail maintained as originally fixed.

The only relief I can grant is to order an immediate

trial of the issues by jury, on the ground of the actual imprisonment of the defendant.

Motion to vacate order of arrest denied, with $10 costs.

SMITH, AS GRANTEE FOR THE BENEFIT OF ADAMS, RESPONDENT, v. LONG, EXECUTOR, ETC., ET AL., APPELLANTS.

COURT OF APPEALS; OCTOBER, 1882.

§§ 1500, 1501.

Affirmance of partition.—What is not.—Who may make, and when.—Grantee of premises held adversely, cannot maintain ejectment in name of remote grantor.—Plaintiff in action of ejectment, claiming an entire lot, cannot recover an undivided part of it without amending his complaint.—Sale by assignee in bankruptcy under bankruptcy act of 1841, *when void.*

Where, after the interest of one M. in a certain farm, amounting to an undivided twelfth part thereof, had vested in an assignee in bankruptcy by virtue of M.'s having been adjudicated a bankrupt, the farm was partitioned in an action to which M. was a party but the assignee was not, and a certain portion of it was allotted to M., who entered into possession thereof, and conveyed a part to one L., and the assignee subsequently sold at public auction all the right, title and interest of M. in, and to said farm, and the description in his deed of the property so sold, was that of the entire farm,—*Held*, in an action for the benefit of a remote grantee of the purchaser at the assignee's sale, to recover from the personal representatives of L. possession of the premises conveyed to him; that the partition was not binding upon the assignee in bankruptcy and if not absolutely void, but voidable it was for the assignee either to affirm or disaffirm it;[1] that this was a right which he was bound to exercise within a reasonable time and by an unequivocal act[2] and one which could not be kept afloat for a series of years and transferred from person to person to be exercised at the pleasure of the last transferee;[2] that the assignee, as owner of the estate, is presumed to know its condition at the time of the sale,[3] and the sale by him of M.'s interest in the entire farm was a disaffirmance of the partition and an election by him not to be bound by it,[4] and that his grantee obtained at the most only an undivided one twelfth interest in the land in question.[5]

A plaintiff in an action of ejectment who claims to recover an entire lot, cannot, without amending his complaint, have judgment for an undivided part of it.[6] If, however, that was the only objection to a judgment in his favor, the complaint might be amended upon appeal.[6]

The provisions of the Code which permit a grantee of land, his heirs, etc., to maintain an action in the name of his grantor when the conveyance under which he claims is void, because the property conveyed was held adversely to the grantor at the time of making it, are limited to the first grantee, and a grantee bringing such an action must bring it in the name of his immediate grantor, and must stand or fall by the validity of his title.[7]

An assignee in bankruptcy, under the act of 1841, held a statutory title to the real estate of the bankrupt as trustee not only for the creditors, but of the bankrupt also. His power to deal with the estate was limited and defined by the statute, and he had no authority to sell it except upon an order of the bankrupt court in which the time and manner of sale should be fixed and determined.[8] Accordingly,—*Held*, where an order did not fix the time and place of sale, but they were determined by the assignee, that the sale was void;[9] that no subsequent act of the court could cure the defect, as it was jurisdictional and it could be raised whenever and wherever the title claimed under such sale was brought in question.[9]

Osborn *v.* Baxter (4 *Cush.* 406), approved and followed.[8] Smith *v.* Long (9 *Daly*, 429), reversed.

Appeal by defendant from a judgment of the general term of the N. Y. court of common pleas, affirming a judgment entered upon the report of a referee. Reported below, 9 *Daly*, 429.

This action was brought to recover possession of certain real property situate in the city of New York.

The premises in question are a part of a farm of which John Hopper died seized in 1819, and which he devised to trustees in three equal undivided parts, each part during the life and for the benefit of one of his three grandchildren, Garrett H. Striker, Miss Ann Striker and Mrs. Winifred Mott, with remainders over as to each share as follows:

(1.) A vested remainder in fee to the issue of each grandchild in that grandchild's share, liable to be defeated by the death of the issue in the lifetime of the parent. (2.) A contingent remainder to the other surviving grandchildren, in case of the death of a grandchild without living issue.

Subsequently, Mrs. Winifred Mott died, leaving four sons: James S. Mott, Jordan Mott, Garrett S. Mott and M. Hopper Mott, in whom, as tenants in common, her undivided third part of said land vested.

October 17, 1863, Garrett H. Striker brought an action for the partition of the farm in which a judgment of partition was rendered in January, 1865. This judgment allotted a certain portion of the farm, including the premises in suit, to Jordan Mott, who soon after entered into possession of the share so set apart to him.

In 1865, Jordan Mott conveyed the premises in suit to one Job Long, who immediately entered into possession, claiming title under said deed. He has since died, and the defendants, John and Martha Long, are the executors of his will, and in possession, under its provisions, and the defendant Sidley is their tenant.

Jordan Mott was duly adjudicated a bankrupt in January, 1843. Prior to that time, one William Coventry H. Waddell had been appointed "official or general assignee" in bankruptcy for the district and had duly qualified. He has ever since held that office and still continues to hold it. In June, 1868, upon application of said Waddell, the United States district court made an order entitled jointly, in the "Matter of Jordan Mott," and in the "Matter of Jacob H. Mott," directing the "sale at public auction by advertising the same one time fourteen days prior to the day of sale in the newspaper called the Times, published in the city of New York," of "all the right, title, interest, property, claim and demand whatsoever, whether in law or in equity, of each and either of said bankrupts of in and to any and all real estate in any manner described or referred to in a certain will of John Hopper, recorded in the office of the Surrogate of the city and county of New York, November, 1819, and which is more particularly described as follows:" (giving the boundries of the entire farm and other property). The order did not name a day for the sale, and the defendant asserts that it is defective on that ground.

The assignee, Waddell, advertised the property for sale in the New York Times, on August 4, 1868. On that day, at the hour and place named in the notice published by him, he adjourned the sale, by public proclamation to September 10, 1868, and inserted in the Times of August 6th, the following notice: "In Bankruptcy. The sale advertised in the Times of the 18th of July for Thursday, is hereby adjourned till the 10th of September next, at the same hour and place. Dated, the 4th day of August, 1868. William Coventry H. Waddell, official and general assignee."

On September 10, he adjourned the sale as before to September 11, and in the Times of the morning of the 11th he inserted a notice of the adjournment similar to that published on August 6.

On the morning of the 11th of September, the assignee sold the right, title, interest, etc., of Jordan Mott and Jacob H. Mott, so ordered and advertised to be sold at public auction, to the plaintiff, James M. Smith, Jr., who was the highest bidder, for the sum of $1,750, which Smith paid, and the assignee then executed to him a deed, describing the right, title and interest sold as it was described in the order directing the sale.

The assignee, thereafter, made a report of the sale to the United States district court, which, February 24, 1869, confirmed the sale.

In November, 1880, Jordan Mott being then dead, his devisees instituted a proceeding in the United States district court to set aside the sale, in which they were defeated in January, 1881 (See *In re* Mott, 6 *Fed. Rep.* 685).

In 1871, Smith deeded the property bought from the assignee to one Tallmadge, who, February 15, 1872, conveyed it to one Veeder G. Thomas, excepting sixteen lots thereof, which he had theretofore conveyed to Charles Buckhalter and John Castor. Thomas deeded the premises so conveyed to him, except a certain portion which he had theretofore conveyed, to William Henry Adams, June 23, 1873. This last conveyance was subject to a certain mortgage, made June 27, 1872, by David Tallmadge and wife, to John Townsend. Adams, thereafter brought this action in the name of Smith. As neither Smith, Tallmadge nor Thomas were ever in possession of the premises so conveyed, of course their several deeds are void.

The action was tried before a referee, who found that the plaintiff was entitled to recover possession of the premises in suit; the general term of the N. Y. court of common pleas affirmed the judgment thereupon entered, and this appeal was taken from its judgment of affirmance.

A. J. Vanderpoel, *William Fullerton* and *William Hildreth Field*, for appellant.

Douglass Campbell and *E. W. Paige*, for respondents.

I. The sale in bankruptcy was valid, and effectually passed the interest of the bankrupt to the plaintiff. *In re* Mott, 6 *Fed. Rep.* 685. . . . . The confirmation of a sale by a court of competent jurisdiction . . . . is an adjudication that the sale is valid, which can never be overhauled except by that court itself. Griffith *v.* Bogert, 18 *How. Pr.* 158, 164; Hogan *v.* Hoyt, 37 *N. Y.* 300. . . . . The effect of these provisions (sections 3 and 9 of the bankrupt act of 1841, 5 *U. S. Stat. at L.* 440, 449), is to vest the title of the property in the assignee, and to give him full power to "sell, manage, and dispose" of it, and the only qualification upon his power is, that he shall exercise it subject to the orders and directions of the court. Barnes *v.* Matteson, 5 *Barb.* 375, 377, 378; Crowley *v.* Hyde, 116 *Mass.* 589. . . . . The order here did direct both the time and manner of the sale within the meaning of the act. Such was the decision on a similar order in Stevens *v.* Hauser, 39 *N. Y.* 305; also, in Stevens *v.* Palmer, 10 *Bosw.* 60, and Barnes *v.* Matteson, 5 *Barb.* 375.

II. The plaintiff is entitled to the premises in severalty. Brown *v.* Wood, 17 *Mass.* 68; Union Nat'l Bank *v.* Kupper, 63 *N. Y.* 617; *Stalman on Election and Satisfaction* (London ed., 1827), 133, 134; *Perk.* § 426; Lessee of Thompson *v.* Gotham, 9 *Ohio* 170. . . . Dispositions made by disseisors and other persons whose titles are defeasible, affecting the estate of which they are in wrongful possession, are for the most part voidable only, and not absolutely void as against the disseisee or other rightful owners of the property, and may be either avoided or affirmed by them, at election. *Stalman on Election and Satisfaction* (London ed., 1827), 133; Rous and Arters, 4 *Rep.* 246; *Co. Lit.* 58 *b;* Clarke *v.* Pennifather, 4 *Rep.* 24 *a.* . . . . Although when the person who "had the right" re-entered, the voluntary dispositions of the intruder affecting the estate were avoidable, yet such was not the case with the acts which "it is compellable to do," but such acts "if there be no covin" were conclusive as against the persons to whom the right of property belongs. *Id.* . . . . To make partition is one of the things which are "*quodam modo judicial*," and which it is compellable to do, within the meaning of the above rule, and, therefore, when he who has the right enters, if the partition be equal he cannot avoid it. If it be unequal or collusive, he has his proper right of action to avoid it; but, in any case, it stands good until avoided. Of the lands of *feme coverts* by their husbands, *Co. Lit.* 170 *b*, 171 *a*, §§ 256, 257, and notes. . . . . Of the lands of infants. . . . . *Stalman*, 40, 58, 60; *Co. Lit.* 171 *a*. Of mortgaged lands by the mortgagors. Harwood *v.* Kirby, 1 *Paige*, 468; Jackson *v.* Pierce, 10 *Johns.* 417; Thurston *v.* Minke, 32 *Md.* 571; Williams' College *v.* Mallett, 12 *Me.* 398. And in the exactly analogous case of the admeasurement of dower by a person in possession but without title, the division is conclusive upon the one who has title, "unless there be covin," and even then it is good until avoided by affirmative action on his part. *Co. Lit.* 35 *a*, "sixthly;" *Id.* 357 *b; Perkins*, § 294; 2 *Scribner on Dower* (ed. 1867), 70–72. . . . .

Conveyances of the undivided portions of those shares to strangers would not be sufficient, in this case, to avoid the partition, because they would be void by reason of the disseisin. Bool *v.* Mix, 17 *Wend.* 119, 133. Nor would they be sufficient in any case; acts of much greater solemnity being required to avoid voidable dispositions as against the parties who hold under them than are available to affirm such dispositions. In the former case no entry is necessary. Dominick *v.* Michael, 4 *Sandf.* 374, 421; Bool *v.* Mix, *supra*; Voorhies *v.* Voorhies, 24 *Barb.* 150. Whereas, in the latter case, slight acts, such as receipts of profits of the one part, or rent, and encouragement to the tenant under the voidable disposition to lay out money are sufficient. *Stalman on Election and Satisfaction* (Ed. 1827), 89, 90, 109, 131, 133, and note *b.* 134; Keech *v.* Hall, *Douglas*, 22. But in this case the plaintiff entered in affirmance of the partition. Smith *v.* Scholtz, 68 *N. Y.* 41. . . . .

A parol partition was good at common law and has always been good in New York. Wood *v.* Fleet, 36 *N. Y.* 499; Taylor *v.* Taylor, 43 *Id.* 578 . . . And the plaintiff's acceptance is sufficiently well evidenced by acts *in pais*, of which entry upon the allotted parcel is a sufficently significant one. Eaton *v.* Tallmadge, 24 *Wis.* 217, 223; Doe *v.* Jewell, 18 *N. H.* 355; Jackson *v.* Richtmyer, 13 *Johns.* 367; Fowler *v.* Griffin, 3 *Sandf.* 385, 391; Millican *v.* Millican, 24 *Tex.* 426 . . .

The plaintiff is entitled to recover the whole of the premises in severalty because of the entire want of title in the defendants, under the rule that one tenant in common, having a right to the possession of the whole premises as against all the world except his co-tenants, may recover the possession of the whole as against a stranger to the title, a simple trespasser having no right to set up the outstanding titles of the other tenants in common to justify his possession. 9 *Viner, Abr.* 456, "Entry," F, pl. 2 and note; Robinson *v.* Johnson, 36 *Vt.* 74; Hibbard *v.* Foster, 24 *Id.* 546; Chandler *v.* Spear, 22 *Id.* 388; Robinson *v.* Roberts, 31 *Conn.* 145; Hardy *v.* Johnson, 1 *Wall.* 371; French *v.* Edwards, 5 *Sawy.* 267; Chipman *v.* Hastings, 50 *Cal.* 310; Collier *v.* Corbett, 15 *Id.* 185; Winthrop's Lessee *v.* Grimes, *Wright* (*Ohio*) 330; Davant *v.* Cubbage, 2 *Hill* (*S.C.*) *311; Logan *v.* Goodale, 42 *Ga.* 96, 118; Truebart *v.* McMichael, 46 *Tex.* 222; Alexander *v.*

Gilliam, 39 *Id.* 476; Dolph *v.* Barney, 5 *Oregon*, 191; Sharon *v.* Davidson, 4 *Nev.* 416.

TRACY J.—The plaintiff's right to recover in this action is resisted upon the ground: First. That if he has any title whatever to the premises in question, it is to an undivided twelfth interest thereof, and not to the entire lot; and having claimed the whole of the premises, cannot have judgment for an undivided part without amending his complaint. Second. That the section of the Code which permits a grantee of land to maintain an action in the name of a grantor, where the grant or grants are void by reason of the actual possession of the person claiming under a title adverse to that of the grantor, at the time of the delivery of the grant, is limited to the first grantee of the premises. Third. That the assignee in bankruptcy had no power to convey or dispose of the premises, except in pursuance of an order of the bankrupt court which should fix the time and manner of such sale; that the assignee's sale to Smith, not having been made in pursuance of such an order, is therefore void.

We will consider these questions in the order stated.

The plaintiff's right to recover the entire lot, was placed by the learned referee before whom the case was tried, upon the ground that the plaintiff had the right to affirm the partition made between the heirs of John Hopper in 1865, and, having affirmed it, was entitled to recover that portion of the premises set apart to Jordan Mott in severalty. We think the plaintiff had no such right of election. The partition made in the action to which the assignee in bankruptcy was
[1] not a party, and in which he did not appear, was
not binding upon him. If the judgment in that case was not absolutely void, but voidable, it was for the assignee either to affirm or disaffirm such partition. It was a right possessed by him, and which he was

bound to exercise within a reasonable time and ['] by an unequivocal act. Such a right, affecting the title to a large and valuable real estate having many owners, is not one that can be kept afloat for a series of years, and transferred from person to person, to be exercised at the pleasure of the last transferee. It is conceded that the assignee never affirmed the partition, and we think the sale made by him in 1868 amounts to a disaffirmance thereof.

The assignee, as owner of the estate, is presumed to have known its condition at the time of sale. ['] He knew therefore that the Hopper farm had been mapped and divided into lots and streets. He knew that the same had been partitioned by the heirs of Hopper, and that Jordan Mott was in possession of that portion which had been set off to him in severalty. Assuming that he had the right to affirm the partition, when he was about to offer the interest of Jordan Mott in the Hopper farm, he was called upon to determine whether he would sell the whole, or whether, ignoring the result of the partition, he would sell the interest of Jordan Mott in the entire farm as it existed at the time of his bankruptcy in 1843. If he affirmed the partition, then he would not sell the interest of Jordan Mott in the whole of the Hopper farm, for his entire interest in such farm had been divested by the partition except as to that portion set off to him in severalty. He would therefore sell the interest of Jordan Mott in that portion of said farm and the purchaser could take Jordan Mott's title thereto, whatever, it might prove to be. But he elected to sell Jordan Mott's interest in the entire Hopper farm, which farm is described in the notice of sale by metes and bounds.

It is conceded by the learned counsel for the plaintiff, that, had the assignee offered for sale and sold Jordan Mott's interest as an undivided twelfth part in the Hopper farm, this would have been a disaffirmance of the partition and an election by the assignee not to be bound by it. But this is pre- [*] cisely what he did do. As the assignee had neither affirmed or disaffirmed the partition, the only interest he had to sell, was the interest of Jordan Mott in the Hopper farm as it existed at the time of his bankruptcy, and that was an undivided one-twelfth interest in the entire farm. However described, the interest which was sold was in fact an undivided interest. Smith purchased a certain and definite interest in that property, and not an uncertain and unknown interest which could only be made definite and certain by some subsequent act of his, or his grantee. We are of opinion, therefore, that Smith at most [*] obtained only an undivided one-twelfth interest in the land in question. The plaintiff's right to recover is placed by the referee upon his right to affirm and his affirmance of the partition. He does not find that the acts of the defendant as co-tenant amount to an ouster of the plaintiff as tenant in common (Edwards *v.* Bishop, 4 *N. Y.* 61).

The plaintiff having claimed to recover the entire [*] lot, he cannot without amending his complaint have judgment for an undivided part. Holmes *v.* Seeley, 17 *Wend.* 75; Gillett *v.* Stanley, 1 *Hill*, 121; Cole *v.* Irvine, 6 *Id.* 634; Cook *v.* Wardens, &c. of St. Paul's Church, 5 *Hun*, 293; affirmed in 67 *N. Y.* 594. If this, however, were the only objection to the judgment, the complaint might be amended upon appeal.

We think the second objection to the validity of this judgment is also well taken. It has long been the policy of the laws of this State to discourage and prevent dealings in pretended titles to real estate by persons out of possession.

By the Revised Statutes of this State it is provided "that every grant of land should be void if at the time of delivery thereof, such land shall be in the actual possession of a person claiming under a title adverse to that of the grantor." (1 *R. S.* 739, § 147; same statute, 3 *Id.* 7 ed. 2196.) "No person shall buy or sell, or in any manner procure or make, or take any promise or covenant, to convey any pretended right or title to any lands or tenements, unless the grantor thereof, or the person making such promise or covenant shall have been in possession of the same, or of the reversion or remainder thereof, or have taken the rents and profits thereof for the space of one year before such grant, conveyance, sale, promise or covenant is made, and every person violating this provision shall be deemed guilty of a misdemeanor." (2 *R. S.* 691, § 6; same statute, 3 *Id.* 7 ed. 2516.)

The Code of Procedure, § 111, provides as follows: "Every action must be prosecuted in the name of the real property in interest, except as otherwise provided in section 113. But this section shall not be deemed to authorize the assignment of a thing in action not arising out of contract. But an action may be maintained by a grantee of land in the name of the grantor, or his or her heirs or legal representatives,* when the grant or grants are void by reason of the actual possession of a person claiming under a title adverse to that of the grantor at the time of the delivery of the grant, and the plaintiff should be allowed to prove the facts to bring the case within this provision." The Code of Civil Procedure, which went into operation after the commencement of this action, contains the following provision in relation to the same subject matter. "Section 1501. Such an action [that is, an action of ejectment] may be maintained by a grantee, his heir or devisee, in the name of the grantor or heir where the conveyance under which he claims is void because the property conveyed was held adversely to

* See Ward v. Reynolds, 25 *Hun*, 385.

the grantor. The plaintiff must be allowed to prove the facts to bring the case within this section." It is now insisted that, by the true construction of the Code, the right to prosecute such an action in the name of the grantor is limited to the first grantee. In this case the property, while held adversely, was conveyed by Smith to Tallmadge, by Tallmadge to Thomas, and by Thomas to the present plaintiff, Adams. To hold that a remote grantee can bring such an action in the name of the original grantor would be to encourage dealings in such claims to real estate and nullify the statute which was intended to prevent the party out of possession from transferring his right to litigate the validity of the title. Sands v. Hughes, 53 *N. Y.* 287, 296.

We think the grantee bringing such an action,
[7] must bring it in the name of his immediate
grantor, and must stand or fall on the validity of his title. We are referred to no case where the action has been maintained by or for the benefit of any one but the first grantee, and we think that a construction, which so limits the right of action best accords with the public policy, which has so long prevailed in this state, relative to this class of assumed titles to real estate held by persons out of possession (*Tyler on Ejectment;* Violett v. Violett, 2 *Dana*, 325; Dubois v. Marshall, 3 *Id.* 336; Webster v. Van Steenbergh, 46 *Barb.* 211; Hamilton v. Wright, 37 *N. Y.* 502, 507; 2 *Hill*, 526*). Chamberlain v. Taylor, 14 *Weekly Dig.* 336; Stevens v. Hauser, 39 *N. Y.* 302, 306, decides nothing to the contrary.

The remaining question to be considered is whether the sale made in 1868, by the assignee in bankruptcy, of the interest of Jordan Mott in the Hopper farm to Smith was valid. Upon this question we are unable to distinguish the present case from that of Osborn v. Baxter, 4 *Cush.* 406. The assignee in bankruptcy

* Livingston v. Proceus.

[*] held a statutory title to the real estate of the bankrupt as trustee, not only for the creditors, but for the bankrupt also. His power to deal with the estate was limited and defined by the statute. He had no authority to sell such estate except upon an order of the bankrupt court, in which the time and manner of sale should be fixed and determined. Section 9 of the bankrupt act of 1841* reads as follows: "And be it further enacted, that all sales, transfers, and other conveyances by the assignee of the bankrupt's property and rights of property shall be made at such times, and in such manner, as shall be ordered and appointed by the court in bankruptcy." In the present case the order under which the assignee sold the property did not fix the time of sale. It was fixed and determined by the assignee, and not by the court. In Osborn *v.* Baxter (*supra*), SHAW, Ch. J., in delivering the opinion of the court, says: "In general when a sale is made under a statute power, it must appear that the requisition of the statute as conditions precedent to the operation of the power to pass the estate had been complied with" (Hogan *v.* Hoyt, 37 *N. Y.* 300). As the order in that case failed to fix the time and manner of sale, it was held that the sale by the assignee was void and no title passed to the purchaser. We think the case of Osborn *v.* Baxter well decided, and for the reasons there stated, the sale in the present case should be held void. It is not a question of mere regularity, but the want of power in the officer making the [*] sale. No subsequent act of the court could cure this defect; it is jurisdictional, and may be raised whenever and wherever the title claimed under such sale is brought in question.

All concurred (ANDREWS, Ch. J., in result), except EARL, J., who dissented.

* 5 U. S. Stat. at Large, 440–449.

DE STUCKLE, APPELLANT, v. THE TEHUANTEPEC RAILWAY COMPANY, RESPONDENT.

SUPREME COURT, FIRST DEPARTMENT, GENERAL TERM, MARCH, 1883.

§ 3253.

Additional allowance—But one can be granted in an action, and that only when final judgment is rendered.

Section 3253 of the Code of Civil Procedure contemplates the granting of but one allowance in an action, and that only upon final judgment. [1, 2] An additional allowance cannot therefore, be granted upon an interlocutory judgment sustaining or overruling a demurrer, with leave to amend or answer over but only, if at all, when the final judgment is pronounced which unconditionally terminates the action and fixes the right of the successful party to tax his costs. [1, 2]

Flynn v. Equitable Life Ins. Co., (18 *Hun*, 212); McDonald v. Mallory (14 *J. & S.* 58), approved and followed. [2]

(*Decided May* 11, 1883.)

Appeal from an order granting an allowance under section 3253 of the Code of Civil Procedure.

The opinion states the facts.

F. R. Coudert (*Coudert Bros.*, attorneys), for appellant.

Albert Stickney and *Edward M. Shepard*, for respondents.

DAVIS, P. J.—The judgment of the special term sustained the demurrer, and ordered an interlocutory judgment thereon for the defendants, but provided that the plaintiffs might at any time within twenty days after service of a copy of the order sustaining the demurrer, and upon payment of the costs of this action, serve an amended complaint herein, and that upon failure to do so, and upon proof by affidavit of such failure, the defendants might enter final judgment in their favor. The additional allowance was made under section 3253 of the Code. It is not contended that this is not a difficult and extraordinary case, but it is insisted that the granting of the allowance was premature.

We are of the opinion that this objection was well taken. The Code contemplates but one allowance,
[1] and that only upon final judgment. None can be granted upon an interlocutory judgment sustaining a demurrer with leave to amend, which is the judgment rendered in this case. An additional allowance after it is properly granted becomes a part of the costs of the action, which the successful party is entitled to recover, and if such allowance be granted upon sustaining or over-ruling a demurrer where leave is given to amend on payment of costs, the unsuccessful party on the demurrer may be compelled to pay, as a condition of leave to answer, an additional allowance in a case where final judgment may ultimately be rendered in his favor. We are satisfied that this result was not in contemplation of the Code. There cannot be two extra allowances granted in the same case, although the case
[2] might have been tried several times (Flynn *v.* Equitable Life Ins. Co., 18 *Hun*, 212). The superior court, in McDonald *v.* Mallory (14 *J. & S.* 58, 63), laid down the correct rule in these words: "The test must be that the action has terminated in such form that the successful party can lawfully claim the payment of the costs on such termination and enforce their payment."

An additional allowance cannot therefore be granted upon sustaining or overruling a demurrer, with
[3] leave to answer over on payment of costs, but only,

if at all, when the final judgment is pronounced that unconditionally terminates the action and fixes the costs absolutely under the Code.

The order should therefore be reversed, without prejudice to a renewal of the application whenever the defendants became entitled to apply for final judgment in the action, with $10 costs of this appeal, besides disbursements.

BRADY and DANIELS, JJ., concurred.

SCHULHOFF, RESPONDENT, *v.* THE CO-OPERATIVE DRESS ASSOCIATION, APPELLANT.

SAME, RESPONDENT, *v.* SAME, APPELLANT.

SUPREME COURT, FIRST DEPARTMENT, GENERAL TERM, MAY, 1883.

§ 531.

Copy of account—Plaintiff is not precluded from giving evidence as to account, where a copy has been demanded, except where there was a total failure to serve one—Failure to serve a copy of account, when demanded, is sufficient answer to motion for reference, on the ground that the action involves a long account, except where plaintiff has served a paper, which he claims is a copy of the account.

The remedy given by the Code, where a party fails to deliver to the adverse party within ten days, after a demand therefor, a copy of an account, the items of which are not set forth in his pleadings, that he is precluded from giving evidence of the account, is only operative in cases where there is a total failure, or refusal to serve any copy of the account.[1] If one is served which is claimed or supposed to be such copy, the provision is not operative, but the remedy of the party is, to apply to the court or a judge for an order, directing the delivery of a further account, on the ground that the one served is defective.[1]

Where a defendant demanded a copy of the account, upon which the action was brought, and the plaintiff served a paper, which he asserted was such copy of account, but which the defendant claimed was not. *Held*, that it was not an answer to a motion to refer the cause, on the ground that it involved a long account, to insist that the plaintiff was, by operation of the Code, precluded from giving evidence of the account on the trial; [2] but that this would be a sufficient answer to a motion to refer, where there had been a proper demand and a total failure, to pay any attention to it.[3]

Appeals from orders referring the issues in these actions to a referee for hearing and determination.

C. C. Prentiss (*C. C.* and *S. F. Prentiss*, attorneys), for appellant.

Blumenstiel & Hirsch, for respondent.

DAVIS, P. J.—These actions we think were referable because each of them would require the examination upon the trial of a long account within the meaning of the provisions of the Code. In one of them this proposition does not seem to be disputed. In the other, it is claimed that the action is one for a conversion, and therefore not referable. But we think the actions in both cases are simply to recover the value of the goods alleged to have been sold, and delivered, and that neither of them can justly be called an action for a conversion.

The question made in the cases is whether the plaintiff is precluded from making the motions on the ground that he failed to comply with the requirements of section 531 of the Code, by not delivering a copy of the account, upon which the actions are respectively brought. It is insisted that his failure to do so has put him into such a position that he cannot at the trial give evidence of the accounts, and that therefore the trials will not require the examination of long accounts.

Section 531 provides, that "it is not necessary for a party to set forth in a pleading the items of an account therein alleged, but in that case he must deliver to the adverse party, within ten days, after a written demand thereof, a copy of the account which, if the pleading is verified, must be verified by his affidavit to the effect that he believes it to be true. . . . If he fails so to do he is precluded from giving evidence of the account." It also provides that where the account delivered is defective, the court or judge may direct him to deliver a further account; and it further provides that the court may in any case direct a bill of the particulars of the claim of either party to be delivered to the adverse party. It is true that this section recognizes a distinction between accounts sued upon, and bills of particulars, and that it requires in the first case the copy of an account verified by affidavit to be served on written demand; and in cases where the action is upon an account, and the account is not served within ten days after written demand, the party so failing is precluded from giving evidence of the account by
operation of the provisions of the Code. But this
[1] severe remedy is only applicable to a case in which
there is a total failure or refusal to serve any copy of the account. If one be served which is claimed or supposed to be such copy, the provision is not operative, but the remedy of the party is to apply to the court or a judge for an order directing the delivery of a further account on the ground that the one served is defective.

In this case the defendant demanded a copy of the account of the sales and deliveries of the goods referred to in the complaint. The plaintiff thereupon in due time served a copy of the items of the accounts each marked on the outside "Bill of items of plaintiff's claim herein" and headed on the inside "Bill of particulars" showing a large number of items of goods delivered and returned from time to time, and items of goods alleged not to have been returned, and these bills of items were duly verified. Thereupon the defendant's attorney gave notice that they had demanded a copy of the accounts mentioned in the complaints in the actions and not bills of particulars of the plaintiff's claim, upon which the plaintiff's attorneys sent notice in writing to the effect that they did not understand the distinction the defendant's attorneys made between a bill of particulars and a copy of the accounts, and saying "if there is any we would be pleased to be informed, and if proper will try to comply with your request" to which the defendant's attorneys replied, "what we want in these cases is a copy of the account which shall show the sales, times of credit, &c." No further copies of accounts were received prior to the making of this motion. Assuming that the accounts or bills of particulars served were defective, it is obvious that they were sufficient at least to prevent the defendant from claiming that the plaintiff was precluded from giving evidence of such account. The defect in them simply set in operation the other provision of the Code which made it necessary for the defendant to apply to the court, or a judge for an order requiring a further account to be delivered. That has not been done in this case.

We think it was not an answer to the motions for reference to insist that the plaintiff was by operation [2] of the Code precluded from giving evidence of the accounts upon the trial. That would of course, be a sufficient answer we think to a motion to refer, where there had been a proper demand and a total failure to pay any attention to it; but not in such a case as this.

The orders should be affirmed with $10 costs and disbursements in one case only.

DANIELS, J., concurred.

TIM ET AL, RESPONDENTS, *v.* SMITH; SCHROEDER AND ANOTHER, APPELLANTS.

BOYD ET AL., RESPONDENTS, *v.* SAME;

SAME, APPELLANTS.

COURT OF APPEALS, JUNE, 1883.

§ 683.

Attachment—A junior attaching creditor, moving to vacate a prior attachment, must prove by legal evidence, a subsequent valid levy, upon the same property covered by the prior attachment.—What evidence is not sufficient.

In a proceeding by a junior attaching creditor to vacate a prior attachment, proof of a subsequent valid levy upon the same property covered by the prior attachment, is a necessary condition to initiating the proceeding.[2] Until this fact is established by legal evidence, the junior attaching creditor is a mere stranger having no right to intervene.[2]

On a motion, by a junior attaching creditor, to vacate a prior attachment, the affidavit of the moving party's attorney that the attachments had been issued, levied, &c., which does not disclose the source of the information upon which it is made, is not sufficient.[1] Such an affiant does not necessarily have knowledge of, and cannot be presumed to know, the several facts, so attempted to be proven.[1]

Where on a motion, by one claiming to be a junior attaching creditor, to vacate two prior attachments, it appeared that after the prior attachments were issued, an agreement in writing was entered into between the plaintiff in the prior attachments, and the assignee of the attachment debtor, by which said plaintiff impliedly abandoned any attempt to perfect a levy upon the property of the debtor, in consideration of the agreement, on the part of the said assignee, to hold the sum of $10,000 in his hands, and to pay it over to the plaintiff in the prior attachment suits, in case they eventually obtained judgment in such suits, and said attachments had not, in the meantime been vacated and set aside, and this agreement was supplemented by an affidavit of the sheriff holding the attachments alleging not only that he had not levied upon, or acquired a lien upon any property by virtue of either of said attachments, but that he had never been able to discover property of the defendant, in such attachments liable to be levied upon: *Held*, that the affidavits of the several attorneys stating that the sheriff did levy upon property under said attachments, without disclosing their means of knowledge or the time when, or the property upon which the pretended levy was made, did not constitute sufficient proof of the fact alleged to raise a question of evidence as to its existence; [4] that there was no legal evidence tending to controvert either the agreement or the facts stated in the affidavit of the sheriff. [4] Also *Held*, that as neither of the parties to the motion had acquired a lien either upon the same or upon any property belonging to their mutual debtor, the moving party had no legal interest in the question as to the validity of the said prior attachments, [6] and was not entitled to move to vacate them; [6] that he had no interest in the agreement between the assignee of the debtor and the prior attachment creditors for the reason that the only obligation of the assignee thereunder, was to the prior attaching creditors, and such obligation could not inure to the benefit of other parties. [7]

Ruppert *v.* Haug (87 *N. Y.* 141; S. C., 1 *N. Y. Civ. Pro.* 411) [6] distinguished, Tim *v.* Smith (3 *N. Y. Civ. Pro.* 347) affirmed.

(*Decided June* 26, 1883.)

Appeal from orders of general term of N.Y. court of common pleas, reversing orders of the special term vacating the attachments issued in these actions.

Reported below, 3 *N. Y. Civ. Pro.* 347.

The facts are stated in the following opinion, and on page 348, *ante*.

A. Blumenstiel and *Adolph Ascher*, for appellants.

Otto Horwitz and *Daniel C. Briggs*, for respondent.

RUGER, Ch. J.—In each of the above entitled actions, the appellant, who was a junior attaching creditor, sought to set aside and vacate prior attachments obtained by the respective respondents, and levied upon the property of the defendant, Clinton H. Smith, an insolvent debtor.

The motion was founded upon the alleged insufficiency of the affidavits upon which the prior attachments were allowed, and the allegation that the appellants had acquired a lien by virtue of a subsequent attachment upon the same property covered by the prior attachments. The only proof of the latter fact was contained in an affidavit made by the appellants' attorney and entitled in the above actions, reading as follows: "That he is attorney for the plaintiffs in an action brought in this court, in which Nicholas Schroeder, and Henry C. Seavers, are plaintiffs and the above named defendant is defendant; that on or about March 17, 1882, an attachment against the property of the defendant was granted in said action by Hon. Charles H. VAN BRUNT, one of said Justices, and the said warrant duly issued to the sheriff of the city and county of New York, who has by virtue thereof attached the property of the said defendant. That the said attachment is in force, and said action is now pending. That prior to the issuing of the same, and on or about March 9, 1882, an attachment was granted in the above action against the property of the defendant, and by virtue thereof the sheriff of the city and county of New York attached the property of said defendant being the same property attached by the attachment in the case in which deponent is plaintiffs' attorney. That the attachment herein constitutes a prior lien to that referred to therein."

The question was raised in the court below that the affidavit furnished no sufficient evidence of the fact that the appellant had acquired a lien upon the same property covered by the prior attachments. We think, for several reasons, that the point was well taken. It does not appear by the affidavit quoted, which attachment was first levied upon the property in question.

The date of the respective levies is not given, and the last clause of the affidavit purporting to furnish this information, is indefinite and equivocal. The only proof of either of the levies in question, is contained in this affidavit of the attorney, and he does not therein disclose the source of information upon which his statements are predicated. He does not even state that the attachment was duly issued or that the
[1] several levies were duly made. Such an affiant does not necessarily have knowledge of, and cannot be presumed to know the several facts attempted to be established by his affidavit in this case. Their existence depends not only upon the official action of several persons acting independently of each other, but also upon the legal sufficiency of the papers upon which their action was based. It is difficult to see how an attorney can acquire such knowledge of the several facts required to be proved on this motion, as entitles him to give legal evidence of their existence.

Proof of a subsequent valid levy upon the same property covered by the prior attachment is a
[2] necessary condition to the right of a subsequent creditor to initiate a proceeding to vacate the prior attachment (*Code Civ. Pro.* § 682). Until this fact is established by legal evidence, he is a mere stranger having no right to intervene. The opinion of an attorney that a lien has been secured, although put in the form of an affidavit, falls short of the evidence required to establish the jurisdictional fact entitling a general creditor to interfere in the disposition of his debtor's property.

In Ruppert *v.* Haug (87 *N. Y.* 141)* and Steuben County Bank *v.* Alberger (78 *N. Y.* 252), the party
[3] intervening was a judgment creditor and his lien was secured by a levy upon execution. A manifest distinction has always been made between the position

* 1 *N. Y. Civ. Pro.* 411.

of judgment and general creditors. The authorities referred to by the appellant, therefore, do not support the propositions to which they were cited.

But a still more serious objection to this motion is disclosed by other undisputed facts. After the prior attachments were issued, and apparently before the attachment of the moving creditor had come into the sheriff's hands, an agreement in writing was entered into, between the plaintiffs in the prior attachments and the assignee of the insolvent debtor, by which said plaintiffs impliedly abandoned any attempt to perfect a levy upon the property of the debtor, in consideration of the agreement on the part of the said assignee to hold the sum of $10,000 in his hands and to pay it over to the plaintiffs in the prior attachment suits, in case they eventually obtain judgment in such suits, and said attachments had not, in the meanwhile, been vacated and set aside. This agreement is supplemented by the affidavit of the sheriff holding each of the several attachments referred to in these proceedings, verified on April 7, 1882, and alleging not only that he had not levied upon, or acquired a lien upon any property by virtue of either of said attachments, but that he had never been able to discover property of the defendant in such attachments liable to be levied upon.

There is no legal evidence in the case tending to controvert either the agreement or the facts stated
[1] in the affidavit of the sheriff. The affidavits of the several attorneys, produced by the moving creditor, stating that the sheriff did levy upon property under said attachments, without disclosing their means of knowledge, or the time when, or the property upon which the pretended levy was made, amount simply to the opinions of the affiants, and
[2] do not constitute sufficient proof of the fact alleged to raise a question of evidence as to its existence.

It, therefore, conclusively appears that neither the

appellant nor the respondents in this appeal have liens either upon the same or upon any property belonging to their mutual debtor, and that the ap-
[6] pellant has no legal interest in the question as to the validity of said prior attachments. Such attachments do not stand in the way of the levy of the appellant's attachment upon any property which he may discover, liable to be seized thereon.

The appellant can have no interest in the agreement made between the assignee of the debtor and the prior attachment creditors, for the reason that the only
[7] obligation of the assignee thereunder, is to the prior attaching creditors, and such obligation cannot inure to the benefit of other parties.

The sheriff has never had possession of, or any interest in the moneys thereby agreed to be retained and paid over by the assignee, and the only effect of that contract is to create a liability upon the part of the assignee to the prior attaching creditors, upon the happening of the contingencies therein provided for. The sheriff can maintain no action upon, or has no rights under such agreement. So far as his attachment proceedings are concerned, the appellant's interest in the property of his debtor can be reached or secured only through his process in the hands of the sheriff, and that is ineffectual to reach a right of action secured by contract to the prior attaching creditors alone. It thus appears quite evident, that the appellant has not brought himself within the
[8] requirements of the Code, entitling him to move to vacate a prior attachment.

The orders must, therefore, be affirmed, with costs.

All concur, except ANDREWS, J., absent.

BUDD, APPELLANT, v. WALKER, AS EXECUTOR ETC., OF SMALES, RESPONDENT.

SUPREME COURT, FIRST DEPARTMENT, GENERAL TERM, JANUARY, 1883.

§ 413.

Statute of limitations.—Proper form of pleading.—It must be distinctly alleged by specific answer that the cause of action did not accrue within the period within which the Code provides that it must be brought.

The provision of section 413 of the Code of Civil Procedure, that the objection that the action was not commenced within the time limited can be taken only by answer, means that it must be distinctly alleged by specific answer that the cause of action did not accrue within the period within which by previous sections of the Code it must be brought.[2]

In pleading the statute of limitations, an allegation that the cause of action did not accrue at any time within six years next before the commencement of the action, where that is the time limited, is the proper form, and there seems to be no excuse for tolerating any material departure from that form.[6]

Where, in an action against an executor of a deceased person, the answer of a defendant set forth "that the claims of the plaintiff mentioned in said complaint, if not wholly fictitious, are stale and outlawed demands, and have been wholly abandoned and lost by the *laches* of the plaintiff in not insisting upon the same during the lifetime of the testator, with whom the plaintiff was in daily intercourse, and the defendant claims the benefit of all statutes or rules of law or equity which may be invoked for the purpose of resisting the same, and which the evidence presented upon the trial may show to be applicable." *Held*, that this is not a plea of the statute of limitations.[1,7,8]

Fisher v. Pond (1 *Hill*, 672; S. C., 2 *Id.* 338);[3] Dyster v. Battye (3 *Barn. & Ald.* 438);[4] Bell v. Yates (33 *Barb.* 627);[5] approved.

(*Decided March* 20, 1883.)

Appeal from judgment in favor of the defendant entered upon the report of the referee.

The opinion states the facts.

Luther R. Marsh (*Marsh, Wilson & Wallis*, attorneys), for appellant.

George W. Van Slyck, for respondent.

The statute of limitations was properly pleaded. . . . . The plaintiff was not misled by the form of the answer as to this defense and at least the allegation was only defective in form, and such defect is cured by the trial. De Grove *v.* Metropolitan Ins. Co., 61 *N. Y.* 650; *Code Civ. Pro.* § 721, subd. 5, and § 723 . . . See also Sharpe *v.* Freeman, 45 *N. Y.* 802, 808, 809.

It was unnecessary to plead the statute of limitations. The complaint set forth a technical trust against which the statute could not run, hence, if by any possibility the plaintiff should be permitted to maintain any other cause of action not founded on such technical trust the defendant is entitled to avail himself of the statute of limitations as no opportunity was given to plead it. The case is similar to that of Arnold *v.* Angell, 62 *N. Y.* 508, 512.

DAVIS, P. J.—The first cause of action set forth in the complaint alleges that: "On or about January 22nd, in the year 1859, said plaintiff entrusted to said testator the sum of $953.72, which sum the said testator shortly thereafter informed said plaintiff he had invested for her at seven per cent. per annum."

To establish this cause of action the plaintiff proved and put in evidence an instrument in the following words and figures:

"NEW YORK, January 22, 1859.

"Dear Mrs. Van Kleeck: I have this day received from Mrs. Meinell, on your account, $653.72, which together with the $300.00 you deposited in my hands about the 1st of September last, are now drawing interest at the rate of seven per cent. If I can find an opportunity of purchasing a mortgage such as I mentioned to you, whereby I can without risk secure a greater profit, I shall do so, unless you wish to make another use of the money. Should you desire to use it please let me know.

"H. SMALES."

In respect to this cause of action, the referee has found against the defendant solely on the grounds that it was barred by the statute of limitations. It was insisted on the part of the plaintiff that the statute of limitations had not been pleaded as a defense. The referee overruled this objection and held that the statute was sufficiently pleaded.

The third answer of the defendant is as follows:

"Defendant further says, on information and [1] belief, that the claims of the plaintiff mentioned in said complaint, if not wholly fictitious, are stale and outlawed demands, and have been wholly abandoned and lost by the *laches* of the plaintiff in not insisting upon the same during the lifetime of the testator, with whom the plaintiff was in daily intercourse, and the defendant claims the benefit of all statutes or rules of law or equity which may be invoked for the purpose of resisting the same, and which the evidence presented upon the trial may show to be applicable."

Whatever this nondescript answer may be we are of opinion that it is not a plea of the statute of limitations. Section 413 of the Code of Civil Procedure, declares that the objection that the action was not [2] commenced within the time limited can be taken only by answer. This means that it must be distinctly alleged by specific answer that the cause of action did not accrue within the period within which by previons sections of the Code it must be brought. The form of pleading the statute of limitations has long been well settled. In Fisher *v.* Pond (1 *Hill*, 672), which was an action on the case against the sheriff [*] for not returning a fi. fa., the defendant pleaded that he was "not guilty within three years next before the commencement of the suit."

A motion was made to strike out this answer as false. The court, BRONSON, J., in commenting on the plea, said, "the plea may be bad because it says not guilty within three years instead of alleging that the action did not accrue within that time," citing 2 *R. S.* 296, and Dyster *v.* Battye, 3 *Barn. & Ald.* 438, but held that the question was not before the court, as neither a demurrer nor a motion to strike out the plea as frivolous was made. Afterwards in the same case in 2 *Hill*, 338, the plaintiff having demurred specially to the plea for not following the statute in its terms, the court held that upon the authority of Dyster *v.* Battye, *supra*, "and the reason of the thing," the plea was bad, and sustained the demurrer. In Dyster *v.* Battye, in speaking of a similar plea, ABBOT, Ch. J., said, [*] "If its import be really the same as an allegation that the cause of action did not accrue within six years, there can be no reason assigned for a departure from the usual forms. And if its import is different, then it is not a plea warranted by the statute, and, certainly, is not a good plea at the common law." In Bell *v.* Yates (33 *Barb.* 627), the answer was that [*] the causes of action did not accrue at any time within six years next before the commencement of this action; and the court held this to be the proper form of pleading the statute of limitations under the Code. Such a plea is concise and plain, and pre- [*] sents the issue of fact which the law requires, to wit: whether the action was commenced within six years after it accrued. There seems to be no excuse for tolerating any material departure from that form. In this case the answer is that the claims of the plaintiff "if not wholly fictitious, are stale and outlawed demands, and have been wholly abandoned and lost by the *laches* of the plaintiff in not insisting upon the same during the life time of the testator with whom the plaintiff was in daily intercourse." The substance of this answer is the *laches* of the plaintiff in not insisting upon the claims during the life time of the testator, and the object appears to be to assert such *laches* as an evidence that they are wholly fictitious. The answer looks more like an attempt to avoid the odium of setting up the statute of limitations instead of one to assert it as a defense.

The question whether it does assert that defense all turns upon the force of the word outlawed, for, if [7] the sentence be read without that word, probably no one would assert that it could be construed to be a plea of the statute of limitations. But the fact that a demand is outlawed, is no defense without a plea of the statute of limitations, for no matter how plainly it may appear upon the face of the instrument that more than six or more than any number of years has elapsed since the demand fell due, yet the omission of the plea of the statute of limitations prevents that fact from operating as a defense. To hold this answer to be such a plea is equivalent to holding that it is a sufficient answer under the statute to assert that the cause of action alleged in the complaint is stale and outlawed, which certainly would not be a good answer, because it would not indicate, according to the requirements of the Code, that the defendant intended to rely upon the force of the statute of limitations. Nor do we think that the conclusion of the answer should operate to make that part already considered, a plea of the statutes of limitation. It is in these words: "And the defendant claims the benefit of all statutes, or rules of law or equity which may be [*] invoked for the purpose of resisting the same, and which the evidence produced on the trial may show to be applicable." The only merit of this part of the answer consists in its novelty. It surely cannot operate to entitle the defendant to the benefit of any statutes which the law requires to be specially pleaded. The statute of limitations is of that character (Code, § 413.) And a general claim of the benefit of all statutes or rules of law or equity which may be invoked for the purpose of resisting a claim, is no compliance with the requirements of the section referred to. Indeed, this whole sentence is nothing more than a declaration of intention to take advantage of whatever may turn up on the trial.

In respect of the other cause of actions set forth in the complaint, there was in the correspondence of the testator considerable evidence tending to establish the allegation that the parties did enter into an arrangement for carrying on a household at their joint expense; and if the learned referee had found that such an arrangement existed, it would not have been difficult to uphold the finding. It being purely a question of fact, however, his construction of the correspondence and other evidence bearing upon that issue, is one with which we are not inclined to interfere, because, upon the question already considered, there must be a a new trial, at all events, as the evidence stood, when the case was submitted, the plaintiff had shown a just claim against the testator for his board for a number of years, and such was the opinion of the learned referee as shown by the concluding remarks of his opinion. He says, "The most that can be inferred is that the testator was a highly favored boarder, and under an implied obligation to pay whatever the services rendered to him were worth. No such cause of action is set forth in the complaint, or attempted to be maintained upon the trial." The parties will, of course, before a new trial be had, be at liberty to make such applications as they shall be respectively advised in respect to the amendment of the pleadings. With leave of the court, the answer can be amended so as properly to set up the statute of limitations as a defense, and the complaint may also in like manner be amended so as to assert a claim for the board, and services rendered to the testator by the plaintiff and with such amendments, the equitable claims and legal defense will be better represented upon a new trial.

The judgment must be reversed and a new trial granted with costs to abide the event.

BUCKLEY, Jr., an infant, by BUCKLEY, his Guardian ad litem, Respondent, v. THE GUTTA PERCHA AND RUBBER MANUFACTURING COMPANY, Appellant.

Supreme Court, Second Department; General Term, January, 1883.

§§ 3268, 3272.

Security for costs.—Right to require, may be lost by laches.—The Code gives plaintiff a right to elect either to make deposit or file undertaking, and restricts court as to form of order.

It seems to have been the intention of the legislature by the adoption of section 3268 of the Code of Civil Procedure to give an absolute right to a defendant to require security for costs, unless he may have lost such right by *laches.*[1] The provisions of that section are intended solely for the benefit of the defendant, and his neglect to promptly avail himself of such benefit would be construed as a waiver.[2]

Section 3272 of the Code gives to a plaintiff who has been required to give security for costs, an election to either pay into court two hundred and fifty dollars, or give an undertaking, and restricts the power of the court as to the form of the order requiring security.[3]

Where the defendant, in an action in which an infant suing by his guardian *ad litem* was plaintiff, appeared and obtained two extensions of ten days each of his time to answer, and upon procuring the last one stipulated to accept short notice of trial, and three days after answering, obtained an order, *ex parte*, that the plaintiff give security for costs, under section 3268 of the Code,—*Held*, that the defendant had been guilty of *laches*, and thus waived his right to require such security, and a motion to set aside the order that security for costs be given was properly granted.[4]

(*Decided May* 15, 1883.)

Appeal from an order of the Kings county special term vacating an order requiring plaintiff to file security for costs.

This action was commenced on September 7, 1882, to recover $10,000 as damages for personal injuries received by the plaintiff through the alleged carelessness of the defendant. The defendant's time to answer was twice extended ten days by consent, and on procuring the second extension his attorneys stipulated to accept short notice of trial for the November 1882 term. October 17, 1882, a copy of the answer was served, and on the 20th of the same month the court, upon the *ex parte* application of the defendant, made an order requiring the plaintiff within ten days after service of a copy thereof on his attorney "either to pay into court the sum of $250 to be applied to the payment of costs, if any awarded against him, or at his election within ten days to file with the clerk of this court an undertaking to secure costs in the usual form and in compliance with the statute in such cases made and provided."

The plaintiff's attorney, October 30, 1882, moved to vacate and set aside this order, and his motion was granted. From the order thereupon entered this appeal was taken.

Pelton and *Poucher*, for appellants.

The right of a defendant to require security is statutory and not discretionary. Code, § 3272; Ashbahs *v.* Coussin, 2 *Sandf.* 632. . . . . An irresponsible guardian *ad litem* will be ordered to give security. McDonald *v.* Brass Goods Co., 2 *Abb. N. C.* 434.

Defendant by obtaining an extension of time and by answering did not waive its right to security. . . . The time within which plaintiff can require security is not limited. Gedney *v.* Purdy, 47 *N. Y.* 676. It is proper to move on pleadings after issue joined. McDonald *v.* Brass Goods Co., *supra.*

James Troy, for respondent.

The practice as settled by the court is that the application, if made to the court, must be on notice to the plaintiff; if made to a judge at chambers the order will be that the plaintiff file security for costs within twenty days after service of the order or show cause on the first day of the next term, and that in the meantime all proceedings on the part of the plaintiff be stayed. Camplin *v.* Pierce, 3 *Wend.* 445. . . . *Graham's P.* 507 (Edition 1836); Blanchard *v.* Nefle, 6 *Hill*, 256. The practice under the Code continued practically the same. Cadwell *v.* Heming, 15 *Abb. Pr.* 271; 24 *How. Pr.* 38. While an absolute order without notice may not be void, it is irregular and should be set aside on motion. Bronson *v.* Freeman, 8 *How. Pr.* 492.

If the defendant ever had a right to the order, it was waived by appearing and answering in the cause before obtaining the order. If the defendant takes any step in the cause he waives security for costs.

Goodrich v. Pendleton, 3 *Johns. Ch.* 520. He must apply as soon as the facts come to his knowledge. Long v. Majestre, 1 *Johns. Ch.* 202. It is not imperative on the court to grant the order under all circumstances. Robinson v. Sinclair, 1 *Denio*, 629; Florence v. Buckley, 1 *Duer*, 705; Feavan v. Gelpke, 13 *Abb. Pr.* 473; Woodman v. Stearns, 11 *Abb. Pr. N. S.* 445.

The motion for security for costs must be made at the first opportunity. Carpenter v. Aldrich, 3 *Metc.* 58; Whiting v. Hollister 2 *Mass.* 102; Samuelson v. Anderson, *L. R.* 3 *Irish C. L.* 575; Koeb v. People, 85 *Ill.* 336. And has been held too late after a demand for a bill of particulars. Johnson v. Glasser, (*M. S.*) *Steven's N. B. Dig.* 373. After a plea in abatement. Randolph v. Emerich, 13 *Ill.* 334. After a demurrer. People v. Cloud, 50 *Ill.* 439. After an appearance and plea. Lincoln v. Hancock, 5 *Ark.* 703. Kasten v. D'Law, 1 *Moo. & Pay.* 30; Clark v. Gibson, 2 *Ark.* 109; Fonville v. Richie, 2 *Rich.* (*S. C.*) 10; Duncan v. Stuart, 5 *B. & Ald.* 702; Jacobson v. Carr, *Cr. & Dix* 107; Watson v. Chadwick, 8 *Irish C. L.* 291; Clapp v. Beach, 3 *Me.* 216; Fletcher v. Lu, 3 *Ad. & El.* 551; Kumbach v. Pelumden, 6 *Bradw.* 539; Wood v. Bellisle, 1 Chanc. 130; Anderson v. Walsh, *L. R.* 2 *Irish C. L.* 303. Although the plea was filed under protest. Henry v. Hackett, *Bl. D. & O.* 248; Bush v. Curran, 9 *Irish C. L.* Appl, XXX. After obtaining time to plead. Eyre v. Duyer, *Lan. & Le.* 653. See also Gurrey v. Key, *Dowl. P. C.* 559; Wilson v. Minchine, 2 *Cromp. & Jerv.* 87; Dowling v. Harman, 6 *M. & W.* 131; Suanzey v. Swanzey, 4 *K. & J.* 237. After an answer. Trustees v. Walters, 12 *Ill.* 154; Myer v. Tysen, 1 *Bland*, 559; Dunning v. Dunning, 37 *Ill.* 306; May v. Power, 2 *Edw.* 294; Schuefer v. Waldo, 7 *Ohio St.* 309; Wyllie v. Ellice, 11 *Beav.* 99; Seider's case, 12 *Sim.* 106; Gray v. Bolton, 2 *Bro. C. C.* 609; Melurucchy v. Melurucchy, 2 *Ves. Sr.* 24. After the expiration of the time for answering, Freel *v.* Traut, 11 *Irish Eq.* 278; Sicleham *v.* Gresham, 2 *Irish C. L.* 139; Alker *v.* Alker, 3 *Irish Jur. N. S.* 50; Beansang *v.* Conden, 13 *Irish C. L.* app. XXX, VII; Smith *v.* Dey, 2 *Ch. Cham.* 454; Granson *v.* Finch, 3 *Id.* 296.

PRATT, J.—It seems to have been the intention of the Legislature by the adoption of section 3268 of
[1] the new Code, to give an absolute right to a defendant to require security for costs, unless he may have lost such right by *laches*.

Section 3272 gives to the plaintiff a right of election to either pay into court two hundred and fifty
[2] dollars or give an undertaking, and restricts the power of the court as to the form of the order. Healy *v.* Twenty-third St. R. R. Co., 1 *N. Y. Civ. Pro.* 15, and cases there cited. Robertson *v.* Barnum, decided at present general term of this court, second department.*

The provisions of section 3268 are intended solely for the benefit of the defendant; a neglect to
[3] promptly avail himself of such benefit would be construed as a waiver. Wice *v.* Commercial Fire Ins. Co., 2 *Abb N. C.* 325; *Broom's Maxims*, 319. The rule is too familiar to require a citation of authorities.

The defendant had been guilty of *laches* and thus waved his right to require security under section 3268, and although he might have moved that that security should be filed, it was discretionary in the court whether or not to grant the order. Instead, however, of moving upon notice to the plaintiff, he obtained an *ex parte* order upon the bare statement of the fact that security had not been filed.

Upon the hearing of the order to show cause why the *ex parte* order so obtained should not be set aside,

* Reported 29 *Hun*, 657.

the defendant offered no affidavit to contradict the proof made by the plaintiff, but relied upon section 3268 of the Code.

Under these circumstances, we think the defendant had waived his right, and that there were no facts [1] shown sufficient to justify an order denying the motion.

Order appealed from affirmed, with costs and disbursements.*

DYKMAN, J., concurred.

* An appeal to the court of appeals taken from the order entered on this decision was dismised June 26, 1883. The court of appeals did not write any opinion.

EDDY *v.* THE CO-OPERATIVE DRESS ASSOCIATION.

SUPREME COURT, SECOND DEPARTMENT; KINGS COUNTY, SPECIAL TERM, MARCH, 1883.

§§ 1788, 1793.

Receiver.—Is simply an official instrument used by the court to execute its orders.—Has no title, personally, to funds placed in his charge, his possession being the possession of the court.—Is not bound in official capacity by injunction issued against him personally.—Injunction restraining a person from interfering with the property of a corporation, does not disqualify him from accepting the appointment of receiver of the corporation, and discharging all the duties of such receivership.—Judgment creditors of corporation are parties to sequestration action against it, and bound by judgment therein.—The court will protect its officers in the discharge of their duties, and see that all persons willfully embarrassing them are arrested and punished.

A receiver is simply an official instrument, used by the court, to execute its orders. He has no title personally to the fund placed in his charge, and his possession is the possession of the court. As receiver he represents a separate and independent legal existence, and therefore an order made in an action brought against him personally and not as receiver, and not in terms in any way purporting to affect him in his official character, has no force or bearing upon him in the latter capacity.[2]

Where in an action brought to set aside the appointment of a receiver of a corporation made in an action by a stockholder of the corporation to preserve its property, he was enjoined from interfering with the property of the corporation, except to preserve it, and the action and injunction order was against him personally, and not as receiver,—*Held*, that he was not restrained from acting in his official capacity as receiver.[1]

Where, in such a case, after the injunction order was granted, the receiver was again appointed receiver of the corporation in a sequestration action, brought by one of its creditors, and judgment was subsequently entered in that action continuing the appointment of the receiver and directing a distribution of the assets, and afterwards final judgment was entered in the stockholder's action discharging the receiver therein, and adjudging that the title to all the property of the corporation was in him as receiver under the judgment of distribution in the sequestration action,—*Held*, that, as no reference was made in the papers on which the injunction order was granted to the sequestration action, the injunction could no more affect the receiver as such in that action, than it could any other person, whom the court might have appointed as such receiver; [3] that the fact that an injunction order, restraining him personally from interfering with the property of the corporation, was outstanding, could not disqualify him from accepting the appointment of receiver in a subsequent action, and discharging all the duties thereof. [4] Also *Held*, that, assuming that the injunction did not restrain the receiver as such, it did not restrain him from distributing the funds in his hands under the judgment; that the plaintiffs in the injunction, being judgment creditors of the corporation, were parties to the sequestration action, and the judgment therein was therefore binding and conclusive upon them, in respect to the matters decided therein; [7] that it was clearly the duty of the receiver to obey the mandates of the judgment, the validity or propriety of which can only be questioned in the usual orderly way by appeal in the action. [8]

The court in the administration of funds, which are taken into its custody, must act through the officers selected for that purpose, and it is clearly its duty, not only in justice to them but in respect to its own dignity, to see that they are duly protected against needless annoyance and interference in the discharge of their duties, and that all parties willfully embarrassing them, are arrested and punished. [9]

Attorney General v. Guardian Mutual Life Ins. Co. (77 *N. Y.* 271), [3, 4,] Butler v. Niles (35 *How. Pr.* 331), [9] followed.

(*Decided March* 19, 1873.)

Application by receiver of the defendant for instruction of court as to the payment of a dividend to the defendant's creditors.

The facts are stated in the opinion here reported.

John L. Hill and *L. W. Emerson*, for receiver and motion.

PRATT, J.—This is an application made by F. H. Smith, Esq., as receiver of the defendant, for instructions as to the payment of a dividend. Ordinarily, it would be a waste of time to write an opinion upon a question of this kind, but the peculiar circumstances involved in this matter seem to require a brief statement of the facts and the reasons for the instructions to be given.

It appears that the moneys in the receiver's hands amount to about $100,000, and the debts proved to $123,000. There are also some claims not yet proved, amounting to about $9,000, besides a claim of Schulhoff & Co. now in suit for about $5,000, which latter demand is secured by a deposit in the Union Trust Company, pending a motion to vacate an attachment issued therein.

It is undoubtedly the duty of the receiver to distribute, without delay, a fair proportion of the moneys in his hands among the creditors whose claims are proved and undisputed, unless the facts which we will now consider render such a course improper.

It seems that on or about December 30, 1882, Simon Danzig and others commenced an action against Mr. Smith personally and the above defendant and Edward H. Cole, upon a judgment recovered by said Danzig against said association, for $383.29, upon which they had issued an execution which was outstanding, alleging that the appointment of said Smith as receiver in an action brought by said Cole as a stockholder against the said association was collusive and void, and praying to have his appointment set aside and another receiver appointed.

A temporary injunction was granted in the action against the defendants, with an order to show cause why it should not be made perpetual, restraining the defendants therein from interfering with the property of said association, except to preserve the same.

On December 30, 1882, Mr. Smith was appointed receiver of said association in a sequestration action brought against it by Lyman K. Eddy. His appointment in the Cole action was made under section 1810 of the new Code to preserve the property.

On January 18, 1883, final judgment was entered in the Eddy action, continuing the appointment of the receiver and directing distribution of the assets, and on the 12th day of February following final judgment was entered in the Cole action, discharging the receiver therein and adjudging that the title to all the property of said association was in him as a receiver under said judgment of distribution in said Eddy action.

It therefore is clear that Mr. Smith took possession of and preserved the property as required in the Cole action until he took the same as receiver in the Eddy action, under which title he now holds the same. Said last mentioned action being a regular proceeding to sequestrate the property of said Dress Association.

Prior to January 8, 1883, an action was brought by the receiver in this court against said Danzig and others, in which an order of injunction was granted and afterwards made permanent, restraining, among other things, all proceedings in the said Danzig's suit first mentioned.

Now, the injunction order in the suit of Danzig v. Smith, as we have seen, runs against Mr. Smith [1] personally, and not as receiver. It, therefore, did not purport to and did not restrain him from acting in his official capacity as receiver, even in the Cole action.

[2] A receiver is simply an official instrument used by the court to execute its orders. He has no title personally to the fund placed in his charge, and his

possession is the possession of the court. Attorney-General *v.* Guardian Mutual Life Ins. Co., 77 *N. Y.* 272. As receiver he represents a separate and independent legal existence, and an order, therefore, made in an action brought against him personally and not as receiver, and not in terms in any way purporting to affect him in his official character, has no force or bearing upon him in the latter capacity.

But if there was any ground upon which the claim could have been made that the injunction order in Danzig *v.* Smith affected the receiver in the Cole action for the reason that the Danzig suit was brought in part to set aside his appointment therein, no such ground can be successfully urged now, for the reason already stated, that Mr. Smith was appointed receiver in the Cole action to preserve the property of the association, and final judgment has in said action long since been rendered, discharging him as receiver therein. And further, also, he now holds the property under a final judgment in the sequestration action brought by Eddy against the said association. No question is raised of the validity of any of the proceedings in the Eddy action, and no reference is made to them in any of the papers upon which the Danzig injunction is based, and it further appears that no appeal has been taken from any order or judgment in the sequestration action.

[3] The injunction order in question, therefore, can no more affect him as receiver in that action (*i. e.*, in the sequestration action) than it could any other person whom the court might have appointed as such receiver.

[4] The fact that an injunction order restraining Mr. Smith personally from interfering with the property of the Co-operative Dress Association was outstanding, could not disqualify him from accepting the appointment of receiver in a subsequent action

and discharging all the duties thereof. He is simply the instrument which the court has used and by its order has directed to take charge of and distribute a fund which it has taken into its possession.

Any other view would inevitably lead to the conclusion that the court, by restraining Mr. Smith, had enjoined itself from distributing the fund of which it had taken control. But, assuming that the injunction order in the Danzig action operated upon Mr.
[5] Smith in his capacity as receiver, it does not restrain him from distributing the funds in his hands under the judgment in this court.

[6] In the case of Attorney-General *v.* Guardian Mutual Life Ins. Co. (*supra*) the court of appeals *held* that "The creditors are parties to the proceeding for the dissolution and winding up of the corporation through the receiver, and as such subject to the control of the supreme court." The Danzigs being judgment creditors of the Dress Association are, therefore, parties to the sequestration action in which Mr.
[7] Smith is receiver. The judgment is, therefore, binding and conclusive upon them in respect to the matters decided therein.

That judgment directs the receiver to distribute the assets among the creditors of the association, and it is clearly his duty to obey its mandates, the validity
[8] or propriety of which can only be questioned in the usual orderly way by appeal in that action.

[9] In Butler *v.* Niles (35 *How. Pr.* 331), where objection was made to complying with the terms of a judgment because of an injunction, MONELL, J., said: "The first answer to the objection is that the acts are authorized by the judgment of this court in a case within its jurisdiction and powers, both as to the subject matter and the parties, which judgment is necessarily a complete justification of all acts done under it.

"It cannot be that an act done by the direction or under the authority of a court of competent jurisdiction and powers, having before it all the parties to be affected, can be questioned elsewhere."

This rule is old and firmly established as any principle of the common law.

If the Danzigs had any valid reason to prevent the distribution of the fund in question they should have appeared in the usual way in the sequestration action and asked for such relief as they desired, or presented their views to this court on the return of this motion, of which they had due notice. Rinn *v.* Astor Fire Ins. Co., 59 *N. Y.* 143. They have done neither, and the court can see no reason against the many in favor of the immediate payment of a dividend.

As we have seen, their judgment amounts to $383.29. The estate will pay probably 75 or more per cent. of the amount of the claims, so that their interest in dispute cannot exceed one hundred dollars, and with that they, alone of all the creditors, are seeking in the ways heretofore described to prevent the distribution of nearly one hundred thousand dollars among the creditors who have proved and represent nearly the total amount of claims against the fund. A bare statement of such a contention renders comment unnecessary.

It appears from the affidavit of Mr. Randall that nearly every judgment recovered and every demand in suit against the association have been proved in the sequestration action.

It is, therefore, difficult to see how the proceedings of the Danzigs are, or are intended to be, other than vexatious and annoying to the receiver. Their rights cannot possibly be affected injuriously by a distribution to the creditors, as a fund far in excess of the amount of their judgment will remain in the receiver's hands after the payment of the first dividend.

This alone is an answer to the position taken by the Danzigs. Butler v. Niles, *supra*.

The most the Danzigs can claim in their action is payment of their judgment, and no court would for a moment entertain the proposition that to secure less than $400 the receiver is bound, or would be justified in holding back from the creditors concededly entitled thereto a fund amounting to a hundred thousand dollars.

I have examined this application for instructions with care, in order that no improvident direction should be given, and have expressed my views thus at length to render it clear that the instructions I shall give will in no way conflict with any order of this court.

[*] The court in the administration of funds which are taken into its custody must act through the officers selected for that purpose.

It is the duty of the court, not only in justice to them but in respect to its own dignity, to see that they are not only properly directed, but that they are duly protected against needless annoyance and interference in the discharge of their duties, and that all parties willfully embarrassing them are arrested and punished, and to that end the court instructs the receiver in this action to report to it forthwith any interference with him in the discharge of his trust.

I am clearly satisfied from all the facts laid before me that the receiver can safely and properly pay a dividend of sixty per cent. immediately to all the creditors whose claims are proved and accepted.

An order to that effect may be entered.

EDDY v. THE CO-OPERATIVE DRESS ASSOCIATION.

SUPREME COURT, SECOND DEPARTMENT; KINGS COUNTY SPECIAL TERM MAY, 1883.

§§ 1788, 1793.

Action against corporation for sequestration of its property.—It seems, that a final decree of sequestration works a practical dissolution of a corporation.—Assets of corporation first subject to claims of creditors existing at time of appointment of receiver in sequestration action.—Claim for damages for breach of contract after appointment of receiver cannot be paid out of such fund.

The provisions of the Code that in an action for the sequestration of the property of a corporation, its property, after the payment of creditors, should be distributed among the stockholders instead of being returned to the corporation, seem to indicate that a final decree of sequestration works a practical dissolution of the corporation.

A corporation entered into an agreement with one "L." whereby it employed him for one year as its superintendent, at a salary of $10,000 per annum. Seven months thereafter, a receiver of its property was appointed in a sequestration action and the receiver forthwith discharged "L." A judgment of sequestrating and directing a distribution of the property of the corporation was thereafter entered and a dividend of sixty per cent. declared by the receiver. "L." presented to him a claim for damages sustained by reason of such discharge, which the received rejected. "L." thereupon moved that his claim be allowed, and the receiver directed to pay him a dividend thereon. *Held*, that while this case could be distinguished from that of the People v. The Globe Mutual Life Insurance Company (16 *Weekly Digest* 225), wherein it was held that a judgment dissolving an insolvent insurance company terminated a contract of employment of an agent made by it, the principle of that case was applicable; also *held*, that "L." was not, at the time of appointing the receiver, a creditor of the corporation; that the assets of the company were subject to claims of the creditors then existing, and such claims must be first satisfied before the fund could be used for another purpose.

Kincaid v. Dwinelle (59 *N. Y.* 548), distinguished; People v. Globe Mutual Life Ins. Co. (16 *Week. Dig.* 225), followed.

(*Decided May* 21, 1883.)

Petition by Charles H. P. Lyman for an order adjusting and allowing his claim against the defendant at $2,000, and directing its receiver to pay him a dividend thereon of 60 per cent.

This action was brought by plaintiff, who is a judgment creditor of the defendant, to secure the sequestration and distribution of the property of the defendant.

Freeling H. Smith was appointed receiver of the defendant December 26, 1882, in an action brought by a stockholder against it to preserve its property. December 30, 1882, said Smith was appointed receiver of the defendant in this action. January 18, 1883, judgment was entered in this action, continuing the receivership of said Smith and directing a distribution of the assets of the defendant among its creditors.

The petitioner, claiming to be a creditor of the defendant, duly proved and presented his claim against the defendant to the receiver, who rejected it. The claim arose as follows: On the 13th of May, 1882, a contract, in writing, between the petitioner and defendant was entered into, whereby the petitioner was employed by the defendant as its general manager at a salary of $10,000 per annum, and he thereupon entered upon the discharge of his duties and continued to perform them until December 30, 1882, when he was discharged by the receiver.

The petitioner endeavored to obtain employment, and on or about February 12, 1883, secured a position with Lord & Taylor, of New York city, at a salary of $300 per month from said February 12, 1883. He has received from the defendant in cash and merchandise $6,426.76, and will receive from Lord & Taylor for his services up to May 15, 1883, $930. By reason of these facts the petitioner asserts that he has been damaged $2,643.24, but he agreed with the receiver that his damages should be fixed and adjusted at $2,000, provided the court should determine upon this application that the assets of the defendant in the hands of the receiver are liable therefor.

The receiver, under instructions from the court, has declared and is paying a dividend of 60 per cent., to the creditors of the defendant, and the petitioner seeks to share in that dividend.

C. C. Prentiss, for petitioner.

J. L. Hill and *L. W. Emerson*, for receiver, opposed.

CULLEN, J.—While this case can be distinguished from that of the People v. Globe Mutual Life Insurance Company,* I am inclined to think that the principal of that case is applicable to the one at bar.

The provisions of the present Code, that the property, after the payment of creditors, should be distributed among the stockholders instead of being returned to the corporation, would seem to indicate that a final decree of sequestration works a practical dissolution of the corporation.

The case of Kincaid v. Dwinelle, 59 *N. Y.* 548, arose before the present Code, and it will be observed that in that case a receiver, *pendente lite* only, had been ap-

*S. C., 16 *Week. Dig.* 225. It was *held* in that case that a judgment dissolving an insolvent insurance company terminated a contract of employment of an agent at an annual salary made by it, and that, therefore, there was no breach of the contract.

pointed, and no final decree had been entered in the action.

But however that may be, I think the petitioner was not at the time of appointing the receiver a creditor of the corporation. There was no breach of the contract between him and the company. It might be that no liability would accrue under such contract. The assets of the company are subject to claims of creditors then existing. Such claims must be first satisfied before the fund can be used for another purpose. If the company continues in existence he may have a valid claim against it, but I do not think he is entitled to share in the fund now in court, to the detriment of creditors.

Motion denied.

CONCORD GRANITE COMPANY, Respondent, *v.* FRENCH, Appellant.

N. Y. Court of Common Pleas, General Term, May, 1883.

§§ 755, 756.

Payment of note by indorser after action brought thereon against maker, does not cause action to abate.—Indorser may ask to be substituted as plaintiff.

Where, after an action was brought on a promissory note against its maker, an indorser paid it, and the maker set up such payment as a defense,—*Held,* that the indorser, by the payment, acquired a cause of action against the maker and might have asked a substitution as plaintiff; that the action did not abate, but was properly continued by the original plaintiff, and that the payment in no way enured as a defense to the defendant.

Concord Granite Co. *v.* French (3 *N. Y. Civ. Pro.* 56), affirmed.

(*Decided June* 30, 1883.)

Appeal from judgment of the general term of the N. Y. marine court affirming judgment rendered in favor of the plaintiff at a trial term thereof.

This action was commenced by the service of the summons and complaint on May 15, 1882, and was brought to recover $500, protest fees and interest on a promissory note made by the defendant and indorsed by the Smith Granite Company of Rhode Island. On May 22 the defendant answered, and about May 24 the indorser, The Smith Granite Company, paid the note, which was thereupon delivered to it by the plaintiff. May 24, 1882, the defendant amended his answer and set up such payment as a defense.

L. B. Bunnell, for appellant.

Cephas Brainerd, for respondent.

Payment by the drawer or indorser does not discharge the acceptor or maker. 2 *Daniel on Negotiable Insts.* § 1237. The drawer or indorser on payment of a bill or note acquires the rights of the holder as against the acceptor or maker. *Id.* § 1223. . . . . Subrogation is the equitable incident of payment by an indorser, and the plaintiff in this action would have violated its duty had it discontinued this action, the indorser having discharged his liability and became the owner of the note, *pendente lite. Dixon on Subrogation*, ch. vi.; *Sheldon on Subrogation*, §§ 181, 182 (where the cases are collected). Griffin *v.* Hampton, 21 *Geo.* 198, and Lancaster Bank *v.* Boggs, 7 *Watts & Serg.* 331, are contrary to the current authority. See *Sheldon on Subrogation*, 163, § 137. The courts of this state are solicitous to maintain the rights of sureties. See cases cited in *Sheldon on Subrogation*, 159, § 137.

Beach, J.—This action was properly brought against the defendant as maker of the note. Thereafter, and before answer, the sum due upon it was paid the plaintiff, presumably by the payee and indorser, and the defendant, among other minor defenses, alleged in his answer, that such payment was made by the indorser, and the plaintiff was not the real party in interest. The learned court below was not called upon to decide any other question. It was found that the indorser did not pay until after the commencement of this action.

It seems the contention between the parties only affects the question of costs. If the payment averred in the answer was in fact made by the defendant it would have been better to have plead the truth. The defendant should now be held to his averment.

The evidence contained in the record shows the truth of the allegation in the answer that the note was paid by the Smith Granite Company, payee and indorser to the plaintiff as holder after this action was brought. This fact in no way enured as a defense to the defendant. His liability could only be met in this case from payment by him (*Edwards on Bills*, 535; *Story on Promissory Notes*, § 401; Havens *v.* Huntington, 1 *Cow.* 387).

The Smith Granite Company, by the payment, acquired a cause of action against the defendant, and might have asked a substitute as plaintiff here; but the action did not abate, and, under the circumstances, was properly continued by the original plaintiff (*Code Civ. Pro.* §§ 755, 756). What may result to the defendant if a correct disposition of the issue be made is of no importance, especially under the supposition entertained by me from the evidence that his answer was interposed with an intention of gaining a technical advantage, or escaping the payment of costs, for which he was properly liable.

In regard to the legal status of the three parties, I

concur in the view so clearly expressed by Judge McADAM in the court below.

The judgment should be affirmed, with costs and disbursements.

DALY, Ch. J., and VAN BRUNT, J., concurred.

WILLIAMS v. THE WESTERN UNION TELEGRAPH COMPANY.

N. Y. SUPERIOR COURT, SPECIAL TERM, JULY, 1883.

§ 885.

Order to take the deposition of witness to be used on motion.—What must be shown in affidavit on which it is granted.

It must appear from the affidavit on which an order to take the deposition of a witness to be used on a motion is granted, that the person sought to be examined refused to make an affidavit of facts which were within his knowledge; it must specify the nature of the motion, and must show that the affidavit or deposition is necessary thereon. Where there was nothing stated in the affidavit on which such an order was granted to show what facts the person sought to be examined was requested to depose to, or what facts the plaintiff believed were within his knowledge,—*Held*, that there was nothing to show how the deposition was material or necessary on the motion, and the order should be vacated.

(*Decided July* 27, 1883.)

Motion to set aside an order appointing a referee to take the deposition of a witness on a motion.

The plaintiff, July 20, 1883, procured an order appointing a referee under § 885 of the Code to take the deposition of Louis Fitzgerald, who was not a party to the action, to be used on a motion therein on the affidavit of the plaintiff's attorney, setting forth that on

July 17, 1883, the defendant served on him an order granted in this action, requiring the plaintiff to show cause on July 23, 1883, at 12 o'clock, noon, why an order entered herein December 26, 1882, restraining the defendant from paying dividends on $15,526,590 of stock of the defendant, declared by the court to be illegal and void, should not be so modified as to allow and authorize the payment by the defendant of a dividend declared by it June 13, 1883; that he intended in good faith to resist said application to modify said order and the affidavit or deposition of Louis Fitzgerald, who is not a party to this action, was necessary to him in doing so; that he had applied to said Fitzgerald to make such affidavit and he had declined to do so; that the said Fitzgerald is president of the Mercantile Trust Company of the City of New York; that an arrangement had been made between Jay Gould, one of the directors and the principal stockholder of the defendant, and the Mercantile Trust Company, by which the said Trust Company undertook and agreed to pay to the holders of said "illegal and spurious stock" the dividend declared by the defendant June 13; and that the said Mercantile Trust Company commenced the payment of such dividend on July 16, and had paid nearly, if not quite, all of said dividend.

This motion was made by said Fitzgerald to set aside the order so obtained by the plaintiff. The motion was made upon his affidavit and the affidavit of one C. C. Demming. Mr. Fitzgerald in his affidavit states that he never refused to make an affidavit in this action touching the payment of the Western Union dividend; that the attorney for the plaintiff called at the office of the Trust Company and said that he wanted to get from him an affidavit as to the payment of the said dividend, and he replied that if he, said attorney, would show the affidavit to the counsel of the Trust Company and they said it was all regular, he would sign it; that in about 15 minutes said attorney returned with Mr. Demming, who was from the office of the counsel for the Trust Company, and Mr. Demming stated, "These people (referring to said attorney) want to make an *ex parte* examination of you, and we advise you not to submit to it without an order from the court," to which he, the deponent, assented; that at no time was any affidavit presented to him with the request to sign the same, nor did he at any time refuse to make an affidavit of the facts, and that "he only refused under advice of counsel as above, which was a refusal to submit to an *ex parte* examination." Mr. Demming's affidavit, besides corroborating Mr. Fitzgerald's account of his second conversation with the plaintiff's attorney, states that he is the managing clerk of Messrs. Alexander & Green, the counsel for the Trust Company; that on July 20 the plaintiff's attorney called at the office of said Alexander & Green and stated to him that he desired to examine the president of the Metropolitan Trust Company in regard to the payment of the dividend of the Western Union Telegraph Company; that he asked the said attorney upon what particular point he wished to examine said president, and said attorney said that he wished to find out where the money came from that paid said dividend; that he, deponent, thereupon said that said president was willing to be examined as to whether or not he paid any Western Union dividends, but was unwilling to be examined as to the personal arrangements between his company and its depositors.

Charles B. Alexander (*Alexander & Green*, attorneys), for motion.

Cited, Brooks *v.* Schultz, 3 *Abb. Pr. N. S.* 124; Erie Railway Co. *v.* Gould, 14 *Id.* 279; Dauchy *v.* Miller, 16 *Id.* 10; Moses *v.* Banker, 7 *Robt.* 131; Matter of Bannister, 1 *Law Bul.* 9; Cockey *v.* Hurd, 36 *Supr.*

Ct. 42; Fish *v.* Chicago R. R. Co., 3 *Abb. Pr. N. S.* 430; Rogers *v.* Durant, 2 *T. & C.* 676.

John Sessions, opposed.

INGRAHAM, J.—It appears by the affidavit of Mr. Fitzgerald that he did not understand that Mr. Sessions requested him to make an affidavit, and that he did not refuse to make one. His statement is corroborated by the affidavit of Mr. Demming. Section 885 of the Code requires it to appear that the person sought to be examined should refuse to make an affidavit of the facts which were within his knowledge. I cannot say from the affidavits submitted that it appears that Mr. Fitzgerald did refuse to make such an affidavit. There is an objection to the affidavit on which the order was obtained which, I think, is fatal to the order. The section in question provides that the affidavit must specify the nature of the motion and must show that the affidavit or deposition is necessary thereon.

There is nothing stated in the affidavit on which the order was granted to show what facts the person sought to be examined was requested to depose to, or what facts the plaintiff believes are within his knowledge, and consequently there is nothing to show how the deposition was material or necessary on the motion.

The motion must be granted, and the order of July 20, 1883, vacated, but without costs.

WILLIARD v. STRACHAN, IMPLEADED, ETC.

N. Y. MARINE COURT, SPECIAL TERM, JUNE, 1883.

§ 3234.

Costs.—Where a complaint was dismissed as to one count, and the plaintiff had a verdict in his favor on the second count, having obtained the only verdict rendered by the jury, he was the only party entitled to costs.

Where there were two separate counts in a complaint to which the answer was a general denial, and on the trial the complaint was dismissed as to the first count, because it appeared that the note therein sued upon was given for the individual debt of a partner of the defendant, which defense was not specially pleaded, and the plaintiff had a verdict in his favor on the second count,—*Held*, that the point on which the complaint was so dismissed was not the substantial issue in the case, and the clerk, under the circumstances, properly refused to tax costs in defendant's favor; that the plaintiff, having obtained the only verdict rendered by the jury, was entitled to the costs of the action. Section 3234 of the Code applies only to cases where the defendant had a verdict on the separate count.

(*Decided June* 21, 1883.)

Motion by defendant for an order requiring the clerk of the marine court to tax costs of the action in his favor.

The opinion states the facts.

James E. Kelly, for motion.

F. A. Burnham, opposed.

MCADAM, J.—Although the defense as to each separate count of the complaint was a general denial, upon the trial it settled down to the single issue of whether the defendants were partners. The first count was dismissed because it appeared by the evidence that the note described in that count was given for the individual debt of the partner who did not defend. This question was not specially pleaded, and arose, as before remarked, incidentally upon the evidence. It was, at most, but a side issue; it was certainly not the substantial issue in the case. Upon these circumstances the clerk was right in refusing to tax the defendant's costs.

Section 3234 of the Code of Civil Procedure is taken from the 2 *R. S.* 617, § 26; 2 *Edm.* 641; and under the statute it was held that section 26 (*supra*) applied only to cases where the defendants had a verdict on the separate count. Briggs *v.* Allen, 4 *Hill*, 538. In the present case the complaint was dismissed as to the first count, and the plaintiff had a verdict upon the second. The plaintiff, having obtained the only verdict rendered by the jury, is entitled to the costs taxed by the clerk in his favor.

INDEX.

WHOLE NO. OF PAGES 508.

Milton Keynes UK
Ingram Content Group UK Ltd.
UKHW012026110124
435898UK00003B/47